Praise for netbooks™

"Thanks to Wolff and friends, the cyber-swamp may just have become a little less murky."—*Entertainment Weekly*

"*NetGuide* is the computer world's online *TV Guide*™."—*Good Morning America*

"*NetGuide* will keep you from wandering around aimlessly on the Internet, and is full of good ideas for where to pull over."—*Forbes FYI*

"*NetGuide* is the liveliest, most readable online guide yet."—*USA Today*

"What you need to connect."—*Worth Magazine*

"*NetGuide* is the *TV Guide*™ to Cyberspace!" —Louis Rossetto, publisher/editor, *Wired*

"One of the more complete, well-organized guides to online topics. From photography to the Church of Elvis, you'll find it here."—*PC Magazine*

"The best attempt yet at categorizing and organizing all the great stuff you can find out there. It's the book people keep stealing off my desk." —Joshua Quittner, *New York Newsday*

"It's changed my online life. Get this book!" —Mike Madson, "Computer Bits," Business Radio Network

"My favorite for finding the cool stuff." — *The Louisville Courier-Journal*

"*NetGuide* focuses on the most important aspect of online information—its content. You name it, it's there—from erotica to religion to politics." —Lawrence J. Magid, *San Jose Mercury News*

"Not only did all the existing Net books ignore Cyberspace's entertaining aspects, but they were process-oriented, not content-oriented. Why hadn't someone made a *TV Guide*™ for the Net? Wolff recognized an opportunity for a new book, and his group wrote *NetGuide*."—Mark Frauenfelder, *Wired*

"Couch potatoes have *TV Guide*™. Now Net surfers have *NetGuide*."—*Orange County Register*

"*NetGuide* is one of the best efforts to provide a hot-spot guide to going online."—*Knoxville News-Sentinel*

"Absolutamente indispensabile!"—*L'Espresso*, Italy

"A valuable guide for anyone interested in the recreational uses of personal computers and modems."—Peter H. Lewis, *The New York Times*

"*NetGames* is a good map of the playing fields of Netdom."—*Newsweek*

"This guide to games people play in the ever-expanding Cyberspace shows you exactly where to go."—*Entertainment Weekly*

"The second book in a very good series from Wolff and Random House."—Bob Schwabach, syndicated columnist

"Hot addresses!"—*USA Weekend*

"Move over Parker Brothers and Nintendo—games are now available online. There's something in *NetGames* for everyone from crossword-puzzle addicts to Dungeons & Dragons fans."—*Reference Books Bulletin*

"Whether you're a hardened game player or a mere newbie, *NetGames* is the definitive directory for gaming on the Internet."—*.net*

"A wide and devoted following."—*The Wall Street Journal*

"*NetMoney* is a superb guide to online business and finance!"—*Hoover's Handbook of American Business*

"[*NetChat*] is...the best surfer's guide out there." —*Entertainment Weekly*

"A product line of guidebooks for explorers of the Internet."—*Inside Media*

In bookstores now!

NetGames 2

NetGames 2 is the all-new, updated addition of the original bestseller. It covers more than 4,000 games, including Doom, Marathon, Harpoon II, Myst, and more than a hundred MUDs, MUSHes, and MOOs, plus demos, tips, and free upgrades!

ISBN 0-679-77034-8
US: $22.00/Canada: $30.00/UK: £20.49 Net

NetChat

NetChat describes more than a thousand places in Cyberspace where people meet to pursue romances, have netsex, or just chat the night away. *NetChat* covers sex spots, fan clubs, political talk, identity forums, gay life discussions, support groups, and ethnic bulletin boards.

ISBN 0-679-75814-3
US: $19.00/Canada: $25.50/UK: £17.49 Net

NetMoney

NetMoney takes you into the world of cyberinvestments, taxes, banking, and budgeting. It is the first personal finance guide to the vast financial resources now available online, from buying a car to paying for college to getting the most out of Quicken.

ISBN 0-679-75808-9
US: $19.00/Canada: $25.50/UK: £17.49 Net

NetGuide—2nd Edition

NetGuide—The Second Edition is the only guide that covers the Internet, America Online, Prodigy, and CompuServe, plus Usenet, the Web, gophers, FTP sites, mailing lists, and chat channels. At more than 800 pages, *NetGuide II* is the most comprehensive guide to Cyberspace.

ISBN 0-679-76456-9
US: $27.95/Canada: $39.00/UK: £25.99 Net

NetTrek

NetTrek charts the amazing world of *Star Trek* in Cyberspace. *NetTrek* includes more than 400 pages detailing Trek-related online forums, chat areas, newsgroups, mailing lists, Websites, sound and picture archives, plus episode guides for all the series.

ISBN 0-679-76186-1
US: $19.00/Canada: $25.50/UK: £17.49 Net

NetSports

NetSports is a guide to sports news, game and player stats, sports talk, team sites, and fan clubs in Cyberspace. *NetSports* covers more than 60 sports, from football, baseball, and basketball to rugby, frisbee, and paintball.

ISBN 0-679-76187-X
US: $19.00/Canada: $25.50/UK: £17.49 Net

NetTech

NetTech is your guide to the tech speak, tech info, and tech support on the information highway. It also includes information on products, user groups, and software resources. *NetTech* is geared to all platforms, product brands, and user levels.

ISBN 0-679-76054-7
US: $19.00/Canada: $25.50/UK: £17.49 Net

NetMusic

NetMusic describes the new world of online music, from rock to techno to jazz to opera. Find chat groups, discographies, and photos of your favorite artists, plus concert information, fan clubs, and hundreds of sound clips. *NetMusic* is your guide to the sound of music in Cyberspace.

ISBN 0-679-76385-6
US: $19.00/Canada: $25.50/UK: £17.49 Net

Continued on other side →

The plain fact is, you alone can't possibly keep track of all that's going on and all you need to know to make money online—but *The NetMarketing Report* can.

Our professional staff of journalists and analysts surf the Web, cut through the clutter, and report only what *you* need to know, *when* you need to know it.

It's really FREE!

Currently priced at $20 a month, we're giving six months of *The NetMarketing Report* to you FREE as a way to say thanks for buying our *NetMarketing* book. Simple as that!

No risk. No Obligation. FREE!

And the quicker you act, the quicker *The NetMarketing Report* can help guide you to big profits in the fastest growing marketplace in the world.

Please tear along this line and mail today!

YES! Please start my FREE 6-month EMAIL subscription to *The NetMarketing Report*™ right away.

$120 Value

Please print clearly

Name: _____

Your EMAIL address: _____

Title: _____

Organization: _____

Address: _____

City, State, Zip/Postal code _____

Country: _____

What other topics would you like to see NetBooks cover? _____

_____

Would you like to receive announcements of new NetBooks by email? ❑ Yes ❑ No

Get Netted!

Instant

Visit our Web guide at

Updates.

http://www.ypn.com

net marketing™

How Your Business Can Profit from the Online Revolution

A Michael Wolff Book

By Bruce Judson

For free updates visit our Website at http://www.ypn.com

WOLFF NEW MEDIA

New York

The NetBooks Series is published by Wolff New Media LLC, 520 Madison Avenue, 11th Floor, New York, NY 10022, and distributed by Random House, Inc., 201 East 50th Street, New York, NY 10022, as agent for Wolff New Media LLC.

NetMarketing has been wholly created and produced by Wolff New Media LLC. The Net Logo is a registered trademark of Wolff New Media LLC. *NetMarketing, NetVote, NetJobs, NetGames2, NetTravel, NetTaxes, NetMusic, NetGames, NetChat, NetMoney, NetTech, NetSports, NetMusic,* NetHead, NetSpeak, and CyberPower are trademarks of Wolff New Media LLC. All design and production has been done by means of desktop-publishing technology. The text is set in the typefaces Garamond, customized Futura, Zapf Dingbats, Franklin Gothic, and Pike.

Published simultaneously in the U.S. and Canada by Wolff New Media LLC

0 9 8 7 6 5 4 3 2 1

ISBN 0-679-77031-3

New York

A Michael Wolff Book

Michael Wolff
Publisher and Editor in Chief

Kelly Maloni
Executive Editor

Ben Greenman
Managing Editor

Senior Editor: Stevan Keane

Senior Writer: Kristin Miller

Associate Art Director: Eric Hoffsten

Assistant Editors: Deborah Cohn, Donna Spivey

Assistant Art Director: Jay Jaffe

Copy Editors: Enid Harlow, David Levine

Vice President, Marketing: Jay Sears

Advertising Director: Michael Domican

Marketing Assistant: Nick Bogaty

Online Director: Jonathan Bellack

Database Administrator: Chaitanya Diwadkar

Systems Administrator: Jon Chapman

Technical Assistant: Patrick Vanderhorst

Administrative Director: Carol Wyatt

Wolff New Media LLC

Michael Wolff
President

Alison Anthoine
Vice President

Special thanks:

Random House Electronic Publishing—Charles Levine, Terry Chisholm, Patricia Damm, Jennifer Dowling, JoAnn Sabatino, Amy Sutton, Tom Willshire

And, as always, Aggy Aed

The editors of *NetMarketing* can be reached at Wolff New Media LLC, 520 Madison Avenue, 11th Floor, New York, NY 10022, or by voice call at 212-308-8100, fax at 212-308-8837, or email at editors@ypn.com.

Editors' Note

NetMarketing is a collaboration between the editors of the NetBooks and Your Personal Net (**http://www.ypn.com**) and Bruce Judson, the General Manager of Time Inc., New Media, a creator of Pathfinder (**http://www.pathfinder.com**), and one of the leading spokesmen for the marketing potential of this new online medium.

NetMarketing is divided into two sections: a comprehensive analysis of the online marketing climate written by Mr. Judson, and site listings and reviews drawn from the NetBooks and YPN database. How does a company create a site? How does it attract customers? How many potential customers are actually online? How many of them are buying products? These are the central questions of current and future Web marketers. Between Mr. Judson's insights and our sites, between his experience helping to steer Time Warner's Pathfinder and our expertise reviewing the online medium, we think we have devised the most effective strategy for explaining the Web both to corporate marketers and mom-and-pop business owners.

A final note about the companies included in this book. The Web is new, and growing rapidly. A month, or even a week, can change the face of the corporate Web. In the weeks before this book's close, Pepsi, KFC, Adidas, and Revlon threw their hats into the ring; these four companies are just a handful of the businesses, large and small, who are making the leap to the online world. Since *NetMarketing* had to be sent to press, certain companies didn't make the cut. For a continually updated list of companies on the Web, visit the *NetMarketing* Website (**http://www.ypn.com/marketing**), an ongoing online initiative that extends the mission of the book.

—The Editors

Contents

Part I. Web Marketing in Theory

Chapter 4. Attracting Traffic to Your Site

Chapter 5. Making an Online Sale

Part II. Web Marketing in Action

Chapter 6. Household Names

Chapter 7. Arts & Entertainment

Chapter 8. High Tech

Chapter 9. Financial Services

Chapter 10. Travel & Hospitality

Chapter 11. Services

Chapter 12. Shopping

Contents

Chapter 13. Politics & Charities

Chapter 14. Appendices

Part I

Web Marketing
in Theory

Chapter 1

Welcome to the Web

Welcome to the Web

Over the past 18 months, a number of significant factors have come together to create an extraordinary tidal wave of interest in the Internet. And much of that interest is being fueled by marketers and advertisers, who have just begun to see how the Internet—and more specifically, the World Wide Web—can be used to benefit consumers. International, increasingly easy to use, and visually appealing, the World Wide Web has all of the necessary ingredients to become the site of a marketing revolution.

As a powerful form of non-intrusive marketing, the Web invites prospective consumers to visit sites—and it has already begun to provide marketers with the opportunity to experiment with different approaches, at low cost, in a market that is already comprised of millions of people. Those marketers who do experiment will help to invent the medium, and benefit as a result. It's worth noting, however, that this opportunity may be fleeting, and the rewards will go to those who act quickly. As more and more Websites are developed, the battles for consumer attention will heat up and the sophistication of the sites being created will increase significantly. Marketers who "get in early" will be building off their initial learning. Everyone else will be in the unfortunate role of trying to play catch-up, as millions of new prospects join the Web.

In many ways, it is useful to think about the World Wide Web as an evolving, entirely new fourth medi-

*Some companies that have already begun online marketing initiatives include (from top) Coca-Cola (**http://www.cocacola.com**), General Motors (**http://www .gm.com**), and Music Boulevard (**http://www.musicblvd.com**). Well-known brands and new retail enterprises alike are making use of the Web.*

um, one that is distinct from existing media such as radio, broadcast, and print. As such, the Web can provide benefits not available through any previously exisiting marketing channel. Unlike traditional media, for example, no one owns the World Wide Web. As a result, there is no gatekeeper setting up hurdles for companies that want to provide different kinds of

Examples of Doing Business Online Maintained by Web Access, this page includes a brief description of the commercial and marketing opportunities available for companies in the online world and furnishes a set of links for visitors interested in investigating the medium.
✓**www**→http://webcommerce .com/webaccess/webcomrc.html

Cyber Sales The May 1995 issue of *Interactive Week* was devoted entirely to questions of online marketing and commerce. Does online advertising empower consumers? Can companies save money by advertising online? What are the drawbacks to online marketing and and sales? The issue includes an interview with Glenn Fleishman, the moderator of the Internet Marketing Mailing List, columns by editor Michael Neubarth and publisher Paul Bonington, and features by Michael Strangelove, Gary Welz, and Carol Blake. All in all, this is an excellent general introduction.
✓**www**→http://pubs.iworld.com /iw-online/May95/toc.htm

Internet Marketing Mailing List Archive Moderated by Glenn Fleishman of Point of Presence Communications, this mailing list is one of the best resources for online marketers, whether they are veterans in the medium or wide-eyed newcomers. The archive can be searched by keyword.
✓**www**→http://www.popco .com/hyper/internet-marketing

experiences for the consumer. The company putting up a Website "owns" a piece of this new medium, and no one except that company sets the rules on what can and cannot be done. Moreover, there is no specific "media charge" (as in more traditional media with limited time or space) for the length of the experience a company creates for consumers.

This atmosphere of low costs and frequent experiments is one of the great strengths of the Internet, and part of what has made it such a hotbed of innovation for marketers. But innovation in the online world cannot be separated from utility. If someone creates a boring site, or one with little appeal for consumers, visitors are unlikely to spend much time there, to return to it, or even to come to the site in the first place. Similarly, a highly creative site may fail if the consumer can't find any valuable product information or services, since companies cannot really compete with creative and editorial content providers in the entertainment market. The balance between the two, and even the very idea of such a balance, is one of the hallmarks of the emerging online medium. Ultimately, the best and most creative innovations survive and prosper (through large numbers of visits by consumers) while subpar efforts utimately fade away because of their low use by consumers. The goal of *NetMarketing* is simple: to help readers profit. Some readers will be starting their own business, and will need help developing an online marketing strategy. Others will be working in marketing departments at large companies preparing to enter the online medium. To realize this objective, *NetMarketing* attempts to explain the tremendous explosion of marketing activity that is happening today, explores how the Web may reinvent entire businesses, describes strategies for taking advantage of the medium, and investigates the finer points of trafficking and sales techniques.

Web Population

How many people are online? As *Time* magazine recently noted, this "seemingly straightforward" question "has produced answers that range from 3 million to 60 million. Most of these numbers are little more than guesses, some highly educated, some less so. But none are substitutes for…statistically defensible research." However, as *Time* also noted, in November of 1995 "hard data finally arrived. Nielsen Media Research—the folks who do the famous Nielsen TV ratings—unveiled the results of what seems to be the first solid, scientific survey of the Internet." Conducted in conjunction with CommerceNet, a consortium of Internet-active companies, the Nielsen study drew heavy fire from some critics, who argued that it used a sample population skewed upward in terms of education and income. Nonetheless, the

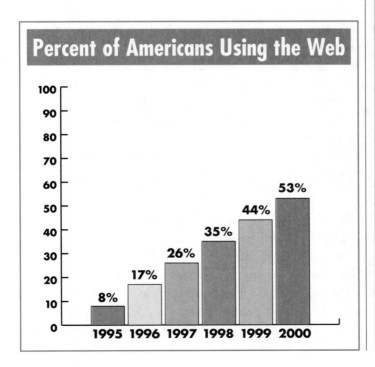

Percent of Americans Using the Web

- 1995: 8%
- 1996: 17%
- 1997: 26%
- 1998: 35%
- 1999: 44%
- 2000: 53%

WORLD WIDE DEMOGRAPHICS

As the Internet population grows, the kinds of people most likely to use the Web change. One of the most comprehensive studies of online demographics is conducted twice each year under the auspices of the Georgia Institute of Technology, with the involvement of the Hermes Project at the University of Michigan. Overseen by the Graphic Visualization and Usability Center, this study is online at **http://www.cc.gate ch.edu/gvu/user_surveys**. The archive of results not only provides a current look at the Web population but also gestures toward some of the changes that are occurring as use of the World Wide Web explodes. As part of its study of the Internet, the A.C. Nielsen Company (**http://www.nielsen .com**) also analyzed the demographics of Web users, although its interest in specific demographic factors is somewhat different from GVU's.

In general, recent research suggests that World Wide Web consumers are an increasingly mainstream and affluent bunch, and consequently an attractive target audience for marketers. It also indicates that women are a rapidly growing segment of the online population. Both the 1995 GVU study (which surveyed 23,000 respondents), and the 1995 Nielsen/CommerceNet survey support these conclusions. What else do we know about Web users? A summary of the two studies appears on the next page, along with a brief annotation.

Age

All available evidence suggests that the typical Web user is in his or her thirties and has Internet access at home. The GVU study found that the average age of World Wide Web users is 33. Nielsen similarly found that 56 percent of Web users were between the ages of 25 and 44, as compared to 43 percent of the total population of the U.S. and Canada. Nielsen also found that 62 percent of Internet users had access at home, 54 percent had access at work and 30 percent had access at school, which is synonymous with college in most instances. (These numbers total more than 100 percent, as a number of people have Internet access through more than one location.)

Income

The Nielsen survey found that Web users are a highly affluent group: 55 percent of those who answered the question about personal worth have incomes at or above $50,000 (as compared to 29 percent of the total population). Similarly, 35 percent of those who answered the question have incomes at or above $70,000, as compared to 14 percent of the total population.

Education

Nielsen found that 64 percent of Web users had completed college, while the GVU placed this number at 55 percent. Both of these totals are significantly above the 28 percent of the general population that has completed college.

Gender

The percentage of women on the Web has been steadily increasing since the middle of 1995,

Nielsen/CommerceNet survey (the results of which are available at **http://www.commerce.net/information/surveys** and **http://www.nielsenmedia.com/whatsnew/execsum2.htm**) remains one of the most important early attempts to chart the numbers of computer users accessing the World Wide Web today. Nielsen found that 37 million people over the age of 16 in the U.S. and Canada have access to the Internet either directly or through a friend, that 24 million people (or 11 percent of the total population) had used the Internet in the past three months, and that 18 million people (8 percent of the total population) were users of the World Wide Web. Whatever the issues with sampling and surveying methodology—and these may well temper the study's enthusiasm—the Nielsen study nonetheless clearly demonstrates that the number of users of the Web already constitute a significant market. The Web, in short, is well on its way to becoming a mainstream medium. Since Nielsen's survey occurred early, and since Web growth will only move in one direction, there is every reason to believe that Web use will continue to increase at a furious pace. By the year 2000 over 50 percent of the total American population will probably be users of the World Wide Web (see the chart on page 7). This startling growth will be fueled by a wide variety of events, innovations, and activities, all of which will reinforce each other over the next several years, and all of which will lead more and more people to become active users.

The starting point for thinking about growth in the use of the Web is the computer itself. Decades ago computer scientists predicted that before the end of the twentieth century, incredible advances in miniaturization would result in computers as small as a bookcase, and capable of fitting in a single room. We know now that their future-vision was near-sighted; with five years to go before the twentieth century ends, computers are small enough to fit on desks, in portable carrying cases, and even in the palm. The widespread use of the computer as a home consumer appliance is inevitable. Jupiter Communications estimates that by 1995, 40 percent of households had personal computers, while 57 percent of these households had modems.

These numbers will certainly increase as the relative costs of computers decrease (see sidebar, page 11). In addition, Net participation will be helped along by the emergence of low-cost Internet-dedicated computers and access appliances. International Business Machines (IBM) and other major companies, for example, have announced plans to introduce a machine completely configured for immediate and simple out-of-the-box Internet access that will retail in the range of $500 or less. The emergence of these dedicated machines has the potential to significantly increase consumer use of the Internet not just because of their low cost, but because they will be extraordinarily easy to use. This ease-of-use is important in bringing the next generation of users—who will be far less computer-savvy than the current generation—to the Web.

In fact, it is entirely possible that these low-cost Internet-access machines will be widely available by the third quarter of 1996. LSI Logic Corp. (**http://www.lsilogic.com**) has already developed a powerful, low-cost computer chip that can process up to 100 million instructions per second. Company officials say that this chip could be the centerpiece of an Internet-access device that sold for as low as $200, provided it used a television set as a monitor. Additional features such as a faster modem, a hard drive, or a PC monitor could bring the machine's cost to $500. A start-up company, ViewCall America (**http://www.viewcallamerica.com**), has already

and women now represent approximately one-third of Web users. Estimates vary slightly—the GVU study found that 33 percent of U.S. Web users identified themselves as female, while Nielsen placed the percentage at 36 percent. Whatever the exact number, the rapid increase in the percentage of female users of the Internet is striking: they represented less than one-fifth of the online population in previous GVU studies and other online demographic surveys.

Occupation
Nielsen found that more than 60 percent of Web users work in professional, technical, and managerial functions. This total stands in sharp contrast to the demographics of the entire population, where only 33 percent fall within these categories.

Time Spent Online
The GVU study also found that people spend a lot of time on the Web: more than 40 percent of United States respondents reported that they spend between 6 and 10 hours per week on the Web, while 27 percent said they spent between 11 and 20 hours per week on the Web. In addition, 78 percent of all respondents reported that they use their Web browser at least once a day.

Uses of the Web
According to the GVU study, the most common use for Web browsers (79 percent) is "simply for browsing." Browsing or searching for "product information" was listed by a majority of online users. Nielsen similarly found that 55 percent of Web users indicated that they had used the Web to search for information on products and services.

The data discussed suggest several important conclusions: First, the Web has moved away from its roots as a college-based media. While the Web user population of a few years ago was limited primarily to those in their late teens and twenties, the average Web user is in his or her thirties. Second, the Web population—with its current average age, high income, and professional/managerial orientation—is a group that is actively sought by marketers.

Another important implication of this research is that women now play a major role in the World Wide Web community. This is vitally important to all consumer-product manufacturers and distributors, because women account for two-thirds of all shopping in the U.S. The growing role of women on the Web is likely to have a positive effect on the growth of Web-based commerce.

Finally, the increasing popularity of the Web as a source of product and service information is interwoven intimately with the statistics on time spent online and browser use. As a non-intrusive medium, the advertising value of the Web is sometimes questioned. If a company invests in a Website, will consumers choose to visit? Given the average number of usage hours that consumers spend willingly browsing sites, as well as the fact that fully half of those surveyed indicated that they used the medium as a place to go for gathering product information, the Web is clearly a medium to be reckoned with as a means of communicating product and consumer-oriented information.

announced a product called WEBster, a set-top box that gives consumers direct access to the Internet and online services through their television sets using a 28,800 bps modem. The expected pricing is below $300 for each unit, along with a low monthly subscription fee. According to Alan McKeon, president of ViewCall America, "The system was developed to give consumers a low-cost, easy-to-use on-ramp to the information superhighway, enabling them to reap the benefits of the Internet without the expenses and learning curve of PCs." ViewCall America trials began in early 1996.

Cheaper computers are part of the growing market penetration of the Internet, but not the only part. Equally important is the growing availability of Web access. Today, all of the major online services, including America Online, CompuServe, the Microsoft Network, and Prodigy provide easy consumer access to the Web. Some of these online services furnish their own browsers and proprietary software, while others have invested in extant browsers like Netscape Navigator. The commercial services are also growing at a rapid rate (America Online, the largest of the Big Four, has more than 5 million subscribers, and is signing up an average of 60,000 new members each week), and their continued health is a great boon to the success of the Internet.

At the same time, major telecommunications companies have begun to provide consumers with direct dial-up access to the Web. AT&T's early 1996 launch of WorldNet, a national Internet-access network with a toll-free number, a year-long free trial offer for consumers, and a $19.95 unlimited-access plan, significantly increased the likelihood of universal Web access. What all this suggests is that the consumer will soon be able to acquire access to the Web as easily as dialing an 800 number today. As a result of AT&T's entry into the market, not to mention the efforts of other large corporations like IBM and MCI, Internet access has become an intensely competitive business. As prices decline rapidly, access providers are embarking upon extensive marketing efforts designed to grab larger shares of this market. The net effect will be three-fold: (1) Extensive marketing efforts by these competitors to educate consumers about the benefits of the Web; (2) a race to develop and deploy software that makes the consumer experience increasingly easy and interesting; and (3) lower prices at every turn.

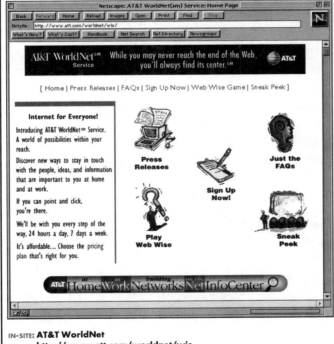

IN-SITE: AT&T WorldNet
http://www.att.com/worldnet/wis

Announced in February 1996, WorldNet is likely to change the face of the online-access-provider industry. By offering special Internet access rates (including five hours *free* per month) to its 90 million long-distance customers, AT&T made its mark. As *NetMarketing* goes to press, AT&T expects to give WorldNet subscribers a free version of the Netscape Web browser branded with AT&T's logo and plans to link to a large database of Website reviews as well as offer a complete guide for online newcomers.

MOORE'S LAW

The dramatic, but still predictable, drop in computer costs is known as Moore's Law, after Gordon Moore, the founder of Intel (the world's largest manufacturer of microprocessors, the hardware brains of computers). Moore predicted that because of advances in technology, processing power for computer chips would double every 18 months while chip costs would remain the same. He was right, and over time we have witnessed dramatic decreases in the cost of computing. In 1979, it essentially cost $1.00 per instruction per second (the operating command telling the computer to do something). By 1995, that cost had decreased to $.00001 per instruction per second.

What is responsible for these extraordinary advances? Transistor density, to name just once cause; with each technological breakthrough, it is possible to include more and more transistors (electronic devices which incorporate instructions) on a single microprocessor chip. Today, for example, a single microchip can contain 20 million transistors. This powerful relationship is shown on the graph below, which demonstrates how the power of Intel's chips have increased over time.

PROCESSING

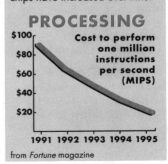

Cost to perform one million instructions per second (MIPS)

from *Fortune* magazine

alt.online-service Although discussions about the various online services (America Online, CompuServe, BBSs, etc.) appear occasionally on this newsgroup, the forum is primarily a place for online services to advertise.
✓ **USENET**→alt.online-service

AT&T WorldNet AT&T's Official WorldNet site includes press releases, pricing information, and a sign-up form.
✓ **www**→http://www.att.com/worldnet

IBM Global Network Big Blue offers Internet access. Visit the site for pricing information about access services, a list of local access numbers, and a description of its Web development services.
✓ **www**→http://www.ibm.com/globalnetwork

Internet Providers A list of Internet providers, both national and international.
✓ **www**→http://www.yahoo.com/Business_and_Economy/Companies/Internet_Services/Internet_Access_Providers

The List Nearly 2,000 access providers, and a search engine that makes locating the closest provider fast and easy.
✓ **www**→http://thelist.com

POCIA (Providers of Commercial Internet Access) A collection of links to sites for almost 1,000 Internet providers.
✓ **www**→http://www.celestin.com/pocia/index.html

Five More Reasons to Care

Many marketers may be skeptical about the growth of the Internet. For those skeptics, here are five more reasons why more and more Americans will soon be joining the online revolution:

1. Access to the Internet will increasingly be bundled with other types of software. The latest version of the popular home finance software package Quicken, for example, includes Internet-access software that takes the consumer to Quicken's Website (**http://www.intuit.com**) for free, at which time it offers an Internet-access subscription offer. This strategy is likely to be used more and more frequently, which will further lead to easy Internet access for consumers.

2. Advances in software and capabilities. Thousands of people, in both large companies and small start-up operations, are developing software for the Web. This entrepreneurial environment is quickening the pace of development of the medium with two clear benefits: the Web will become increasingly easy for consumers to use as more consumer-friendly software is developed, and Web content providers will be able to create sites that are increasingly entertaining and useful.

3. Growing business uses. The single greatest factor in the growth of the Web is increased use by businesses. This increase meets several business needs, including Internet Web-based networks (or Intranets), customer-service systems, and extended secure Enterprise Networks for each company's customers and suppliers, as well as business-to-business connections (see pages 220-223).

4. The availability of quality content and applications will draw consumers. It also seems that almost every day, a major media company announces that it has established a site on the Web. As more and more content becomes available to consumers on the Web, its popularity will certainly grow. To date, major magazine publishers, newspapers, and cable and broadcast television networks have all established information and entertainment sites on the Web. These companies are, in some cases, spending tens of millions of dollars to develop new and interesting content for the Web. Some of the media giants with initiatives to develop sites on the Web include Time Warner (with its Pathfinder super-site at **http://www.pathfinder.com**), Disney (**http://www.disney.com**), CNN (**http://www.cnn.com**), ESPN (**http://www.sportszone.com**), *The New York Times* (**http://www.nytimes.com**), The Discovery Channel (**http://www.discovery.com**), and National Public Radio (**http://www.npr.org**). All of this activity by large information and entertainment companies will operate as a self-reinforcing circle: Great content will draw consumers to the Web; the presence of more consumers will lead media companies to become even more active in creating content on the Web; the increased content creation will draw even more consumers online; and so on. These media companies are also aggressively publicizing their activities to consumers who are not presently on the Web. ESPN, CNN, and the Sci-Fi Channel regularly promote their Websites on their telecasts. *The New York Times* promotes its site on the front page of the newspaper. And some movie studios are resorting to innovative ways of publicizing their sites (see the illustration on the following page). Media companies are both providing more reasons for consumers to come onto the Web, and using their ability to communicate with consumers to secure the legitimacy and create awareness of the medium.

METCALFE'S LAW

As it matures beyond its infancy, the Web will continue to grow, and its growth will be influenced by something called the Law of Networks. The Law of Networks, aka Metcalfe's Law, says that the value of a network increases as the square of the total power of the computers attached to it. What this means in layman's terms is quite simple: the more people who are connected to a network, the more valuable it becomes—and increased value attracts even more people to the network.

George Gilder, the author and theorist of Metcalfe's Law, explains the social mathematics of the law as follows: "Every new computer, therefore, both uses the Net as a resource and adds resources to the Net in a spiral of increasing value and choice." One clear example of this is the phone system: if only 10 percent of the population had phone service the system would be a lot less valuable than it is today—where almost the entire population has phone service. The service would be less valuable to those with phones, because they would be unable to reach by phone the many people who did not have service. The World Wide Web follows the same basic dynamic as the telephone system, another common carrier and another national network. As more people are able to access the Web, its value to everyone active in the medium, especially marketers, increases. For more information on network growth, see George Gilder's writings at **http://www.seas.upenn.edu/~gaj1/ggindex.html**.

Metcalfe's Law has several important corollaries, many of which can be tailored to marketing needs. One of the corollaries works as a sort of peer-pressure generator—since a network becomes increasingly valuable as more people are part of it, the more it grows the more imperative it becomes for everyone who is not on the network to join. The phone system once again serves as a useful analogy. If 90 percent of the population has phone service, then it is very valuable for the last 10 percent of the population to get this sevice: they are missing out on the ability to connect to everyone else.

This corollary also suggests that the dramatic growth of the World Wide Web, most of which has occurred in the last 18 months, is likely to continue and even accelerate in upcoming months. As more and more people have Internet access, it will be increasingly valuable for those without access to join. As marketers see that they can reach more and more consumers through the Web, they will be more likely to devote resources to the development of valuable information and applications for online consumers. From the marketer's perspective, as more and more people *choose* to use the Web, companies can begin to offer new types of product information and incentives on the Web. As more companies do this, more consumers will *need* to get online to take advantage of these resources. In fact, if a large percentage of product information is moved from traditional, offline media to online media, getting online will become an absolute necessity for most consumers.

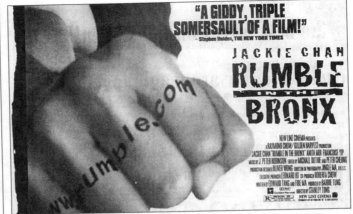

The top image, an ad for Jackie Chan's Hong Kong action movie Rumble in the Bronx, *appeared in the* New York Times Sunday Arts & Leisure *section and testifies to the increasing currency of Website addresses in print, radio, and television ads.*

5. Finally, the growth of the Web will be aided and abetted by the widespread growth of high-speed access to the Internet. A consideration of speed topics is offered in the next section.

The Need for Speed

The experience of the Web is significantly conditioned by the speed at which the consumer is able to connect to the World Wide Web. In this regard, a number of events will occur over the next several years. The cost of 28,800 bps modems—the emerging modem standard, and a speed twice as fast as the 1995 standard of 14,000—will continue to decline and can already be purchased for less than $100.

In addition, local phone companies are also introducing high-speed data line services known as ISDN (integrated services digital network). ISDN allows telephone companies to provide consumers and small businesses with at-home Internet service at speeds of up to 128.8 Kbps, or four times faster than a 28.8 modem. How? Well, with traditional transmission, a computer sends a digital signal from his or her computer to an analog modem, which transmits the information along copper phone wires to another digital modem, which re-encodes the information. ISDN technology uses digital modems, allowing for greater speed, clarity, and complexity in the transmission of information.

So why aren't massive numbers of consumers biting? Price and ease of set-up. But the prices of equipment for consumer hook-ups to ISDN are starting to drop, and may soon be in the range where consumers will find them affordable. In the fall of 1995, prices for a full complement of ISDN equipment dropped from approximately $1,200 to less than $500, reflecting new offerings from equipment manufacturers. Over time, these prices are likely to decrease even further. In addition to price, a central issue in the deployment of ISDN has been the limited technical acumen of the appropriate personnel at local phone companies. Customer service personnel are often unfamiliar with

EXTRA POINTS
ISDN CONNECTIONS

comp.dcom.isdn As ISDN hook-ups become an affordable option in most places, many people are choosing to upgrade their connections to the Net. The newsgroup offers informed discussions about costs and connectivity issues using ISDN as well as a fair amount of telephone company bashing.
✓**USENET**→comp.dcom.isdn

ISDN Need help troubleshooting problems with your ISDN connection? Want more information about ISDN technology? Marketers interested in discussion about low-cost, high-speed Internet connections should subscribe.
✓**EMAIL**→isdn-request@precipice .v-site.net ✍ *Write a request*

ISDN FAQ What is ISDN and should you get it? How much does it cost? The multi-part FAQ offers detailed answers to the most basic ISDN questions, complete with ASCII diagrams. And if all these acronyms are confusing, check out the section titled "What do all these acronyms mean?"
✓**WWW**→http://alumni.caltech .edu/~dank/isdn/

ISDN for Microsoft Windows Microsoft is signing up Windows Netsurfers for home ISDN access at its Website. The successful software company, which also runs the Microsoft Network (MSN), has set up a Website that not only takes orders but also pitches the virtues of ISDN and promises to simplify the process of upgrading

customers to high-speed access.
✓**www**→http://www.microsoft
.com/windows/getisdn

ISDN Informationbase A
mix of ISDN information and
resources that includes descriptions of ISDN telephones, fax
machines, and modems; downloadable Linux device drivers;
links to ISDN vendors and suppliers; information about three
major ISDN providers; and an
ISDN glossary and reading list.
✓**www**→http://igwe.vub.ac.be
/~svendk

ISDN Technical Page Reference guides to the hardware,
software, and standards of the
ISDN world.
✓**www**→http://fly.HiWAAY.net
/~jfrohwei/isdn

Low Cost ISDN Dedicated to
discussions about the cost of
ISDN, discussions on this mailing list range from rate comparisons to analysis of telephone
company expenses to tarrifs.
✓**EMAIL**→listproc@tap.org ✍
Type in message body: subscribe
isdn <your full name> *Archives:*
✓**www**→http://www.essential
.org/listproc/isdn

MSG's ISDN Info Center Includes reviews of ISDN equipment and an ISDN glossary.
✓**www**→http://www.msg.net
/ISDN

Pacific Bell Pacific Bell, one of
the major West Coast telephone
utilities, has been the most aggressive of large phone companies in offering ISDN to consumers. The Website includes a
technical guide to ISDN and information about PacBell's services.
✓**www**→http://www.pacbell.com

ISDN technology, and consumers have typically needed some technical understanding of their ISDN equipment in order to describe it to the local phone company and establish the appropriate service. A final issue is the availability of ISDN services. Today, approximately 62 percent of the nation is equipped for the service—primarily in or around large and medium-sized cities. This coverage is expected to increase to 70 percent by the end of 1996. There is unquestionably a demand for higher speed access to the Web, but the ultimate growth of ISDN will depend on how quickly prices for ISDN equipment and services decrease, and the ease with which consumers can have such equipment and services installed.

Although ISDN speeds are impressive, they may soon be eclipsed by another technological advance—high-speed Internet connectivity through cable TV lines. The availability of this service, capable of offering extraordinary speeds, will have a dramatic impact on the quality of the services that will be available over the Internet. Imagine clicking on a huge graphic, video, or sound file and experiencing no delay in downloading it to your computer. This incredible speed stands in sharp contrast to the Web today, where memory-intensive files can take up to an hour to download to the consumer's computer, even with a 28.8 modem As a result, the entire experience of the consumer on the Web will be transformed: everything will happen in the blink of an eye.

The technology for delivering access to the Web through TV cables to personal computers already exists. In fact, two of the nation's largest cable carriers, Time Warner Inc. and Tele-Communications Inc. (TCI), have indicated that they anticipate major initiatives in this area. In the summer of 1995, Time Warner began operating a live test with several hundred users of this high-speed delivery system in

Elmira, New York. The company is dedicated to rolling out this service on a national basis and has established a separate subsidiary, whose product is called LineRunner. Time Warner has announced that it will launch the full-scale LineRunner service in certain cities in 1996, with a broad roll-out in 1997. Paul Sagan, Time Inc. New Media's editor and president, stated in *Wired* magazine, "We want to take it to all of our cable systems. And we would make the same thing available to any other cable company." Sagan noted that "Everybody wants it." TCI has also announced that it will support a high-speed cable-delivery system as part of a joint venture called @Home. This joint venture plans to launch its first Internet-access service in Sunnyvale, CA, in early 1996, with a broader roll-out during this same year.

These services will not cost much more than current access. First of all, cable-to-PC connections will probably provide an unlimited amount of usage time for a flat monthly fee. Second, valuable content—both local and national in its orientation—may be provided as part of this basic service. No one knows for certain what the roll-out pricing for a basic service will be, but it appears likely to be in the $25 to $35 per month range for unlimited access time. In the Elmira test, Time Warner Cable is providing unlimited Internet access along with electronic content (such as the local *Star-Gazette*) to consumers for $25 per month.

It seems likely that cable-to-PC delivery will create entirely new opportunities for local and regional marketers to become involved in Web-based marketing, and even true local, community environments. The system Time Warner is testing in New York State includes links to local government offices, the local library, and the local schools. In such environments, the development of local retail-oriented initiatives is virtually a foregone conclusion.

EXTRA POINTS
CABLE DELIVERY

@Home This site incorporates a description of the @Home service, which is designed to deliver Internet access and other online capabilities to the personal computers of consumers via cable systems. The joint venture of Tele-Communications Inc. and Kleiner Perkins Caufield & Byers, a venture capital firm, will first deploy service in 1996 in Sunnyvale, California. The site states that the monthly charge for @Home is "expected to be $30-$50 for unlimited use of basic services."
✓www→http://www.home.net

CableLabs This research and development consortium of cable television system operators publishes an industry calendar, links to related Internet sites, and serves as a clearinghouse for issues in the cable industry community, including cable modem service.
✓www→http://www.cablelabs.com

Cablevision In addition to offering real-time video on the Web, Cablevision plans to create regional news and feature content for its subscribers.
✓www→http://www.cablevision.com

Comcast Corporation The Pennsylvania telecommunications company spent the early part of 1996 developing PC Connect, a cable modem distribution plan. In addition, Comcast plans to offer Comcast Online, a regional news and infor-

mation service.
✓**www**→http://www.comcast
.com

LineRunner A very brief description of the Time Warner cable online service project known as LineRunner.
✓**www**→http://pathfinder.com
/pathfinder/LineRunner

Online Services See Cable in Future This article addresses the efforts by online services to integrate cable delivery and includes a useful chart of cable-delivery efforts to date.
✓**www**→http://www.jup.com/e
droom/newsletters/ic/ic4-11.htm

Rogers This Canadian company plans to offer cable modem service for businesses, schools, and homes.
✓**www**→http://www.rogers
.com

Sam's Interactive Cable Guide Sam's annotated and enthusiastic guide "keeps tabs on Internet access via cable TV" and links to relevant news clips, Websites, and statistics. Sam provides hefty doses of industry analysis and vigilantly monitors the experiments run by the cable companies. See the Cable Modem Trials feature for a table comparing the Internet-access ventures of major cable companies.
✓**www**→http://www.teleport
.com/~samc/cable1.html

TCI-MET TCI's cable-delivery system, which debuted in the Lansing, MI, area, will soon be expanding its operating base and delivering Internet service to homes nationwide.
✓**www**→http://198.109.160.4
/default.htm

Finally, cable delivery creates new options for software developers. Entertainment and learning applications developed at Websites will certainly include far richer graphics and video than current Websites, and will, in fact, even exceed the multimedia sophistication of a CD-ROM. In addition, cable delivery will allow for the sale of complex software and information products over the Internet. Prohibitive in today's slower-speed climate—the significant time involved to download all of the data, which are now often contained on multiple disks, effectively limits such activities—full-service software distribution online will be more than possible in the era of cable delivery.

Online Commerce

Studies have established that there are a lot of people on the Web, surfing from site to site, examining content, and learning about this new medium. But what about online commerce? Are the Web faithful actually spending their money? What is the size of the online economy? Well, the short answer is this: whatever size it is today, you can bet it will be much bigger tomorrow. In 1994, the business of the Internet barely existed. Now, analysts predict that by the turn of the century it will approach $50 billion. One noteworthy study was conducted by Forrester Research. Forrester estimated that the total size of the Internet economy—which includes all Internet-related revenues from infrastructure investment, access services, content, and transactions—would grow to more than 20 times its current size between now and the year 2000. The firm estimates the current size of the Internet economy at $2 billion ($1.5 billion of this derives from online services) and sets the total at the millennium at $45.8 billion.

In fact, business use is the fastest growing area of the Web. Today, it is estimated that more than 50,000

Expenditure Category

Infrastructure	$14.2	billion
Business Transactions	15.0	billion
Consumer Content	2.8	billion
Consumer Transactions	6.9	billion
Business Content	6.9	billion
Total	**$45.8**	**billion**

(Source: *Interactive Week*, Oct. 23, 1995)

THE SOFT SELL AND THE WEB

Why would consumers voluntarily visit a Website created by a company? Don't consumers dislike advertising, in particular advertising on the Internet? The short answer to this last question is both "yes" and "no." The Internet was not originally zoned for commercial use, and many members of the online community feel that Cyberspace should not be paved over so that shopping malls and ad billboards can be erected. But smart online marketers have already begun to understand that the Web does not make advertising impossible—it only makes a certain kind of advertising more difficult, and other kinds of advertising more desirable. Because of its unique architecture, in fact, the Web is the first mass-medium whose ad content is primarily non-intrusive.

What exactly does this mean? Well, in short, it means that ads don't come to consumers—consumers come to ads. The remote control greatly diminished the power of television ads by giving consumers the power to click away from commercials that didn't interest them. The Web represents a further evolution of this principle, where virtually all content is optional. Online marketers must subscribe to a conditional version of the *Field Of Dreams* theory: "If you build it, they will come...but they may not stay." No site can forcibly hold an audience captive; the job of the marketer is to convince the consumer to visit and stay voluntarily, because the content is interesting or the services valuable. In fact, any attempt to prolong a visitor's stay without reward may be considered a transgression of the rules for successful online marketing and advertising. And the language of television ads doesn't have the same hypnotic effect online. Still, companies are not powerless to capture the market. If they have valuable information deployed intelligently and innovatively, they can draw consumers to their sites and keep them there. Consumers have product needs and Websites can serve as an efficient means of delivering information about those products.

Product information is only one example of a powerful general principle—Websites must deliver valuable information to consumers. All Websites, including those put up to educate consumers about products are a form of content. And unlike other media, the Web has an unlimited content window. What does this mean? Only that the amount of information a company can place online is virtually infinite. In traditional media, marketers are typically limited by time (television) or space (print). With a Website these issues don't exist. Moreover, the low cost of creating information—a thousand-page site is still considerably cheaper than a television spot—creates a higher standard of excellence. Many companies, including Toyota (**http://www .toyota.com**), the National Basketball Association (**http:// www.nba.com**), and Alamo Rent-A-Car (**http://www .freeways.com**), explore ways in which a medium without a content window creates an opportunity, and even a mandate, for commercial sites to deliver quality information to consumers.

businesses have established Websites; 10,000 businesses register for new Internet addresses each month; and about 5,000 new commercial sites actually launch each month.

Dramatic growth of marketing and sales activities through the Web is inevitable. Since online information delivery will only become cheaper and easier, accessing product information and making purchases on the Web will soon be as simple as dialing an 800 number. In fact, the development of the Web is probably the most significant innovation to hit the sales process since the dramatic growth of shop-at-home catalogs in the 1980s, and reviewing the catalog and direct-sales explosion may help to explain the explosive growth potential of the Web. The evolution of on-demand shop-at-home services followed a fairly clear evolution. First came the 800 number, which provided consumers with instant interactivity and an immediate way to request a catalog and order merchandise. The 800-number infrastructure triggered a catalog-shopping boom. Consumers who already had a catalog could see items and order them by phone or by mail and follow up on their orders with a customer service hotline. The only major drawbacks of catalogs, in fact, are physical ones. Consumers need to have a catalog in hand when they call to buy, and they need to be able to find the desired products in the catalogs, which can be hundreds of pages long. (Spiegel's twice-a-year tome, for example, isn't easy to tote around.) The Web has the potential to eliminate these two limiting factors.

No one doubts that the Web will change the way companies advertise and sell. The only questions are "How?" and "How soon?" The next part of this book, in fact, will explore how the Web can directly improve a marketer's effectiveness.

Chapter 2

Why the Web is Different

Why the Web is Different

In the first part of this book, we looked at some of the reasons why the Web is quantitatively different from other media, and why the medium's rapid growth and low costs make it a vitally important part of the future of marketing. In this chapter, we'll look at some of the reasons why the Web is qualitatively different from other media, and, particularly, why its unique technology enables marketers to change the ways in which they interact with customers. As the world's only bi-directional mass medium—in other words, the only content-based network that permits two-way communication between content providers and content consumers—the Web creates an entirely new set of opportunities and challenges for companies.

Customizing Customers

The Web has revolutionized business not only because it allows companies to make unlimited content available to millions of people all over the world, but also because it has introduced a new form of interaction between merchants and customers. With fairly basic technology like email, Web forms, and bulletin boards, companies can provide information to potential and existing consumers. Before the Web, consumers who needed information on products were obliged to read instruction booklets, call toll-free numbers, or phone a local store staffed with authorized dealers or representatives. In the era of the Web, all these functions can be centralized at a Website and conducted far more efficiently than ever before.

One of the most important concerns of a company is how to furnish product information to potential customers. Hypertext, the associative technology that underlies the Web, allows marketers to use a "tree and branch" approach to addressing consumer needs. In other words, a consumer can enter a company's Website through a central point, and then move to more specific levels based on their needs. Let's use a hypothetical example and consider how this approach would work for an insurance company's Website. A potential customer would visit the site, view a range of possible products, and "click" on the life insurance category. This choice would transport the visitor to another page with a new set of options. These options might include the opportunity to view an explanation of the difference between whole life and term life, a description of relevant term life policies, and a description of relevant whole life policies. Choosing the third option would summon up another list of options highlighting several whole life policies. When a customer finally settles on a product, the company can

---

EXTRA POINTS
CUSTOM FIT

American Express University Visually compelling, American Express's site uses familiar graphics (doors, a telephone, familiar buildings, etc.) to make the visitor comfortable. The site is also packed with information about the American Express line of cards for college students. Potential card holders can click door number one—Which Card is Right for You—for a "quickie quiz" that will help them choose between an Optima Card and an American Express. Features elsewhere on the site will help those same students budget their money.
✓**www**→http://www.american express.com

Avis Trying to rent a car? Customers can send Avis their travel information (including the flight they're arriving on) and the car rental company will take the next step. Within minutes of submitting an online car registration form, Avis will email customers complete reservation information.
✓**www**→http://www.avis.com

Beech-Nut Beech-Nut walks parents through the process of feeding their children with easily navigable product information. What should children be eating at 3 months? 9 months? Beech-Nut has broken down its product information in terms parents can readily grasp—the age of the baby (click the big number 3 button if your child is nine months or older).
✓**www**→http://www.beechnut.com

Pacific Coast Need help selecting a pillow or a Down comforter? The site will walk you through the process and offer sleeping instructions along the way—"if you sleep in healthier ways, you'll feel better and live healthier."
✓**www**→http://www.pacific coast.com/welcome/welcome .html

New Balance New Balance has created CyberPark USA, an athletic online park, where customers can click on mountains, rivers, and forests for information on running, health, and fitness; customers can also shop for the perfect shoe. First, they're invited to click "the perfect shoe" button. Then, New Balance walks them through a series of questions to help them decide on the right sneaker.
✓**www**→http://www.new balance.com

Royal Caribbean The Cruise'O'Matic promises to find visitors the "cruise of their dreams" *if* they answer a few questions. Customers plug in a dream destination and options like whether or not they are bringing kids, going on a honeymoon, or prefer activities that slow down their blood-pressure (beaches, museums, golf). When a cruise has been chosen, information about the trip such as maps, ports of call, and other cruise details are provided.
✓**www**→http://www.royal caribbean.com/royal/main.html

Sony Consumer Product Guide Sony has set up a site to help customers navigate a number of consumer electronic product choices. Shopping for a Camcorder? What about the

direct them to a purchasing page (for more information on selling, see Chapter Five of this book). If the insurance company can successfully anticipate all of the questions a prospective policy-holder might ask, it can design a site that maximizes the possibility of a purchase (beware of designing overly elaborate Web pages; product decisions should be streamlined not complicated). Products that are easily explained, and even those that until now have required knowledgeable, salespeople, can be presented to consumers over the Web in a persuasive, coherent presentation.

Companies can also recommend products to potential customers based on their personal profiles. To understand how this approach differs from the product-information approach, let's return to our hypothetical insurance site. In this model, when the potential customer arrives at the site, he or she enters personal

IN-SITE: **At Home with Hamilton Beach/Proctor-Silex**
http://www.hambeach.com

Hamilton Beach (the Big Name in Small Appliances) is using current Web technology to personalize the shopping experience. Visitors entering the At Home Website are asked a series of questions about their commuting habits, community, and lifestyle, after which the Hamilton Beach site retrieves one of five custom product catalogs (apartment house, ranch house, country house, brownstone, and suburban home). For anyone equipping their home with appropriate appliances, this is a witty site to visit.

information, either into an online form or via a series of "clicks" in an online questionnaire. Has the customer recently had a child? What is the customer's age? Is the customer the sole source of financial support for his or her family? Does the customer hold any other life insurance policies? With this information the company's computer can direct the customer to relevant advice and product information.

This "recommending function" can occur either with or without a request for the customer's name, address, phone number, etc. In some cases, it may make sense for companies to try to collect this information at Websites, but that benefit should be weighed against the possibility of provoking a negative reaction. Remember, privacy is very important to consumers. The gigantic Amazon.com bookstore (**http://www.amazon.com**) goes so far as to display an "Amazon.com Bill of Rights" that describes the privacy protection it provides each customer, and Preview Vacations (**http://www.vacations.com**) promises that information divulged by the consumer "will not be made available to any outside parties." Providing this type of privacy is essential for any company that wants to build a successful ongoing relationship with its online visitors.

Digital Handycam? How about the Handycam Camcorder? Once the customer has decided what product line, they then must decide what model to buy. Customers begin by clicking a button (the product category) on an illustration of large remote control. For each of its product categories (discman, TVs, VCRs, laser disc players, etc.), Sony has set up graphs that compare the features of each product line and model as well as linking to detailed spec sheets.
✓**www**→http://www.sel.sony .com/SEL/consumer/index.html

Virgin As a company run by entrepreneur Richard Branson, tailoring service to the needs of the customer is the key to Virgin's success. Visitors to its Website are offered a unique itinerary feature which gives them the opportunity to enter their names, where they're traveling from, and where they're headed. The airline will return the customer a flight plan, and also give fliers the chance to select their class of choice.
✓**www**→http://www.fly.virgin .com

Warner-Lambert The manufacturer of cold and allergy products—Actifed, Sudafed, Benadryl, Halls, Sinutab, and others—has developed one of the most unique product matching services online. Customers check off their symptoms (itchy eyes, runny nose, headache, sore throat, aches), age, preferred form of medicine (tablets, caplets, capsules, etc.) and Warner-Lambert recommends the cold product most appropriate for them.
✓**www**→http://www.allergy -cold.com

ONLINE EVOLUTION

In the offline world, some companies are primarily catalog businesses—Spiegel, Avon, J Crew. Other companies are retailors that also run succesful direct-marketing businesses—Talbots, Eddie Bauer, the Pottery Barn. But what happens when a traditional company goes online and begins selling products directly to consumers? Have all online stores essentially gone into the catalog business? The Net is a direct selling medium. If a company is selling online, it is fufilling orders for customers and bypassing distributors. In other words, companies selling online have gone into the electronic catalog business. The Net makes the cost of entry into this market significantly lower than ever before by eliminating printing and mailing costs although a company still must develop the resources to fufill consumer orders, whether they're getting those orders in Cyberspace or on the telephone. So who's running online catalogs? Lands' End (**http:// www.landsend.com**), for instance, is selling its merchandise on the Web—women's casuals, men's haberdashery, luggage, etc.—but is also setting up special areas where customers can add their names to the print catalog mailing list, and running regular new features on new items. The Internet Kitchen (**http://www .your-kitchen.com**) is selling discounted kitchen supplies on its site. And, for animal lovers, Austin's Wholesale Pet Shop (**http://webcom.com/~pets /austins/welcome.html**) lists its products online.

Catalogs of Change

The Web not only greatly increases the convenience of company-consumer interaction; it greatly decreases the cost of that interaction. Let's consider another hypothetical situation, this one uses a catalog company doing business in the early-eighties. Every quarter, this company—it may sell soap; it may sell books; it may sell clothes—sends its new catalog to thousands of interested customers across the country, highlighting new products as well as discounted and discontinued merchandise. Then, one day, an enterprising young woman in the mail-order department suggests to her boss that the company move its catalog operation "online." With "Web technology," the woman explains, the company can display its product information, along with pictures, and make it available to millions of potential consumers instantly. In addition, the company can collect the "email addresses" of visitors and (with their permission) apprise them of important developments—new products or discounts, for instance—at practically no cost to the company. The boss lowers his head to his desk. "That's brilliant," he sighs. "If only I had the slightest idea what you are talking about."

Well, some years later, every direct selling business should understand what the young woman was talking about. The Net has revolutionized the industry by significantly reducing the cost of entrance and changing the cost structure of products sold directly to consumers. Catalog printing, postage and paper, which can consume a large portion of a direct marketer's revenues, are eliminated in Web catalogs, replaced by a one-time production cost and then minimal updating and revision costs. Because the Web permits instant publication, merchandise listings can be updated at any time, whether to reflect new products or to tailor a

IN-SITE: Spiegel
http://www.spiegel.com

With a name that is almost synonymous with catalogs, Spiegel's online operation lets its customers fill out an online credit application, ask company experts questions about fashion and interior decorating, browse an online magazine with lifestyle articles for Spiegel shoppers, and, most importantly, shop, shop, shop. Spiegel merchandise ranges from furniture to clothes, and while the entire catalog isn't online, a significant proportion of it is.

sales message. If a product is selling poorly, a company can move it to the front page of its Website and tout it as a "special offer." And with new personalizing technologies, companies can even customize their online catalogs, asking all new Website visitors some basic questions and then displaying only items that are likely to be of interest to those specific individuals. Web-based sales technology also lets companies provide customer service, both front-end and back-end at lower costs.

ATTRACTING CUSTOMERS

Not every catalog company has its own Website; many that don't (and many that do) have listed their catalogs at clearinghouses like the CatalogSite (**http://www.catalogsite.com**). Customers can order free print copies of catalogs from these sites. Here is a small selection of those currently available at CatalogSite:

Austad's Golf
The Bombay Company
Chocolats Le Francais
Coors and Company
Creative Health Products
Diamond Essence
Egghead
Hadley Fruit Orchards
Hold Everything
J. Crew
Lands' End Direct Merchants
Lenox Collections
Lifestyle Fascination
The Mac Zone
Marshall's Fudge
Motherwear
National Baseball Hall Of Fame
Nordstrom—The Catalog
Okun Bros. Shoes
Orvis Hunting And Fishing
PaperDirect!
Par Excellence—Golf Awards
Pottery Barn
Pourette Candle Making
Quartermaster
Raven Maps & Images
REI
Ski Limited
Smith & Hawken
Steuben
Sundance Catalog
Talbots
Thompson & Co. Smokers Catalog
Tool Crib Of The North
Williams-Sonoma

Aetna Want a quote request? There's a form. Have a question about home insurance? There's a form. Hate the site? Let 'em know. The Insurance company anticipates many reasons why customers would want to speak with them. Its "Let's Talk" Website feature has fill-in-the-blank email forms for dozens of customer concerns related to personal and business insurance.
✓ **www**→http://www.internet mci.com/marketplace/aetna

The As Seen on TV Superstore All those products sold on the television airways are also being sold online, at this site, which bills itself as "The Infomercial Super Store on the Internet." The site prominently features a "Customer Service" button which customers can use to ask questions and even request help finding that extraspecial, super-sharp potato peeler they saw on television late, late last night.
✓ **www**→http://www.internet mci.com/marketplace/tv

Aveda This beauty-products company accepts customer questions at its Website and promises to respond by email within one business day—guaranteed. Beautiful.
✓ **www**→http://www.aveda .com/dear/custserv.html

FedEx Since FedEx delivers in excess of two million overnight packages per day, the company has a pressing need to track the status of these packages, and to track them quickly and accu-

For Whom the Web Tolls Free

By adding customer service features to its Website, a business can make money even before it makes a sale. In the last decade many companies have come to recognise that customer service is a critical market battleground. In those industries where products and prices are similar, what makes the difference between success and failure is customer loyalty, and what builds customer loyalty is attentive and intelligent customer service. Unfortunately, this can be expensive. For years it has revolved around toll-free (or "800") numbers, which allow customers to contact companies at no cost. To date, they remain the preferred method for answering consumer questions, collecting orders, and responding to complaints. But toll-free numbers are not toll-free for the merchant. Typically averaging $1 per minute (between the cost of the phone service and the person taking the order), calls to place orders can take in excess of 5 minutes. These costs are eliminated on the Web. Consumers acquire their own Internet access, and there are no additional costs associated with receiving online visitors unless the Website is staffed with personnel to respond to questions in real-time (usually not necessary). As a result, today's typical order cost of $5 for 5 minutes is avoided. When a customoimer makes an order of $40-50, that's a saving of 10 percent. The savings add up and can produce a substantial increase in yearly profits for a company that escapes a large volume of calls by interacting with customers via the Web. In addition, many companies with customer service features on their Websites have found that although calls to their toll-free number have remained stable, they've reached a whole new customer base.

A Website can do everything a toll-free number can, and more. A toll-free number is a source of product information and an ordering mechanism, but the Web adds another dimension. Websites allow companies to provide a much higher level of product information and support—high quality photos, illustrations, spec sheets, product reviews, user manuals, FAQs (Frequently Asked Questions), and more. However, it is important to note that like a toll-free number, a company's Website only has value if a consumer "dials it up," or decides to pay a visit. (See Chapter Four for a discussion of building traffic at your site.)

As the Web becomes increasingly familiar to families across America, companies that rely on toll-free numbers, whether to provide information to their con-

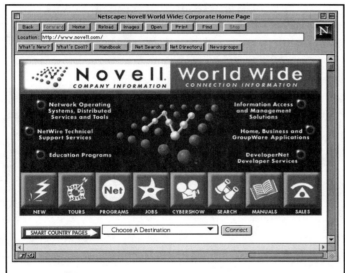

IN-SITE: **Novell Computer**
http://www.novell.com

In the past year, Novell has seen the number of customer accesses to its online customer support service expand dramatically, while its business increased and its customer support telephone calls remained at more or less constant levels. In the month of December 1995, Novell reported that it received more than 5.6 million accesses to its customer service site through the Web. Novell's experience suggests not only that providing easy online access makes the demand for customer support more obvious (since many customers may be reluctant to pick up the phone), but also that by providing this support through the Internet, companies can both lower overall support costs and better meet the needs of the customer. In effect, easy access to online support through the Internet creates a more valuable total product experience for the consumer and each customer access through the Internet that would have otherwise come by phone represents a very real cost savings for Novell.

rately. Thousands of customers need to know at the same time where their deliveries are. Since November 1994, FedEx has put its entire package-tracking operation online; customers can visit the Website, type in the bill tracking number for a specific package, and read an online report on the whereabouts of their package. By the end of 1995, an estimated 10,000 people per day visited the site to make use of this facility.
✓ **www**→http://www.fedex.com

Fingerhut Fingerhut, one of the nation's largest catalog marketers, has a Website filled with product descriptions and ordering instructions. In addition, the Fingerhut site includes an extensive customer service page that lets visitors submit questions and comments via a Web-based form.
✓ **www**→http://www.fingerhut.com/html/mail.html

Interplay This game manufacturer uses its Website to answer questions about its products, and to collect information on its customers' hardware and software purchases so that it can better orient itself toward their needs.
✓ **www**→http://www.interplay.com/website/csfiles/csform.html

Malloy Lithographing, Inc. What's a Michigan-based book production company to do when it wants to communicate with its customers? Well, Malloy decided to take its customer service department to the Web—its electronically-published site contains a form on which customers can submit questions and comments, and even specify their preferred method of reply (email, phone, fax, etc.).

✓ **www**→http://www.malloy
.com/inforqst.html

L.L. Bean By exploioting Web opportunities, the catalog and customer-service pioneer may have struck the first blow in the a move to shift consumers to the Web from toll-free numbers. In the 1995 year-end issue of *Martha Stewart Living*, L.L. Bean's entry in the Advertiser Directory invited consumers to "check out" its new Website and *did not* include an 800 number as an alternative mechanism for contacting the company. No toll-free number? Is this the future of customer ordering and-service? Bean thinks so. This promotion of the Website instead of the toll-free number is a genuine sea-change.

✓ **www**→http://www.llbean
.com

Sprint's World of Communi-cations One of the big three in the national telecommunica-tions industry, Sprint works hard to communicate with cus-tomers via its Website. Online, customers can notify the com-pany of address changes, inquire about their bills (balance and other account information), and even sign up for Sprint service. Sprint is also looking for "Sprint stories"—good times, bad times, that sort of stuff—to post on its Website. This tactic of letting consumers comment on their experiences with products at length, is possible only on the Web, where additional content costs nothing. By employing this strategy, Sprint is pioneer-ing new types of company-con-sumer communication.

✓ **www**→http://www.sprint
.com

sumers or respond to customer concerns, will almost certainly begin expanding their Web presence. The Web may even offer the means to diffuse customer anxiety about interacting with companies and lead to higher customer satisfaction. Some customers, for instance, don't like to "bother" service reps, and others find calls to companies intimidating. Websites appear to give complete control of the "conversation" back to the consumer while still delivering product informa-tion, this can be a major advantage. Many businesses that began as toll-free number services are already migrating to the Web. 1-800-Music-Now, for example, MCI's over-the-phone music sampling and purchasing service, has moved online, and the 1-800-Music-Now Website (**http://www.1800musicnow.mci.com**) anachronistically retains the number in its URL.

Staying in Touch

The Web will revolutionize customer relations. The various ways in which companies communicate with prospective and existing customers will be transformed. Even the simplest electronic communciations technology, email, dramatically reverses all of the previous assumptions held by businesspeople about communicating with consumers. It moves the focus of customer relations away from cost of communication and toward the quality of the message.

Offline and pre-Web, a marketers primary concern when considering communication with consumers was cost. What would it cost to create and mail this letter or brochure? What would it cost to telemarket this new product to a customer base? What would it cost to create a toll-free number and invite customers to call in with their ideas and recommendations for improving old products? Some of the best customer relations ideas have died on the drawing board because they weren't financially feasible. Email effectively removes the cost factor from the decision-making process by offering an alternative to the relatively high expense of postal and telephone communication.

With the cost issue minimized, new questions arise. What interesting messages can product marketers create? Can they hold the attention of consumers? How do they avoid violating any online codes of ethics by being too intrusive? Online communications— whether a monthly newsletter, a daily update of new product offerings, or a personalized message sent to each customer on his or her birthday—need to be requested by consumers, need to be engaging, need to be desirable. Otherwise, they violate Net consumer ethics, and are likely to send a previously loyal customer elsewhere.

WEB SERVICE MANUALS

Companies who distribute their product manuals online are gratifying two kinds of customer: those whon bought a product and lost their own manual, and those who may make a purchase but who want to take a virtual test drive first. Online manuals and instructions are also potentially easier to understand. Using hypertext, companies could link simple instructions to more detailed discussions, glossaries, spec sheets, and diagrams. A good, innovative online approach for instructing consumers could lead to higher sales of "assemby required" products, more satisfied customers, and savings for companies with 800 numbers.

Manuals are not nearly as common online, however, as technical support libraries, FAQs, and tip sheets. Computer companies like Apple (**http://www.apple.com**), Microsoft (**http://www.microsoft.com**), and Novell (**http://www.novell.com**) all give customers access to huge technical support libraries with answers to hundreds, if not thousands, of customer questions and problems. In fact, the information in these libraries is often the same information to which the technical support staff answering 800 calls has access, and most of these libraries include powerful search engines for easy access. But it's not just the customers of computer companies who are looking for this type of information. Buyers of consumer products also need directions sometimes, and such an evolution is likely here.

Amazon.com This innovative online bookstore has established a service called "Eyes," a personal notification service which allows consumers to identify the kinds of books he or she likes and then emails them when a new title is available that meets the consumer's profile.
✓**www**→http://www.amazon.com

American Airlines Subscribers to the airline's mailing list get the the latest Net SAAver Fares for different destinations each week.
✓**www**→http://www.amrcorp.com/aa_home/aa_home.htm

PC Flowers & Gifts Consumers can sign up for the company's "E-Mail Holiday Reminder" service at no cost. First, they need to input the dates of important events (birthdays, anniversaries, graduations), and then the store emails them reminders to send gifts. PC Flowers also emails gift suggestions.
✓**www**→http://www.pcgifts.ibm.com

Preview Vacations The travel company can email consumers who join their "Preferred Member" club—fill out an online form that asks for detailed information about travel preferences—with vacation deals that match the consumer's areas of interest. Preview Vacations also emails members a monthly newsletter with travel tips and bargain suggestions.
✓**www**→http://www.vacations.com

Many Websites now include links that ask customers if they would like to be added to an email service. Consumers who demonstrate an interest can be added to mailing lists, and any future information about the company can be sent to them. At the same time, companies can use these email request forms to tailor their message to the needs of individual consumers. A record label, for example, may make contact with thousands of customers, but only a small number of those customers will have interest in specific artists signed to that label. With the help of a simple email program, companies can deliver the most relevant product or service information to the most relevant buyers.

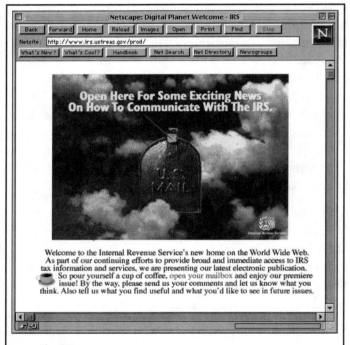

IN-SITE: **The IRS**
http://www.irs.ustreas.gov
The IRS works overtime trying to improve its image, clarify its information, and provide service to the public. The 1996 revamp of its Website positioned the tax collecting agency and its Website as a friendly source of tax information written "in plain English," a place where "customer service standards" are important, and, perhaps most soothing to the tax payer, a place with "tax info for you" about "exactly what you need." All the information a taxpayer is likely to need is available here.

R&D on the Web

Especially cautious marketers may be forgiven for stepping carefully through the risks and rewards that surround Net commerce, but no marketer should ignore the Web's power as a marketing research tool. Direct communication with prospective and existing customers, as well as indirect communication with customers via analysis of market data, can help a marketer answer key questions during product development.

What sales messages are needed for what products?
The Web is an extremely effective tool for gauging what sales messages are most effective and what questions customers typically have about a specific product. With the help of traffic-analysis software, companies can determine which sections of their Websites are visited most frequently. In addition, companies can create "product question areas" within their Website that solicit answers to a series of short questions about existing and potential products. However, once such an area is established, a company must commit to staffing it, processing responses quickly, and even creating incentives for consumers to participate.

Alternatively, marketers might create an area on the Website that displays answers to the most frequently asked product questions. This lowers the staff requirements. By monitoring which FAQs are accessed most frequently, companies may also gain valuable insights into how their products are performing. Companies attempting this strategy should update their Frequently Asked Questions list often; if questions reflect outdated concerns, it will not please customers nearly as much. Companies may also want to link their FAQ to other Net resources. This feature carries one significant risk: consumers may leave the site and not return.

EXTRA POINTS
MARKET RESEARCH

The Web is an incredible storehouse of information which can assist in the development and analysis of new markets. In many cases, the Web has turned what was formerly a difficult, expensive process into something that is fast, easy, and inexpensive. In addition to general demographic sites, there are sites that analyze specific companies and industries, and even sophisticated business-news services. More sites can be found in the appendix to this book (pages 310-319).

American Demographics
Browse the current issue of *American Demographics* magazine; search an archive of previous issues by keyword (the archive holds articles from the past year); download a data table of "America's Hottest Markets"; or pick up details on how to subscribe to the offline version of this marketers' magazine.
✓**www**→http://www.marketing tools.com

Business Week Online BWO offers marketers in-depth company and industry news and topical feature articles (many of them with an online slant) as well as offering message boards geared toward the needs of marketers. Coverage is generally good.
✓**www**→http://www.business week.com

The CNN Financial Network
Timely data and articles about the business community and the financial markets, advice on managing your business, a daily

business discussion ("Interact with Us"), and an annotated collection of links to other financial resources online make the CNN site well worth a visit.
✓**www**→http://www.cnnfn.com

Corporate Financials On-line CFO tracks recent press releases, earnings reports, filings, and shareholder information for several publicly-traded companies. In addition, the site links to online business news services.
✓**www**→http://www.cfonews.com

Fortune Articles on business topics often focusing on issues in marketing and technology.
✓**www**→http://www.Pathfinder.com/Fortune

Hoover's Business Profiles Search the full text of Hoover's Handbook for detailed profiles of nearly 2,000 of the largest and fastest growing public and private companies in the U.S. and the world.
✓**www**→http://www.hoovers.com

U.S. Census This treasure chest of facts and figures will help marketers get a handle on who makes up the market today, how much they earn, and who will form the market of tomorrow. The Ask the Experts topic lets you pose specific demographic questions to Census personnel.
✓**www**→http://www.census.gov

The Wall Street Journal's Money & Investing Update News about the U.S. and world financial markets from the third section of the WSJ. Continually updated and registration required.
✓**www**→http://update.wsj.com

How can companies improve existing products?

As the only two-way mass medium, the Web provides marketers with a unique opportunity to probe the difficulties users encounter with existing products. Complaint and suggestion areas should be prominent parts of any Website, and companies can even prompt consumers to answer specific questions, including whether or not a product seems reasonably priced and whetheror not a product met or fell short of a buyer's expectations.

What do consumers want from new products?

Marketers can use the Web to engage consumers in a dialogue about products that don't yet exist. This discussion can either take place in the form of a set of questions ("What other features would you really like to see in our product?"), a careful analysis of the FAQs accessed at the Website, or a "Coming Attractions" area in a company's Website. The downside? An area of this type can leak valuable information to your competitors about product plans. Entertainment companies have long been wary of this tactic because it increases the possibility that a consumer will take credit for a product, claim partial ownership and attempt to sue for part of the profits.

Marketers should remember that the demographics of the Internet deliver a "self-selected" population that may differ significantly from the population at large. As we saw in Chapter One of this book, online users are wealthier and more educated than the general population, and companies may not want to base their product development on such a narrow slice of the market. A recent study by the Minneapolis-based Customer Research Inc. (CRI) concluded, however, this did not cause significant concern. With the help of an online service, CRI conducted a survey related to cellular telephone usage. CRI also conducted a similar survey using telephone interviews. The firm found that within 36 hours of announcing the survey online, over 7,600 responses had been received. This is, in short, a staggering amount of feedback—telephone response accumulated at less than 2 percent of the online rate, and it would have taken 2,000 hours of telephone calls to amass a similar number of responses. CRI also found that the results from the two survey methods were similar, although the online audience was younger, more affluent, and more male. Even with this skew, however, the study suggests that as the Web population becomes more representative of the population-at-large, it has the potential to signifcantly change the way surveys are conducted and dramatically reduce their costs.

Chapter 3

Building a Better Website

Building a Better Website

Web marketing is in its infancy. Young and stillevolving, the Web is already attracting huge numbers of consumers who want to play, socialize, conduct business, and spend money. For the time being, the cost of entry into this interactive medium is relatively low—even new businesses can afford to set up a Website—and marketers who get online early have the opportunity to make their mark with Net-savvy consumers and to get comfortable with online marketing before the balance of the business world gets wired.

If there's a single piece of advice for Net marketers at this early stage of the industry, it's this—don't wait too long. Marketers should jump right in: set up a site, start experimenting, and make themselves known. It's easy to create content online and equally easy to change it. In early 1996, Spiegel was publishing a fashion and fitness magazine online; Molson was running a Canada-centric site with a live chat area, concert listings, and hockey news; American Express had dedicated an entire area of its site to college students and their needs; and other companies were trying online soap operas, advice columns, daily tips, games, free downloads, store locators, and other ideas. Some online marketing initiatives are successful; others, less so. But no company was locked into an approach.

Making a mistake in this new medium or even producing a Web dud is far better than waiting on the sidelines. Consumers expect the Web to change constantly, and a Website heading in the "wrong direction" can be redirected quite easily. A company that waits too long (more than a couple of months) before launching a Website risks that rapidly evolving Web technology and online trends will make a company's ideas seem dated. As technologies get more powerful and expensive, and sites begin to compete on the basis of these technologies, marketers will be forced to be more conservative, but for now they don't have to be.

Marketers may not know exactly what they want to include on their Websites (searchable product databases, chat clients, technical support bulletin boards, magazines, games, product demos, etc.), but as in any other marketing medium, they should understand what they want to accomplish. Do they want to target a specific demographic group? Do they want to make the consumer feel as if the product fits in with the consumer's lifestyle? Do they want to compete with other products on the basis of price? Do they want to enhance the value of a product? Do they want to deliver product information? Do they want to respond to the needs of longtime customers? Do they want to make a direct sale? Once a marketer clarifies what a company wants to accomplish with its Website, the marketer will be in a better position to direct the development of the Website and to filter good ideas from bad ones.

EXTRA POINTS
ONLINE MARKETING

@dMarket Co-sponsored by *Advertising Age* and *HotWired*, @dMarket lists a variety of marketing, advertising, public relations, and media sites on the Internet, and offers marketers a forum for discussing branding, trafficking, and maintenance issues. Check the "Resources" section for Web demographic info.
✓**www**→http://www.admarket.com

Advertising Age Give 'em an A. Give 'em two A's. *Advertising Age* has created an excellent resource for marketers online, with breaking news in the marketing industry, reviews of new Websites, statistics on Web use and demographics, a calendar of upcoming conferences and events, online discussion boards, and even a gossip column called Roadkill. The publication also sponsors a mailing list on which professional marketers can discuss the interactive industry and marketing opportunities.
✓**www**→http://www.AdAge.com

The Advertising Media Internet Center Covering more than the online industry, this site links to an enormous range of resources for marketers and media professionals. Filling out the registration form gains you access to discussion forums, comprehensive lists of media-related Websites, and even media planning advice.
✓**www**→http://www.telmar.com

American Association of Advertising Agencies The American Association of Adver-

tising Agencies, a goliath in the advertising world, includes at its site *BackChannel*, an electronic newsletter that interviews executives at leading advertising agencies, reports on technology and advertising, links to sites and surveys online that advertisers just shouldn't miss, and even tracks "Interactivity Events."
✓**WWW**→http://www.commerce park.com/AAAA/AAAA.html

CyberSmart Marketing
Martin Interactive, an online ad agency, weighs in on marketing in Cyberspace with short features on the culture of Cyberspace, online consumerism, the dos and don'ts of marketing, and more. The site also regularly reviews good and bad Websites.
✓**WWW**→http://www.martin agency.com/cybersmart.html

The Internet Advertising Resource Guide Links to Net advertising resources, including advertising magazines, marketing associations, shopping malls, and stats on Web use.
✓**WWW**→http://www.missouri .edu/internet-advertising-guide .html

Internet Marketing Discussion List With several thousand members around the world, this moderated marketing discussion forum is one of the most active on the Net. Marketers share stories from the trenches, exchange advertising strategies, debate surveys and demographic statistics, announce conferences, brainstorm ideas for their sites, and discuss trends and technology. Moderator Glenn Fleishman keeps discussion focused on the issues.
✓**EMAIL**→im-sub@i-m.com ✍
Type in message body: subscribe

Setting Your Basic Goals

Online advertising and marketing not only depend on different technologies than their offline counterparts, but also employ different strategies. At the moment, the Net is a much smaller mass medium than either radio or television, much more limited in its demographics and much more tentative in its consumer patterns. But if the online world is limited in ways that may frustrate a marketer accustomed to television and radio, it also creates new options in branding, interactivity, product description, product enhancement, targeting, customer service, and customer community. What elements of online marketing should you foreground? Any marketer new to the Web should take some time to clarify his or her goals in entering this new medium.

• **Do you want to reinforce your brand image?** Because of its graphic and sound capabilities, the Web is immensely helpful for building an image of a particular brand—particularly if you're interested in an image that is cool, hip, fun, or technically sophisticated. And companies with recognizable identities can have a field day online, where numerous Website features—from background wallpaper to navigational buttons—can carry logos or slogans.

• **Do you want to find a cheaper way to provide product information?** The online world offers several exciting options for companies wishing to provide consumers with information about products and services—and all of them are extraordinarily effective and affordable. Not only can companies use the Net to deliver vast amounts of information about specific products (specifications for automobiles, for example); they can also build awareness of customer readiness (reminding a customer when he or she is likely to need new tires, for example). And in some cases, companies can even use the Web to distribute their products (software that simulates driving conditions of a new car) or increase the value of their products (creating a car-repair Website that helps automobile owners do their own basic repairs).

• **Do you want to improve customer service and heighten consumer interest in your products?** The defining characteristic of the Net is its interactivity, and the Web may be the best mass medium yet devised for two-way communication with consumers. Consumers can contact companies to complain about faulty products, ask product-support questions, or suggest new products; companies may respond to these complaints and concerns, and also announce the launch dates of new products, run contests and promotions, and offer savings to any Netsurfers interested in their products or services. And since the Internet charges no usage fees, the cost of these interactive initiatives is minimal.

• **Do you want to build a community of consumers?** The Web offers a unique opportunity for marketers to identify consumers and even communicate with them. In addition, Websites can both reinforce ties between consumers and products and reinforce ties among consumers.

Media Central: Interactive Monitor What's at the Interactive Monitor? Well, a little bit of everything. Top stories in interactive marketing. Reviews of Websites. A monthly list of Website dos and don'ts that, while relatively general, is indispensable for marketers arriving online ("Don't use multimedia applications in essential, information-intensive areas"). And don't forget to consult the *Media Central Digest*—an invaluable insider's report on "new and noteworthy" developments on the Web.
✓**www**→http://www.mediacentral.com/IMonitor

NetNews Members of this moderated list regularly exchange advice about Website development and opinions about new Websites and online promotions. It's a great place to keep on top of what everyone else in the industry is doing—and thinking about doing.
✓**EMAIL**→NetNews-request@cue.com ✍ *Type in message body:* subscribe
Info: ✓**www**→http://www.sundaypaper.com/general/netnews.htm

WebTrack One-stop shopping for the hard data that online marketers crave, including lists of major U.S. advertisers, directories of sites soliciting advertising (including the all-important rate card information), a who's who of Web marketers, surveys about advertising online, and brief news reports about the industry. When it comes to statistics about consumer Web use, there's no site quite like WebTrack.
✓**www**→http://www.webtrack.com

REGISTERING A DOMAIN NAME

Starting a business on the Net is simple, but you still have to follow the rules. Rule number one: All domain names must be registered with Network Solutions Registration Services, a company that does its business on the Web (**http://rs.internic.net/rs -internic.html**). If you don't register your address, it won't work. It's that simple.

But don't despair. The registering process is almost as simple. Companies or individuals can download an online registration form from **http://rs.internic.net/ reg,** fill it out, and email it in. New domain names carry a fee of $100, which covers maintenance for two years, after which a $50 fee must be paid annually. Don't register the night before your business is set to open; processing may take weeks.

Marketers visiting InterNIC for the first time may have a rude awakening awaiting them—hundreds of thousands of domain names are already registered, and chances are that most simple alphanumeric combinations are spoken for. If you're curious who's using or trying to use your company's name—or you want to play the domain-name lottery—you can. Visit InterNIC's update form at **http://rs.internic .net/cgi-bin/reg/** (domain-update-form), type in the desired domain name, and InterNIC will call up the original application, which includes the identity of the company planning to use the domain name for online business and contact information.

What's in a Name?

Like toll-free phone numbers, Website addresses live or die by their recognizability and catchiness, and in the early years of the Net, companies have scrambled to register commercial URLs with the Network Information Center, the Virginia-based organization that oversees domain-name registration. The rules for address assignment are very simple—it's first come, first served, so long as you have a legitimate right to the name. It doesn't matter if you're a Fortune 500 corporation—if a two-man consulting firm with the same name registers first, you're out of luck. As a result, companies considering a Web presence should rush to InterNIC and start registering any name that might fit into their business plans (instructions are at left). Some examples of this proactive strategy: Kraft Foods registered 132 domain names in August 1995; while Procter & Gamble reserved 52 names, including **pampers.com**, **tide.com**, and **toiletpaper.com**.

Domain-name competition isn't just a theoretical problem. American Airlines doesn't own the online rights to **aa.com**; the name belongs to a Japanese design firm named Architech and Arts, Inc. And the American Broadcasting Company can't do business online as **abc.com**, unless they convince the Seattle-based ABC Design to surrender (or sell) the registered domain. The gold-rush mentality of the domain-name landscape has resulted in a number of land-grabs by enterprising Netsurfers. Two years ago, journalist Joshua Quittner highlighted the issue when he registered **mcdonalds.com** and then offered to sell it back to the fast-food giant. After making his point, Quittner gave the name to McDonald's in exchange for a donation to a New York City school. While corporate trademark lawyers have moved to curtail this practice—and InterNIC has added legal restrictions to the effect that applicants must have legitimate claim to a name—small businessmen or individuals can often reserve names before larger corporations can. Who owns **bigmac.com**? James McDonald of San Jose, California. And **coke.com** belongs to fellow Californian Rajeev Arora, although the Coca-Cola Corporation is fighting to reclaim it. The Disney Corporation registered many domains named after its most popular animated characters—**mickeymouse .com**, **donaldduck.com**, and **minniemouse.com**— but couldn't secure **goofy.com**, **pluto.com**, or **poca- hontas.com**, the last of which is held by Native American Treasures, a company in San Jose, Cali- fornia. The sports world has been harmed by this prac- tice as much as any other major industry—**baseball .com**, **mlb.com**, **worldseries.com**, **nfl.com**, **foot- ball.com**, and **basketball.com** have all been snatched up by private citizens or smaller companies with legiti- mate claims to the name, leaving more specific options (**nba.com**, **nhl.com**, **superbowl.com**) for the profes- sional sports leagues.

Domain name registration has also had a profound effect on corporate identity. Many companies have unified several product-specific Websites under one domain name; Warner-Lambert, whose product line extends from Rolaids to the e.p.s. home pregnancy test, markets many of its products through a single site, **http://www.warner-lambert.com**. This is power- ful if a product is indistinguishable from its corporate parent (AT&T TrueVoice); however, an unfamiliar corporation name may require additional promotional efforts to build consumer interest. It may even pay to register products and slogans (Burger King has regis- tered **whopper.com**; Nike has registered **justdoit .com**). In general, it's a good idea to think carefully about the market magnetism of your company name and your products before selecting an online strategy.

MASTERS OF THEIR DOMAIN

Picking a domain name can be tricky—you can't be too obvious, but many of the best ones are already taken. Here's a list of some commer- cial domains registered with Inter- NIC. You may be surprised.

burgerking.com
Burger King Corporation

whopper.com
Burger King Corporation

nytimes.com
The New York Times

bandaid.com
Tim Young, private citizen

jello.com
John Shelepet, private citizen

geoffrey.com
Toys 'R Us

bugsbunny.com
Bugs Bunny Software
**In trademark dispute

soup.com
Ingress Communications

coke.com
Rajeev Arora, private citizen
**In trademark dispute

dietcoke.com
The Coca-Cola Company

baseball.com
Green Diamond Data

levi.com
Levi-Strauss

levis.com
Stateside Garment Traders

Web Page Designers This a huge list of Internet consultants, regularly updated. How huge? Well, huge enough to exhaust the memory of most Netscape browsers. How do you search this huge list? Well, it's not easy—Yahoo hasn't really sorted them and companies provide their own descriptions—but you can try to limit the field by geographical area or preferred client type, and you can even search for familiar companies—some of them may turn up on the client lists of firms listed here.
✓**www**→http://www.yahoo.com/Business_and_Economy/Companies/Internet_Service_Providers/Web_Page_Designers

The Black Point Group The Black Point Group, a California graphic design firm, assumes your Web pages look terrible and offers its services. If you disagree, you can email the company your URL.
✓**www**→http://www.slip.net/~themook/bpg/welcome.htm

Blitz Media This Boston-based media-buying company designs Websites for businesses, including the Boston Museum of Science and the Kaplan Educational Center. The site includes links to general marketing resources, a full list of Blitz's clients, and fun quizzes.
✓**www**→http://www.blitzmedia.com

Events On Line Events On Line, a Web-based marketing and public relations firm, has created sites for clients like

Calculating the Costs of a Site

What are the costs of creating a Website for your company? Well, they vary depending on the size and complexity of the site involved—not to mention the constantly fluctuating cost of technological expertise. Whether you hire a firm to design and maintain your Website or create the site in-house, with freelance help, you should know the general costs of an online presence:

• Companies in search of a very basic Website— approximately 10 pages of content, along with a simple online form for ordering or customer response— can expect to pay about $2,500.

• Companies that wish to create a more complicated site—perhaps including an online catalog with graphics, audio, or multimedia—can expect to spend anywhere between $5,000 and $50,000, depending on the numbers of the products and services and the quality of the graphics. There may also be monthly storage fees (if you locate your site on a shared computer or rent space from a business set up for this purpose) and monthly maintenance fees. The maintenance fees depend entirely on the degree of customization required—and can be estimated fairly accurately at the time the site is designed.

In addition, there are two types of high-end sites, those that are primarily promotional and those that permit direct sales over the Web. Companies that want large (200-plus pages), highly complex sites with lots of interactivity may spend $100,000 to $150,000 or more on site construction. These sites are terrific for building product recognizability and brand-name recognition, but do not necessarily include a transaction capability that permits the direct sale of products to a consumer. Even without this, it is important to recognize that these sites may require an additional cost of as much as $200,000 for yearly maintenance. The essential point here is that the costs of maintaining a significant corporate site can exceed the costs of construction.

A second type of high-end site is one that is custom-designed to include direct sales of a marketer's products. At this point, companies may need to design custom software of transaction systems (with links to distribution and inventory systems, for example) and annual costs can exceed $1 million. However, it's worth noting that in this case a company has developed a direct sales channel to the consumer, and this investment may be quickly offset by lower customer service costs, lower costs per order, reduced catalog printing and distribution costs, and increased sales.

It is also worth noting that a number of companies are developing "plug and play" solutions for businesses that want to build Websites and *sell* products over the Net. Products such as Merchant Solution from OpenMarket (**http://www.openmarket.com**) can enable even small businesses to easily engage in electronic commerce.

These estimates are by no means authoritative—some studies have placed the cost of online presence at half these numbers, others at twice them. But the cost of a Website, as compared to almost any other medium, is low, and companies can enter the world of online marketing for far less than the cost of creating a single television commercial.

America's Cup and GNN.
✓**www**→http://www.events online.com

M/B Interactive Website for this New York-based interactive design agency.
✓**www**→http://mbinter.com

NetCreations A Web design and promotion company.
✓**www**→http://www.net creations.com

On Ramp Inc. The Web development company founded by former MTV VJ Adam Curry counts Sprint, BMG, Broadcast Music Inc. (BMI), Reebok, NEC, and other large companies as clients.
✓**www**→http://metaverse.com /vibe/onramp/onramp.html

Organic An online design firm that counts among its clients Planet Hollywood, Netscape, Octel, and 1-800-Collect.
✓**www**→http://www.organic.com

Razorfish Hip and well-connected, this New York design firm has The New York Botanical Gardens and Bankers Trust as clients and has worked on projects with many of the big names in the advertising and online industry.
✓**www**→http://www.razorfish .com

SiteSpecific This Web design agency has captured major clients—Duracell, *The New York Times Fax*, and the American Museum of Natural History—and designed innovative campaigns. The Duracell online home was named one of the top ad sites of 1995 by *Web Review*.
✓**www**→http://www.site specific.com

Web Design Guidelines

Blue Marble Advanced Communications Group Enriched with "an irreverent cartoon history of the world from the Big Bang to the Information Highway," the Blue Marble ACG site is as impressive as the list of clients the agency presents at its site: AT&T, General Motors, GT Interactive, and more.
✓**www**→http://www.blue marble.com

Chiat Day: The Idea Factory Evolution, exploration, vision, community, invention, and interaction are the buzzwords at the famous ad agency's Website, which tours visitors through Chiat Day's Virtual Office, hosts online focus groups, and traces the history of Chiat Day, which created the Nissan Pathfinder site, among others.
✓**www**→http://www.chiatday.c om

Dahlin Smith White An innovative introduction to this ad agency for high-tech companies—Intel, Netscape Communications Corp., Novell, Sybase, among others. The site features a witty "doodle" motif (click on the lightbulb, for instance, and link to sketches of ads and TV spots that the company's produced). You can even download a Windows program to create your own doodles.
✓**www**→http://www.dsw.com

DDB Needham Interactive Communications The interactive division of this large international advertising agency offers services ranging from data-

When the Web was created, the rules of site design were vague and inchoate. Now that the medium has progressed past its early infancy, Website designers have begun to codify some of the basic principles that make sites work.

• **Design an attractive "door," or front page, for your site.** Websites aren't all about first impressions—they run too deep for that—but a bad first impression can stop an effective site dead in its tracks. For that reason, you should think long and hard about your "door" page. Should you display your logo prominently? Should you entice a consumer with a more enigmatic set of images? Should you create a streamlined front page, or one that showcases all your resources? For most Websites, the "door" page (the first page a visitor sees when arriving at the site) is also the home page (the main menu); some sites, however, split the duties between two pages. While there are no rigid rules, it's never a good idea to create a crowded or confusing page: since the online medium is already perceived as complex and high-tech, simplicity is golden. And don't forget about the limits of human perception. While there are no real restrictions to the number of links or images a Netscape page can contain, the human mind can only absorb five to seven choices at a time.

• **Make navigation buttons easy to find and easy to understand.** If consumers get lost in your site, they'll get out eventually—and never come back. No one wants to feel disoriented, stupid, or frustrated, especially in a medium that bills itself as interactive. As a result, your site should be logically designed, and the buttons that move consumers through it clearly labeled. Buttons that lead to the home page should say "Home Page" or include small graphics that communicates this concept (a house, a bull's-eye, the hub of a wheel), and they should be displayed prominently throughout the site. A lack of clarity is deadly. This doesn't mean, of course, that your links can't be stylish or humorous; like a magazine cover, links should encourage customers to explore what's behind them.

• **Include a search engine on your site.** If your company intends to provide consumers with large amounts of content, you should allow for keyword searches of your material. Otherwise, visitors looking for specific information (a piece of software, a brochure, or a press release) may get frustrated with the "stab and see" strategy and leave your site empty-handed—and unlikely to return.

• **Notify visitors when something new debuts.** In a medium where every month seems to bring an important technological development, companies are constantly changing their approach, and they need to keep their customers apprised of their shifts. A "What's New" page not only helps you orient consumers to the newest features, but it offers a history of how the site has changed to meet consumer needs.

• **Create both low-graphics and high-graphics versions of your site.** While no company should ignore the possibilty of amazing graphics and multimedia wizardry, it's foolish not to be sensitive to visitors' varying connection speeds. Nothing can turn off a consumer like a long wait, especially in an electronic medium. Site designers should also be aware of the color composition of their graphics. While using thousands of colors in an illustration may create a spectacular effect, it can result in swollen loading times.

• **Design intelligent image maps.** Image maps—the practice of embedding a set of links in a single illustration or photograph—can set the tone for a site, communicate information, and give a more elegant look to

base development to Website design and counts Pepsi, American Airlines, GTE, and Tabasco sauce as clients.
✓**www**→http://www.ddbniac.com

JWT The giant ad agency's Website includes video clips of its advertisements, including popular spots for 7-Eleven, the American Red Cross, and Kodak Film.
✓**www**→http://www.jwtworld.com

The Martin Agency With Coca-Cola under its roof, Martin is one of the players in the online advertising world. The agency's site includes links to other sites reporting on Web marketing, and weekly lists of must-see advertising sites.
✓**www**→http://www.martinagency.com

Modem Media Highly successful and innovative, the Connecticut-based Modem Media has designed sites for Zima, AT&T, Delta Airlines, and JC Penney.
✓**www**→http://www.modemmedia.com

The Online Ad Agency This company, with clients such as 1-800-Flowers and The Monster Board, runs seminars on Web marketing and writes the *Web Digest for Marketers*.
✓**www**→http://advert.com

Poppe Tyson Take a drive through the Website for this $88 million advertising agency that developed the first home page for Netscape and redid the White House home page.
✓**www**→http://www.poppe.com
for more ad agencies, see pages 86-87

a Web page than a set of buttons or textual links. For instance, store locators on several commercial sites use a map of the U.S.; customers can just click the state they're interested in for the names and addresses of stores. But image maps have risks as well as rewards. If maps are not intuitive, or if they are too large, they will confuse or frustrate visitors rather than guide them.

• **Link to your company's email address.** Companies shouldn't miss the opportunity to encourage direct customer feedback about their products. There should always be a link, or several links, to an email address for the company. Don't combine a direct email link with an online customer survey; the click-and-communicate simplicity of the email link has indisputable appeal.

• **Offer a table of contents or a site index if your Website is really large.** If a company is running a deep Website with several layers of content, then its home page cannot (and should not) try to list all the content available on the site. In such cases, the site should include a simply designed table of contents accessible from the site's home page.

• **Consider using RealAudio and video clips.** Increasingly, sites are welcoming visitors with RealAudio clips or integrating video technology. Multimedia content can make visitors more comfortable, entertain them, and add to the ways a site can deliver information.

Key Marketing Strategies

So, you've set your broad goals, figured the cost of your site, and done the basic research into site design. What's next? Well, you might want to check out the competition, and see how the early entrants into the world of online marketing are dealing with strategies such as branding, positioning, targeting, and customer relations, as well as new Web-based strategies such as interactivity and hypertextual marketing. Over the next 30 pages, we have examined in detail how companies are tailoring these tactics for the online world. From the product-information databases at companies like U-Haul and Goodyear to the online content at sites like Toyota's Hub and The Prudential, from the community-building of companies like Gund and Heineken to the localizing of companies like Home Depot and Jolt, companies across the Web are trying innovative ways of getting their company names and products before consumers.

GET YOUR HOT JAVA NOW!

If your Web consultant is talking about abstract classes, applets, and packages, never fear. Increasingly, Web page designers are using Java, a cutting-edge programming language that permits animation and greater customization of Web pages. HotJava, a browser that showcases Java, is currently available for Solaris, Windows 95 and Windows NT systems. Netscape 2.0 for Windows also supports Java. Mac users are still waiting, but not for long—Java browsers for Macs are already being beta-tested, and should be on the market before summer 1996. If you're still confused, or interested, check out the sites listed below for more info on Java, Java chat, and even (in the case of *HotWired* and the Rolling Stones) examples of Java technology at work.

comp.lang.java
✓**USENET**→comp.lang.java

Hot Java and Java Links
✓**www**→http://www.inch.com/~nyjava/java2.html

HotWired
✓**www**→http://www.hotwired.com

Java Home Page
✓**www**→http://java.sun.com

Java Programming Language
✓**www**→http://www.acm.org/%7Eops/java.html

Rolling Stones
✓**www**→http://www.stones.com

Positioning & Branding

An important rule of marketing, of course, is that marketers must be aware of how their brands appear to consumers—the connotations of company names, the familiarity of product names. Websites work differently than radio ads (where tone is often as important as content and endless mention of a product is a tried-and-true strategy) and television spots (where sensual overload is the rule), and enable powerful new strategies for building and reinforcing a specific image with the consumer.

As any Netsurfer knows, Websites are more than print—they are fluid, interactive, able to integrate sound and video, and located within a vast virtual environment of linked and cross-linked sites. As a result, Web ads can demand new branding and positioning strategies, strategies that rely on deeper content and a heightened awareness of context. On the Web (at **http://www.snapple.com**), Snapple successfully translates its concern for consumers into the online medium by emphasizing its mailroom, which collects letters from customers. In addition, Snapple demonstrates an admirable understanding of the online community, linking to unofficial fan sites and unauthorized branding that would be anathema in any other medium. IBM (**http://www.ibm.com**) uses a different strategy, positioning itself as an industry and global leader; IBM Planetwide summarizes the corporation's business in two dozen countries across the globe. Chrysler (**http://www.chryslercars.com**) positions itself as a technological leader by including in its site a visit to the Chrysler Technology Center, where potential buyers can "fully appreciate the fruits of our technical labors like our world-renowned cab-forward design and all-wheel drive technology." A tour across the Web will turn up as many strategies as there are

EXTRA POINTS
BRANDING

Ben and Jerry's In the online world as well as the offline world, this Vermont-based ice creamery stands for entertaining marketing with a social conscience. Sure, customers can play games and visit the Flavor Graveyard, but Ben & Jerry's also uses its Website to reinforce its political identity—on Martin Luther King, Jr.'s birthday, the front page displayed a large picture of King and linked to related civil rights sites.
✓**www**→http://www.benjerry .com

The Body Shop The environment, animal rights, social issues, and education get as much—if not more—play on the Body Shop's Website than its products do. In other words, Anita Roddick's company is marketing itself online exactly like it does offline.
✓**www**→http://www.The-Body -Shop.com

Duracell Though the Duracell site includes information on batteries, an interactive toy trivia contest, and a large area devoted to the Puttermans, the battery-operated family that has dominated the company's commercials for the past few years, the real star here is the coppertop battery itself, which dominates the opening page.
✓**www**→http://www.duracell.com

Ferrari With all its content printed in both Italian and English, the Website of the famous sports-car manufacturer capitalizes on the rearing-stallion

IN-SITE: Levi-Strauss
http://www.levi.com

In its ongoing struggle to get a leg up on the jeans competition, Levi's site targets the MTV generation with extensive graphics, interactive attitude, and interviews with such Gen X luminaries as video director Spike Jonze. But what's most noteworthy about this lavish and entertaining site is its relentless branding—the opening page, which contains dozens of animated frames, unleashes a fusillade of red Levi's logos, blue jeans, and brown leather patches. You're probably familiar with Levi's already, but a visit to this site will make you a virtual expert.

companies—from sites peppered with logos and slogans (Budweiser, at **http://budweiser.com**) to sites that forgo traditional branding entirely, instead positioning companies as added-value participants in the online medium (Barnes and Noble, at **http://www .loci.com**).

trademark and the legend of founder Enzo Ferrari.
✓**www**→http://www.ferrari.it

Frito-Lay Subtitled "A Happenin' Place in Cyberspace," this site capitalizes on Frito-Lay's universe of snack brands, including Doritos, Tostitos, Fritos, Lay's, and Chee-tos. Consumers who recognize these names—or the company's mascot Chester the Cheetah—will feel right at home.
✓**www**→http://www.fritolay.com

Hollywood Records Hollywood Records has designed a cartoon world to promote its artists—Queen, Wickerman, etc. Music fans touring the "city" will bump into sound clips, videos, pictures, and concert schedules for bands playing on the label.
✓**www**→http://www.hollywoodrec.com

Maytag If you were Maytag, and you had a marketing campaign as recognizable as the lonely repairman, you wouldn't be likely to abandon the campaign simply because someone invented a new medium like the Web, right? Right. Ol' Lonely oversees a site rife with product information, contests, and more.
✓**www**→http://www.maytag.com

Ragu With Italian recipes, Italian language lessons, a chance to win a trip to Italy, information about Italian art and architecture, and even an ongoing soap opera called "As the Lasagna Bakes," Ragu has done everything humanly possible to position itself as an ethnically-flavored company.
✓**www**→http://www.eat.com

Interactivity

If branding is a central rule of marketing, interactivity is the cardinal rule of Net marketing. Websites can work subtly or blatantly, but if they do so without an eye toward the interactive possibilities of the Net, they risk rapid extinction. What kinds of interactivity work? Any kind that involves consumers in the decision-making, from clickable maps to trivia quizzes to online games; interactive technology is most effective when it works in conjunction with other marketing goals, from the delivery of product information to the surveying of consumers to the branding of a company's identity. Jack Daniel's (**http://www.infi.net/jack-daniels**), for example, offers screensavers for both Mac and PC platforms (although the company preserves its rough-hewn image, warning Netsurfers not to expect

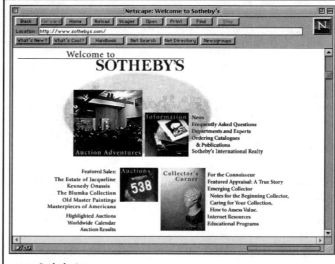

IN-SITE: **Sotheby's**
http://www.sothebys.com
The renowned international art auction house is online, and its Website encourages visitors to explore the high-stakes, high-glamour world of art auctions through guides, glossaries, articles, images of auctioned works, and even links to related Internet resources for art collectors, art historians, and auctioneers. The site is directed at Netsurfers curious about auctions; Sotheby's has netted special praise for its Auction Adventures, an interactive program which generates auction scenarios and lets visitors try to figure out how to bid successfully.

IN-SITE: Blockbuster
http://pwr.com/blockbuster

Once simply an immensely profitable video rental chain, Blockbuster has now expanded into all corners of the entertainment business, including the awards business. The Blockbuster Entertainment awards, broadcast March 6, 1996 on the UPN network, are based on fan votes, and the Web arm of the awards represents a new level of interactivity. Viewers can submit online ballots in the music category and in the video/theatrical category. And in another groundbreaking experiment, the awards themselves were simulcast over the Net, at Blockbuster's Website.

"bouncing geometic shapes, electronic noise or flying toasters"). Nabisco (**http://www.nabisco.com**) encourages its visitors to participate in an online scavenger hunt called "Where's the Nabisco Thing?" And Microsoft's home page (**http://www.microsoft.com**) includes a pull-down menu that lets customers locate specific product-support documents; if you're looking for system requirements for Microsoft Word 6.0, you can jump directly to a page about the program. To date, there are many examples of interactivity and few failed experiments, except for those sites that disingenuously promise consumers options and then proceed with a choreographed sales routine.

ter). Fox Monday Night Football fans are invited to play fantasy football on the site. And everyone else can head to the Entertainment section for games like the Dating Game—just type in a description of a your perfect mate and you'll be matched to a character selected from the Fox Network's prime time lineup (Ned, Stacey, Martin, etc.).
✓**www**→http://www.foxnet work.com

Sega Sega, a leader in the interactive gaming industry, couldn't exactly go online with a simple, low-key Website—and it didn't. The busy Website holds live chat sessions for gamers, contests, and even a place for gamers to upload their own add-ons and patches. And that's just the Sega Live! section—the site also includes a product info area, a company info area, and a section devoted exclusively to Sega sports games.
✓**www**→http://www.segaoa .com

The Singapore Online Guide The Singapore Tourist Promotion Board is using the Web to attract visitors with a searchable guide to Singapore that offers information about shopping, restaurants, festivals, nightlife, and hotels on the island. The interactive guide also features a downloadable movie clip, and an interactive tour guide that will prompt travelers for answers to a few basic travel questions (trip dates, interests, etc.) and then return a customized itinerary. Times and dates link to more detailed information.
✓**www**→http://www.travel.com. sg/sog

Bookworks Bookworks is the online home of Warner Books and Little, Brown and Company. The site regularly runs author interviews and excerpts from books. It has also mastered the medium, offering live chats with favorite authors and frequently linking to related sites—the Mysterious Press Homepage, for instance, might link to the Sherlock Holmes Page.
✓**www**→http://pathfinder.com/twep/Library/Library.html

Grolier's Online Grolier's is in the information industry, and fittingly, its Website is as well, with links to history, literature, science, philosophy, sports, religion, and technology.
✓**www**→http://www.grolier.com

The Nissan Pathfinder The 1995 Nissan Pathfinder was also called the Practical Guide to Outdoor Adventure. Using a series of outdoor adventure stories and outdoorsman tips, the site both showed off the features of the car and linked to a seemingly endless number of Internet resources for the outdoorsman—from scuba diving sites to mountain-biking discussions to sled dog racing FAQs.
✓**www**→http://www.nissanmotors.com/pathfinder/me_path.html

Panasonic Interactive Media Homepage Along with information about the 3DO home gaming system and 3DO game titles, the site links to

Hypertextual Marketing

What is hypertext? It's text with index fingers, specially coded pages that conceal a number of links to other pages. And it's also how the World Wide Web works. Each and every page on the Web carries with it the power to connect to an infinity of other pages: the personal page of a Seattle pediatrician can link to the corporate home page of a pharmaceutical company; the page of a Rolling Stones fan in Hamburg can link to the band's official home page; a page from an online sports 'zine can link to the official site of the National Basketball Association. The interconnections are endless, and endlessly fascinating.

In the era of Net marketing, many companies have taken it upon themselves to emphasize the hypertextual aspects of the medium. Link-heavy sites not only help build traffic as they move consumers from one page to another, but they also serve as important navigational aids; in this vast new medium, any site that helps Netsurfers orient themselves provides a valuable customer service and a reason to return to the site. For example, Alamo Rent-A-Car's Freeways site (**http://www.freeways.com**) positions itself as a rudimentary guide to the Web's travel resources, with a valuable set of links to sites such as Travel Web and Airlines of the Web. Grolier's Online (**http://www.grolier.com**), the Website of the popular encyclopedia, has created a set of general knowledge links. And American Recordings (**http://american.recordings.com**), the record label of rap-metal impresario Rick Rubin, has earned much of its online popularity as a result of the Ultimate Band List, a huge hyperlinked directory of musical resources.

As these examples demonstrate, many companies use hypertextual marketing to increase awareness of (and interest in) their own products; this strategy creates an

IN-SITE: **MasterCard International**
       http://www.mastercard.com
While some companies have held themselves apart from the online world, MasterCard has opted to immerse itself in Net culture. The company's site offers extensive Web tutorials and tours, fiction for the cybermedium, an ATM locator, and an extensive directory of online stores accepting MasterCard. But the site is most noteworthy for its pointers, quotations that include unexpected links (a Thomas Edison quote, for instance, connects to lightbulb jokes). The pointers, updated daily, establish MasterCard as a gateway to the unexplored corners of the Web.

association between the riches of the Web and the company's riches, and positions the company as a Net-savvy organization with a vested interest in the consumer's online comfort. Increasingly, though, companies are building collections of links that extend beyond the narrow boundaries of their corporate identities. The Guinness brewery site (**http://www.itl.net /guinness**) not only links to various British entertainment and media sites, but also lets visitors submit their favorite URLs—or take a spin on the Web courtesy of a program that generates a random destination.

dozens of gaming sites on the Internet, ranging from *Computer Gaming World* magazine to the 3DO FAQ.
✓**www**→http://www.MITL .Research.Panasonic.COM/cool

TurboTax Online Intuit's highly successful tax program may make preparing taxes easier, but the Website tries to make tax time a little more fun. A Fun On the Net section links customers to sites they might want to explore when they "just want to avoid even thinking about taxes." Intuit also uses the Website to deliver customers a wide range of tax tips and technical support.
✓**www**→http://www.intuit.com /turbotax

Visa Expo Visa elegantly integrates links to other relevant Websites. In its Visa Worldwide section, for instance, customers can link to the Websites of banks accepting Visa cards in countries all over the world. In its travel section, the site links to Internet resources for virtually every nation in the world. Visa often features spectacular Web pages on big events it sponsors—including links to related sites online.
✓**www**→http://www.visa.com

WNEW WNEW (102.7 FM), a New York City alternative-rock station, offers an extensive collection of connections to Internet sites, including large lists of links to music, television, movie, weather, and New York City sites. It also links its weekly playlist to artist sites on the Web, thus enabling fans of Joan Osborne or Pulp to get their news and sound clip fix.
✓**www**→http://www.wnew.com

Fidelity Investor Center Fidelity successfully blurs the line between selling advice and giving it away, with its site, which is jam-packed with financial information for potential customers. Visitors can use the site to design a retirement plan, determine which type of investor they are, or learn about mutual funds—all the while absorbing information about a wide range of Fidelity's investment opportunities. The generally somber site even has a section partitioned off for contests and games—everybody should play Guess the Dow and win a financial CD-ROM!
✓**www**→http://www.fid-inv .com

Kodak Throughout this Website Kodak positions itself as a company on the cutting edge of image-processing techniques. Along with an extensive company history and an online photography gallery, the Website includes a vast product information archive, which divides the company's products into conceptual categories such as "Capture," "Storage," "Manage," and "Share."
✓**www**→http://www.kodak.com

Magnavox With the help of innovative navigational graphics—an online remote control and console buttons—the consumer electronics giant has created an elegant and well-designed guide to its products and its customer-support services. What's here? An electronics reference area that includes a glos-

Product Information

Offline, any sales force spends the lion's share of its time answering questions about products. How much do they cost? What do they do? How well do they do it? When will new models be introduced into the marketplace? Can old products be repaired and serviced? Online, the process of providing product information and product support is at once more affordable and more comprehensive. For example, the U-Haul moving company's Website (**http://www.uhaul.com**) presents its products—boxes, moving equipment, and trucks—in terms the average mover understands, with easy-to-follow directions for packing homes and apartments. Geffen/DGC Records (**http://www.geffen .com**) not only describes its most recent releases, but also gives consumers the ability to make an instant purchase with the help of an online record store. In moving product information and support onto the

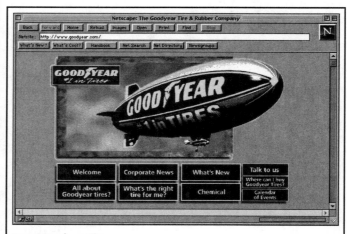

IN-SITE: **Goodyear Tires**
         http://www.goodyear.com
Goodyear knows its tires, and the people at Goodyear want you to know their tires too. Customers visiting the blimp-laden site can use the store locator to find out who's selling Goodyear tires, learn safer driving with a list of road tips, and motor to other car-related sites online with Goodyear's collection of automotive links. But the real draw is the tires, and specifically tire-buying. To help consumers in the market for new tires, Goodyear has created an online "Tire School," an illustrated primer on selecting, purchasing, and maintaining tires.

Web, many companies have designed innovative updates on old traditions of product-information delivery. Customer-service hotlines have been replaced by email forms; question-and-answer sessions with salespeople have been replaced by Frequently Asked Question lists, complete with answers. Web technology not only allows companies to track consumer concerns (an automobile manufacturer whose Website is suddenly flooded by Netsurfers worried about a minivan's air-conditioning can move air-conditioning information to the top of the site), but also to link to related products (an electronics manufacturer can place related models in close proximity, so that a consumer buying a new television will also learn about videocassette recorders) and related processes (a winery site that teaches visitors about Australian wines can then offer specific information about the wines that company has in its inventory).

The Web even permits companies to employ combination strategies—for example, using hypertext technology to create a virtual product-support department. For example, Apple Computer's large list of product-support documents and resources (**http://www2 .apple.com/documents/productsupport.html**) is not a unified effort, but rather a set of links to various companies and Apple subdivisions across the Web, including QuickTime (**http://quicktime.apple.com**) and Claris (**http://www.claris.com**).

sary of all electronics terms mentioned on the site, a store locator, and a steady stream of TV giveaways and links to entertainment sites. And, of course, there are specs for each product in Magnavox's catalog with hypertext links that explain product features.
✓**www**→http://www.magnavox .com

People's Bank With an airy design and bright, unthreatening graphics, the Website of the Connecticut-based People's Bank plays straight into the heart of traditional bank positioning, casting People's as a dependable institution, largely faceless but comforting. In addition to offering a message from the CEO, the company's quarterly financial reports, and links to financial newspapers across the Web, People's includes an area devoted to describing various products and services such as PC Banking, Tele-Banking, Correspondent Banking, and even Supermarket Banking.
✓**www**→http://www.peoples .com

Professional Association of Diving Instructors Known by its acronym, PDI, the professional Association of Diving Instructors runs diving centers, international diving conferences and events, diving schools, and resorts. For detailed information on any of these places or events, customers can search the comprehensive directories on its Website. And there's even a large online catalog with videos, instructional booklets, and other equipment targeted at beginning, intermediate, and advanced divers.
✓**www**→http://www.padi.com

Product Recommendations

Companies advertising in radio or on television are restricted to showcasing a few products; companies advertising on the Web are not. The unlimited space, and the ability to show each customer only the part of the site that interest him or her, makes customized product information a real possibility. This both enhances the sales of the company's products, and in appropriate categories positions the company as the leading expert in the industry.

Here, different industries employ similar strategies. In late 1995, the Intel site (**http://www.intel.com**) included a section titled "What PC is right for you" in which Intel advised consumers on how to choose the

IN-SITE: L.L. Bean
http://www.llbean.com

L.L. Bean's site is rugged and polished at once—rugged in its graphics and ambiance, which evoke rock-climbing and cross-country skiing, and polished in its execution, which uses state-of-the-art Web production techniques. In addition to Park Search, a database of more than 900 national forests and state parks, Bean provides links to sites on outdoor activity of all kinds. But the real draw is the online catalog, which not only describes products, but guides customers to related items—for instance, the Gore-Tex boots page links to a page on lightweight socks.

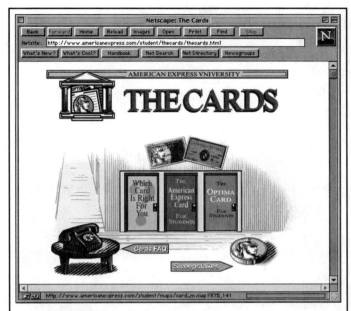

IN-SITE: AmEx University
http://www.americanexpress.com/student
College students must be important to AmEx, because they're targeting them with style online. This intensely interactive site is fast, fun, and focused entirely on the needs and interests of college students. Clickable image maps (a train station, a street corner, and a clubhouse, for instance) lead to programs that plan trips, list scholarships, and sample sound clips from bands. Where are AmEx's products? In The Cards, of course—a section of the site that pairs undergrads with the credit card best suited for them.

best personal computer; factors included price, computing power, and platform. Fidelity Investments (**http://www.fidelity.com**) helps consumers make appropriate product choices by allowing visitors to use a self-scoring worksheet to put together a mix of mutual funds that are appropriate for that visitor's specific goal, and to calculate the cost of college for a child of a specific age.

The auto aftermarket, which relies on occasional purchases that require some preparation, is particularly concerned with this sort of marketing. The Goodyear Tire Company (**http://www.goodyear. com**), for example, provides detailed information on choosing the right tires for the consumer's vehicle and needs.

dealer, runs two mailing lists where customers can discuss the products and Pentax can send out product announcements, and offers easy-to-navigate product catalogs. It also has simple walkthrough guides to choosing a camera or a pair of binoculars. A series of simple questions and nontechnical equipment descriptions guide the customer from choosing a general type of camera or binocular to picking a specific model.
✓**www**→http://www.pentax.com

Ping Sports equipment is a growing market online, and the manufacturer of golf clubs has created a small but useful site that includes an online club selector. How does it work? Well, Netsurfers input their body dimensions, and a program at Ping's end picks a club. Ping doesn't rely on puns about "links"; this site does, however, demonstate the power of customized consumption. Fore!
✓**www**→http://www.pinggolf.com

Toro Toro knows that the average person doesn't buy a landscape sculpting vehicle often, so its Website is set up to give customers the guidance they'll need. Customers can select a product class (snowblower, lawnmower, etc.), answer a few simple questions (how long is your driveway? what is the average snowfall in your area?), and Toro will recommend particular products. The site also runs a Dealer Locator to track down the products and offers an extensive searchable database of lawn care information. Discolored grass? Insects? Just ask Earl The Yard-Care Answer Guy.
✓**www**→http://www.toro.com

American Airlines Home Page One of the best airline sites on the Web, the American Airlines Home Page lets travellers view their personal mileage summaries, check flight schedules (including movie listings), and read about several American Airlines travel programs.
✓**www**→http://www.amrcorp.com/aa_home/aa_home.htm

Amtrak How does a national rail company without many competitors market itself? In Amtrak's case, it concentrates on the past and the present, not only detailing the company's history, but also publishing an online rail map and schedules. And for consumers who haven't been getting the most out of their train-travel experience, Amtrak also furnishes a list of train trips that help make vacations more enjoyable.
✓**www**→http://www.amtrak.com

Godiva Chocolatier The gourmet chocolatier's site includes a huge recipe section so that chocolate lovers can explore their passion's dietary versatility.
✓**www**→http://www.godiva.com

International Channel Network The International Channel Network provides programming in more than 23 languages. The Website offers visitors updated programming information (click the name of a language for a list of programs playing on the network in that

Enhancing the Product

By providing services or information to the consumer through its Website, a company can actually enhance the value of its products. This type of activity can range across a wide variety of product categories— Websites can include software upgrades, recipes, and even (in the case of Federal Express and United Parcel Service) package-tracking services.

One example of how a company can use the Web to create an enhanced, more valuable product is the case

IN-SITE: **Federal Express**
http://www.fedex.com
Aggressive branding, intelligent design, and fast-loading graphics have made the Federal Express Website one of the most successful experiments in the early phases of online marketing. But aggressive branding, intelligent design, and fast-loading graphics are merely reasons to like the site—for a reason to love it, visit the package tracking feature, which lets FedEx customers locate their airbills with the aid of an online form. FedEx also delivers on its promise of customer response, with numerous email links to the company's home offices in Memphis.

of CUC's Shopper's Advantage, a rapidly growing subscription service that finds its members the best prices on over 250,000 brand name items—largely thanks to a vast database of retailers, inventories, and shipping costs. CUC's principal business operates by phone; customers call up seeking specific products and CUC finds the best available price, with delivery, on that specific item. But phone service has its limits. Customers may be hesitant to occupy a customer service representative for a long time. Moreover, even customers presented with dozens of options may find them difficult to remember. And finally, long phone calls, all of which are trafficked through CUC's toll-free number, are costly for the company.

In contrast, CUC's Website (**http://www.cuc.com**) allows the consumer to research—and even purchase—more than 250,000 name-brand products online. A customer can visit the site looking to purchase a specific television, obtain a description and a price, and then use the online search features to investigate hypothetical adjustments of expense (What if I want to spend $50 more? What if I want to spend $50 less?). By providing the customer with absolute control over all the available information—and eliminating the costs of the 800 number—the Web allows CUC to create a superior product. And Web subscription technology even enables CUC to offer skeptical Netsurfers a three-month trial membership for the nominal cost of $1.

language) and, perhaps, more impressively, links to Internet resources to assist students learning languages and the educators teaching them.
✓**www**→http://www.i-channel.com

Land 'O Lakes This buttery yellow (and incredibly fast) Website is packed with cooking tips and recipes for cookies, cake, pasta, and other treats made using Land 'O Lakes products.
✓**www**→http://www.landolakes.com

United Parcel Service Like Federal Express, UPS offers a package tracking service. But the shipping company's Website also includes software for making the delivery process quicker and easier—a cost calculator, a ground time estimator, and rate charts.
✓**www**→http://www.ups.com

Virtual Vineyards What goes best with a T-Bone steak, red or white? Virtual Vineyards capitalizes on the average consumer's interest in wine, and the concomitant intimidation with traditional wine ratings systems. Using Peter Granoff's "trademark tasting chart," the site helps customers compile a personal menu that reflects their individual tastes in stomped, fermented grapes.
✓**www**→http://www.virtualvin.com

Visa The credit card company offers its cardholders an extremely valuable service—an ATM locator, which helps Netsurfers find money machines worldwide.
✓**www**→http://www.visa.com

Advil The painkiller company's Website includes information on its product, but a valuable draw of the site is its health education forum, which gives Netsurfers the lowdown on everything from headaches to fitness to lower back pain.
✓**www**→http://www.ahpc.com

Freeways by Alamo Rent-A-Car Booking a car may lead the list of things to do at the Alamo Website, but Alamo doesn't just hand travelers the keys and wave goodbye. The site delivers travel tips, information on driving destinations, games for "cooped-up kids," an Alamo locator, directions for getting around popular U.S. cities, coupons for tourist sites, and even links to other travel, map, and weather sites. Knowing that travelers like to talk about their trips, Alamo even offers a forum for drivers to compare notes on roadside food, hotels, and sightseeing.
✓**www**→http://www.freeways.com

Gatorade Gatorade has always advertised its product in the context of sports, and the Website stays true to form. Sure, there's an icon customers can click for information about the drink, but other icons lead to reports and features about sporting events, as well as to a section devoted to Michael Jordan (Chicago Bulls game reports, Jordan stats, Jordan photos, and personal tidbits).
✓**www**→http://www.gatorade.com

Added Content

The Web gives companies virtually infinite marketing space—the challenge is to fill that space with valuable content. One technique popular among companies is to provide information that is, in some way, likely to be of interest to the users of a product, to position the company as an expert in its industry and pass on the fruits of that expertise to the consumer. For example, Alamo Rent-A-Car's Freeways site (**http://www.freeways.com**) furnishes a list of handy travel tips, with a variety of suggestions for harried parents on the finer points of entertaining grumpy children. Advil (**http://www.ahpc.com**) has created a large health education forum, and L.L. Bean describes its Website (**http://www.llbean.com**) as one of the premier sources online for "outdoor sporting information and expert advice." If these are obvious examples of this strategy, the Web is filled with less obvious ones, too. Guardian Alarms (**http://www.stayout.com**) offers detailed instructions on keeping homes secure, noting that "all exterior doors should be either metal or solid core, and that glass or thin wood panels, in or near the door, can be protected by installing polycarbonate glazing and secured with one-way screws." And the Armstrong Funeral Home in Ontario (**http://www.funeral.net**), provides information on twentieth-century thanatology, as well as links to related sites. The universe of companies online covers everything from home decorating to cooking to travel to personal fitness, and most of those companies have a vested interest in drawing customers to their site with industry-specific content.

Companies designing online content should keep in mind that the Web, while perhaps the best means of delivering information, is not the only means—added content can also be transported to consumers in news-

IN-SITE: Hot Hot Hot
http://www.hot.presence.com

This Pasadena, California-based hot sauce shop was one of the first businesses to harness the power of the online medium, and the company's site remains one of the most entertaining, playful, and visually pleasing on the Web. In addition to mapping its sauces according to country of origin and listing the ten hottest sauces known to man—the undisputed champ is Dave's Insanity Sauce, which comes wrapped in yellow caution tape—Hot Hot Hot furnishes an FAQ that addresses such scorched-mouth topics as Scoville units (which measure chile potency).

groups and mailing lists. Mailing lists are especially effective; for a modest initial investment, companies can install a piece of software on their server that fields all subscription requests and automatically emails the list to subscribers. The Internet search engine Lycos (**http://www.lycos.com**), for example, hosts an interest-based mailing list that helps consumers "keep…on top of the latest sites in favorite areas of interest."

Holiday Inn Along with its directory of Holiday Inn hotels worldwide and online reservation system, the site challenges its visitors to compete in an Internet version of the travel trivia game Travel Buff. Players choose a level of difficulty and are then asked questions which they must answer within a fixed period of time. Visitors can either play the game online or download versions to play offline.
✓**www**→http://www.holiday-inn.com

Lexus Delivering more golf content than most sports sites, Lexus's Website has tournament schedules, a course locator, an equipment shop, links to golf-related sites online, golfing news, putting advice, and contests. Cars, on the other hand, surface subtly, and occupy only a small segment of the site.
✓**www**→http://www.lexuscar.com

SallieMae One of the largest financial services companies in the U.S., SallieMae delivers a Website packed with financial aid advice, worksheets, and calculators. Targeted at students, parents, and college financial aid advisors, it manages to serve the needs of all three groups at once. If you need to learn the basics of paying for your college education, come here.
✓**www**→http://www.salliemae.com

Simmons The mattress company's Website includes enough information on sleep to keep an insomniac occupied all night long—sleep quotas, a sleep debt analyzer, and more.
✓**www**→http://www.simmonsco.com

Bank of America Each day customers are invited to click the piggy bank on the opening screen for a new money tip. Bank of America has filled its site with weekly columns, monthly features, and economic news and data to draw customers back as well.
✓**www**→http://www.bofa.com

MTV Online MTV's putting on quite a show on the Web, with regularly updated music news briefs, music industry gossip and rumors, album reviews, music charts, and a multimedia feast of sound clips and videos. And that's just the music section! The Animation section goes all out promoting network stars like *Beavis & Butt-Head, Aeon Flux, The Maxx,* and *The Head.* Enough changing content on this site to keep pop culture and music fans coming back regularly.
✓**www**→http://www.mtv.com

The Prudential Prudential has put so much financial planning information on its Website that visitors have plenty of reasons to keep coming back, but the people who want you to own a piece of the rock have also broken new ground in innovative Web marketing. The site is running a campaign that puts a face on financial planning decisions, makes them easier to understand, and uses the interactive potential of the Web. Visitors are given details about a financial decision faced by a virtual Prudential customer and asked to vote on what the customer

Encouraging Repeat Visits

To build brand image and product awareness—and to increase the chance of an online sale—companies want consumers to return to their Website frequently, and one of the best ways to encourage return visits is to provide fresh information with some regularity. The online record store CDNow! (**http://cdnow.com**) includes an area for music news, which apprises visitors of the latest record releases, award nominations, and rock-star arrests. Dreyfus, the financial services company (**http://www.dreyfus.com**), is finalizing plans for an enhanced effort to attract return customers. When Dreyfus first launched its Website, it included a weekly financial review from the company's top economist. Now the site is expected to change

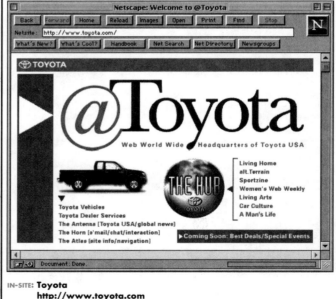

IN-SITE: **Toyota**
http://www.toyota.com
When you think of cars, you probably think of engines, brakes, and tires—not restaurants, women's health, or opera. But if Toyota has its way, you may soon be associating all of these topics with the Japanese automaker. While the Toyota Website does contain information on vehicles and dealer services, the site's front page also promotes *The Hub,* an online magazine created and maintained by the corporation. The site demands higher levels of maintenance. Our question: Will Toyota be able to sustain it.

IN-SITE: The NBA
http://www.nba.com

With so many marketable properties—Michael Jordan, Charles Barkley, Shaquille O'Neal, Dennis Rodman, Damon Stoudamire, and so on—the National Basketball Association is in an enviable position, and the league's Website spotlights its star personalities. In addition, the NBA offers hoop fans enough resident content to fill Bob Lanier's shoes—not only last night's scores, but also biographies for every single player in the league and extended feature articles. And then there's the NBA Theater (pictured), a collection of on-court highlights updated weekly for maximum fan satisfaction.

daily, with contributions from a rotating panel of Dreyfus's financial experts: one day the firm's top stock analyst might discuss the prospects for the stock market; the following day the firm's top bond market analyst might forecast bond performance. Increasingly, companies are opting for frequent content updates, whether product-related or not (some companies, like Toyota, have created general-interest online publications). Not only do these updates position the company as an organization that has fully embraced the online medium, but they also create compelling reasons for customers to return to the site.

should do. Every three weeks votes are tabulated and a new decision is featured. Visitors, however, can continue to follow the progress of the former featured customers and track how smart their decisions were.
✓**www**→http://www.prudential.com

Spiegel The clothing and furniture catalog house has put highlights from its product line online, and minimized loading speeds by showing images only when customers choose a specific product. But this site is more than just an online catalog. Spiegel is trying to keep customers coming back with an extensive online magazine and an advice column that focuses on fitness, fashion, and nutrition issues.
✓**www**→http://www.spiegel.com

The Travel Channel The Travel Channel has created a Website that is successful as an online travel resource as well as a promotion for a cable network. The site runs weekly travel features and columns, sponsors and hosts message-based and live travel discussions, carries a huge gallery of travel photos uploaded by visitors, offers travel advice and info, maintains a searchable database of more than 26,000 electronic travel brochures, and links to other travel sites. And all of the additional information hasn't obscured the site's primary mission—cable customers interested in the channel's televised offerings can use the Website for programming and schedule information.
✓**www**→http://www.travelchannel.com

Amazon.com "Earth's largest bookstore" has come up with a truly innovative way of standing out among the hundreds of bookshops in Cyberspace. They offer "Eyes & Editors," a free personal notification service to keep avid readers apprised of new releases by favorite authors, new titles in any field, and any other bibliophile news.
✓**www**→http://www.amazon.com

Epson The Epson technical support staff runs several discussion forums for its lines of products on the Epson Website. The boards are simple to use and are supplemented with FAQs and a substantial amount of product information. The site also includes Web-based problem report generators that customers can use to alert Epson to problems they might be experiencing.
✓**www**→http://www.epson.com

Firefly Firefly used to be known as HOMR, and before that RINGO, but it's always been something similar to what it is now—an online music recommendation agent. With the help of a fairly simple computer program, Firefly lets its visitors input their musical tastes, and then recommends albums appropriate to those tastes. In addition to this, the Firefly site attempts to build a community of like-minded music fans, furnishing an extensive online environment for speaking to other Firefly users.
✓**www**→http://www.ffly.com

Creating a Dialogue

Companies can use the Web's communications potential to gather feedback from their customers and participate in an ongoing dialogue with them, even create Cyberspace versions of "focus groups," in which consumers give instant feedback on existing and proposed products. But any company planning to solicit online feedback should remember that consumers will expect a reply. When former President Lyndon Johnson was a Texas Congressman, he forced his staff to answer every letter from a constituent, and any company planning on doing business online should heed the Johnson Rule. The athletic-shoe manufacturer Reebok (**http://www.planetreebok.com**), an early entrant in the online marketing arena, made a decision to answer each and every email it received; similarly, Sega's Customer Service Link (**http://www.segaoa.com**) promises a response within five days. Websites can collect complaints about products and service, suggestions for new products, and even allow consumers to schedule repair and service visits—and they are at once more efficient and more substantive than toll-free numbers.

In addition to responding to consumer concerns, companies can use the Web to encourage ongoing dialogue with their customers and build product sales by providing unique value. This may be the single most powerful means of using the Web to build increased sales. But any company attempting this strategy should heed the cardinal rule of manufacturer-consumer dialogue—a consumer will eagerly participate in a dialogue if he or she receives something of value in return. The massive online bookstore known as Amazon.com (**http://www.amazon.com**) asks visitors to fill out an online questionnaire that includes questions about their interests and hobbies, and then noti-

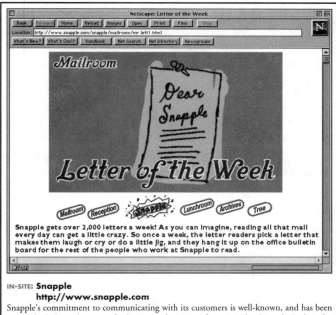

IN-SITE: **Snapple**
http://www.snapple.com

Snapple's commitment to communicating with its customers is well-known, and has been established through years of television advertising featuring the Snapple Lady, who answers customer mail with the help of humorous skits. Although the familiar Snapple lady doesn't show her face online, the strategy of communicating directly with customers is still very much in evidence at its Website, especially in the popular Letter of the Week feature, which electronically posts one of the thousands of letters that Snapple receives each week.

fies them about the publication of books they might want to buy. PC Flowers (**http://www.pcgifts.ibm .com**) invites visitors to participate in the Gift Reminder Service which collects relevant information from participants—including birthdays, anniversaries, etc.—and then emails them when an important event is approaching. Meanwhile, industries like the auto aftermarket have experimented with a more sales-oriented variation, conducting basic interviews with consumers and then notifying them when they need to replace an infrequently purchased product. In general, consumers are happy to receive targeted sales messages and participate in a dialogue when it solves a problem, makes life easier, or helps individuals pursue their specific interests. The Web has proven an extraordinary medium in this regard.

Ford Customers who register with the Ford Customer Link are eligible to be chosen to test-market Ford products and can request notification when Ford produces a new product or offers a special incentive for its car buyers.
✓**www**→http://www.ford.com

Godiva Chocolatier Website visitors can request that Godiva email them a reminder to send chocolates before a gift-giving occasion.
✓**www**→http://www.godiva .com

GT Web GT Interactive Software sells some of the most popular PC and Mac games on the market, including Doom II, Locus, and Island Casino. Customers can sign up for Web-Flash bulletins at GT Interactive's site, and when new products become available or there are developments with popular games, the company will send email customers.
✓**www**→http://www.gtinter active.com

Nordstrom The department store is online, where it offers its customers a free personal shopper. How does personalization work? Well, a customer can email Nordstrom with a product request (shoes in a size 12?) and the shopper will email the customer back suggestions. If the customer wants to buy, he or she can send an email order and Nordstrom will FedEx the goods. As a personal shopper gets to know the customer's tastes, the company will send the customer email about special promotions or new items.
✓**www**→http://www2.pcy.mci .net/marketplace/nordstrom

Barnes & Noble: The Loci
Barnes & Noble isn't selling books online. It's building a community of college students who log on to chat, attend weekly events with authors and celebrities, read book and movie reviews, play games, opine on world events, and pick up after-college advice (job hunting, graduate school, etc.). While the bookstore funds and supports the site, it's turned over the tone and editorial direction to college students, positioning the company as a social gathering place, a bookstore that understands both the needs of college students and the culture of the Net.
✓**www**→http://www.loci.com

Gund Gunderland is a community for teddy bear buffs that offers product information (a bear family tree), a program to find the nearest Gund retailer, games and activities, and even a live chat channel for teddy bear talk.
✓**www**→http://www.gund.com

Heineken The Dutch Heineken site takes an old hospitality strategy and reupholsters it for Cyberspace: have visitors sign a guest book. The rest of the site isn't too shabby either, with pages devoted to major Heineken promotions worldwide (for a concert, for instance, the site featured dozens of video clips and artist bios of performers); a history of Heineken; the Heineken Quest, an interactive game of traveling, gambling, and bribing that requires players to check their email daily; and a

Building a Community

For years, marketers in other media have tried to build a sense of community for their consumers. These might be communities of people who share an interest in the product itself, or they might be communities of people who, through their involvement, share a similar lifestyle or outlook on life. Whatever the case, auto manufacturers, clothing companies, television networks, breweries, and any other companies with identifiable constituencies have all developed online marketing efforts that work to unify these consumers.

IN-SITE: **Bell Atlantic**
http://www.bell-atl.com/sbs
Bell Atlantic's entire site is presided over by James Earl Jones, whose voice is featured on the company's commercials. But Jones's *basso profundo* isn't the site's only special feature. Bell Atlantic's Small Business Center, which opens with a lavish clickable map, offers a variety of online services oriented toward the needs of small businesspeople, including classified advertising, listings of free business seminars across the country, links to small-business sites on the Net, and even a Web-based bulletin board on which small business owners can communicate with one another.

Since the online world is full of small communities—newsgroup members, mailing list subscribers, visitors to commercial service forums—the early stages of Net marketing have seen dozens of examples of this kind of collective identity, from the strategic placement of ads in newsgroups to the creation of Web-based discussion groups. Barnes & Noble's Loci site (**http://www.loci.com**) holds regularly scheduled chat sessions that encourage interaction among its visitors. This strategy inverts traditional branding and positioning tactics, creating a set of associations for a product based on consumer rather than on corporate personality. The Fox television network (**http://www.foxnetwork.com**) has established Web-based message groups for each of Fox's prime-time shows, as well as hosting real-time chat sessions about shows like *Martin*, *The Simpsons*, *The X-Files*, and *Melrose Place*. And companies like Egghead Software (**http://www.egghead.com**) have stressed the financial aspect of community, founding online clubs that offer participating consumers special deals on products and services. Finally, there are those companies that have chosen to appropriate communities already in existence. The mattress manufacturer Simmons (**http://www.simmonsco.com**), for example, links to Usenet newsgroups like **alt.support.sleep-disorder** and **alt.dreams**. Whether this practice of superimposing commercial categories over noncommercial ones will prove popular depends on how well companies integrate their concerns with the larger online community. Still, community creation—whether for financial gain or as a positioning issue within the emerging online medium—reinforces consumer-product identification. A consumer's identification with the product and participation in the community can provide new ideas on how to use or enjoy a product and guarantee return traffic to a site.

form to send an illustrated electronic postcard to a friend.
✓**www**→http://www.Heineken.nl

Reebok One of the first non-computer companies to develop a presence on the Web, Reebok has turned its planet into a hangout where sports and fitness enthusiasts gather to chat with each other, check in for fitness tips, browse features about the Olympics and women's sports events, keep tabs on the causes that Reebok supports (including human rights and Project America), and get Reebok's guidance about other sites to explore on the Web. The site is full of multi-universal rhetoric like, "We believe in life on other planets, so here are the places we like to visit." The focal point of Planet Reebok is its Cyberbok, an online auditorium that Reebok uses to host live chats with big sports personalities like Roger "Rocket" Clemens, Frank "The Big Hurt" Thomas, Dominique "The Human Highlight Film" Wilkins, and UConn women's basketball superstar Rebecca Lobo.
✓**www**→http://www.planetreebok.com

Zima Zima's doing a little bit of everything on its Gen-X-cellent site—contests; merchandising, product information, and stories that trace the adventures of the Website's faceless, hapless, and Zima-drinking antihero Duncan. And those Netzurferz who want more Zima than the zite providez can join Tribe Z, a online club that gives them access to otherwise hidden corners of the site. All in all, an innovative and hypnotic site for fans of clear malt liquor.
✓**www**→http://www.zima.com

Beech-Nut Babies cannot surf the Web, and as a result, the baby-food manufacturer Beech-Nut has wisely targeted *parents* of newborns. In addition to a product guide, the site includes dozens of features directed specifically at new parents—news about pesticides, Internet birth announcements—and even links to an independent Website called Babycare Corner, which is sponsored by Beech-Nut.
✓**www**→http://www.beechnut.com

Black and Decker They're a dying species, the American male, and the venerable tool manufacturer wants to do its part to save men from the influx of other genders. As a result, the Website never strays far from Home Improvement territory—although the androcentric fixer-upper content is offered with tongue firmly planted in cheek, there are some real payoffs (check out the "Real Men Bake Bread" Contest, which has as its grand prize a trip to Paris).
✓**www**→http://www.bdhome.com

Dole 5-A-Day Homepage Dole has turned its Website into a campaign to get kids to eat five servings of fruits and vegetables a day. While the Fun section is aimed at young children (Play the 5-A-Day Game!), the rest of the site is for teachers willing to preach the 5-A-Day gospel.
✓**www**→http://www.dole5aday.com

Targeting

Target-marketing—the growing practice of increasing returns on marketing dollars by directing campaigns at the consumers most likely to respond—is alive and well on the Web, although with an interesting twist. In the past, marketers could advertise in publications associated with target groups; cosmetics companies bought ads in women's magazines and shaving companies bought ads in men's magazines. Online, where companies have created their own "magazines," the dynamic is reversed—companies must draw specific demographic groups to their site with tailored information, incentives, or promotions. As a result, many media and entertainment companies have used sections of their sites—if not their entire sites—to appeal to the interests of valuable Gen X consumers. Similarly, beer companies, razor companies, and auto manufacturers have targeted men with androcentric resources like sports guides and information about hair-regrowing drugs. Pharmaceutical and cosmetic firms have aimed their pitch at women. And kids are as huge a market online as they are on television and in movie theaters, defining the strategies of cereal companies, toy companies, clothing companies, and even entertainment mega-corporations (Disney and Fox both run sites geared toward the little people).

Because of the Web's informational demands, these sites are almost all content-intensive; Budweiser (**http://budweiser.com**), which has long been a sponsor of auto racing, has created online forums and features for auto racing. And the Campbell's Soup Website (**http://www.campbellsoups.com**) is geared toward homemakers, although Campbell's is careful to use gender-neutral language. Finally, targeting is, of course, closely connected with strategies for building traffic at your Website. As discussed in Chapter Four

IN-SITE: Bristol-Myers Squibb
http://www.womenslink.com

For its lavish, high-production Website, the large manufacturer of beauty and health products has chosen to minimize its corporate identity (a tiny logo appears at the bottom of the window) and instead target women. Bristol-Myers promotes Women's Link—which contains information on skin care, hair care, and even career management, as "the place for women-in-the-know…a library, a cafe, a wellness center, and a spa—all in one," and ends its welcome message with the now-correct observation that "Cyberspace isn't a men's club anymore."

of this book, the evolving technology for tracking online use is likely to increase the potential for targeting individuals with even more specific demographic characteristics. Ultimately, the Web allows marketers to enter into a true one-to-one dialogue with both prospects and customers.

Kellogg Cereal is for kids, and so is Kellogg's Website, which uses a clubhouse motif to guide young breakfast-eaters through a series of interactive games and coloring exercises with the help of puffed-rice pixies Snap, Crackle, and Pop.
✓**www**→http://www.kellogs.com

Ryka Since Ryka's athletic shoes are exclusively for women, it's only fitting that the shoe manufacturer's Website is targeted at those Netsurfers with XX chromosomes. In addition to a an online forum and a direct email link, Ryka has created the Link Tank, a collection of links to other women-oriented resources around the Web, including the National Organization for Women, the Global Fund for Women, and the National Alliance of Breast Cancer Organizations.
✓**www**→http://www.ryka.com

Stuart Hall: Virtual Notebook Choosing the right notebook is important to kids, and the notebook manufacturer Stuart Hall wants to help. The company's colorful Website invites visitors to participate in contests (win a diskman!), peruse fashion tips (what's awesome, what's not), and get a rundown on hip new school accessories.
✓**www**→http://www.stuarthall.com

Target The discount department store's Website is oriented toward new parents, with a Lullaby Club that not only helps expectant Netsurfers pick out a name for their bundle of joy, but also allows them to set up a gift registry for their new baby.
✓**www**→http://www.targetstores.com

Burlington Coat Factory
The Burlington Coat Factory has over 150 locations nationwide, and its Website features a store locator to help customers find them. Great URL, Burlington!
✓**www**→http://www.coat.com

Gund Gotta getta Gund and uncertain where the plush animals are being sold these days? Just enter your ZIP code and the online locator will retrieve the name of the nearest Gund retailer.
✓**www**→http://www.gund.com

Mobil Mobil has put its huge database of service stations and lubricant distributors online to help customers locate a station near them. Customers can specify if they want a bare-bones station or one with several options (convenience store, service bay, car wash, or diesel pumps).
✓**www**→http://mobil.crcmedia.com

Home Depot The Home Depot phenomenon has swept suburban America, with more than 400 of the giant hardware stores nationwide. Customers desperate for a lug wrench, hammer, or a new toilet seat for the master bathroom can use the color-coded map on the Website to find the store closest to them.
✓**www**→http://www.homedepot.com

Jolt How much caffeine do you need? How much caffeine can you endure? The Jolt site rates caffeine products—chocolate,

Localizing

Geographically, the Web is a unique medium, since all of its content, no matter how provincial, is available from anywhere on the globe. A Netsurfer in Calcutta sees the same Zima site, or American Airlines site, as a Netsurfer in Grover's Corners, New Jersey, and while locally-oriented companies (funeral homes, amusement parks, etc.) can earn worldwide market presence faster on the Net than in any other medium, this technology works against companies (large or small) who want to make their goods and services locally relevant. Companies have remedied this problem with several

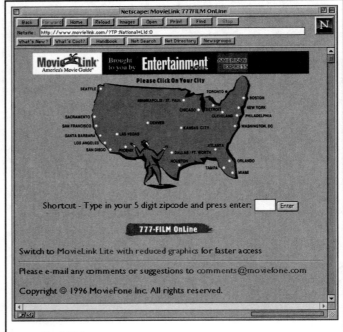

IN-SITE: **MovieLink**
http://www.movielink.com
The online outgrowth of the MovieFone service, which allows moviegoers to research showtimes and purchase tickets from home, the MovieLink site opens with a screen that lets Netsurfers select from more than two dozen cities or enter their ZIP code into a geographic search engine. While all movie-related content—downloadable previews in QuickTime or AVI format, cast information, plot summaries, and reviews—is available from anywhere in the site, this initial page ensures that MovieLink visitors will only have to view showtimes from their area.

strategies, all of which use Web technology to emphasize (or simulate) a local orientation. The most common tactic is the store locator, a search engine connected to a comprehensive database of a company's stores. When visitors input their location, the site generates a list of the closest stores; while the Calcutta Netsurfer would probably come up empty in the search for a Sir Speedy outlet, he or she might be surprised to learn that the company has franchises in Argentina, Indonesia, and Saudi Arabia, not to mention dozens in New Jersey.

Store location is not technologically demanding and provides an indisputable customer service; perhaps that's why it has proven such a popular technique in online marketing. But it is by no means the only form of localization. PolyGram Records (**http://www .polygram.com/polygram**)—the media giant that owns such record labels as A&M, Def Jam, Deutsche Grammophon, Island, London, Mercury, Motown, Polydor, and Verve—has a worldwide database that not only locates record dealers, but also lists tour dates for PolyGram artists. Some companies, like Southern Comfort (**http://www.SouthernComfort.com**), have started to build city-specific guides that not only list entertainment events, but also help forge a sense of community between consumers in the Northeast, Midwest, or West. And Toyota's site (**http://www .toyota.com**) promises that it will soon provide a "regional 'deal finder' search engine, to help you find the greatest values close to home. And a calendar of special events from coast to coast." As the Net evolves, localizing is a growing issue for marketers, combining the problems of product enhancement, community-building, and targeting.

tea, caffeine tablets. Here's a hint: Jolt is high on the list. Where do you find Jolt? Like the rest of the Jolt site, the be-cool-and-drink-Jolt theme sets the tone for the store locator. Visitors can send email if they want to distribute Jolt, sell it in their stores, or just find a store that sells it.
✓**www**→http://www.joltcola.com

Sir Speedy With a super-glossy front page that looks more like a 21st century art gallery than a print shop, this Website also has an online store locator that allows Netsurfers to find the nearest of the more than 800 Sir Speedys.
✓**www**→http://www.sirspeedy .com

Southern Comfort Living in Austin and looking for a music club, restaurant, or new radio station? Or maybe you're from Buffalo, Philadelphia, Boston, Chicago, or San Francisco? The folks at Southern Comfort are trying to create the ultimate guides for cities across the country, and they're using the Website to survey young people "who really do the things and go to the places named."
✓**www**→http://www.Southen Comfort.com

Ticketmaster Online The national ticket broker puts derrieres in the seats for major concert, arts, and sporting venues, and its Website lets customers search for upcoming events in their area. If you live in New York or Los Angeles, you're especially lucky; Ticketmaster has created a special online guide for your fair city.
✓**www**→http://www.ticket master.com

Energizer World What keeps going and going and going? The Energizer Bunny, of course. And the troublemaking-bunny-with-an-attitude is the star of Energizer World, a relatively sparse Website with company news, product information, battery guides, tips for buying toys for kids, and bunny trivia.
✓**www**→http://www.eveready.com/main.html

Hershey Foods Corporation Hershey's Website uses several easy-to-follow metaphors to put customers at ease. Customers can take a "Chocolate Tour" which walks them through different parts of the Hershey chocolate factory, visit Hershey's kitchen for baking tips and recipes, or head out to Chocolate Town, U.S.A., to explore the sweet town of Hershey, Pennsylvania.
✓**www**→http://www.microserve.net/~hershey

Merrill Lynch's Internet Center The opening graphic of Merrill Lynch's virtual village uses familiar settings—a university, a suburban home, a skyscraper, and a radio tower—to explain financial concepts and opportunities with the investment company. Each "building" includes a RealAudio clip that welcomes visitors stock quotes, advice on retirement planning, and tips for writing a business plan. The site is easy to navigate and packed with a series of guides and interactive exercises to help focus its customers' financial and business concerns

Creating an Environment

The novelty of the online world is tremendously exciting for marketers and consumers alike; as a result of hypertext, interactivity, and vast online databases, companies have had to rethink traditional models of consumer-product interaction. However, this radical newness can be a source of discomfort if not handled skillfully, since consumers may be intimidated by the unfamiliarity of the Web or disoriented by its seemingly endless series of ramified pages. In light of this problem, many online marketers have developed sites that create a sense of comfort for consumers by simulating familiar environments—an auto showroom, a movie theater, or a restaurant. Bass Ale (**http://www.guinnessimportco.com**) employs a virtual pub envi-

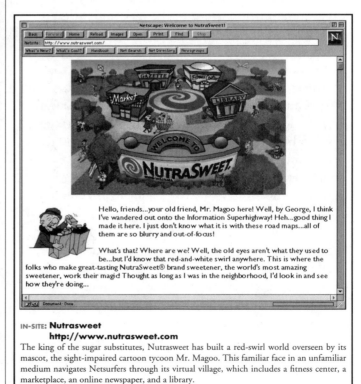

IN-SITE: **Nutrasweet**
http://www.nutrasweet.com
The king of the sugar substitutes, Nutrasweet has built a red-swirl world overseen by its mascot, the sight-impaired cartoon tycoon Mr. Magoo. This familiar face in an unfamiliar medium navigates Netsurfers through its virtual village, which includes a fitness center, a marketplace, an online newspaper, and a library.

IN-SITE: MCA/Universal Home Entertainment
http://www.mca.com/home/index.html
With an opening screen that looks like a home theater, complete with a bowl of popcorn on the table, MCA/Universal not only emphasizes its ability to deliver pieces of its products—in this case, video and sound clips from *Apollo 13*, *Casper*, and *The Land Before Time III: The Time of the Great Giving*—but also creates a prepossessing online environment where sections of the screen lead to extensive online press kits for each movie.

ronment to tap its rich storehouse of company history and cultural information, while Kellogg's Website (**http://www.kelloggs.com**) is designed around a clubhouse metaphor. But by far the most popular virtual-environment strategy has been the online village. A number of companies, including Snapple, Volkswagen, Nutrasweet, Nabisco, Land's End, and Jack Daniels, use the organizing principle of a small town—complete with general stores (which contain product information), newspapers (news releases), museums (cultural resources), town halls (customer chat), and more—to render their sites more accessible and navigable, and sometimes less overtly corporate.

or to illustrate the types of services Merrill Lynch provides.
✓www→http://www.ml.com

Nabisco Nabisco makes strong use of the neighborhood theme at its Website, which is targeted both at consumers and at companies looking to buy food products. Tips for healthy living, company info, merchandise, games, product histories, recipes, and screensavers are packed into areas known as the kitchen, the museum, the store, and the town hall. Visitors can even take a guided tour of the neighborhood (click on a tram icon at the bottom of each Web page). Nabisco also has a fairly extensive consumer survey—fill it out and the company will keep you updated on new products and new developments in the neighborhood.
✓www→http://www.nabisco.com

Volkswagen Volkswagen's site puts visitors on a map of a virtual highway and invites them to click on the destinations that interest them. They can head to the spot on the map marked Dealer Showroom for the name of dealership near them, to the Newsstand to collect company press releases, or to the Technology Center for updates on new Volkswagen technology. But this being Volkswagen, there are also plenty of cultural pit stops: the Museum of VW History, with photos of VW's from the past (Adolf Hitler's role in developing the *Kraft durch Freudewagen* is reduced to a single phrase, "backed by government financing"); and Shakedown Street, where dead Grateful Dead frontman Jerry Garcia is lovingly memorialized.
✓www→http://www.vw.com

Sampling

Britannica Online The encyclopedia publisher offers customers a free seven-day trial subscription (customers must register with a password) to the online version of the product as well as a brief interactive demo of the encyclopedia's features.
✓**www**→http://www.eb.com

Electronic Arts How do you market visually compelling sports and space-combat game? Well, if you're Electronic Arts, you put demos and even movies of its games online.
✓**www**→http://www.ea.com

id Software How does a company get its game on almost every PC in the known universe? It creates texture-mapped, animated, morphed, open-architecture shoot-em-up games like Doom and Heretic, and then uses the Net to give away the first few, fully functioning levels of the games. At least that was id Software's strategy, and it helped make id's programs must-have products for online gamers.
✓**www**→http://www.idsoftware .com

Inspiration This Oregon software company is best known for its eponymous bestselling idea-management program. Inspiration's Website, which includes technical support documents and an email link to the company's sales staff, is anchored by its free-demo offer; Netsurfers can download a limited version of the program to help them decide whether or not they should

Almost everyone has experienced sampling as a marketing strategy in other media. Movie previews, record-store listening booths, free time on online services, and even trial-sized detergents sent through the mail are all examples of this tactic, which allows manufacturers and retailers to give customers the illusion they are receiving something for nothing—and consequently, to encourage purchase of an official version of the product. Online, sampling has taken on new life—with the power of downloading (that is, moving data from a host computer to a user's computer), software and entertainment companies can provide consumers with product samples directly from their Website.

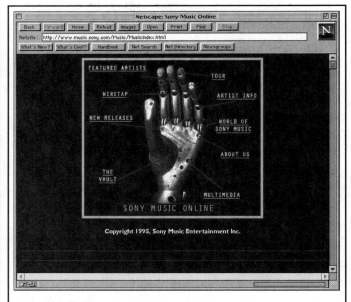

IN-SITE: **Sony Music**
http://www.music.sony.com
It may or may not be possible to tell your future from your palm, but it is certainly possible to tell the future of online marketing from Sony Music's site. With extensive coverage of artists ranging from Ozzy Osbourne to Frank Sinatra to Kriss Kross, Sony delivers press releases, publicity photos, tour dates, lyrics, and links to related sites. But the big draw of Sony's site is its extensive archive of sound samples—there's no other mass medium that permits consumers to play Ol' Blue Eyes's version of "Birth of the Blues" on command.

IN-SITE: Netscape
http://home.netscape.com

As the company that manufactures and distributes the most popular Web browser in the world, Netscape has a vested interest in drawing Netsurfers to its site, and it does so with a steady stream of information about new product releases, new Websites, and general Internet navigation resources. But what has turned Netscape from a freeware enterprise to a major corporate force is its sampling strategy—its ability to attract customers to the site for browsers, software demos, and updates.

Record labels as large as Warner Bros. (**http://www. music.warnerbros.com/**) and as small as the Nashville independent label, Hey Baby! (**http://songs.com /noma/hb/**) have online samples of songs. Movie studios joing the trend too, by uploading trailers for upcoming films onto the Web. But sampling isn't limited to sound and video clips. For a time, the Website of AT&T's Global Electronic Media Solutions (**http://www.att.com/gems**) offered to convert Netsurfers' content (technical information especially) into a temporary Web page, and to send potential customers the URLs for free. Virtually any product or service with an electronic component can be offered to Netsurfers free of charge, on a sample basis, across the Web.

buy the full software package.
✓**www**→http://www.inspiration .com

Metro-Goldwyn-Mayer
The major movie studios, including MGM/United Artists, have set up elaborate advertisements for their current blockbusters that include free downloads of video clips from the movies.
✓**www**→http://www.mgmua .com

Microsoft Who says you can't profit by giving things away? Microsoft's mammoth Website includes lots of "Free Stuff"—libraries of demos, add-ons, and beta versions for each of Microsoft's software products. Customers interested in Microsoft Word, for instance, can download beta versions of an Internet Assistance for Microsoft Word, converters, a demo of Microsoft Office, and much more.
✓**www**→http://www.microsoft .com

1-800 Music Now The unforgivably long URL aside, this company has extended its tollfree phone business onto the Web without sacrificing its sampling ethic. Customers can select a song from any album that they might be interested in, listen to a sound clip online, and then order the album online if they like what they hear.
✓**www**→http://www.1800music now.mci.com

21st Century Eloquence
This Florida voice-recognition software dealer includes online demos of its PC-platform based products.
✓**www**→http://pbol.com /eloquent

Incentives

Like any medium, the Web can also be used to create and deliver enticements and incentives. The most popular example of this technique, of course, is the same example that has been popular in print for years—coupons. Coupons are well-suited for the online medium, since most consumers have access to a printer. For the time it takes to send a print command, shoppers can earn savings on goods and services. The obvious problem that arises—consumers who collect multiple copies of the same coupon—can be addressed in a number of ways.

In fact, online technologies can restrict customers to a

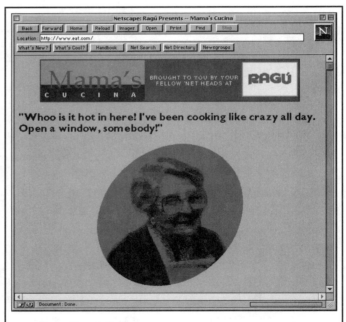

IN-SITE: **Ragu: Mama's Cucina**
   http://www.eat.com
Ragu's Website is one of the stars of the first phase of Net marketing, largely because of the company's success in creating a unified online identity. Positioning itself as an advocate of home-style ethnic cooking, Ragu has created various kinds of online content—product information, recipes, online contests—but filtered them all through the site's central icon, the Italian "Mama." Mama's Cucina even promises to send Netsurfers a coupon book if they complete a brief online form.

IN-SITE: Rogaine
http://www.igroup.com/rogaine
The Upjohn Company, which manufactures the topically applied hair-replacement drug Rogaine, wants to make your loss your gain, and they're using the Web to do so. Jointly targeting men and women with basic information about the hair-regrowing process, the Rogaine Website includes a doctor locator that finds dermatologists nationwide. And for those balding Netsurfers wary of chemical remedies, Rogaine includes an incentive offer—any visitor who fills out an online questionnaire receives a $10 gift certificate for an initial hair-loss consultation.

single coupon. How? By requiring visitors to complete a rudimentary registration form before giving them access to the coupon. This technique is already in use at sites such as Casual Male (**http://www.thinkbig.com**) and Rogaine (**http://www.igroup.com/rogaine**), both of which withhold coupons from Netsurfers until after they have completed a short online form. Registration serves corporate needs in a number of respects, both as a means of tracking and controlling coupon use and as a means of collecting basic data about consumers. And sites like Coupon.Net (**http://www.coupon.net**) are experimenting with even more sophisticated technologies for ensuring the one-to-one mapping of coupons to consumers.

free gift.
✓**www**→http://www2.vivid.net/~petunltd

Healthy Choice Who wouldn't click the "free stuff" button on the opening screen of the Website for the makers of the Healthy Choice line of food products? Customers who do will get $1 coupons as well as other incentives (a free magazine, a free demo of personal health management software, etc.). Resembling an online magazine, the site also publishes recipes, health and fitness tips.
✓**www**→http://www.healthychoice.com

Little Caesars Pizza! Pizza! Coupons! Coupons! Little Caesars' Website advertises promotions and distributes coupons.
✓**www**→http://pages.prodigy.com/L/I/S/LittleCaesars/main.html

The Original Cookie Company Continuing its long tradition of serving cookie-deprived Netsurfers, the Original Cookie Company has created an online coupon kiosk full of specials. Just print the page and use the coupons you'd like at any Original Cookie Company store.
✓**www**→http://www.originalcookie.com

3M Office Market Companies want customers to try their products and they want customers to complete their online surveys. 3M has solved this problem by offering to send customers free samples of its products (Post-it notes, transparency film, etc.) if they complete the online survey.
✓**www**→http://www.3m.com/market/omc/index.html

Blackwell's Bookshop The celebrated Oxford purveyor of knowledge, sponsors a monthly literary quiz with really fabulous prizes—how about all 900 Penguin Classics?
✓**www**→http://www.blackwell .co.uk/bookshops

Cathay Pacific Airways As much as any company online, Cathay Pacific is associated with promotions and contests—the Faststart Contest, the Mileage Millionaire Contest, and especially the CyberAuctions, which create an open market for tickets and travel packages.
✓**www**→http://www.cathay-usa .com

Crayola Crayons While Crayola packs its Website with coloring contests and promotions (an online version of Crayola's big "find the 100 billionth crayon" promotion), the site also includes stain-removal tips for parents, trivia, and product information.
✓**www**→http://www.crayola.com

From Dusk Till Dawn Though the Quentin Tarantino vampire movie will certainly be on video by the time this book is released, its promotional Website may still be up. Why? Because the makers of the film have invited Netsurfers to create promotional pages of their own, and cast their contest as the latest stone thrown in the ongoing war over Internet censorship.
✓**www**→http://www.obs-us .com/obs/english/films/mx /dusk/contest.htm

Events and Promotions

The interactivity, immediacy, and multimedia potential of the Web makes it a medium particularly conducive to contests. Customers can answer trivia quizzes, submit their names and emails for use in a random drawing, or participate in an online scavenger hunt that promises valuable prizes to the winner, all for a relatively small initial investment. Not only have huge national promotions like Diet Coke's "Who's Gonna Drink the Diet Coke?" recognized the Web by

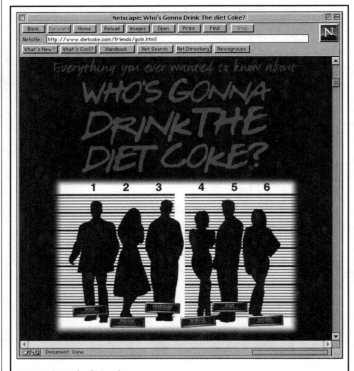

IN-SITE: **Diet Coke/Friends**
http://www.dietcoke.com/friends
The media tsunami created by Coca-Cola's "Who's Gonna Drink the Diet Coke" promotion, which managed to unite the nation's most popular sitcom (*Friends*), the largest soft-drink manufacturer in the world, and the most widely-watched television event of 1996 (the Superbowl), didn't stop at the borders of the Internet. For most of January, in fact, the Diet Coke Website was dominated by the promotion, which supplemented the TV-centric contest with behind-the-scenes information, a calendar of college-campus events, and an online trivia quiz.

designing an online component, but smaller companies wary of spending the money to advertise on television have created online contests and competitions. To date, online contests have demanded more of the consumer than their offline counterparts—writing contests like the Faux Faulkner event sponsored by Jack Daniel's (**http://www.infi.net/jackdaniels**) and the free-verse free-for-all at Hugo Boss's Word Slam (**http://www.wordslam.hugo.com**) are qualitatively different than traditional sweepstakes, and increasingly common.

In addition to contests, special events, especially chat events featuring celebrities, have begun to proliferate online. If your Website has a chat client—a program that allows visitors to communicate in real-time with other visitors—you may want to consider staging talk shows, interviews, or even promotional appearances with celebrities. Though this practice has been most common on commercial services—America Online has been particularly successful at drawing traffic by hosting chats with rock stars, movie stars, and political luminaries—sites like Planet Reebok (**http://www .planetreebok.com**) and Barnes and Noble's Loci (**http://www.loci.com**) have experimented with online chat events.

Hugo Boss Word Slam Although Hugo Boss is a fragrance company, Hugo Boss's Website makes almost no mention of scent. Why? Because online, Hugo Boss has remade itself as a company interested in promoting all forms of poetry, from Jenny Holzer to Robert Frost. In the last months of 1995, the site also included a contest in which site visitors were encouraged to submit their own poems of 75 words or less. First prize? Publication on the Website and $1500 in cash.
✓**www**→http://www.wordslam
.hugo.com/contest.html

Jack Daniel's Faux Faulkner William Faulkner liked his whiskey, and for that reason, Jack Daniels likes Faulkner enough to take over the Faux Faulkner contest, one of the country's oldest literary parody competitions. In addition to offering Netsurfers recipes and a Jack Daniels screensaver, the company invites scribes to try their hand at doing the Yoknapatawpha thing—entries can even be submitted online.
✓**www**→http://www.infi.net
/jackdaniels

Trojan The condom company is online, with a site that dispenses interesting facts about human sexuality and STDs. Until May 1996, though, the centerpiece of the site is its free condom offer—any Netsurfer 18 or over can fill out an online form and receive a prophylactic absolutely free. And don't worry if you don't want your neighbors to know that you're practicing safe sex—the product will be mailed in "a discreet envelope."
✓**www**→http://www.linkmag
/trojan

Greatest Hits: Popular Strategies

WHY DO WEBSITES FAIL?

Maybe you're the kind of marketer who has an intuitive understanding of the online medium, who understands instantly how to integrate interactivity and multimedia into a text-based page. And maybe you're not. In case you're floundering a bit in the Netsurf, take the time to look over this list of Definite Don'ts—marketing tactics that guarantee unpopularity for a company and something less than success for its Website.

- The door (the first page) fails to catch the consumer's attention. If you don't grab customers immediately, they may grab their mouse and click away to another site. First impressions are important online.

- The site's pages take too long to load because of too many graphics. Graphics are visually stimulating and as effective for communicating information as text; they also frustrate visitors with slow connections. Before you launch your site, you may want to test-surf it on an "average" computer, a Macintosh or PC from three or four years ago, just to be certain that users will be able to navigate smoothly and quickly.

- The site fails to treat the World Wide Web as a new, interactive medium. Don't just present content that's readily available elsewhere; if you do, people will begin to refer to your site as an online "brochure," and before you know it, no one will be visiting.

What are you going to do with your Website? Innovate. Experiment. But don't forget to track on what your neighbors and competitors are doing; in a medium this new, keeping up with the Cyberjoneses is all important. Here are some of the features frequently found on company Websites:

Advice Columns. Since companies want customers to see them as the experts in a particular field, many companies are running advice columns on their sites and answering questions about more than their products.

Chat. Whether on bulletin boards or in chat rooms, online communication is an enormously popular and, for some, addictive activity. Chat rooms can also be used to sponsor events with celebrities.

Contests. Free trips, money, clothing sprees, computers, and more! Many companies are using contests to generate interest in their Websites and to get customers to answer questions. Some sites even run regularly scheduled contests—daily, weekly, or monthly.

Coupons. It works in newspapers and magazines. Why not on the Web? Customers can print them, clip them, and head to the stores.

Cyberdirectories. As the range of Web resources continues to grow, Web directories and cyberguides are becoming more and more valuable. Airlines, for instance, might link to travel sites; camera companies might link to online photo galleries; shaving cream companies might link to sports directories.

Electronic Giveaways. Computer toys such as screensavers, icons, and wallpaper, usually with a company's logo or slogan on them, can be valuable publicity tools.

Building a Better Website Greatest Hits: Popular Strategies

Fun & Games. Absolutely everybody is doing it—even mutual fund companies—and if they're not designing special sections for fun and games, then they're turning the entire Website into a virtual playground, hosting everything from trivia contests to multiplayer, graphical games. Prizes are sometimes offered.

Postcards. Visitors can design their own colorful postcards to email to friends. The postcards invariably include company logos and Website addresses.

Store Locators. Many companies include searchable databases with the names and addresses of every one of their store locations.

Surveys/Guestbooks. Companies are generally interested in gathering information about their customers. Many sites have put up online surveys and encouraged visitors to fill them out by offering incentives. Other sites have taken a subtler approaching, asking visitors to fill out a guest book, which sometimes includes basic questions.

Tours. Companies are offering interactive "tours" of their manufacturing plants and production processess. Customers click through a description, both textual and graphical, of how a product is made.

Virtual Villages. Companies have built entire Websites around the theme of fictional village settings, often using graphics of recognizable town institutions to help visitors navigate. Where will customers find product news? The village newsstand, of course.

What's new. Companies also list new features, which draw visitors back to the site time and again.

- The site is insufficiently creative and overly stiff; it lacks a sense of fun or imagination. The Web is not as conservative as some other media; pitches should come at the consumer a little off-center, with attitude.

- The site has no content. Multimedia is flashy, sure, but it will only hook customers if it's working in harmony with interesting content. At the same time that it's dangerous to build a site that's composed entirely of content (boring), a site that depends entirely on effects will be quickly written off as flashy and insubstantial.

- The site is overtly commercial. In keeping with the Internet ethos, a site should include valuable information or entertainment.

- The site is difficult to navigate. One rule of thumb is that content should never be more than three clicks away. Always give visitors plenty of chances to return to the home page.

- The site is not updated regularly. Even the coolest site needs to be changed over time, so don't create content you can't afford to update.

- The site does not allow customers to contact the company. Without an email link, sites can seem offputting and unfriendly; also, you won't get the benefit of your customers' opinions.

- The site is always under construction. The Web is an evolving medium, but the sense of unfinished business can frustrate visitors.

It's a Mall World

If Website design seems like an overwhelming prospect—so much to think about, so many new developments, such a complex calculus of risks and rewards—you may want to think about joining an online mall. The decision to use an Internet shopping mall as your primary connection to the Internet is similar to the decision as to whether to purchase space in a physical shopping mall. Will the uniformity in design required by the mall eclipse your company's identity? Will the services and publicity provided by the mall be worth the extra costs involved? How much extra traffic will the mall bring? To answer these questions, you should know the basic facts about online malls.

• The mall will maintain a publicity and advertising effort to build traffic for its stores. In theory, consumers who come into the mall are likely to visit multiple stores.

• The mall will typically develop a sophisticated shopping and security mechanism. If you are selling products through the Web, this will be of significant value.

• A mall run by a large, established consumer-oriented company, such as MCI, may have a positive halo effect for small companies that are not well-known to consumers. In a sense, the mall itself may act as a brand that implies quality to consumers.

• The operator of the mall is likely to have lots of experience in both the front end of online business (designing a site) and the back end (operating the transaction and billing system). Companies that join the mall will benefit from this experience and expertise.

• Malls may build traffic by developing sophisticated

"intelligent agents," or personal shopping programs. If a business is located in a mall with this capability, the businesses' products will be recommended to consumers who are looking for items that match this profile.

It is important to understand how the mall will charge prospective customers. Some malls look for a percentage of every transaction in return for all of the services provided. This type of compensation may be appropriate if the mall is the only entity driving traffic to the marketer's site. However, if the marketer is also executing traffic driving efforts, such as those described in the next chapter, then such compensation is probably inappropriate: the marketer pays the mall operator for sales created through its own advertising and publicity. In many cases, it's possible for an online store to join several malls. Companies can then comparatively evaluate the effectiveness of these malls. In fact, while some stores set up separate sites in each different mall, others merely offer front doors that link to a single Website. The best way to assess the desirability of operating through an Internet mall is probably to price-out all of the services you will receive from the mall and compare it to the cost of setting up an independent shop. Don't forget to factor in the level of traffic and all added services that malls provide. This will give you a sense of the value the mall is placing on the traffic (and any unique shopping services) it is providing.

Internet Shopping Pages
✓www→http://community.net/~csamir/aisshop.html

Internet Web Shopping Center
✓www→http://www.internetweb.co.uk/centres/shopping.htm

Internet Mall Listings
✓www→http://www.shop-the-net.com

Internet Plaza
✓www→http://storefront.xor.com/index.html

London Mall
✓www→http://www.micromedia.co.uk

MarketPlace MCI
✓www→http://www2.pcy.mci.net/marketplace/index.html

Online World Wide Mall
✓www→http://www.olworld.com/olworld/mall/mall_us

ParentsPlace.com
✓www→http://www.parentsplace.com/shopping/index.html

RockMall
✓www→http://www.rockmall.com

Shopping 2000
✓www→http://www.shopping2000.com

Shopsite
✓www→http://www.shopsite.com

VirtualPlex Mall
✓www→http://www.virtualplex.com/vplex

World Wide Marketplace
✓www→http://www.cygnus.nb.ca

Ad Agencies on the Web—A Selection

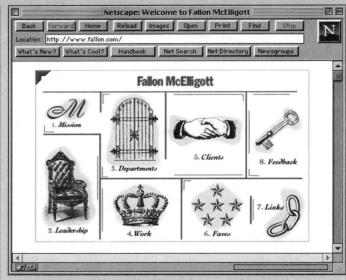

A screenshot from Fallon McElligott's Website

Ad Methods: Halpern & Eurich, Inc. Clients: Axios, Micro Vision Software Inc., Mitsubishi International
✓**www**→http://www.li.net/ad method

Adajecency Clients: Patagonia, Specialized, Sram Corporation
✓**www**→http://adjacency.com

Advanced Media Services Clients: Viking Technologies, Peace Frogs, Georgetown Tobacco
✓**www**→http://www.amsmain .com/amsmain

Advernet Clients: The Kissimmee-St. Cloud Convention & Visitors Bureau
✓**www**→http://www.advernet .com

Ambassador Marketing Group, Inc. Clients: IBM, Motorola, Pfizer, Woolworth
✓**www**→http://www.napi.com /clients/AMB/index.html

Anderson & Lembke Clients: Microsoft, Hewlett Packard, Texas Instruments, Dun & Bradstreet
✓**www**→http://www.lembke.com /clients.html

Arnold Advertising Clients: Federal News Agency, Distribution Resource Center
✓**www**→http://www.arnoldnet .com

Austin Knight Clients: Pizza Hut Australia
✓**www**→http://www.ak.com.au

Bandy-Carroll-Hellige Advertising Clients: McDonalds (local), Bank of Louisville
✓**www**→http://www.bch.com

Bates Dorland Interactive Clients: Perrier, Rover Group, Safeway U.K.
✓**www**→http://www.bates-dor land.co.uk

BBDO Worldwide Clients: 20th Century Fox, U.S. Navy
✓**www**→http://www.techsetter .com

Bernard Hodes Advertising Clients: Career Mosaic, Cole-Haan
✓**www**→http://www.hodes .com

Black Box Clients: Crayola, Liquitex, Graphics Express
✓**www**→http://www.ot.com/black box

Carter Waxman Clients: San Jose Magnet Schools, Devcon
✓**www**→http://www.carwax .com

Charron & Schwartz, & Partners, Inc. Clients: ABC News, Martex, Quaker Oats
✓**www**→http://www.inx.net/~cs pad

CKS Group Clients: MCI Telecommunications, Motorola, Norwegian Cruise Lines
✓**www**→http://wwww.cks.com

Colle & McVoy Clients: Winnebago Industries, 3M, Land O'Lakes
✓**www**→http://www.collemcvoy .com

Duval Woglom Brueckner & Partners Clients: General Electric, Polaroid
✓**www**→http://www.dwb.com

EMA Multimedia Clients: Citizen America, BMG Music Publishing, MGM/UA
✓**www**→http://www.emamulti .com

Ad Agencies on the Web—A Selection

Fallon McElligott Clients: Coca-Cola, Black &Decker, Time Magazine, BMW, Jim Beam
✓**www**→http://www.fallon.com

Grey Interactive Clients: Seagram's, Hasbro, Procter & Gamble
✓**www**→http://www.grey-interactive.de

Hill Holliday Clients: Reebok, Lotus, Sony, Bank of Boston
✓**www**→http://www.hhcc.com

Ingalls, Quinn & Johnson Clients: United States Postal Service, Spyglass
✓**www**→http://www.iqj.com

Ketchum Advertising Clients: Bank of America, Miller Brewing, Acura
✓**www**→http://www.ketchum.com/advertising/advertising.html

The Kilgannon Group Clients: Southern Communications, Techsonic Industries
✓**www**→http://www.kilgannon.com

Kirshenbaum Bond & Partners Clients: Snapple, Columbia House, Keds, SaraLee, NBC
✓**www**→http://www.kb.com

Leo Burnett Clients: Dewer's, Marlboro, McDonald's
✓**www**→http://www.leoburnett.com

McCann-Erickson Worldwide Clients: 1-800 Flowers, Buick, Black & Decker
✓**www**→http://www.meric.com/index.htm

McMann & Tate Clients: Nationwide Recovery Sytems, AT&T. Witches, Ltd.

✓**www**→http://www.mcmann-tate.com

Merkeley Newman Harty Clients: American Stock Exchange, Forbes, Casio
✓**www**→http://www.hooked.net:80/buzznet/mnh

Ogilvy & Mather Clients: World Wildlife Federation, Duracell, Lipton
✓**www**→http://www.ogilvy.com

Porter/Novelli Think Link Clients: Amtrak, Kellogg's Gillette
✓**www**→http://www.porternovelli.com

@Radical Media Clients: ELLE, George, Nike, Sci-Fi Channel
✓**www**→http://www.radicalmedia.com

The Richards Group Clients: Tabu Lingerie, Volant Skis, Hummer
✓**www**→http://www.x-ads.com

Richardson, Myers & Donofrio, Inc. Clients: Rubbermaid, Baltimore Orioles, American Institute of Architects
✓**www**→http://www.rmd.com

Saatchi & Saatchi Business Communciations Clients: Kodak, Du Pont, The Prudential
✓**www**→http://www.saatchibuscomm.com

Weiss, Whitten, Stagliano, Inc. Clients: A/X Armani Exchange, Buck County Coffee Company
✓**www**→http://www.wwsworld.com

Winkler McManus Advertising Clients: Sony, LSI Logic, Nikon
✓**www**→http://www.winklermcmanus.com

A screenshot from BBDO Worldwide's Website

Chapter 4

Attracting Traffic to Your Site

Attracting Traffic to Your Site

More than five thousand new commercial Websites open their doors each month, and this phenomenal boom in online traffic has intensified the battle for consumers' time and attention. As a result, effective marketing on the Web now demands a two-pronged strategy—not only the creation of an engaging and goal-oriented Website, but also the development of an active strategy to draw in online consumers.

There are eight broad areas of Web marketing which should be considered when contemplating Website traffic: (1) using traditional media, such as magazines and television, to alert consumers to the site, (2) buying advertising links or "gateways" from high-traffic Internet sites, (3) ensuring the site is listed in all appropriate Internet indexes, (4) buying space in Internet shopping malls (as discussed in the previous chapter), (5) joining or linking the Website to an industry hubsite, (6) generating free publicity through Internet discussion groups, (7) encouraging links from Internet sites with desirable audiences, and (8) employing an electronic mailing list to notify consumers about developments on a Website. These approaches are discussed in greater detail in this chapter.

Advertising in Traditional Media

A Website cannot deliver product information, offer customer support, sell products or services, give away samples, or do any of the other things for which a marketer turns to the Web if consumers don't know about it. For many years companies have faced a similar dilemma when it comes to their toll-free numbers. An 800 number can do a lot for a company—in fact, just having an 800 number is reassuring to a consumer—but only if the consumer knows about it. An essential goal of the marketer, then, is to publicize these important company resources. If customers are aware, for instance, that they can track packages at the FedEx Website (**http://www.fedex.com**) or search for answers to technical support questions at the Microsoft Website (**http://www.microsoft.com**), the marketers for these companies have made an impact. And just as companies have long advertised their toll-free numbers in magazine, newspaper, radio, and television ads, they are now using the same strategy when it comes to URLs. Within the next few years, it will become commonplace for ads in more traditional media to include URLs.

Companies can use traditional media to publicize a Website address in two very different ways. The first method is for a company to simply assume that all advertising materials—ranging from print ads to brochures to television ads to the product packaging—will include the company's Website address, and that the Website address is only part, albeit an integral part, of a company's marketing efforts. Many software companies already follow this approach, and other consumer-oriented companies are likely to adopt this form of broad awareness-building over the next few years. Take the movie industry, for instance. In the summer of 1994, it was unheard of for movie ads in

PROMOTING THAT URL

You want people to come to your Website, but frankly, you're not so sure that the people you're targeting even know what a Website is. You know you want to try to build awareness among the offline crowd (the hundreds of millions of consumers you might be able to reach with a more traditional advertising campaign), but you're not sure where to start. What to do? You can probably achieve your primary goal—increasing awareness of your company's online presence among consumers—by designing ads for newspapers that mention your company's Website, putting Website addresses on product packages, setting up billboards touting your Website, or producing television spots, but how do you get consumers to remember the string of numbers and letters in your URL? Will marketers write witty slogans to help consumers learn their URLs? Will they create elaborate television commercials to advertise URLs? Will radios play URLs set to melodies on the airways? These creative strategies have proved effective for advertising toll-free numbers and they will probably be used for Website addresses as well.

Before marketers spend a lot on advertising campaigns, however, there are some basic principles of promoting a URL that they should understand. URLs, like toll-free numbers, are easier to remember if they include phrases associated with the product, or better yet, the company name. In fact, URLs should be as intuitive as possible—**http://www**

.yourcompanyname.com is often the best approach. A company may also want to consider reserving several URLs that all point to the same site. For instance, **http://www.bofa .com** and **http://Bankof America.com** both point to the Bank of America site. Some companies such as Nike (**http:// www.justdoit.com**) or Warner-Lambert (**http://www .shaving.com** for its shaving page) will have an easy time advertising their URLs. Their addresses are familiar and even fun. Another way to reinforce a company's URL in the public's mind is for the company to make the URL the same as the site's name. This tactic has been used to promote toll-free numbers like 1-800-music-now and is now popular online; the shareware distributors Software.com, the bookstore Amazon.com, and the Superbowl site Superbowl.com are just a few of those doing this.

Keeping the URL simple is imperative. In most cases, consumers should be directed to a site's home page even if the marketer is advertising a specific feature on the Website. The home page should, of course, include an obvious link to the part of the site that consumers will be looking for. In line with the keep-it-simple principle, marketers should consider dropping the beginning of a URL—**http://**—in its advertisements. In the future, as consumers become more familiar with the medium, First Federal, for instance, could advertise its site as **www.firstfederal.com** rather than **http://www .firstfederal.com**, and eventually **firstfederal.com** might be most effective.

newspapers to include Website addresses; by the summer of 1995, more than half of the newspaper and magazine ads for movies included Website addresses. In part, the studios were early adopters of this strategy because of the spectacular multimedia capabilities for movie Websites—but any company can push consumers toward the Web this way. Toyota (**http://www .toyota.com**) and Magnavox (**http://www .magnavox.com**) were including URLs in most of their advertising campaigns by early 1996.

Site marketing, the second approach to building Website traffic through traditional advertising mediums, involves developing a media campaign that is actively oriented toward sending visitors to a Website. The Website, in this case, is not just mentioned in an advertisement for a company or product; it is the focus of the advertisement. Just as marketers used ads to publicize company toll-free numbers, they can also create ads to highlight the special services that companies provide on the Web—like detailed product information, interactive support, and convenient delivery. Site marketing is already a recognized phenomenon in magazines oriented toward online users, and is now

c/net's October 1995 ad, which used TDI's Super King Size bus posters, placed the computer news company's URL in a new context—the streets of New York—in the Internet industry's first "Information Superhighway meets the West Side Highway" campaign. The advertisement appeared on 1 out of every 12 buses in Manhattan.

Honda's extremely subtle, extremely effective ad, which ran on the back cover of print publications like Wired, *used a traditional offline symbol (a car key) as a means of communicating a nontraditional piece of information (a URL).*

taking off on network television and in mainstream magazines and newspapers. The Sci-Fi Channel, for example, advertises its Website (**http://www.scifi .com**) on the air, with long spots that are essentially infomercials about the online medium. In all likelihood, the early efforts at this second approach represent only the tip of what will become a giant iceberg for marketers.

WEAVING THE WEB OFFLINE

It sounds like a science-fiction plot—in the span of months, the entire advertising world is infested by http's, colons, and virgules. But that's exactly what has happened in the early days of World Wide Web marketing. Website addresses, which just months ago were the equivalent of a secret language for online wonks, are now common parlance in the advertising world. The National Basketball Association displays its Website address, **http://www.nba.com**, prominently during games at Madison Square Garden and other arenas. And even small businesses—like the New York-area moving company Galil Moving (**http://www.galil .com**), have started to display their Website addresses on cable television commercials. Where else are they turning up? CNN (**http://www.cnn .com**) follows up news broadcasts by offering its URL. Superbowl announcers give URLs on the air. The blockbuster movie hit of 1995, *Toy Story* (**http:// www.toystory.com**), included a URL in all of its television and newspaper ads. *Toy Story* even listed its Website address in the movie's credits. Zima, the clear malt liquor, promoted its advertisement with on-pack URL advertisements. Zima's URL appeared on all of the bottle labels. TV shows even began including URLs in previews of the coming week's episode. But what's next? Will companies hire skywriters to spell out URLs over sunny, crowded beaches—**http://www .sunblock.com**?

CATCH 'EM WHILE THEY'RE HOT

What if you're designing a Website or a feature on a site that has a short-term life span? If you're going to invest a lot of money in such a Website, you're going to want to start drawing traffic immediately. The most effective way to do that is to offer information that the consumer can't get elsewhere—to run a pre-event. For instance, when *Sports Illustrated* decided to set up a site for its famous swimsuit issue (**http://swimsuit.pathfinder.com/swimsuit**), the magazine revealed who was going to be on the cover (a vigilantly guarded and much anticipated secret every year) a few days before the issue hit the newsstands. The online event drew press coverage that gained the site attention—and traffic. Superbowl.com (**http://www.superbowl.com**), which Microsoft, the NFL, and NBC launched only weeks before the actual event, ran events before and during the game that drew huge online audiences. But getting consumers interested in SI's swimsuit issue or the Superbowl site isn't incredibly difficult to do, and that may be the most important lesson for marketers. Sites with short-term lifespans should be natural draws, places that consumers don't need to be given reasons to visit. Then, the only job of the marketer is to let the consumer know the site is there and to communicate the urgency of visiting before it's gone forever. The 1996 Olympics site (**http://www.atlanta.olympic.org**) didn't take any chances—it went up over a year before the event.

IN-SITE: **Batman Forever**
http://www.batmanforever.com

In the summer of 1995, *Batman Forever* set the record for the highest box office receipts during the opening weekend of a movie, with a total of $58 million. According to *USA Today*, one of the reasons for this success was the highly popular *Batman Forever* Website, which launched before the release of the movie in March of 1995. From the outset, Warner Bros. used the site to build excitement about the movie, and integrated the site into its overall marketing efforts. The week the site opened, ads appeared in small type at the bottom of the front page of *The New York Times* that included the URL; the Website address also appeared in other newspaper ads and on bus-stop advertisements. This site was particularly effective because of the strength of its design, including attractive front pages (above) and map pages (below). To generate a loyal audience (i.e. repeat traffic), the site also incorporated contests built around the Riddler. The site stayed up beyond the movie's theatrical run, and subsequently added announcements about the video release.

Advertising Online

Companies, in addition to advertising offline, can advertise online, drawing traffic to their Websites by placing advertisements on other sites. As more and more consumers get online, the Net will prove to be one of the most effective places to advertise company Websites. For the moment, there isn't a set of rules for how to do it—and very few dos and don'ts. Marketers overseeing the design of a Website are not the only ones who need to experiment in this new medium. Media buyers and advertisers do, too.

Those companies that are making a spirited attempt to get Netsurfers to stay at their sites are aggressively taking advantage of the different and unique advertising opportunities of the online world. The Net delivers an audience already familiar with the medium and offers an incredible number of potential advertising spaces—online magazines, Internet directories, services, other company sites, general interest sites, etc. Some of these spaces cater to niche markets and specific demographic groups, while others deliver huge numbers of people. The Net also promises to provide whole new ways of attracting consumers to Websites through the technological—and particularly the interactive—potential of the medium.

A number of high-traffic areas on the Web, especially media sites like Time Warner's Pathfinder (**http://pathfinder.com**) and directories like Yahoo (**http://www.yahoo.com**), have begun to actively solicit ads. For the most part, these ads have taken a single form—the "gateway advertisement," also known as a "link ad." This gateway is typically a graphic displayed on the editorial or directory site; if consumers choose to click on the graphic, they are transported to the advertiser's own home page. This form of non-intrusive advertising has proven to be an effective means of

EXTRA POINTS
HIRE IT OUT!

So much to do, so little time. Generating publicity for a Website often involves a tedious process of listing sites in the right places online—many, many of the right places. These resources—some free, some not—are available online to assist marketers:

Apollo Web Referencing Kit This annotated guide to "the most effective directories" on the Web offers links to directory home pages and site registration forms for each.
✓**www**→http://apollo.co.uk/web-kit.html

How To Announce Your New Web Site FAQ An annotated hypertext guide to the places online and offline where companies and individuals can announce their Websites—from a list of search engines and directories to books and magazines covering the Web. Instructions included for sites when needed.
✓**www**→http://ep.com/faq/webannounce.html

onLine Web Promote A hypertext list of more than 300 sites online where you can promote your Website. The list is divided into well-known directories and search engines, sites with free classifieds, free multi-submit services, sites that will add a URL, sites that will exchange links, free-for-all links pages, yellow pages, URL randomizers, and site-for-the day sites. All onLine Web Promote asks in return is that you pro-

mote its site on your site.
✓ **www**→http://online-biz
.com/promote

Pointers to Pointers Covering more than just the same Internet directories that most of the other services list, this free service lists a large selection of mailing lists and newsgroups, commercial sites and malls, and topical or local Websites that marketers should consider. Users check off the sites they want to notify about their own sites, fill out the form, and then press the submit button. *Voila!*
✓ **www**→http://www.homecom
.com/global/pointers.html

The PostMaster Once your company has a Website, it will need to get listed in online directories and written about in the media to attract attention. For a fee ($500 and up), the PostMaster will send a description of your site to over 300 different Net sites and media outlets. Want attention without shelling out the cash? The PostMaster will even send your description to about 20 of the Net's most popular directories (Yahoo, OpenText, Web Site of the Week, GNN, etc.) for free.
✓ **www**→http://www.net
creations.com/postmaster/index
.html

Promophobia Promophobia uses its site to promote its Website marketing services. The company does everything from evaluating Websites to submitting listings to directories to contacting the press. They charge for their services, but they've put together a list of links to shopping malls, general and specialty directories, search engines, and more cool stuff

building Website traffic; as the Web becomes more populated, this form of advertising will become even more essential.

How do gateways work? First, high-traffic sites sell other companies space on their Web pages for displaying these gateway ads—banners or icons that also work as live links. At the moment, the most popular ad size is an inch-tall strip as wide as the Netscape screen; this is known as a banner ad, an ad band, or just a banner. Some sites offer different dimensions, including ads that are exactly one-half the width of the banner ad, square ads, full-page ads, and even ads in the form of logos or icons. When consumers visiting high-traffic sites see these gateway banners, they can either ignore them, or—if they are intrigued by the image or message—click on them, at which time they are transported from the high-traffic site (Yahoo, for instance) to the advertiser's site (Microsoft, the romantic trivia game "Get a Little Closer," Sprint, or any of the other companies who advertise on Yahoo). In this way, gateway ads placed within editorial sites operate

IN-SITE: **Pathfinder Places**
http://pathfinder.com
Time Warner's Pathfinder offers single, page-wide ad banners on many of its pages.

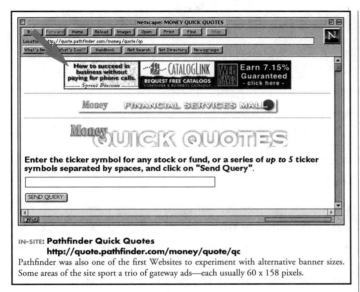

IN-SITE: Pathfinder Quick Quotes
http://quote.pathfinder.com/money/quote/qc
Pathfinder was also one of the first Websites to experiment with alternative banner sizes. Some areas of the site sport a trio of gateway ads—each usually 60 x 158 pixels.

just like ads in print publications: consumers voluntarily participating in the editorial environment are given a nonintrusive invitation to learn more about the company.

Gateway ads are certainly not the only way to use the Net to advertise a Website. Marketers should also make certain that they list their sites in the major Web indexes and notify Website announcement services to have them reviewed. In addition, they should consider linking their site to an industry hubsite (a site which brings together companies in a related field). These Websites often garner more publicity than sites for single companies and, because they become online idustry resources, other Web pages link to them voluntarily.

Promoting a Website is a time-consuming effort. Many companies employ the services of online promotional companies to cover the basics, but marketers should continue to experiment, innovate, and pay attention to what the competition is doing if you don't want to fall behind.

that is totally free.
✓**www**→http://www.interbiz net.com/ibn/promophop.html

Promote-it The ultimate do-it-yourself resource for the marketer who wants to hit all (or a significant chunk) of the Web directories, sites of the day sites, newsgroups, and mailing lists that allow companies to submit descriptions of their sites. This is just a hypertext list. You'll have to do the work yourself.
✓**www**→http://www.iTools .com/promote-it/promote-it.html

Submit-it A free service that submits a description of your site to over 15 different Internet indexes and search engines (check the ones you want), including Yahoo, WebCrawler, Lycos, infoseek, and Alta Vista.
✓**www**→http://www.submit-it.com

WebPromote This for-profit company will send announcements to all major directories, "what's new" sites, and award sites. The company will also evaluate the cost-effectiveness of banner advertising for your company and help you assess your Website's design.
✓**www**→http://www.web promote.com

Web Site Promotion Services One of the best listings of places online to advertise sites.
✓**www**→http://www.meh.com /meh

WebStep WebStep offers companies several levels of marketing assistance, including basic information about where to advertise online and more advanced promotion services.
✓**www**→http://www.mmgco .com/online/source.html

You want your gateway ad to make a good impression. You think you've created a real grabber, an ad that's virtually guaranteed to get consumers clicking—unless, of course, they don't see your ad at all. Consumers navigate the Web using a variety of browsers, including text-based browsers which can't display graphical gateway ads. In fact, many commercial Websites get more than five percent of their traffic from consumers without graphic capabilities. Unless companies are willing to throw away these potential customers, all gateway ads should include an ALT tag, a text-only description of the ad that also serves as a hypertext link to the company's Website. As technologies change, there will be even further differences in how users see Web pages (tables, frames, animation, etc.). Marketers will have to balance the appeal of cutting-edge capabilities with rates of accessibility. For the time being, however, the biggest challenge to the gateway ad comes from Web users who've voluntarily turned off image loading on their graphical browsers and for users who are running programs to hide gateway ads. (Marketers should be aware that some Net-surfers have created extension programs for use with their Web browsers—like WebFilter (**http://emile.math.ucsb.edu/~boldt/NoShit**)—that block all graphics in the fairly standard dimensions of gateway ads.) But never fear—only a very small percentage of Web users employ these programs.

Making Gateway Ads Effective

Marketers want consumers to visit their sites, and one way to accomplish this is to get consumers to click on gateway ads in high traffic sites. By using advertisements that solicit an immediate response from consumers, Web marketers have embraced a direct marketing approach. And, as in most direct marketing models, a one-to-three percent response rate is the goal.

Online marketers should anguish over gateway ads in the same way that direct mail marketers labor over the look of envelopes in home mailings. The design of the banner can make a significant difference to how the consumer responds to this nonintrusive invitation. Marketers should experiment with different approaches, recognizing that some approaches will draw large numbers of consumers, while others will draw the "right" kind of people, and still others just won't work. All assumptions should be challenged, from the size of the ad to the philosophy of nonintrusion. Gateways may currently be nonintrusive and designed in a few standard (and very small) sizes, but these are trends, not laws. For example, MovieLink (**http://www.movielink.com**) regularly features intrusive ads. If you want a half-page ad, an ad that breaks out of a box, or an intrusive ad that viewers must visit before moving on, open negotiations with Websites or look around until you find a site that will do it. Unsuccessful attempts are inevitable, at least until the dos and don'ts of gateway advertising are ironed out. But early observations suggest the following guidelines:

• **Create action-oriented messages.** Gateways with a specific call-to-action message have a far greater likelihood of engaging consumers; in other words, a banner ad that says "Click here for giant savings" is more likely to drive customers than a banner that says "Discount products."

• **Give the consumer a sense of what's behind the door.** A simple logo or company name is less likely to intrigue a consumer than a gateway that communicates fun, excitement, or mystery—or even one that previews the flavor or personality of the site. Don't be afraid to use bold colors, interesting fonts, or enigmatic images.

• **Rotate the creative design of the gateway.** Frequent changes in the gateway presented to consumers has two major benefits, both of which are likely to increase visits to the Website. First, they give a sense that the site itself is fresh and vital; and second, they diversify the attraction of a site, drawing new customers with each different design.

• **Let consumers know if there's something new behind the door.** As marketers change Website content, they should announce this new content on the gateways. New gateways increase return traffic from consumers who have already visited and also attract new visitors.

• **Consider using Java.** The use of Java is expected to increase in the coming months, enabling marketers to create affordable gateways that incorporate eye-catching animation. As always, companies must balance what is technologically possible with what is philosophically sound. However, if a marketer wants to keep his or her gateway non-intrusive (which is in line with the current Internet ethos), using Java to create hyper-animated banners might yield undesirable results.

Interactive Publishing Alert Online Advertising Index Consider it a searchable directory of rate cards for the online world. The IPAOAI Website lists all the major sites soliciting advertisers—from *Penthouse* to Pathfinder to Prodigy. Each listing includes rate information, traffic stats, names of sponsors, and a brief description of the site's content.
✓ **www** → http://www.net creations.com/ipa/adindex

The Traffic Resource Designed as an "online media planning tool," Traffic Resource offers its subscribers information on planning online campaigns, describes the fundamentals of advertising online, evaluates sponsorable sites, and maintains a database of sites accepting sponsors. The site also sponsors the I-Traffic 40, a list of the top sites that a media planner should consider.
✓ **www** → http://www.traffic resource.com

WebTrack's Adspace Locator WebTrack breaks down the online advertising market into Websites actively soliciting advertisers and those potentially accepting advertisements. These sites are further broken down into categories such as Web services, Web publishers, shopping malls, entertainment sites, and special events. Each listing includes rate card information, the names of past advertisers, and a link to the site.
✓ **www** → http://www.webtrack .com/sponsors/sponsors.html

Beginning in earnest in 1995, Websites began selling ad space to media buyers. This is a selection of such sites, excluding directories and search engines which are listed on pages 110-111:

Advertising Age The electronic spinoff of the weekly bible of the advertising industry not only chronicles advertiser activities online, it also takes sponsors. NBC, the Alcone Marketing Group, *The New York Times*, and Silicon Graphics have had gateways here.
✓ www→http://www.adage.com

Boston.com Run by the *Boston Globe*, the mammoth Website is an excellent online resource for New Englanders. Site resources range from job listings to features on the Boston Marathon and major tourist attractions to a section devoted to the arts (movie listings, restaurant reviews, etc.) to sports, weather, and national news. Advertisers range from NYNEX to Computertown.
✓ www→http://www.globe.com

CMP's TechWeb Computer magazine and newsletter publisher, CMP, has a lineup that includes *CommunicationsWeek*, *HomePC*, *Windows Magazine*, *InformationWeek*, and *NetGuide Magazine*. The company's Website has a calendar of online events, an award-winning daily newsbrief about online developments, Website picks of the day, a techie job board, and more.

Types of Gateway Ads

Gateway advertisements can employ a wide variety of strategies, ranging from simple-draw banners ("Click Here For More Information") to more complex and playful treatments (Duracell, for example, has created ads that suggest that the Websites on which they are advertising are powered by the Copper-Top battery). Gateway design depends on the company paying for the advertising, the site at which the advertisement will appear, and the kinds of consumers companies want to attract, but even a fairly narrow sampling of gateways can illustrate some of the some of the issues that marketers face when placing their banners in sites. Consider these four major gateway strategies, illustrated by ads collected from Yahoo (**http://www.yahoo.com**), Pathfinder (**http://pathfinder.com**), and HotWired (**www.hotwired.com**) in February 1996.

I. Product Information

Insignia Solutions (http://www.insignia.com)

Windows For Power Mac — INSIGNIA SOLUTIONS.

Insignia solutions sends a simple message with its banner: if you're interested in running Windows on a Power Macintosh, the company has products that meet your needs. The ad boldly associates a consumer's need with a company's name.

Saturn (http://www.saturncars.com)

No salesbots. No hyper talk. No anonymous electric anything. A DIFFERENT KIND *of* COMPANY. A DIFFERENT KIND *of* CAR. SATURN.

Saturn's gateway ads continue to drive home the "we're different" message that Saturn has been sending since it first launched its first car. The ad creatively mixes car and cyber references, and it's made clear to consumers what clicking the ad means: more information about why Saturn is a different kind of car. And, like many banners focused on product information, the ad serves its purpose even if the consumer sees it and doesn't click.

Excite (http://www.excite.com)

Like Saturn, Excite uses its gateway to define itself in terms of what it is not—in this case, Yahoo. Since most Netters are familiar with the Yahoo Internet directory and search engine, Excite describes itself to consumers through a comparison with Yahoo's product. Just by mentioning Yahoo in Excite's ad, the consumer has a general idea of what Excite is.

II. Promotion

RentNet (http://www.rent.net)

AmEx University (http://www.americanexpress.com)

These two gateways use promotions to attract Netsurfers to their sites—RentNet offers visitors a chance to "Win Free Rent!" and American Express University promotes its Spring Breakaway Sweepstakes. Both banners employ large lettering and bold colors to appeal to consumers, and both of them indicate that Netsurfers who visit their site may win valuable prizes.

Advertisers have included Sybase, Intel, Lotus, Jupiter Communications, and Netscape Communications.
✓**www**→http://techweb.cmp.com/techweb

CNN Interactive CNN's searchable site delivers frequently updated news reports, a daily news quiz and link of the day, daily CNN programming listings, and even a collection of CNN video clips. Sponsors have included AT&T Business Network, Intel, and Lexis-Nexis.
✓**www**→http://www.cnn.com

c|net The computer network is part magazine, part reference center, part technical support line. The Website (which has a television show counterpart) reports on news affecting the computer industry, runs features and reviews on new software and hardware, offers a marketplace for buying and selling computer products, and maintains—or links to—valuable online resources for computer owners. Advertisers have ranged from Apple to MCI Marketplace to Amazon.com (a bookstore). clnet carries a list of all its advertisers.
✓**www**→http://www.cnet.com

CouponNet/RebateNet How do you get consumers to visit a site? One way is to give them discounts and incentives. CouponNet/RebateNet distributes coupons and rebates for companies who advertise with them. Coupons are organized by category for consumers, but companies can buy advertisements on the site's home page as well.
✓**www**→http://www.coupon.com

ESPNET SportsZone One of the Net's leading sports sites, SportsZone is packed with images, articles, games, sports talk, live events with sports personalities, and sports news. Sponsors have included Gatorade, Toyota, Levis, and Pizza Hut. The site includes a sponsors' index.
✓ www→http://ESPNET.Sports Zone.com

Hoover's Online Business people, job seekers, and others interested in company information can use this site to search databases of company information, quotes and earnings, businesses news and industry reports, and a marketplace with business software and books. Subscription required for some services. E*Trade, a "fully-automated stock and option trading system on the Web," and IBM have been big advertisers.
✓ www→http://www.hoovers.com

HotWired Breaking new ground in design and online editorial ambitions, *HotWired* was one of the first sites to use the clickable banners at the top of Web pages (they now offer smaller ads strategically placed on its pages). The magazine reports on culture, technology, politics, and the Net from the-future-is-digital perspective. Advertisers that have flocked to the magazine have included Toyota, Checkfree, and Silicon Graphics.
✓ www→http://www.hotwired.com

Mecklermedia's iWorld Publisher of several Internet magazines, including *Web Developers*, *WebWeek*, and *Internet World*, Mecklermedia's site also actively encourages discussions

III. Convenience

Shareware.com (http://www.shareware.com)

The Shareware.com gateway, which appeared on a number of Yahoo directory pages, celebrates the immediacy of the medium; by exhorting consumers to "Click here to download free software," the banner promises an instant payoff for any consumer who follows the link. With its imperative message, this gateway clearly marks itself as a live link, thereby offsetting the passivity of most online ads.

PoliticsUSA (http://www.politicsusa.com)

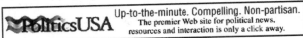

PoliticsUSA follows a similar tactic, emphasizing its store of cutting-edge political news and promising up-to-the-minute updates "only a click away." While this approach is subtler than Shareware.com's, it does cast the gateway as a translucent link that can, with only the smallest consumer investment, yield great gains.

Interactive Yellow Pages (http://www.niyp.com)

NYNEX's Interactive Yellow Pages gateway adopts a third strategy for allaying consumer fears about the time commitment of gateways. NYNEX doesn't offer any specific information about the contents of its site; rather, it emphasizes the fact that consumers can use the Yellow Pages "in seconds," after which they can return to their previous Web activity.

IV. Enigma

The Discovery Channel (http:// www.discovery.com)

This gateway, which contains only a detail of a photograph, the mysterious slogan ("What is this?"), and an imperative tagline ("Click here to find out!"), doesn't reveal the identity of its advertiser unless clicked, thereby forcing the consumer to visit the site to satisfy his or her curiosity.

Finally, when marketers purchase ads in editorial sites or directories, it makes sense for them to look for subject areas that are the most likely to attract the type of person who typically purchases their product. A software producer might, for instance, look to purchase banners in technology-related areas. On the other hand, if a certain section of a Website attracts a high level of traffic (say, the Entertainment section of Yahoo), the space may be desirable regardless of the demographics.

about the medium on its bulletin boards and live chat areas, and produces a daily news report called *Net Day*. Past advertisers have included the search engines infoseek and Excite, the Internet Shopping Network, and PC Gifts and Flowers.
✓**www**→http://www.meckler web.com

Pathfinder Time Warner has created one of the most popular Websites with digital content and online services from such popular brands as *Time, People, Money, Sports Illustrated, Fortune, Life*, and *Entertainment Weekly*. Special features include "New Now," with updated news, weather and stock reports, as well as discussion areas for its visitors. Pathfinder has been one of the most successful sites to date in attracting advertisers, which have included Advil, 7-Up, Saturn, and Fidelity Investments. The site offers an ad directory.
✓**www**→http://pathfinder.com

USA Today Designed to deliver the news quickly and clearly, *USA Today* leads with stories from each of its sections: news, sports, money, life, and weather. A big yellow starburst on *USA Today's* home page highlights the site's sponsorship index. Advertisers have included Career-Web, CE Software, Inc., and the Baltimore/Washington International Airport.
✓**www**→http://www.usatoday .com

Word It's a hip, smart electronic magazine for twenty-somethings. Past advertisers include Sun, Zima, and Mastercard.
✓**www**→ http://www.word .com/index.html

SPONSORING A WEBSITE

One potentially promising area for online advertisement is the sponsorship model. Unlike the direct marketing model of gateway advertisements, a company's objective through sponsorship is to brand itself in association with something valuable or interesting—in this case, Net resources. A credit card company seeking college-aged customers might buy a new computer for a popular MUD (a chatting or gaming environment designed to create the illusion of rooms and worlds through text descriptions) in order to associate itself with MUD-ding, an activity college students enjoy. A modem company might sponsor a useful gaming Website to ensure that the page designer can continue to afford upkeep on the page and the modem company gets associated with computer games—a shaving products company, like Gillette, might sponsor a sports news service. America Online has been one of the first companies to actively pursue this strategy. The company runs the Give Back to the Net Program and through the program has already sponsored Tid-BITS (a weekly electronic newsletter that reviews Internet and Mac services), the University of Wisconsin-Parkside music archives, the PC/Windows FTP Archive, and more. The Net community is accustomed to getting things for free, and is used to others giving up their time and building resources for them. Companies may want to start thinking like a member of this community when planning their marketing strategies.

Targeting Specific Audiences

The underlying principles guiding audience targeting are the same as in traditional media and affect both site design and gateway design. As we have discussed in earlier chapters, marketers can orient their sites' content and look toward narrow demographic groups (e.g., college students or frequent travellers). In this chapter, we'll consider how they can also design gateways with a targeting strategy.

• **Marketers can buy links in areas likely to be frequented by users of that product.** A company that makes kitchen products might buy gateways in sites that are cooking-oriented, while a company looking to reach young men might place ad links in sports-related sites. Internet directories are also starting to offer marketers the opportunity to have their gateways appear whenever specific categories or word searches are performed. The theory behind such offerings seems straightforward: consumers who are searching for information on specific products or specific topics are more likely to be potential buyers of specific products. The gateways, which appear during searches, serve as nonintrusive invitations to these prospective consumers to visit Websites.

• **The message on the gateway can be oriented specifically toward a particular type of consumer.** Sites that target specific demographics should, in the spirit of this new form of direct marketing, have banners that speak directly to the targeted demographic group. If companies have chosen to build areas on their Websites that target or carry information relevant to a specific demographic group, then targeted gateway ads should link directly to that area rather than sending these particular consumers through the front door of the site.

• **As technology evolves, it is likely that banners can be customized to the needs and interests of individuals.** Marketers employ a variety of techniques to encourage consumer participation in online surveys, including mandatory registration for access to the site and running contests. By asking customers to fill out surveys, sites can collect potentially valuable information about consumers' interests, gender, income, or shopping needs. In the future, developing technologies combined with this information will most likely allow marketers to target a consumer with a customized gateway ad. If a consumer, for example, indicates in a registration survey that he or she is planning to buy a specific item (such as a car) in the next six months, then that consumer may be presented with gateways and promotions that have been tailored to consumers who are at this point in the product-purchase cycle. Customized gateways have the potential to enhance the entire experience of visiting a Website for a consumer. The ultimate development of these types of individualized ad deliveries will depend on the extent to which sites invest in collecting information from their users and the development of the necessary technologies.

Consumer information can be highly valuable; in Chapters Two and Three of this book, we have discussed how companies like the online bookstore Amazon.com have used innovative approaches for gathering this information. What are the rules for collecting and using this consumer data? The Net community is highly sensitive to privacy issues and marketers need to balance a respect for personal privacy with their commercial objectives. As a result, many companies collecting information about users promise their customers that they will not release the information to any other companies.

EXTRA POINTS
NARROW CASTING

MovieLink MovieLink is a national directory of movie listings that lets consumers search by theater or title. Ticket ordering is also available. MovieLink sells full-page movie ads to movie studios which are automatically seen by all visitors using the site (before visitors can see listings they're directed to a movie ad). Companies may also buy small sponsorship gateways at the top of MovieLink's Web pages. Besides movie studios, advertisers have included American Express and *Entertainment Weekly*.
✓**www**→http://www.movielink.com

Musi-Cal This worldwide listing of live musical performances—a huge concert calendar—lets visitors search by performer, city, venue, or event. Advertisers have included musical events, netradio.net, and Lawrence Financial Services.
✓**www**→http://www.calendar.com/concerts

Rolling Stone The popular rock magazine's online site takes advertisements from the likes of Sun Microsystems and the film studio Thinking Pictures.
✓**www**→http://www.next.com.au/music/rstone

SnoWeb Consider it an avalanche of skiing, snowboarding, and winter sports resources. The site includes skiing articles, resort guides, slope reports, and travel links. Advertisers have included radio stations, ski resorts, and ski magazines.
✓**www**→http://www.snoweb.com

TALKING THE TALK

The advertising world is buzzing with terms like hits, impressions, and adclicks. In a frenzy to quantify the value of online advertisements, media buyers are hollering for numbers—and numbers they're getting. Here's a quick primer for navigating the language of Web stats.

Webmasters count **hits** (or **raw hits**) as the total number of pages and graphic files requested by visitors to the site. Pages with multiple graphics register as multiple raw hits. In other words, if a site has a home page with four graphics on it, each visitor to the home page would add five hits to the total raw hits for the day. Slightly more informative are **page hits** (also known as **page views**), which consider just HTML pages, not the graphics on them. In the example above, a visit to the home page would count as one hit, whether the page had 4 or 40 graphics.

As might be expected, a **visitor** is an individual, or to be more accurate, an IP number, who visits a Website. (An IP number is the address of a computer on the Internet.) A visitor may register one or more page hits to a site in a single visit. Webmasters keep track of the number of visitors to a site during a given time period—an hour, a day, a week, etc. The total number of visitors to a Website, however, includes repeat visitors. The **unique visitors** or **unique sessions** measurement is used to determine how many unique individuals have visited a site in a given time

Evaluating Gateway Success

How do you know if your gateway is doing its job or if the Website you bought space on was a good choice for your company? How do you justify your gateway budget to your boss? Don't think in terms of CPMs. It's too early for Websites to be generating the numbers that television and magazine ads generate. Besides, raw numbers aren't the issue—results are.

Websites selling ad space and marketers looking to buy space, nonetheless, continue to talk about numbers—number of visitors, hits, impressions, etc. The Web appears highly accountable. It's relatively easy for a high-traffic Website to track how many times a marketer's gateway was seen by visitors and how many people moved through a gateway to visit an advertiser's site. But how valuable are these numbers? Until there are standard interpretations of traffic numbers, marketers should attribute less importance to stats and more to the goals of a site.

Based on the goals for their online presence—goals that range from collecting consumer names to selling a product directly to introducing a new product—marketers have to decide what they need from their gateways. Would they rather have 100 people link to their Website or 1,000 people exposed to their banner (which tells consumers they are available on the Web)? Do they care more about the number of people visiting their site or the type of person visiting? As in other marketing venues, it may be better to reach the people who count than count the people you reach. The interactivity and selectivity benefits of a gateway advertisement need to be factored into any "formula" that evaluates its cost-effectiveness and success. Traditional media can deliver a higher raw number of impressions and will continue to outrank the online medium for quite some time. Yet the Web both lends itself to a much higher response rate than other media—consumers can link directly from the ad to the marketer's Website—and can provide more in-depth product information. In addition, many Websites that sell advertising links are able to provide advertisers with a demographic profile of the types of people sent from their site to the marketer's site. If marketers are trying to reach specific target audiences, then the kind of person passing through the gateway plays an important role in determining the value of the number of visitors. For many companies the pre-qualified audiences (specific demographics and interest areas) that Websites deliver combined with the interactivity of a gateway (click to go to the site for more information about a product) make gateway advertising much more powerful than conventional advertising. Using information culled from registration surveys, IP number analysis, and other means of qualifying visitors, marketers will soon be able to create different gateways for the same site, customized for different types of consumers.

Measuring the success of a gateway necessarily involves considering the larger goals of the company's online presence. Websites have the potential to match consumers with products, offer consumers personalized or unique promotions, and even sell products directly to consumers. The marketer just has to figure out how much a visit to its site is worth—and that figure may be different for every site and every online ambition.

The final piece of the evaluation puzzle is an auditing mechanism. As the industry matures, sites that sell advertising will need to be audited by an independent third party to verify that the sites have provided advertisers with the exposure that they promised in return for a specific fee. Several industry participants are working to develop valid audit procedures and these are likely to be available by the end of 1996.

period. This number can only be accurately tracked if a site incorporates a registration requirement and tracks individuals signing onto a site. Why is registration effective? Sites cannot distinguish between different people using the same IP number. Many people, for instance, share computers in an office or school. If a university student uses a public computer to link to the Snapple Website, and a few minutes later a different student uses the same computer to link to the site, the site counts only one unique IP number despite the fact that there have been two people visiting. Much more troublesome are circumstances where several computers on the same network share the same IP numbers. This is most pronounced in the case of commercial online services in a situation known as "dynamic allocation." Services such as America Online and Prodigy maintain a certain number of IP numbers that are continually reassigned to users wishing Internet access. Thus, the millions of users on these services are masked by a few IP numbers used by all of the service's members.

So how many people saw your ad? **Impressions** are the number of times an ad was *presented*—the number of times the ad graphic was downloaded by a user. **Adclicks** or **clicks** is a much more straightforward measurement of response (unless you're attempting to count clicks by unique visitors). This is the number of times that visitors have clicked an ad and visited the advertiser's site. The **clickrate** is the percentage of all impressions (as measured by page views) who actually clicked the ad.

How do you measure traffic? Netscape and other server software often include the ability to track raw hits, HTML hits, and unique IP addresses. For those without access to server logs (a business can run its Website on someone else's server) and for those who want more sophisticated analysis and presentation of server stats, stat services and software are available. These are just a few different options:

Getstats Getstats is written for GCC and is used to report basic Web server statistics and generate a dozen different reports. No analysis, just numbers. Requires compiling and access to the Web server.
✓ **www**→http://www.eit.com /software/getstats/getstats.html

ICS Webstats This freeware program is written in perl script and generates an easy-to-read log summary in HTML format. Another program available at the site converts the data into graph format.
✓ **www**→http://www.ics.uci .edu/WebSoft/wwwstat

Internet Audit Bureau Targeted at Website owners who are not techies, this free Internet service lets users monitor the number of unique visitors to their Websites. Site owners just add a few lines of HTML code to their Websites and the code displays the Internet Audit Bureau's logo. Every time the page is downloaded, the IAB's logo is downloaded, which is monitored on the IAB site. Statistics

The Price of Gateways

Selling gateways is an evolving phenomenon. As a result, there are no fixed rates for marketers looking to buy gateways. However, a number of approaches to charging for gateways have emerged. These include:

• **A flat price for a monthly or quarterly placement.** This pricing plan has the virtue of simplicity. Marketers sign on for a period of time, assess the value they receive, and continue advertising in flat-rate sites as long as they receive high value.

• **A specific number of viewers, or guaranteed page views.** In this approach, ad sites guarantee marketers that their gateways will be seen by a specific number of individuals (as measured by impressions); they guarantee a number of exposures. One important aspect of this guarantee: it is still up to the marketer to cause customers to "click" on the gateway and visit the marketer's site. The marketer is guaranteeing the number of users who will receive invitations to the site, by being exposed to the gateway, not how many consumers will actually visit the marketer's site.

•**A Dutch auction.** A few sites have been experimenting with an auction model. In theory, this sales method perfectly matches market demand and supply. Specific advertising areas are auctioned to marketers for a period of time (such as a month). Marketers bid by filling out forms online. In keeping with Dutch auction rules, the winning bidder pays the price bid by the next highest bidder.

•**A pay-per-visitor model.** Some sites have begun to experiment with charges that reflect the actual number of people who "click" on the marketer's site and move through the gateway. There are, however, certain drawbacks to this approach: advertisers are effectively not charged for any of the exposure they receive from consumers who see that they are on the Web, but decide not to visit at that particular moment. In addition, these sites have an incentive to sell gateways to advertisers with the most interesting Websites or most compelling banners—which may not be in the best interest of every marketer.

What's the bottom line on pricing? As a new medium, it's appropriate that many different approaches are at work. Clearly, Web advertising is in its infancy, and lots of experiments are taking place. Whatever pricing approaches remain viable over time will do so because they have delivered clear value to advertisers buying gateways.

Top Web Advertisers for 4Q95

(based on placement spending)

1. AT&T	$567,000
2. Netscape	556,000
3. Internet Shopping Network	329,000
4. NECX Direct	322,000
5. Mastercard	278,000
6. American Airlines	254,000
7. Microsoft	240,000
8. c|net	237,000
9. MCI	231,000
10. SportsLine	218,000

(Source: http://www.webtrack.com)

---

are updated regularly.
✓**www**→http://www.internet-audit.com/

I/PRO In partnership with Nielsen Media Research, I/PRO is offering services to measure Website usage for both site owners and advertisers. The company offers a program that allows site owners to check number of visits, origin of visitors, most frequently sought destination within the site, and more. I/PRO also offers an auditing program that lets advertisers or media buyers monitor Web audience usage and demographics. Includes customized statistics and analysis.
✓**www**→http://www.ipro.com

WebAudit This subscription-based stats service is run via email. Website owners with difficulty compiling statistics for their site (perhaps they don't have access to server logs) can use this service. WebAudit sends customers regular reports with statistics that are easy to sort and manipulate. Free trial service available.
✓**www**→http://www.wishing.com/webaudit

WebStat Download or register perl-cgi script programs that record the number of total hits, unique IP visits, duration an HTML file is read, and other stats.
✓**www**→http://www.huntana.com/webstat/about.html

WebTrends Designed for Windows systems, WebTrends software generates reports and graphs that measure and analyze Web traffic. Demo available on site.
✓**www**→http://www.egsoftware.com/webtrend.htm

Alta Vista Far-ranging? The farthest. Alta Vista offers quick searches of more than 6 million Websites; the problem, as with any search engine this comprehensive, is that any set of search terms calls up an inexhaustible list of links.
✓www→http://www.altavista.digital.com

Commercial Sites Index The most comprehensive listing of corporate and other commercial Websites, and consequently an invaluable resource for marketers.
✓www→http://www.directory.net

ElNet Galaxy Search the Web, gopher, Hytelnet, and Einet's own Web pages for a listing of up to 240 sites at a time. Einet has also created its own topical index of the Web.
✓www→http://www.einet.net

infoseek Infoseek lets you search Web pages, Usenet news, over 50 computer magazines, newswires, press releases, and more.
✓www→http://www.infoseek.com

Lycos Lycos claims over 3.5 million Web pages in its searchable database.
✓www→http://lycos.cs.cmu.edu

Opentext A huge search engine, and the only one to allow full-text searches of the Web.
✓www→http://www.opentext.com

WebCrawler An incredibly

Getting Listed in Directories

The online world is a vast and sprawling place, and can be difficult to navigate. That's why it needs its navigation services, and in the early days of the Internet, a dozen or so services have emerged as the leaders in helping Netsurfers get around online. There's Yahoo (**http://www.yahoo.com**), which started as the project of two Stanford University students and has expanded into one of the quickest and most reliable maps of the Net. There's YPN (**http://www.ypn.com**), a more detailed, if less comprehensive, guide to the Net that grew out of the popular NetBooks series (of which this book, *NetMarketing*, is the thirteenth). And then there are the dozens of online search engines, from Opentext (**http://www.opentext.com**) to Altavista (**http://www.altavista.digital.com**) to Webcrawler (**http://www.webcrawler.com**), each of which has its own strengths and weaknesses. Content-based sites, such as Time Warner's Pathfinder (**http://pathfinder.com**), CMP's TechWeb (**http://www.techweb.com**), and WMMS 100.7's, BuzzardWeb (**http://www.concourse.com/wmms**), are also beginning to incorporate directory services that provide indexes of materials within their own sites as well as on the Internet as a whole. In most cases, these indexes, directories, and guides are among the first places that a consumer seeking specific information will go in order to find facts on a particular product or service. Listings in these directories can generate large numbers of hits for Websites. Any well-developed marketing campaign should contact these sites and ensure appropriate listing.

Marketers should begin by deciding whether they want to tackle the project of getting their site listed in online directories or whether they want to hire someone else to do it. The process of getting listed can be tedious and time-consuming. Marketers must write descriptions for their sites that meet the criteria for different directories, decide where they want to be categorized in each, denote which keywords they wish to be associated with, and include other information specifically requested by the sites. Major indexes are flooded with new submissions every day and it can take up to a few weeks before a site is listed (assuming the submission hasn't been overlooked), which means that someone has to follow up on all submissions. If a site hasn't appeared after a couple of weeks, a marketer should resubmit a description for it.

Several sites have sprung up online to help companies and individuals get listed in these directories with a minimum of hassle and cost. These sites solicit information from site owners and then automate the submission of site descriptions to a specified group of directories. The free sites, however, do not follow up to make sure a company is actually listed. Marketers can instead hire an online promotional company to do the submission and the follow-up.

Listings are usually accompanied by a big increase in traffic for a site, particularly at the beginning. Often new sites are given prominence in a special section for new additions, or an icon or label is slapped next to a site description, highlighting the site as a new addition to the directory.

quick, no-frills search engine.
✓**www**→http://www.webcrawl er.com

DIRECTORIES

GNN Whole Internet Catalog Based on one of the first mainstream Internet how-to books, the Whole Internet Catalog is GNN's guide to the best sites online. Sites are categorized and reviewed.
✓**www**→http://gnn-e2a.gnn .com/gnn/wic/wics/index.html

Point These are the guys behind those "Top 5%" graphics plastered all over Cyberspace. Point maintains an extensive, searchable directory of site reviews and distributes the graphic to highly rated sites.
✓**www**→http://www.pointcom .com

Yahoo For a long time, the site has reigned as the Web directory of choice for most serious Netters, in large part because of its small graphics and sparse text. There isn't a ton of information at Yahoo, but there are tons of sites, and they're updated regularly.
✓**www**→http://www.yahoo .com

YPN Based on the popular Net-Books series, YPN (Your Personal Net) lists more than 15,000 of the Net's best sites, and divides them by topic. What distinguishes YPN from other services? The breadth of its coverage (not only Websites, but also newsgroups, commercial service forums, and bulletin boards) and the quality of its writing (the site offers pointed, literate mini-reviews of sites).
✓**www**→http://www.ypn.com

AttorneyNet AttorneyNet has created an international directory of attorneys. Clients come to AttorneyNet to use the site's legal resources, link to other legal sites online, and find an attorney. Similar to the benefits of being in the telephone book under "Attorneys," AttorneyNet provides practicing lawyers a valuable place to advertise their services. AttorneyNet will design Web pages or link to an attorney's outside Web page for a fee.
✓ **www**→http://attorneynet.com

CatalogLink Shoppers are invited to CatalogLink to collect all the catalogs they can click on. CatalogLink's clients—the companies advertising their catalogs—feature short descriptions of their catalogs, and CatalogLink then sets up a program to collect the names and addresses of consumers interested in the merchandise of their clients. The process is especially easy for consumers: just click the "send free catalogs" button under the catalog description.
✓ **www**→http://www.cataloglink.com

CatalogSelect Pathfinder's entry into the online catalog clearinghouse industry not only collects catalogs, but allows consumers to sign up for the mailing lists for a wide variety of direct mail enterprises. At Catalog Select's checkout point, consumers can also opt to receive special offers on merchandise; to keep everything electronic, noti-

Joining an Industry Hubsite

Location! Location! One of the most important decisions a businessperson makes is where to set up shop. This is increasingly becoming important online as well. The idea of location, to the extent that it exists at all online, is tied up in one site's association with another site. Location in Cyberspace isn't geographic—there are no physical corners, no Madison Avenues, no Main Streets. It's about links to other sites

IN-SITE: **AutoWeb Interactive**
http://www.autoweb.com

"The Nation's Electronic Auto Mall" brings together car dealerships and car buyers. Dealerships and individuals can post information about new and used cars in searchable databases that consumers can easily access. For a fee, the site will build an Internet presence on AutoWeb for a car company, develop online ordering and email customer communication features, release quotes for new makes, advertise promotions, and offer sponsorship opportunities for various areas of AutoWeb. Car dealerships can buy gateway ads throughout the site. To make the site a more comfortable place for consumers to use and to keep them coming back, AutoWeb offers consumers detailed information about dealers, free quotes on new and used cars, and special deals. To increase traffic to its site, AutoWeb offers a link exchange program. If a car company already has a Website, AutoWeb will include a link to it in exchange for the site linking to AutoWeb.

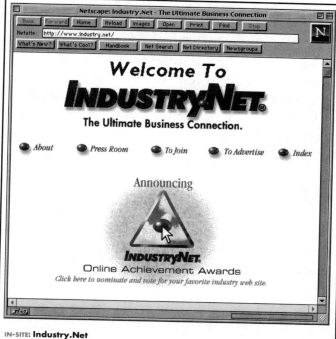

IN-SITE: Industry.Net
http://www.industry.net

The only reason companies are online, ultimately, is to move their products and services. Industry.Net operates under the assumption that manufacturing, automation, and computer companies move their products best when they're networking with their peers and customers. More than 4,000 companies have set up "business centers" (home pages with company profiles, product info, options to send faxes, etc.) on Industry.Net and thousands of other companies list information about themselves at the site. Distributors or those interested in a company or its products can search the site by industry, geographical location, or product. The site also includes a daily newsletter, discussions with other industry leaders, a job board, and a shareware repository. Many companies with their own Websites also maintain a "business center" here.

and shared resources. Companies are joining or linking their sites to malls (see pages 84-85) and industry hubs to take advantage of—and create—high-traffic, virtual spaces.

Industry hubs bring together related businesses for the convenience of the consumer—one-stop shopping. Companies, associations, stores, professionals and others choose to join industry hubs because of the advantages they offer. Some industry hubs offer to create and maintain home pages for their members (includ-

fication of those offers will be sent by email.
✓www→http://www.Catalog Select.com

CatalogSite Eddie Bauer, J Crew, Beehive Botanicals, and other catalog companies list contact information, and often a general description of their merchandise at this huge catalog clearinghouse. The site helps generate interest in a company's catalog in two ways: It lets consumers search for a specific catalog and order it online at no cost, and it encourages a visitor to register with a service that sends consumers catalogs similar to the other ones they pick (this is a great way to get less well-known catalogs seen).
✓www→http://www.catalog site.com

DealerNet Car dealerships from all over the country list information about their businesses and inventories with DealerNet, and the large number of companies promoting their services on the site attracts car buyers. Customers use DealerNet to check their credit histories, apply for credit, read car reviews, search for information on new car models, locate dealerships selling the type of car they want to buy, and even search the inventories of dealerships for used or new cars. It's an easy way for even small-town dealers to establish a Web presence.
✓www→http://www.dealernet .com

DineNet This restaurant guide, which includes basic information about a large selection of eateries in major U.S. cities, encourages restaurants to submit menus, pictures, and even re-

views; DineNet, which is also trying to attract paying advertisers, will build a Web page for them on the site at no cost.
✓**www**→http://www.menusonline.com

DVC Corporation Airline Database Companies may submit general contact information for their airlines at no cost. The site includes a database of airline information with links to Websites when available. Airlines may also buy advertising space and home pages on the site.
✓**www**→http://www.checkin.com/database/airlines.html

The Electronic Newsstand *The Economist, Playboy,* and *Smithsonian* all have their own sites on the Internet, but like hundreds of other publications, they also maintain a presence on the Electronic Newsstand. Each magazine offers selections from its current issue, a form to subscribe to the print edition of the magazine, and a form to communicate with editors. The newsstand also links to hundreds of other online publications and is a popular place for advertisers—including Check-Free and Britannica Online—to place gateways.
✓**www**→http://www.enews.com

Hotel Net This guide to European lodging is an ideal place for hotels to advertise their services. Each hotel gets a home page on which it may include incentives, coupons, and images. In addition, hotels may choose to buy additional gateways on the site.
✓**www**→http://www.hotelnet.co.uk

ing store locators, shopping programs, mailing lists, etc.), set up powerful search engines that let consumers search and sort through all of the resources on a hub, develop interesting content and promotions for the site to keep consumers coming back, and even offer offline promotional assistance. These sites also facilitate business-to-business transactions. The synergy of sharing the same space with other similar businesses is often highly valuable. The most important advantage that industry hubs offer, however, is increased visibility for sites.

Except for the Websites of the most well-known companies, industry hubs are easier to find online than are sites for individual companies. Like online malls, industry hubs are often more prominently featured in

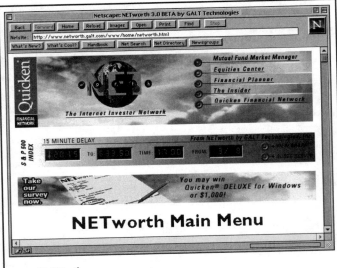

IN-SITE: **NetWorth**
 http://www.networth.galt.com
Several mutual fund companies such as the Alger Fund, Dreyfus, and Wright Investors' Service have built home pages, or "NETworth storefronts," on this Quicken-owned site. Companies have customized their pages with fund family information, services, contests, and other features to attract investors, but they also capitalize on the resources shared by all members of NETworth. The site offers analysis and information about mutual funds, free stock quotes, a financial planner, links to hundreds of financial-related resources, and a searchable atlas of funds. Visitors who register with the site may also track their portfolios online.

directories and the press, they are more likely to be added as hotlinks to personal home pages, and they are usually more equipped to generate publicity (after all, the site is making money on its ability to generate traffic for its members).

Industry hubs are a business. Some ask businesses to pay membership fees, while others are free and rely on the sale of gateway advertisements to generate revenue. Many offer a combination of both approaches. If an industry hub is successful, advertisers are usually easy to find. A successful industry hub with a lot of members and steady stream of visiting consumers (consumers interested in very specific products) is prime media space for advertisers. In many cases, industry hub members choose to buy gateway ads on the front door of the hubsite to increase their visibility and draw consumers to their page.

InsuranceNet This no-frills site is an index to insurance companies and resources online. It also runs discussion forums about insurance topics. The site was designed to promote the industry's presence online and to offer consumers a "no hassles way to make first contact with providers of insurance." When reviewed, the site was not performing any services for insurance providers (creating home pages, etc.) except for linking to their separate Websites.
✓**www**→http://www.insurance net.com

Mall of Catalogs This site has more than 1,600 catalogs to select from, some already with Web pages, and each fitted with a concise review and an email button to facilitate easy ordering. There is also a special green button which customers can use to submit their name to a "never send me anything list"—marketers with ties to catalog houses should consider adding a feature like this to their sites to allay the fears of junk-mail- and junk-email-phobic consumers.
✓**www**→http://www.csn.net /marketeers/mallofcatalogs

Realty.Net Realty.Net is positioning itself up as a "comprehensive information resource on the Internet dedicated to the real estate marketing, lending, construction and related industries." The site offers to build home pages on its site for real estate professionals and then advertise them on several big Internet directories. The site offers consumers the functionality of searching by geographical location or type of service.
✓**www**→http://www.builders .com

Participating in the Online Community

An extraordinarily valuable way of building traffic at a Website is to generate interest in the site within the Internet community. There are two principal means of getting this attention: hotlinks, or pointers, from appropriate sites; and announcements in appropriate Usenet discussion groups or mailing lists.

Let's treat hotlinks first. Companies should try to get listed on popular home pages that are related topically to their business. Many Websites that address specific interests, whether rock music or the finances of senior citizens, include "hotlists," or sets of Web links editorially chosen and likely to be of interest to Netsurfers visiting the site. The first step in building free hot-list links to your commercial site is to think of your site as a resource for another site with editorial content. Then, ask yourself what sites have editorial content that harmonizes with yours. Sports-related sites, for instance, might feel they are providing value to their users by linking to Reebok's site. Big gaming sites often choose to link to gaming companies like Nintendo, Sega, or Sony. Travel sites benefit from linking to online ticket agents. Many popular sites are receptive to linking to commercial sites and the payoffs for companies can be immense.

How can you encourage these links? You can use Internet search tools and directories, or an inexpensive consultant, to compile a database of all of the Websites that might, because of their topical focus, be interested in providing a free link to your site. When you launch your site (or add new features to it), you could then email the Webmaster at each of these sites. The tone of your email should be casual and the note should be brief. In a related strategy, you could maintain your own hotlist and operate on a principle of reciprocity, listing those sites that consent to list your site. The

SPAMMING & OTHER SINS

Any marketer beginning an online advertising campaign is likely to hear the First Commandment of Online Advertising: Thou Shalt Not Mass Email. For marketers not intimately familiar with the online community and Netiquette (a neologism that refers to online manners), this is also known as "spamming," which refers to the bombardment of newsgroups with off-topic, often commercial, posts. Intuitively, this may seem like a good strategy—to announce your Website's launch in hundreds of newsgroups, and thereby reach hundreds of thousands of Netters for free. But don't do it.

Companies that have mass emailed Usenet have become Internet pariahs, accused of tainting a Utopian medium with poisonous avarice. The prime example, of course, is the law firm of Laurence Canter and Martha Siegel, which in April 1994 emailed a post advertising their services to more than 6,000 newsgroups, touching off months of furious conterposts, boycotts, and even death threats. Canter and Siegel never expressed remorse—in fact, they have reported profits of more than $100,000 from the campaign, and even written a book to promote their new online marketing agency, *Cybersell* (for a review of the book, see **http://www.well.com/user /paulkies/iway.html**).

If you want your company to be respected by the online community, be very careful about posting to multiple newsgroups. As a rule of thumb when trying to get free links is simple: don't be demanding and don't be annoying.

A second approach to generating interest within the Internet community is to post messages about a company's site in appropriate newsgroups. Before you post, though, make certain that you understand what a newsgroup is, and what it is not. Some newsgroups are designed only for discussion; some, for buying and selling; some, for moderated news announcements; and still others, for postings related to very specific topics. Be careful not to violate the social code of the Net by posting to too many newsgroups indiscriminately. There are nine **comp.sys.ibm.pc.games*** newsgroups, for instance. A gaming company should never post to all of them, but if the company announced that it was running a challenge ladder on its site which pitted Netters who played its game against each other, the company could probably post to one of the groups and expect a positive response. While brevity is important, companies should be wary of posts that are too

rule of thumb, post only to newsgroups that are explicitly connected to your product—if you are advertising a book about the Presidential election, for example, feel free to post to **alt.elections** or **alt.politics.bob-dole**, but don't post to **alt.fan.woody-allen** or **alt.sex.fetish.hair.** And don't post a new announcement every day. One or two posts are enough.

To prevent spamming, a number of watchdog newsgroups like **news.admin.net-abuse.misc**, **news.admin.net-abuse.announce**, and **alt.current-events.net-abuse**. have sprung up on Usenet. And the famous Blacklist of Internet Advertisers (**http://www.cco.caltech.edu/~cbrown/BL**) which collects an ongoing list of spammers, along with a detailed FAQ on inappropriate commercial advertising, recommended retaliation measures, and other aspects of Usenetiquette. Newsgroups are not the only tempting targets for marketers. Electronic mailboxes are, too. As marketers begin to collect more information about online consumers, some companies will have the means to send consumers customized email. Most Netizens consider their email address to be a form of private property. Getting unsolicited email, then, is a form of intrusion, and virtually certain to hinder rather than assist a marketer's efforts to forge a relationship with customers.

For a collection of articles and FAQs on the proper use of the Internet for marketing purposes, marketers should visit net.acceptable at **http://arganet.tenagra.com/Tenagra/net-acceptable.html.**

IN-SITE: Point Communications
      http://www.pointcom.com/
Want Point to point to your site? Point's staff reviews and lists the top-five percent of Websites in several categories, from Kids to Computers to Health. It also runs weekly top-ten lists and offers a mailing list to keep visitors informed of new sites.

The All-In-One Cool Sites Page This supplement to the All-Internet Shopping Directory collects a list of links to the "best of the Net sites"—that's the sites doing the ratings, not those judged highly. Each link is annotated to help guide those seeking cyberexcellence.
✓**www**→http://www.webcom.com/~tbrown/coolsite.html

Cool Site of the Day Many have started to collect Net hot spots, but Cool Site was one of the first. Now there are actually two cool sites of the day: one grab-bag site and a "categorically cool" pick for every weekday. Stop by for a knowledge site on Monday, an art choice on Tuesday, a home page on Wednesday, a bizarre site on Thursday, and a commercial choice on Friday.
✓**www**→http://cool.infi.net

HotWired's Net Surf *HotWired* continues to deliver hip, cybersaavy analysis of the medium with annotated links to daily choices for best sites on the Net.
✓**www**→http://www.hotwired.com/surf

PC Magazine The Top 100 Web Sites The venerable computer magazine has created an elaborate Web gallery of top Websites. Updated frequently, this site lets visitors browse the best in e-zines, commerce and marketing, or government and politics, among others.
✓**www**→http://www.zdnet.com/pcmag/special/web100

generic. Don't expect to generate a lot of enthusiasm over a post that says "check out our cool, new Website."

What is the key to successfully using a newsgroup to build traffic? Downplay the commercial aspect of your site, and instead focus on how your company is making a real contribution to the specific newsgroup. It is easiest to post an invitation to your Website when your site has relevant information; Warner Bros. Records (**http://www.wbr.com**), for instance, would be entitled to post a message on **alt.fan.madonna**, even if the message announced a profit-making endeavor.

A few newsgroups are specifically designated for announcements of new commercial sites and initiatives. If you launch a site, be certain to notify the moderated newsgroup **comp.infosystems.www .announce**, which is one of the two or three most important places online to announce new sites. Guidelines for submitting announcements are posted on the Web, along with the group's charter, at **http://boutell.com/%7Egrant/charter.html**. Another popular forum for announcing new Websites, commercial and otherwise, is the Net Happenings mailing list (**listserv@lists.internic.net**, *Type in message body*: subscribe net-happenings <your full name>). Net Happenings also exists in newsgroup form (**comp.internet.net-happenings**).

Another way to generate interest is to get noted as a site-of-the-day. Hundreds of sites offer picks of the day. Many avid Netsurfers regularly check in with these sites to discover new places to visit. Some sites encourage site owners to email them URLs for consideration, while others choose to find sites themselves. The net result of being listed as one of the select few is an increase in traffic!

Sending Out an Invitation

You want consumers to visit. Couldn't you just email them an invitation? Throughout this chapter, we've discussed strategies for getting consumers to visit your site for the first time, but a personal invitation might be a way to get them to come back again. To truly build a steady flow of traffic at your site, you're going to need repeat visitors. Interesting content and useful services might encourage consumers to return, but a friendly email reminder is also a valuable strategy.

Before companies can email an invitation, they must capture the names, addresses, and profiles of visitors. The more information they get, the more customization is possible. Contests, visitor guestbooks, voluntary mailing lists, registration forms, and other incentives have been a successful means of garnering this information. Conscious of the Net community's sensitivity to privacy, many companies are promising consumers that they will keep the information they collect about consumers private, that they won't sell a mailing list of their visitors to another company.

It's important to avoid antagonizing consumers by getting visitors to your site to ask for the email you want to send them. One increasingly popular approach is to let consumers check off reasons why they'd like to be contacted (e.g., "check if you'd like to be notified of any special sales or promotions" or "sign up if you'd like to be notified of new resources on the site"). The consumer retains control over what he or she is sent, the company is seen as offering the consumer a valuable service, and the visitor gets a reminder to come back and visit the site.

EXTRA POINTS
SIGN 'EM UP

Good Stuff Cheap Specializing in close-out merchandise, this online store gets its customers to sign up for a free personal shopping agent. The agent then notifies the customer by email whenever merchandise arrives which might be of interest.
✓**www**→http://www.onramp.net/goodstuf

IBM Telecommunications and Media IBM lets customers sign up for an email notification service that announces new technological breakthroughs, laws, and industry moves.
✓**www**→http://webster.ibmlink.ibm.com/telmedia

Metropolitan Museum of Art The Met runs an email service that notifies art lovers every time a new exhibit is mounted on the Web or on the actual walls. Each month's schedule of lectures, movies, and events is also emailed.
✓**www**→http://www.metmuseum.org

Pathfinder Pathfinder encourages visitors to sign up for *Compass*, a weekly newsletter which updates visitors about what's new on Pathfinder.
✓**www**→http://pathfinder.com

WebSaver Annuity This financial company offers customers an email notification service that lets them know when new annuity rates are available.
✓**www**→http://www.websaver.com

Chapter 5

Making an Online Sale

Making an Online Sale

For marketers, the Web today is principally an advertising vehicle, a powerful new way for companies to provide in-depth corporate and product information to potential buyers of products. However, as it moves toward the future, increasingly the Web will be a place for active, actual shopping. With new technology, consumers can submit online payment information (whether in the form of a credit-card number, a billing number for an online account, or even electronic "cash") and have products shipped to them by overnight delivery—and sometimes delivered immediately over the Web itself.

Although not every company has decided to use the Web to sell its products directly, as the convenience and minimal costs of taking online orders are understood, more and more companies will add sales features to their sites. But legitimate concerns remain. What happens to local bookshops when online bookstores become a major competitor as publishers sell directly from their Websites? What happens to record stores when consumers can sample and order music online? How do banks and newspapers change their businesses as more consumers access these services and content—bolstered with added features—from their computers? As companies try to carve out opportunities to sell their products online, entire industries are likely to change in accord with the new medium and its way of selling.

Are People Buying?

So long as consumers are buying goods online, companies will be interested in the medium. In fact, any marketer trying to convince his company to build a Website will have to consider consumer online buying habits. So are they buying? The most noteworthy effort to track consumer habits online is the Hermes Project (**http://www.cc.gatech.edu/gvu/user _surveys**), which is overseen by researchers at the University of Michigan. In the fall of 1995, the Hermes Project surveyed Websurfers in a study conducted in collaboration with the GVU center's fourth WWW user survey. The most interesting results relate to survey respondents who used the medium to assist them in purchasing computer hardware and software. The Hermes Project results in these categories suggest that the future for Web-based product advertising is bright; in fact, between 54 and 68 percent of respondents (depending on the specific type of product involved) used Websites as sources of product information for shopping. As other businesses establish similar, sales-oriented Websites, and as the number of active Web users increases, the integral importance of the Web to product and service suppliers as a place to help consumers learn about products in order to influence purchases will be taken for granted.

But product information and sales are by no means growing concomitantly. The Hermes Project also found that for hardware and software only 13 to 27 percent of respondents actually used the Web to purchase products (with the least expensive software products receiving the higher share of online purchases)—statistics that suggest that a far smaller percentage of Websurfers use the Web for making purchases. Other online demographic studies have yielded similar results. The A.C. Nielsen Company, which conducted

---

EXTRA POINTS COMMERCIAL USE

CommerceNet/Nielsen Internet Demographics Survey The 1995 study found that almost 40 million people age 16 and over in the United States and Canada have access to the Internet, and that almost 20 million of them have been on the World Wide Web in the past three months. Get executive summaries of the survey's findings.
✓**www** ...→http://www.commerce.net/information/surveys ...→http://www.nielsenmedia.com/whatsnew/execsum2.htm

The CommerceNet/Nielsen Survey: Is It Representative? In this article, the authors assert that the CommerceNet/Nielsen survey skews education and income upward, thereby significantly inflating the numbers of online users and distorting the influence of the medium.
✓**www**→http://www2000.ogsm.vanderbilt.edu/surveys/cn.questions.html

The Hermes Project Named for the Greek god of commerce, the three-year-old Hermes project was one of the first attempts to survey business and consumer use of the Internet, and to use that data to draw conclusions about the medium's future. Hermes visitors can read the survey results, sign up for the Corporate Panel (composed of businesses using the Web), and even customize Hermes information with the InfoMyWay service.
✓**www**→http://www-personal.umich.edu/~sgupta/hermes

Nielsen Online Recognized as one the world leaders in market research, the A. C. Nielsen Company—which has become a household name for creating "Nielsen households," the ratings-determining factors for American television—has arrived online in force, with an extensive Website that contains information on demographic measurement and its relationship to consumer behavior. However, if you're a marketer looking for the much discussed CommerceNet/Nielsen online user survey, look at the other Nielson site at **http://www .nielsenmedia.com**—information here is restricted to the company's more established market-research products.
✓**www**→http://www.nielsen .com/home/nie-ol.htm

NAFTAnet Electronic Commerce/Electronic Data Interchange A huge, hypertext document with information on electronic commerce (EC), electronic data interchange (EDI), and doing business on the Internet. Sponsored by the software company, Key Software Solutions, which offers services related to EDI and network applications.
✓**www**→http://www.nafta.net /ecedi.htm

The Toner Group Survey Companies which are conducting business online as well as consumers who are shopping online are invited to fill out this survey about business on the Internet. In exchange, The Toner Group promises to send copies of the results to everyone participating.
✓**www**→http://cymetric.com /toner

a substantial study with CommerceNet in 1995, found that 55 percent of daily Websurfers search for information on products or services, but only 14 percent use the Web to actually make purchases. And an *Advertising Age* survey of U.S. adults found that 60 percent of respondents were interested in using interactive services for "research before purchasing" but only 24 percent were interested in "computer home shopping." So the evidence would seem to indicate that Web users today typically go online to help make product purchase decisions, but go elsewhere to actually buy the products. Nonetheless, given the relatively low cost of building a Website with a sales feature, setting up shop online is becoming an attractive option for many companies, particularly small companies.

For large companies, selling through the Web can raise other issues. Relationships with distributors are vital to manufacturers, and companies must now balance the rewards of selling through the Web with the potential consequences of undercutting their distributors. Nevertheless, online sales are increasing at a rapid rate.

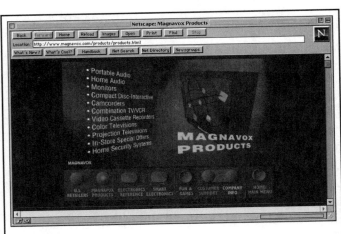

IN-SITE: Magnavox
http://www.magnavox.com
Magnavox will walk you through your television purchase decision and even follow up with online customer support, but don't expect to order a TV at the Website. The company directs its customers to offline Magnavox distributors.

The Business of the Future

While the Web is still perceived primarily as a means for delivering information, online sales will blossom as increased consumer and corporate confidence in the medium grow—not to mention advances in software, hardware, and online sales technique. A study by ActivMedia (**http://www.activmedia.com**) concluded that sales generated through the Web (excluding revenues for Web consultants and service providers) jumped to $400 million in 1995, up from only $18 million in 1994. While $400 million still pales in comparison to the $53 billion catalogue industry, more than half of those sales occurred in the last quarter of the year. And SIMBA, an affiliate of Cowles Business Media, has projected that the interactive retail industry will net $7 billion annually by the year 2000.

As a radically new medium, and one that only recently opened for business, the Web is a fascinating commercial experiment, and one whose initial growth will be largely determined by two factors—consumer perceptions about online financial security and perceptions of product value. By considering them together, we can crystallize much of the current debate about online sales.

Security Fears. The single greatest fear about online buying is security. A clear majority of respondents to the Hermes survey cited security concerns as a primary reason for not buying online. The main concern is credit card fraud—the fear that an enterprising hacker or cracker will decode the encrypted transmission, extract the customer's credit card number, and then use it to charge thousands of dollars worth of goods, or that the credit card number will be stolen from the system where it resides. A seemingly endless number of articles have been written about the safety of online

EXTRA POINTS
WEB SECURITY

About the Clipper Chip This page provides dozens of links to information about, in the words of its author, Francis Litterio, "the U.S. government's attempts to restrict the privacy of its citizens via the Escrowed Encryption Standard (EES), a.k.a. 'the Clipper Chip.'" A collection of papers, statements, and letters representing both sides of the issue are linked to the site.
✓ **www**→http://draco.center line.com:8080/~franl/clipper /about-clipper.html

alt.security.pgp A very active newsgroup covering Pretty Good Privacy issues: where to get it, problems with it, information about it and, of course, discussions (often heated ones) of the export restrictions placed on it. Several FAQs have been created to answer frequently asked questions about the Pretty Good Privacy encryption program and to list where Netters can get the latest versions of PGP.
✓ **USENET**→alt.security.pgp *FAQ:*
✓ **www**→http://www.cis.ohio -state.edu/hypertext/faq/bng usenet/alt/security/pgp/top .html

Basic Flaws in Internet Security and Commerce This outline of possible security holes on the Internet was assembled by Netters quoted in a *New York Times* article about online security flaws and their effect on commerce.
✓ **www**→http://http.cs.berkeley .edu/~gauthier/endpoint-sec urity.html

Computer Professionals For Social Responsibility

Eschewing the belief that technology alone will improve our world, CPSR, an organization of computer scientists founded in 1981, polices government organizations interested in tapping your telephone or raiding your computer's database. The CPSR Website has an automated letter of protest against the Clipper Chip that users can send to the White House. The heart of the site, however, is its archive of academically-oriented texts on computing responsibility in such areas as computer crime, the Freedom of Information Act, privacy and encryption, commerce and security issues, and more; it's a good clearinghouse for information on the sociology of the online world. CPSR also maintains a list of more than twenty mailing lists covering specific issues from security in the workplace to Bay Area CPSR member concerns.
✓**www**→http://www.cpsr.org /dox/home.html

The International PGP Home Page

Besides carrying the latest version of the Pretty Good Privacy protocol (PGP), the site also includes information on the program, the legal issues surrounding PGP, and links to other PGP resources on the Web.
✓**www**→http://www.ifi.uio.no /~staalesc/PGP/home.html

MIT Distribution Site for PGP

MIT maintains current versions of PGP, programs to integrate PGP with other programs, and an FAQ about PGP.
✓**www**→http://web.mit.edu /network/pgp.html

purchasing, encryption technologies, PGP protocols, and related issues. But any marketer thinking of selling online need know only one fact about online transactions—they are as safe as many accepted methods of payment. Online transactions take place in a datastream that contains billions of bits flowing across wires every second, billions of pieces of information, whether alphanumeric, hexidecimal, or binary. The chance of a thief correctly identifying one string of data as a credit card number, and then matching that number to a consumer's identity or breaking into systems to steal the resident credit card numbers, is far slimmer than the chance of a thief skimming credit-card information from a cellular phone conversation, or from discarded receipts. The technology of the Web is new and consequently quite intimidating, but cooler heads should prevail in the discussion of secure transactions. Programmers are constantly working to develop new methods of encryption and to distribute that software to the community of Web users at no cost. And finally, major credit card programs, such as the AT&T Universal Card Service (when customers use the AT&T WorldNet service), have suspended the $50 fraud deductible in an attempt to encourage online purchasing. The consumer, then, has essentially no liability.

As secure software becomes more readily available, and consumers increasingly trust this security, online sales are likely to increase dramatically. But the absence of a secure system—or even the perception of the Web as insecure—forces merchants to employ costly measures. L.L. Bean, for example, has placed its products for sale online (**http://www.llbean.com**), but, apparently for security reasons, lists a toll-free ordering number for interested consumers to call and provided an option for consumers to fax their orders. Under this system, the typical consumer, who has only one phone line, must disconnect from the Internet to place an order.

Now, not only does this mean the customer has to leave the Web, but the connection between merchant and customer is interrupted. It is difficult to calculate how many potential sales are lost as a result of this additional step; one way to approximate is to examine the fluctuating fate of companies that have designed methods for secure online transaction. On August 15, 1995, NECX Direct, a Web-based computer products store (**http://www.necx.com**), began offering consumers the option to purchase products using a secure credit card transactions system on the Internet. The day after NECX Direct began promoting this secure online transaction capability, its business doubled. It now averages more than $500,000 in business each month.

Savings. A key factor in the initial growth of catalog sales was the consumer perception of lower prices. The Web has the same potential to offer consumers high-quality merchandise at reduced cost. It has been estimated that Web-based selling can lower a merchant's overall costs by as much as 50 percent. The reasons for these dramatically lower costs, discussed in Chapter One, are largely commonsensical—reduced order costs, reduced service costs, reduced overhead. When the majority of merchants recognize that their lower costs enable them to offer lower prices and still achieve a healthy return, Web-based buying will increase. It's worth noting that this transformation is already starting: some of the most popular Web-based shopping areas are, in fact, taking advantage of their lower operating costs to provide consumers with better prices. The Internet Shopping Network (**http://www.internet.net**) offers more than 25,000 computer and software items for sale on the Web at prices well below those you would expect on the street. Similarly, a number of Web-based music and book stores have begun offering meaningful discounts.

Open Market One of the leading suppliers of software that enables companies to conduct business (secure transactions) over the Web, Open Market has created a Website with a treasure trove of information about Web security and secure online commerce. The site includes an extensive discussion of how two Open Market products, the Merchant Solution, and OM-Transact (a transaction link) enable online companies to "quickly and easily sell" products on the Web. The site also includes an excellent discussion of the general issues involved in Web commerce; the "Merchant Solution Business White Paper" is written for "executives, managers, and other decision-makers evaluating electronic commerce on the Internet."
✓**www**→http://www.openmarket.com

PGP: A Nutshell Overview A reference guide to PGP.
✓**www**→http://www.engin.umich.edu/~jgotts/underground/pgp-nutshell.html

PGP—Pretty Good Privacy A repository of information, news, and documentation (user guides to quick command reference charts) about PGP. The page also links to sites that carry the PGP program and utilities.
✓**www**→http://draco.centerline.com:8080/~franl/pgp/pgp.html

Secure Electronic Transactions (SET) A consortium of major Internet and financial service companies, including MasterCard, Visa, Netscape, IBM, GTE, SAIC, Terisa Systems, and Verisgn, recently agreed on a common standard for handling credit-card transactions

over the Internet. According to the MasterCard site, SET has "developed a single method that consumers and merchants will use to conduct bankcard transactions in Cyberspace as securely and easily as they do in retail stores today." SET will be tested in the second quarter of 1996.
✓**www**→http://www.Master Card.com

Security-Related Net Pointers A list of pointers to security-related information online, dealing with both commercial and non-commercial issues.
✓**www**→http://www.cs.cmu .edu/afs/cs.cmu.edu/user/bsy /www/sec.html

Security Mailing Lists Information about several Internet mailing lists related to security issues, including the Firewalls list, the Best of Security list, and the Privacy forum.
✓**www**→http://iss.net/iss/mail list.html

The World Wide Web Security FAQ Are CGI scripts insecure? How do I accept credit card orders over the Web? This elaborate and regularly updated treatment of Web security issues offers answers to questions ranging from server security to email privacy to online ordering.
✓**www**→http://www-genome .wi.mit.edu/WWW/faqs/www -security-faq.html

WWW Security Mailing List A forum for the discussion of security issues on the Internet.
✓**EMAIL**→www-security-request @nsmx.rutgers.edu ✍ *Type in message body:* subscribe www-security *Info:* ✓**www**→http://www -ns.rutgers.edu/www-security /index.html

The joint effect of these two factors—consumer fears about security and desire for lower prices—will direct the course of online sales. But when thinking about the future of online commerce, it is important to remember that any new computer technology will always seems forbidding to begin with. It takes time for consumers to become confortable with new systems, especially where money is involved. Take the example of Automated Teller Machines (ATMs). When ATMs were introduced, many consumers found them forbidding and uncomfortable to use. People forgot their PIN numbers; they were used to the relationships they had built with bank tellers. However, as consumers came to recognize three key factors— ATMs' extraordinary convenience, their high reliability, and their easy-to-use interfaces—their popularityskyrocketed. These same factors apply to the Web.

Product Comparisons. The hypertext element of the online medium creates one additional advantage for Web-based consumers: comparative shopping power. The online shopper has the ability to link to a wide variety of stores, and consequently, to be better informed than his or her offline counterparts. At one level, shoppers can compare prices and services using the traditional search tools of the Internet—Opentext, Altavista, Webcrawler, Yahoo, and other indexes. Consumers can visit one of the search engines, input the type of product desired (toaster or sweater), and find every place on the World Wide Web that mentions home appliances or cable-knit outerwear. However, this search software has not been designed for gathering information for product comparisons. It was designed for more general information searches, and can be somewhat cumbersome. Do you really want a list of hundreds of sites that mention "flying toasters?"At a more advaceed level, a wide range of initiatives are underway to develop software specifically for product shopping and comparisons, which will be easy for the consumer to use. Such software will *inevitably* be created for common use on the Internet. The type of software that performs such searches is sometimes referred to as "agents," (see pages 140-141) but what matters is that potential buyers will ultimately have an ability to find out what's out there, and to compare product prices and features literally "at the click of a button."

An example of one such experimental initiative is BargainFinder (**http://bf.cstar.ac.com**), a music-selection system developed by Andersen Consulting. In a live test of this technology, Bargainfinder allowed consumers to select a CD and search multiple stores on the Internet, many of which each carried over 100,000 titles. The result of a search led to a listing of prices for the specific CD in question, order terms, and hot links to each of the stores searched. It is worth noting that some music stores responded to Bargainfinder by blocking the agent's entry: presumably they did not want to participate in the comparison process. However, it seems likely that the use and sophistication of such agents on the Internet will grow significantly over time. Indeed, other product categories which appear to be particularly well-suited to the use of such agents include software, travel, and consumer electronics.

There may still be a few skeptics straggling behind the curve, insisting that the Web will not work as a means for consumer transactions, that security concerns are only a small part of larger concerns about the stability and legitimacy of the Internet. If consumers cannot hold and touch the product, how do they know the merchandise is reliable? If consumers cannot carry the product home with them, how can they know that shipping will not delay it indefinitely? One answer: consumers trust brand names and store reputation. Where inspecting products is a logistical impossibility

CAN THE WEB COMPARE?

It seems so natural. Consumers go online, search for a product, and get a list of brands and prices. A click here and a click there and the customer knows the differences between brand s and is ready to make a purchase. Unfortunately, it's not that simple and search engines aren't that smart—yet. Without the cooperation of the companies manufacturing products, it is extremely difficult to establish which products are comparable. Today, for such a program to have any value, companies would have to give up some of their rights to position the product and enough companies would have to participate. SmartStore (**http://smart store.ac.com**) avoids this dilemma by focusing on a single product—music CDs. Its BargainFinder search engine compares the cost of a CD at several online music stores. The magazine *PC Today* offers an alternative in the form of the PC Cyber Shop (**http://web2.pc -today.com**). The magazine, a third party in the computer sales industry, has set up a catalog that compares the cost and features of over 4,000 products from mail order vendors. Then, there's what *NetMarketing* is calling an Industry Hubsite (see pages 112-115). Companies join these Websites and either create pages on the site or link independent Websites to it. Industry Hubsites may not always make direct product comparisons but they offer the consumer a single, searchable site from which to explore options.

FAMILIARITY BREEDS CONTENT

Online shopping employs a diversity of approaches. Some stores let consumers purchase products with a single click, others make them jump through a series of registration and security hoops. Some stores change their featured specials every day, others keep the same sale product on display for months at a time. It almost seems like the real world, doesn't it? Well, yes and no. At the most basic level, the majority of offline stores share the same shopping procedures. Shoppers enter the store, inspect merchandise, handle products that interest them, and then purchase those that hold their interest. Any variation from this familiar procedure—security gates at the front of a store or product giveaways—disrupt the experience and must be introduced carefully and explained in great detail, lest the consumer become uncomfortable. Marketers on the Web, with hundreds of new technological possibilities, would be foolish to ignore the consumer's need for familiarity. Websites do not need to duplicate the experience of in-store shopping, but they do need to find a shopping standard that cuts across product types and industries. Arriving at consensus about some conventions of the online shopping experience is as important as using the new medium to build unique online environments that reinforce product branding and attract consumers. Online malls, where consumers are required to learn the procedures for a single shopping experience, are helping to forge this consensus.

and the sales environment or distribution system is unfamiliar, brand names serve as shorthand for concepts like reliability, affordability, and quality. As familiar brands appear for sale on the Web, consumer confidence will increase, and with it online purchases. This has already begun to happen. For example at the Shopper's Advantage Website (**http://www.cuc.com**), products manufactured by brand names such as Sony, Nike, and Corning are available for purchase. There are a number of reasons for the Web's expected commercial growth, including improved transmission speeds, improved security, demographic shifts, and software advances. However, the decision of familiar brands to enter Web commerce may prove to be the single greatest boost to the medium. Online stores will live or die on their reputation to get goods to consumers quickly and effectively. For the consumer, the convenience of shopping online is ultimately weighed against the experience of shopping in stores.

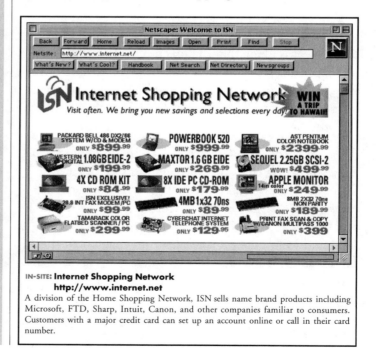

IN-SITE: **Internet Shopping Network**
        http://www.internet.net

A division of the Home Shopping Network, ISN sells name brand products including Microsoft, FTD, Sharp, Intuit, Canon, and other companies familiar to consumers. Customers with a major credit card can set up an account online or call in their card number.

Who is Selling?

Earlier, we cited a survey that estimated 1995 Web sales at $400 million. But $400 million of what? In the early going there are a few industries that have already (and predictably) proven excellent matches for the Web, including computer hardware and software, financial services, information services, and entertainment-based retail industries like music, video, consumer electronics, and books. In part, these industries have ascended because the Web was initially dominated by men—and these are areas of the economy also dominated by men. However, women are joining the Web at a faster rate than any other demographic group. Since women control two-thirds of all retail spending in the United States, it seems likely that online shopping will become both more prevalent and more diversified in the future. But for the most part, these products have taken off online because of their affinity with the medium, their ability to take advantage of the technology. The Web can carry stock quotes and portfolio info which helps sell financial services. The Web can distribute demos efficiently which helps sell software. The Web can make excerpts of books available which helps sell books. But what can the Web do to sell other types of products?

The Net has proven a fertile sales medium for a wide range of professionals, including lawyers, career counselors, and psychologists. Attorneys OnLine (**http://attorneys-on-line.com**) offers legal advice over the Web at relatively low cost. Michael Sklar (**http://pages.prodigy.com/CA/internetcpa**) provides accountancy services, including income-tax counseling. And there are even songwriting consultants like Molly-Ann Leiken (**http://www.earthlink.net/~songmd**), a music-industry vet who has written for Tina Turner, Cher, and Placido Domingo, and who

EXTRA POINTS
YELLOW PAGES

What's the difference between an online mall and a list of links to online stores? All the difference in the world. Malls provide companies with a presence, possibly a look, and often times a means of collecting payment from customers. Lists of online stores, on the other hand, are simply links. However, for marketers interested in investigating how other companies are selling their products online, these directories of cybermerchants can be an invaluable resource, whether they are so local as to be almost provincial (the Madison Virtual Store List) or so general as to be difficult to digest (Online Stores and Malls).

The Madison Virtual Store List Part of a larger directory devoted to business and commerce in the Madison, Wisconsin area, this list includes a travel agent, a record label, a brewery, and an accountancy firm. The Madison Virtual Store List is a trailblazer of sorts, demonstrating how marketers can go against the internationalizing grain of the Internet and restore local focus to their businesses. ✓**www**→http://www.toracorp.com/name.html

Online Stores In addition to online giants like CDNow! and NECX Direct, this directory of merchants includes operations like Dial-A-Book, Inc., and the AmCan Travel Store. Its primary focus, however, is on computer stores. ✓**www**→http://utelscin.el.utwente.nl/users/jelle/onlinesu.html

Who is Selling? **Making an Online Sale**

Online Stores This list links to both malls and free-standing stores; the major Web-based businesses like Amazon .com, CDNow, and NECX are all here. Drawbacks to this list? No annotation, and some of the addresses aren't quite current—so don't be surprised if you get a faulty connection every once in a while.
✓**www**→http://www.vt.edu:10 021/C/cbower/stores.html

Online Stores and Malls This huge list of online stores and malls isn't very well-organized—it has no category breakdowns and isn't alphabetized, and the date-of-posting organization serves the needs of neither consumers nor businesses researching competitors. On the other hand, it is one of the few large virtual-store directories to be completely user-created, inviting visitors to add their own businesses to the list with the help of an online form.
✓**www**→http://www.nauticom .net/users/future21/users/onl .html

Stores Online The high-tech, high-end, consumer-products company known everywhere as The Sharper Image has posted a working catalog online, and this site links to it, as well as linking to businesses that aren't quite online stores but do conduct online sales of one kind or another (United Parcel Service, TicketMaster, and Peachpit Press, all of which extend the definition of an online store in important ways). In addition, the site links to more traditional retail operations like Tower Records.
✓**www**→http://www.pe.net /~snowwis/store.html

charges Netsurfers for polishing tunes. For a more detailed discussion of marketing professional services online, see pages 256-261.

As this brief rundown of industries and professions reveals, much of the Net's sales power results from the fact that it is a bidirectional medium. Customers can not only order place orders, but manufacturers can actually distribute products—whether tax tips, newspaper articles, or word processors—over the Web. Many of the most successful online industries thus far have been those that have discovered ways of providing such direct and immediate distribution. Recorded

IN-SITE: 1-800 MUSIC NOW
    http://www.1800musicnow.com
Music chat rooms. Sure. DJ recommendations. Of course. Music news. Yup. But the heart and soul of this colorful music store is its huge archive of soundclips (in the most popular computer formats) that let consumers listen before they buy. Customers open an account with the MCI-owned store and use PIN numbers whenever charging.

music, for example, is especially conducive to this strategy of direct delivery; almost every record label and music store lets Netsurfers download parts of songs, and a few sites have even begun to experiment with the delivery of entire songs. And this is only the beginning—in fact, even conservative prophets admit that the online distribution of entire albums is a distinct possibility, and that one day soon home customers will be able to use the Web to download digital sound files that they can store on recordable CCDs (Custom Compact Discs).

Not every company will be able to rely upon sampling to move products on the Web. Food and beverage companies, cosmetics and clothing companies, health care and lawn care services, and many other businesses are developing their own strategies (see Part Two of the book). Unquestionably, one of the most important pieces of advice for marketers is this: Keep track of your industry. Music retail companies now have a sizeable online industry; as a result, Net music retailers can participate in online industry directories, compare their services with those of more established companies, learn from those companies' errors and profit from their successes. Real estate agencies, on the other hand, have not yet appeared on the Web in force, so new sites for real estate agencies will have less of a clear notion of what works online. Nonetheless, the history of consumer products generally suggests that the companies that jump in first—both because they are able to build their brands and their knowledge base—are generally the long-term industry leaders even after extensive competition develops.

GIRL SCOUT WEB-COOKIES?

Although Web commerce is barely in its infancy, consumers can already stock a home with the products available for sale online—books, record stores, computers, clothes, and more. Individual Avon representatives are online, as are lingerie catalogs, auto aftermarket companies, and even credit-card programs. So it was only a matter of time before the most modest of direct sellers, the Girl Scouts, showed up on the Web. That's right—Girl Scouts. The Boston-based Patriots' Trail Girl Scouts Council (**http://www.ptgirlscouts .org**) has extended its entire 1996 cookie campaign to include online marketing. Netsurfers who suddenly have a need for Lemon Pastry Cremes, Shortbread, or the perennial favorite Thin Mints can view pictures and nutritional information for the cookies (a box of thin mints will furnish roughly half of the day's recommended daily allowance of dietary fiber). But cookie information is only part of the Patriots Trail masterplan. With the help of Merchant Solution, an online sales package developed by OpenMarket (**http://www .openmarket.com**), the Girl Scouts have moved their sales operation online. Just place an order for cookies, select from several payment options, and then wait for the cookies to arrive. The Girl Scout Cookie season closes April 1, but the Patriots Trail Girl Scouts will probably be back in future years, along with the dozens of other small businesses and direct-sales operations who discover the Net.

In Chapter Three of the book, we discussed how the Web's worldwide reach created an enviable set of problems for online marketers—upon arriving online, companies find that they have instant international credibility, and consequently an instant international clientele. Some companies have risen to this challenge (and promise) by creating sites that target specific international populations. This development is most noticeable in the travel industry, where airlines originating in other nations court both American and foreign customers. The Asian airline Cathay Pacific (**http://www.cathay-pacificair.com**), for example, has reproduced its site's contents in English, Korean, Chinese, and Japanese. Air France's site (**http://www.mexicana.com**) includes both French and English descriptions while Mexicana Airline's site (**http://www.mexicana.com**) is written for both a Spanish and English audience. Other non-travel companies like the Japanese film company Fuji (**http://www.fujifilm.com**), and the Italian sports-car manufacturer Ferrari (**http://www.ferrari.it**) have also mounted bilingual sites. While bilingual sites are a useful exploration of the Web's personalizing and localizing function, it remains to be seen whether companies can develop entirely independent online sales pitches tailored to specific nations—culturally-sensitive advertisements that appeal to a variety of consumers, depending on the target nation.

Setting Up to Sell Online

Online sales have specific technical demands, chief among them the capacity for online ordering and billing. Online businesses must have some means of collecting billing information from customers (a direct email link, a secure online form, a toll-free number, etc.). How a company chooses to bill customers depends upon the size and character of its business—specialty shops that expect to work with a limited customer base may opt for email transactions, while larger catalog companies should certainly invest in an online ordering and shipping form. These forms—interactive areas of Web pages that require visitors to supply key pieces of information, such as the preferred credit card and the shipping method—are relatively simple and affordable programming tasks, and they greatly enhance the commercial power of a site.

As we have mentioned earlier, consumer interest in online sales is tempered by a dearth of consumer confidence, and a great reluctance on the part of consumers to supply payment information online. To avoid this problem, companies can set up internal customer accounts backed by credit cards, and any online purchases can be billed to those accounts. The music retailer CDNow (**http://www.cdnow.com**), for instance, requires all new customers to supply basic financial information, including a credit card number, after which they can make an online purchase with only their name and a unique CDNow account number. To allay security fears, some companies give consumers the option of supplying all of the necessary information online except for the consumer's credit card number, which can be communicated separately by phone. However, as security standards evolve and consumer concerns diminish, this less than optimal mechanism should no longer be necessary.

Is an online billing capability the only aspect of a Website that should concern an online marketer interested in selling over the Internet? Hardly. In fact, marketers designing Websites with sales capabilities need to think about the psychology of the shopping experience, and to simulate parts of that experience online. Innumerable studies of market psychology have demonstrated that consumers feel pleasure during shopping—the processes of travelling to the store, interacting with salespeople and other customers, as well as handling and inspecting items before purchasing them. As we have discussed in Chapter Three: Building a Better Website (see page 37), there are a number of ways to simulate the in-store environment and, by doing so, to increase the customer's enjoyment of online shopping.

An important rule of online shopping is that customers must be able to express their interest in products without committing to a purchase. Most online stores have designed a virtual shopping cart, or something equivalent, to dramatize this unspoken contract of retail transactions—that products can be inspected without being purchased, that customers have time to think about their purchases before making them. For example, the online wine shop Virtual Vineyards (**http://www.virtualvin.com**) has equipped its Website with a "Remember This Item" function that stores a customer's items in the computer's memory while they continue shopping, delaying actual purchase until a checkout procedure at the end of the shopping session.

ONLINE SALES STRATEGIES

There are two marketing strategies particularly well-suited to online sales.

Creating an environment. Stores like Barnes and Noble build on the pleasure of offline shopping with coffee bars, large magazine-browsing areas, and comfy sofas. The online world permits a similar kind of environment-creation. Online music stores like Music Boulevard (**http://www.musicblvd.com**), do more than just make CDs available for sale. The store employs sound samples, album art, *Billboard* charts, reviews, and more to create an environment for online music lovers.

Offering free product samples. While florists can't yet send flowers electronically, the Net lets many companies provide consumers with low-cost or even free versions of their products over the Web (in part because the Web eliminates almost all distribution costs). Netscape, for instance, originally gave away its popular Web browser at its Website (**http://www.netscape.com**), and bookstores, record stores, magazine publishers, and other information providers have also embraced this strategy. The software and gaming industries have profited most from this strategy—by giving consumers a free taste of addictive games like Doom (**http://www.idsoftware.com**) or Marathon (**http://www.bungie.com**), companies can bank on consumers coming back for more.

EXTRA POINTS
CHECKOUT LINE

eShop The shared marketplace for companies such as Spiegel, Tower Records, and 1-800 Flowers has tried to advance the online shopping experience for consumers by offering secure transactions, fast graphics, coupons, shopping assistants, personalized shopping features, and more. The catch? Consumers have to download special software to work in conjunction with their Web browser—and they have to be operating a Windows machine. The check out line is closed to those who don't download first.
✓**www**→http://www.eshop.com

The Sharper Image The nifty gadget store has a searchable catalog of its merchandise online, and highlights monthly specials, new merchandise, and browsable product categories. Customers can order by fax, phone, or in person (the site sports a store locator as well), but they can also use their Web browsers for purchases.
✓**www**→http://www.sharperimage.com/tsi

SoundWire This searchable online music store has a large inventory and a well equipped check out line. After tallying up a customer's order (including tax and shipping and handling), Soundwire offers several payment options: Visa, MasterCard, American Express, CyberCast, Netcash, and First Virtual's Digicash. Customers can telephone in their orders as well. At any point during the transaction, the customer can click the

$59.95

Show someone special you care with a breathtaking bouquet of long stem Roses elegantly decorated with greenery in a traditional vase.

Choose Color:
Red ▼

Delivery: FTD Select Florist
From: FTD

[PLACE ORDER]

FLOWERS
ROSES

BIRTHDAY
ANNIVERSARY
ROMANTIC/LOVE
CONGRATULATIONS
THINKING OF YOU

HONIG
Vineyard and Cellars   **A Honey of a Wine**

Honig's 1994 Reserve Sauvignon Blanc is not a "honey" because the wine is sweet (although Mike and Elaine Honig certainly are!), but because the family name translates as "honey" in German. So, my corny sense of humor got the better of me. This dry wine is flying out the door. Offer good while supplies last.

[Remember this item] **3 bottles $39.90 (save $2.10)**

[Remember this item] **6 bottles $75.60 (save $8.40)**

[Remember this item] **12 bottles $142.80 (save $25.20)**

Amazon.com Books

The Stinky Cheeseman and Other Fairly Stupid Tales

by Jon Scieszka , Lane Smith(Illustrator)

School & Library Binding
List: $16.99 -- Amazon.com Price: $13.59 -- **You Save: $3.40(20%)**
Published by Viking Pr
Publication date: July 1993
ISBN: 067084487X

Availability: This item can be shipped on the next weekday.

[Add This Book to your Shopping Basket] (You can always remove it later...)

*It's all in the buttons. Online stores such as PC Flowers & Gifts (**http://www.pcgifts.ibm.com**), Virtual Vineyards (**http://www.virtualvin.com**), and the bookstore Amazon.com (**http://www.amazon.com**) have designed buttons for ordering that are both clear in their function and non-intimidating to the customer. Amazon.com goes so far as to write a brief message next to each button explaining that the customer can always change his or her mind.*

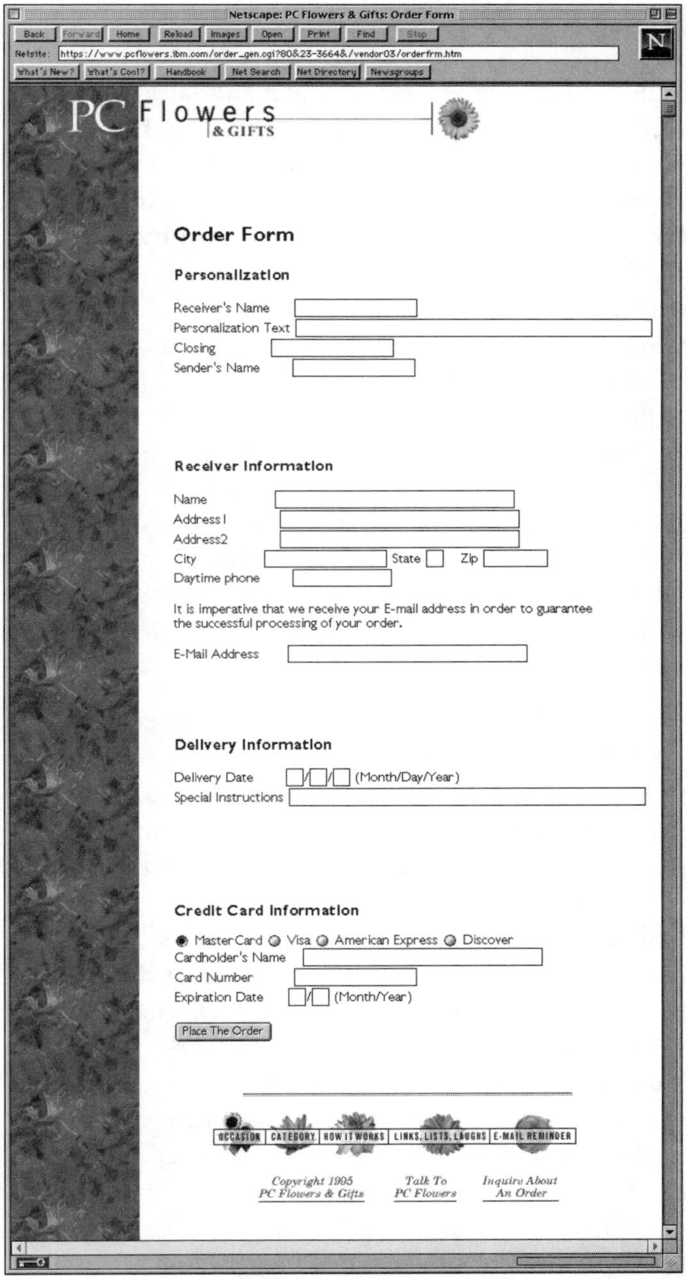

Making an Online Sale Setting Up to Sell Online

Order Form

Personalization

Receiver's Name
Personalization Text
Closing
Sender's Name

Receiver Information

Name
Address1
Address2
City   State   Zip
Daytime phone

It is imperative that we receive your E-mail address in order to guarantee the successful processing of your order.

E-Mail Address

Delivery Information

Delivery Date   / / (Month/Day/Year)
Special Instructions

Credit Card Information

● MasterCard ○ Visa ○ American Express ○ Discover
Cardholder's Name
Card Number
Expiration Date   / (Month/Year)

Place The Order

OCCASION CATEGORY HOW IT WORKS LINKS, LISTS, LAUGHS E-MAIL REMINDER

Copyright 1995   Talk To   Inquire About
PC Flowers & Gifts   PC Flowers   An Order

How do online customers get flowers delivered? If they don't already have an account, PC Flowers &Gifts has them fill out an online order form like this which specifies the item ordered, payment method, where the gift is going, and what the card should say.

"Modify Cart" button to change an order.
✓**www**→http://SoundWire.com

Spice Merchant So you want some Madras Curry Powder or Hunan Style Chili Sauce? Fill out a very simple order form—name, email address, item numbers and quantity, address, and credit card information and then click the button "Click here to electronically place your order now." The store is part of the eMall.
✓**www**→http://eMall.com /Spice/Spice1.html

TravelWeb Hotel Database Using this all-purpose travel site, customers can search for a hotel room. They begin the process by filling out a form which asks them for information about their destination, their preferences for hotel chains (Best Western, Hilton, Hyatt, Ramada, etc.), the type of hotel they want (condominium, conference center, resort, etc.) and several other desired features (pets allowed, heated pool, hairdryer, modem lines, etc.). The site then walks the traveler through a simple online reservation process. Say the customer wants to book a room at the Waldorf-Astoria in New York? The customer is first prompted to check for availbility at the hotel and then the site returns a list of room types and rates. After selecting a rate, the bill is totaled and the customer is then prompted to enter his or her name, address, and credit card information. A comment box is also available for special customer requests .
✓**www**→http://www.travel web.com/thisco/global/fast -search.htm

THE WEB VS. PRINT CATALOGS

Does a Website offer advantages over a paper catalog, whether that catalog is distributed in stores or mailed to consumers? Unless you have a romantic attachment to the printing process, the answer is yes. The cost of creating an online catalog is significantly less than that of printing a catalog. In the online world, you only have to create a single copy, not as many copies as customers, and if you need to revise content—perhaps there's a slow-selling product you'd like to highlight—it's as easy as uploading another file to your server. Online catalogs or brochures are always available; customers don't need to worry about losing or misplacing their copies. Customers can also find what they want quickly and easily. With the installation of simple search engine, a Website visitor can type in a keyword or key phrase and retrieve a list of appropriate products. Consumers no longer need to "thumb through" an unwieldy, phone-book-sized catalog looking for specific items. This kind of technology is already in place at sites such as the Shopper's Advantage (**http://www.cuc.com**).

Print catalogs and Web catalogs aren't always mutually exclusive. Software products are emerging that allow companies to publish catalogs in both online and offline mediums simultaneously. A cooperative effort between Pindar Systems and the Interactive Catalog Corporation, for instance, lets merchants compile one central catalog and then publish it to a variety of mediums,

Direct Selling

Will the Web make floor salesmen and sales representatives obsolete? That's unlikely. No matter how many virtual shopping carts and visually stimulating sites appear online, the Web will not eradicate offline retailors. But the Web does have the opportunity to significantly shift the buying habits of Americans if marketers respect and react to consumer needs.

Companies that are already selling products directly to consumers—from florists to travel agents—have an opportunity to capture a larger market. They can use the Web to present their merchandise and communicate with potential buyers, which are the two most important aspects of a direct selling business. In fact, Web commerce has extended the reach of the direct sales industry, blurring the line between catalog sales and retail operations and letting small retailers function as catalog houses.

The whole history of consumer goods suggests that over the course of time, a share of the sales of any product moves out of stores into direct-sales mechanisms that bypass traditional forms of distribution and save money by reducing overhead. This shift typically starts to occur when consumers, comfortable with the basic features of a product, permit new low-priced direct sellers to enter the market. Consider the example of the home-computing industry. Originally, personal computers for home use were sold through retail outlets. Over time, as consumers became more familiar with computers, a number of manufacturers and catalog houses entered the business as direct sellers. Today, direct sales represent a significant portion of the total sales of the personal computer industry. Life insurance has experienced a similar transition. Whole life insurance, a sometimes a complex mix of life insurance and investment benefits, can be difficult for consumers to understand, and consequently it is sold primarily by agents. But term life insurance is significantly simpler, its economics well within the grasp of the average policyholder. As a result, the balance of sales of term life insurance has moved to direct channels. In essence, whenever a sales agent is no longer needed to familiarize consumers with a product, direct sales replace retail. The Web increases the number of products capable of being explained without human agents. The extensive product and service descriptions at most Websites, from Hot Hot Hot (**http://www.hot .presence.com**) to Fidelity financial services (**http:// www.fid-inv.com**) to Spiegel (**http://www.spiegel .com**), assume this "explaining function" and facilitate direct sales.

Marketers should also entertain the possibility that the Web will evolve toward an even more aggressive direct-sales model along the lines of televised home shopping. Using the graphic and interactive capabilities of the Web, merchants could display product descriptions and illustrations, and then offer low prices to the first two hundred customers who email, for instance. This technique is radically different from the soft-sell strategies we have discussed thus far—involving high pressure and demanding a fast response from consumers—but it is technologically possible.

including paper, the Web, and CD-ROM. In other words, any company with a catalog can prepare its products—with accompanying photos and prices—a single time, in a raw-data format, and then take advantage of the Web, as well as traditional paper distribution, quickly and cost effectively. Office Depot, the world's largest office products retailer, has already taken advantage of this capability. It used Pindar's Catalog Management System and the Interactive Catalog Corporation's iCat Electronic Commerce Toolkit to publish in bothmediums. Visit the Interactive Catalog Corporation's Website (**http://www.icat.com**) for more information about this technology, including a list of corporations intending to use Pindar's Catalog Management System and press releases about other advances in catalog-publishing technology.

The Web even enhances the opportunities for offline catalog publishers. Websites such as CatalogLink (**http://www.cata log link.com**), CatalogSite (**http://www.catalogsite .com**), and CatalogSelect (**http://www.pathfinder .com/CatalogSelect**) are set up to market print catalogs to online consumers. These sites feature descriptions of hundreds of catalogs, often organized into categories, and offer consumers the chance to order these catalogs online at no cost. Consumers can click a button, fill out their name and address, and the catalogs of their choice are sent directly to their homes. In the end, print catalogs and Web catalogs may not be competing for the same market as much as they are covering all bases.

EXTRA POINTS
ONLINE AGENTS

AgentNews A mailing list that treats current topics in agent technology, including the application of agents to Internet searching, user customization, and commerce. The Website contains archives and a subscription form.
✓ **www**→http://www.cs.umbc.edu/agents/agentnews

Business and the Internet This overview of information about conducting business online includes a section dedicated to intelligent agents.
✓ **www**→http://falcon.cc.ukans.edu/~wlewis/project/hpage.html

comp.ai A newsgroup devoted to artificial intelligence topics, incuding knowbots and search engines. Discussion of shopping agents isn't plentiful, but this theoretical symposium does turn up fascinating insights into AI's role in commerce.
✓ **USENET**→comp.ai

Defining the Role of Agents in Web Malls Written by Robert E. Calem, this *WebWeek* article investigates the use of intelligent agents in online malls such as eShop, DreamShop, BargainFinder, and the Internet Fashion Mall.
✓ **www**→http://pubs.iworld.com/ww-online/Dec95/commercial/webmalls.html

Intelligent Agents—A Technology and Business Application Approach Created for a class in telecommunications, this long, academic paper examines how agents can assist

Shopping Agents

Among the most exciting development for online marketers is the evolution of intelligent-agent technology. "Intelligent agent" is a term used to describe any piece of software that makes an adaptive, autonomous decision based on an initial state of information collection; in a retail economy, it refers more specifically to programs that record buying habits and recommend products to consumers.

A few online shops have already begun to apply the technology. At Nine Lives Clothing Consignment Store (**http://www.los-gatos.ca.us/nine.html**), visitors can contact a Personal Shopping Assistant. Nordstrom's (**http://www2.pcy2.mci.net/marketplace**) puts visitors in touch with a shopping agent who charts past purchases and recommends new ones. Other intelligent agents select products from a wide range of retailers. Firefly (**http://www.agents-inc.com**), billed as "Your Personal Music Recommendation Agent." is a registration-based service that matches music fans with appropriate products, and then remembers each user's tastes for future reference. Continuum Software's Fido—the Shopping Doggie (**http://www.continuumsi.com/cgi-bin/ Fido/welcome**) searches a database of more than 100 vendors and retrieves a list of appropriate products. And Bargain Finder (**http://bf.cstar.ac.com/**), the most commonly cited online intelligent agent, compares prices of compact discs from online music stores.

To date, the greatest area of growth for intelligent agents has been online malls. Because they usually have one main gateway and a significant amount of return traffic, malls are perfectly suited to make customized recommendations to consumers. During the 1995 winter holiday season, for example, Marketplace MCI—which included stores such as Cyberwarehouse,

Damark, Hammacher-Schlemmer, Intercontinental Florist, Borders Books and Music, and Lady Footlocker—invited visitors to create a personalized holiday catalogue. Consumers making purchases input their relationship to the gift recipient, a description of the recipient and his or her interests, and the "size" of the buyer's "wallet." After completing the form, the consumer was presented with a customized selection of recommended products available for purchase within the mall.

One example of a shopping environment that remembers past purchases is eShop (**http://www.eshop.com**). The initial tenants in this service include, among others, Tower Records, Spiegel, and Insight (a computer software and hardware store). By remembering consumers' purchase histories, eShop allows the consumer to experience the online equivalent of walking into Tower records and meeting a sales assistant who knows his or her personal tastes; in addition, it can furnish relevant coupons or other types of incentives with each visit. In an article in *Advertising Age*, Matt Kursh, the CEO of eShop, suggested that the future of online shopping lies in an expansion of intelligent-agent software: "Sell-side agents will help you find the best products for you." And companies are even starting to design intelligent agents sensitive enough to tell when they're not wanted; both eShop and Dream Shop (**http://www.dreamshop.com**), an interactive shopping venture on Time Warner's Pathfinder service, have added "anonymous shopper" features that let customers turn off their agent so that they can browse in peace.

businesspeople, and includes a special section on shopping agents.
✓**www**→http://haas.berkeley.edu/~heilmann/agents/index.html

Intelligent Agents/Information Agents A review of recent advances in intelligent-agent technology, focusing on the subtleties of shopping services and search engines.
✓**www**→http://www.pulver.com/netwatch/topten/tt9.htm

Intelligent Agents Make Shopping a Pleasure A review of Web-based intelligent agents written by the Bradenton (FL) *Herald* business correspondent Sean Savage.
✓**www**→http://www.gate.net/~savage/cols/col7-13.htm

Intelligent Software Agents Resources This huge directory of links connects to nearly every intelligent-agent related resource online, and divides them into several categories, including "Agent News," "Agent Theory," "Agent-Related Projects," and even "Agent Sex" (although curious, prurient Netsurfers who click on this link will be rewarded with the message, "You've got to be kidding").
✓**www**→http://www.cs.umbc.edu/agents

What are Intelligent Agents? Sponsored by the California Software company, this page outlines the broad characteristics of intelligent agents and includes an email link so that interested Websurfers can request more information.
✓**www**→http://www.calsoft.com:80/interap/agents

CyberCash Home Page Promising secure shopping transactions at any CyberCash, CheckFree, or CompuServe store on the Web, the Cyber-Cash system uses a software program called Get Wallet that works in conjunction with a consumer's Web browser to protect their credit card number. The site also offers shopping tips and a list of merchants accepting Cybercash (Novell and Dreisbach's Steaks, for instance). ✓ **www**→http://www.cyber cash.com

Digicash If you're baffled by terms like "smart card chip mask technology," you should begin your long climb toward electronic-payment literacy at the home page of this pioneering digital-payment company. Although much of the site is devoted to marketing DigiCash's electronic payment schemes—including Ecash (electronic cash for computer networks), facility cards (cash replacement for closed systems), and assorted encryption tools—it also links to the Cybershop, a collection of stores that accept digital dollars. ✓ **www**→http://www.digicash .com

Digital Cash This fairly basic introduction to the principle of digital cash and the issues behind it includes a set of links to electronic payment resources across the Internet, including the First Bank of the Internet, Carnegie Mellon's NETBILL project, and more. ✓ **www**→http://violet.berkeley

New Payment Methods

Earlier in this chapter, we discussed the options for billing and payment, noting that merchants could accept payment from consumers by check though the mail, with a credit card over the phone, or with a credit card via an online form. New forms of direct electronic payment are also being developed which let consumers buy products online without paper (checks, cash) or plastic (credit cards). How would these transactions work? Funds would be transferred from a consumer's bank account to a merchant's bank account immediately and invisibly, and the consumer's digital account would be debited in the amount of the purchase. The potential advantages of digital cash include anonymity for the buyer, the ability to handle purchases that may be too small (in price) to justify credit card transactions, and possibly certain security advantages.

In fact, there are already at least two well-developed electronic payment systems working to convince merchants and consumers that they can manage secure transactions. DigiCash (**http://www.digicash.com**) is working to bridge the gap between traditional credit-card accounts and paperless debit systems. DigiCash's Website links to online shops that accept their currency, and also includes detailed Unix instructions on how to become an ecash-accepting merchant. Without requiring complicated encryption tools, First Virtual Holdings (**http://www.fv.com**) also permits companies and individuals to set up shop online; if your bank account accepts direct deposits through the U.S. ACH system, $10 will get you a First Virtual Seller Account and the ability to take payment online. Already more than 100 thousand consumers pay for their products using First Virtual's systems. Both digital currency companies run online malls, although First Virtual's public-access marketplace, the InfoHaus,

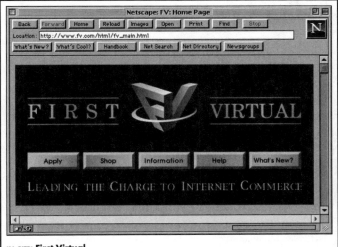

IN-SITE: First Virtual
http://www.fv.com
First Virtual uses financial transaction tools familiar to consumers, such as credit cards. Its payment system offers a secure way for consumers to buy products and merchants to sell them online. Without having to encrypt orders, customers can make transactions via email, FTP sites, and Websites using First Virtual accounts. Oriented toward information sales, First Virtual is thoroughly described at the Website. See the site for a list of InfoHaus merchants (the InfoHaus is First Virtual's online information shopping mall).

specializes in Information Products (defined as anything that can be encoded and distributed over the computer, or created on a computer, whether video sequences, audio samples, software, or articles).

As the major players to date in electronic credit payment systems, First Virtual and Digicash can be used for almost any application. Online lawyers can receive payment for their services. Online non-profits and advocacy groups can accept contributions. Online publications can collect subscription fees. If you're a merchant investigating payment systems, you'll probably want to consider adding these options. For more information, Michael Peirce, a student at Trinity College Dublin, has conducted a research project on the variety of online payment systems, and a summary of his findings is available at **http://ganges.cs.tcd.ie /mepeirce/project.html**.

.edu/~maddogg/project/project.html

Digital Money The software programs AutoPay and AutoReg are directed at shareware developes, and allow them to collect payment for their programs over the Internet.
✓**www**→http://www.digimoney.com

NETBILL Designed to faciliatate electronic network payment, Carnegie Mellon's NETBILL project creates an electronic debit-card system. Find out more about it here.
✓**www**→http://www.ini.cmu.edu/NETBILL/home.html

NetChex This service allows consumers to create virtual extensions of their checking accounts using special software available for download at the site. Currently, few merchants accept these virtual checks but the company is advertising for new merchants at its site as well.
✓**www**→http://www.netchex.com

Payment Mechanisms Designed for the Internet An annotated list of links about the dozens of electronic payment methods designed for the Internet, including Cybercash, the First Bank of the Internet, the FSTC Internet Check Project, BankNet, CommerceNet, Secure Electronic Payment Protocol, Secure Commerce on the Internet, and Brand's Cash. With new payment methods added each day, this is the place to go for new information on online commerce.
✓**www**→http://ganges.cs.tcd.ie/mepeirce/Project/chaum.html

Absentee Computer Auction Services On most Saturdays during the year, computer equipment is auctioned off in Texas. Can't make the bidding? Mountain Parameters will bid on your behalf. The company posts on Thursday evening a catalog of the merchandise to be auctioned and Netters then email in their bids by midnight on Friday. The company then sends a representative to bid on the equipment (they'll try to get you an even better deal than you offered) and, if successful, will email you back notice. On top of the bid, customers pay 10% to the auction house and 10% to Mountain Parameters. This service isn't a new way to price products *online*, but it uses the Net to extend the reach of the consumer.
✓**www**→http://199.185.139.51:80/MParam

Auction Gallery The site auctions off art, antiques, glassware, and collectibles. Bids may be made by phone, email, or in person, and a 10% premium is charged by the site. Auctioned items are listed on the site and bidders can click on them for a photo and the current bid.
✓**www**→http://www.bonk.com/auctions/auction.html

AuctionLine The site has set up an online auction house and a place where registered users can browse merchandise on the block and make a bid. Auctions are scheduled regularly.
✓**www**→http://www.auctionline.com

The Online Auction House

Among the other innovations in selling inspired by the new medium, companies are experimenting with the way products are priced and purchased. One of the most exciting developments in this vein is the Web's worldwide auction capability. In an auction, a product goes on sale, and members of the online community "bid" for it, offering a price that meets their needs. The bidder offering the highest price within a certain amount of time is awarded the item. These are not "fringe sales schemes." It is entirely possible that auctions could become an important force in product retailing online.

The theory of an auction is that for the quantity of goods available, the seller maximizes the amount he or she can receive for these goods, while buyers pay what

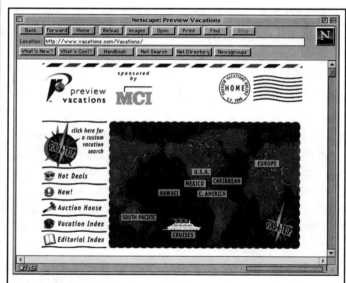

IN-SITE: **Preview Vacations**
http://www.vacations.com
Preview offers travelers a colorful Website packed with vacation ideas. It also provides a glimpse of how online travel auctions can be organized. Its Auction House feature lists a new vacation for two (accomodations only) each month. All bids can be made directly from the Website and there's no minimum bid.

the goods are worth to them. Since the value of one-of-a-kind items (like Van Gogh paintings) is "in the eye of the beholder," auctions are a common way of selling specialty and collectible goods. But can auctions encompass a broader range of product types? Some early online experiments have involved sporting goods, software, computer equipment, and even scouting memorabilia (**http://www.tspa.com**).

Although only a small number of consumers currently know about online auctions and a limited number of merchants and manufacturers participate, if auctions were to become more common, they might recalibrate the relationship between supply and demand. In fact, Chuck Martin, an IBM vice president and the former publisher of *Interactive Age*, has suggested that auction sales may ultimately lead to a tighter relationship between sales and the volume of products manufactured. According to Martin, "As companies start to regularly sell products over the Internet through auctions, they will be able to more precisely manage supply and demand for their products. The number of items manufactured will directly reflect auction prices."

Cathay Pacific Airlines ran one of the most interesting online auctions. When Cathay Pacific upgraded its Business Class service from Los Angeles to Hong Kong, it auctioned 50 round-trips, at this class of service, with no minimum bid. This auction appears to have served two purposes: the intriguing copy describing the auction served as a way for Cathay Pacific to tell its market how it had upgraded its service and since auction participants needed to register with Cathay Pacific, the auction enabled the airline to build a database, with email addresses, of consumers that were interested (and willing to spend money) to travel between Los Angeles and Hong Kong. The airline indicated that it might contact registered consumers in

Auction List A list of links to Web pages devoted to both online and offline auctions and auction houses.
✓ **www**→http://www.syspac .com/usaweb/auction.html

Auction.Net Auction.Net designs home pages for auctioneers, maintains a state directory of auctioneers, and runs a service called Electronic Auctions, which runs online liquidation sales of furniture and office equipment. The company provides the site for auctions but is not involved in the transactions.
✓ **www**→http://auction.net

Auctions On-Line Home Page The name of the site is slightly misleading: auctions aren't actually held here. The site maintains a large database of catalogs from fine art, antiques, and collectible auctions worldwide as well as a calendar of upcoming auctions. It offers an entirely new way to publicize offline auctions.
✓ **www**→http://www.auctions -on-line.com

AuctionWeb Going once. Going twice. Sold to the bidder in Cyberspace. Popular, easy to use, and free to most customers, AuctionWeb held 10,000 auctions in its first six months online. How does the site work? People can list merchandise (free for items under a $100) and set a bidding schedule (usually between 7-14 days). At the end of the bidding, they are then given the names and email addresses of the highest bidders. Since the site merely facilitates these auctions and does not get involved in the actual transactions, the person auctioning items must contact the bidders

directly. In addition to the standard auctions, the site also runs Dutch auctions. AuctionWeb regulates itself according to well-established practices within the Internet community. Buyers and sellers are held to public scrutiny if claims of foul play are made, and the site offers a forum to let people air their gripes and bans those who've been accused several times. Rules, registration information, auction schedules, current listings, and even a personal shopping service that alerts bidders by email when items they might be interested in are being auctioned.
✓**www**→http://www.ebay.com/aw

Glenn Johnson's Internet Coin Auctions Series 1928 $1 silver certificate sold for $28. Six Standing Liberty Quarters sold for $14. 10 New York City subway tokens from the mid 1960's sold for $6. Exclusively serving the online community, Glenn Johnson's coin auction site lets collectors browse items on the Website and bid via email. Interested buyers can check in over the course of the auction (ususally several days) for the most recent bids and continue to place their bids until shortly before bidding closes.
✓**www**→http://www.intac.com/~wb2mpk

Mother Lode Gold Head for the cyberhills. There's gold on the Internet! Mother Lode auctions gold nuggets, jewlery, and other gold products on its Website. Customers enter their bids and are kept are informed about the bidding via email.
✓**www**→http://www.motherlode.com

the future by email about special offers. Cathay Pacific is only one example, but Internet-based auctions hold tremendous promise for the travel industry, where prices already shift dramatically based on the supply and demand at any given time of the year. Airlines, villas, and resorts could all use Net auctions. Other likely candidates for Internet auctions include traditional categories such as art, antiques, classic cars, stamps, and even real estate.

The Web is not the only place on the Internet where auctions are held. Although the items up for bid may not be as glamorous (or as pricey) as those at Sotheby's (**www.sothebys.com**), an online underground economy has developed around Usenet's newsgroups. These discussion groups are home to people who are passionate about their interests and hobbies, and hence, perfect customers for certain merchandise. Although the newsgroups are usually free-from discussion forums, many have set up rigid rules to control and legitimize the bidding wars that takes place among members. Many of the marketplace newsgroups—groups designated exclusively for commercial use—get hundreds of postings a day related to trading, buying, and selling. Items up for sale on the **rec.games.board.marketplace** newsgroup, for instance, commonly gather six or seven bids for each. What's being auctioned on these groups? Antique Gibson Mandolins on **rec.music.makers.marketplace**, Chinese sewing boxes on rec.antiques.marketplace, first edition *Spiderman* comics on **rec.arts.comics.marketplace**, etc. And it's not just the little guys who use the newsgroups. More than half of the postings on **rec.arts.books.marketplace** consist of catalogs from dealers in rare and antiquarian works.

Part II

Web Marketing in Action

Chapter 6

Household Names

Apparel

Clothing manufacturers want consumers to be excited about their particular brand of

trench coat, or underwear. It makes sense, then, that their online offerings are strongly oriented toward branding and positioning the product, often to a young, sporty audience. Jeans, reinvented for fresh consumption with every generation, are now sold as the signature piece of the MTV generation at the **Levi Strauss** site which is packed with pop figureheads (Spike Jonze, Kurt Cobain). With the advice, super shoes, and apparel available at **Pearl Izumi,** it would seem anyone can be a world-class athlete with dedication— and a fair amount of pocket change. **GildaMax** shows young women what aerobics can do for them with 3-D movies of toned bodies. And on **Planet Reebok** there's a brave new world where hip, young superhumans hang out by the weight machine.

On the Net

Footwear

Adidas Webzine Adidas, the athletic footwear designer, has launched its name on the Internet in the form of an information-packed Webzine that's all about

sports, sports, sports. Highlighting a handful of fascinating themes (women in sports, Olympic memories) every month, the Adidas Webzine also provides hyperlinks for further sports info. The site also includes regular sports news updates and athletic product information.

✓**www**→http://www.adidas.com

Birkenstock Birkenstock is giving away free sandals! Customers can enter its online contest for a shot at a pair of Arizonas, and for first-time sandal wearers, Birkenstock offers an FAQ and size-fit-

ting tips to guarantee that the customer orders the right shoe.

✓**www**→http://www.birks4u.com

Minnetonka Moccasin Minnetonka's site is clear in its mission—to have its entire line of shoes and hats available to everyone in Cyberspace. Minnetonka also offers special coupon incentives for Internet customers.

✓**www**→http://www.minnetonka mocc.com

New Balance New Balance has created CyberPark USA, an athletic online park, where customers

IN-SITE: **Joe Boxer MegaCorp**
http://www.joeboxer.com

Joe Boxer promises to put a customer's name in lights.... From this site, anyone can type in a message which will later be flashed across a mock stock market ticker in Times Square, NY. Joe Boxer's site, called "the Fairgrounds," is a cyberamusement park jam-packed with attractions such as interactive email postcards. Who knew that underwear could be so much fun?

can click on mountains, rivers, and forests for information on running, health, and fitness. New Balance will even walk them through the process of picking out the right shoe (customers can print out a shoe chart) and point them in the direction of the closest store.

✓**www**→http://www.newbalance.com

Saucony "Welcome! I'm George, and I'll be your guide to the Saucony story," begins Saucony's friendly and casual Web guide. After meeting George, customers are invited to hang out in the locker room for training tips or use the store locator. The company also

offers news about the upcoming athletic events it sponsors.

✓**www**→http://www.saucony.com

Sports apparel

Amspirit The first image to assault the visitor on this home page is a stern American eagle in front of Old Glory above the tag-line, "The Power Of A Nation." Taking the Made In America theme to new heights, this is a site chock full of pride and nationalism with quotes from Thomas Jefferson, and emphatic praise of the company's official sponsor—The American People. Heartwarmingly, Amspirit doesn't want famous sports celebrities as representatives, it

wants everyday Joes and Janes, because everyday Joes and Janes built this country.

✓**www**→http://www.amspirit.com

Eastbay Geared toward the young team athlete and sports fan, this sportswear site is filled with images of high school track matches and football games, driveway b-ball and little league games. Fandom and fitness share the spotlight—there are sports trivia quizzes and opinionated evaluations of all the major league teams, as well as a guide to matching the proper footware to each sport. The quirkiest feature is called Deep Thoughts, a contest where cyberjocks send short essays to the site on questions like "What made you fall in love with your favorite summer pastime?"; winners get their prose published in the next Eastbay catalog. While it's rather hard to determine what kind of gear Eastbay actually sells, the company earns loyalty through its almost sentimental affection for the game, and most fans will likely leave the page having ordered the free offline catalog.

✓**www**→http://www.eastbay.com

GildaMax The women's sportswear company famous for giving the world "breathable" workout panties enters the Web fray with guns blazing. Cybersavvy and sexy, this site is targeted at Gen-X hardbodies (and wannabes)—especially the Trixie line, which uses Vargasesque photos and Japanimation-style cartoons to showcase its ultra-hip excercise gear. The catalog uses multimedia almost to the point of abuse—each outfit is presented with a sound clip to describe it and a 3-D video clip to show it off. Visitors with Quicktime VR players can move the models around their screen—allthe better to view Gilda's outfits.

IN-SITE: **Levi Strauss & Co.**
http://www.levi.com/menu
In its ongoing struggle to get a leg up on the jeans competition, Levi's site targets the MTV generation with graphics, interactive attitude, and interviews with such Gen X luminaries as video director Spike Jonze. But what's most noteworthy about this entertaining site is its relentless branding—the opening page, which contains dozens of animated frames, unleashes lots of red Levi's logos, blue jeans, and brown leather patches. The site also offers sizing and style info for the original Levi jean. Customers are probably familiar with Levi's already, but a visit to this site will make them virtual experts.

Apparel Household Names

✓**www**→http://gildamarx.com

Pearl Izumi Pearl Izumi aims straight for the professional or super-serious athlete with a substance-over-surface campaign, profiling partnerships with pro-athletes involved in product development (and not just sponsorship), and by focusing on the apparel's fabric and utility (and not just style). In addition, the catalog matches an informative feature to every clothing line. For example, the Fall Classics line ties into illustrated tips on layering in different weather, while the Pro Collection ties into an interview with a world-class mountain biker. Each item of clothing in a collection gets its own page, with images, a description of its utility and features, and a link that uses diagrams and semi-scientific words like "microfilament hydrophobic fibers" to describe the fabric. One of the world's leading sportswear manufacturers, Pearl Izumi has created a home page of appropriate magnitude.
✓**www**→http://www.sportsite.com /cedro/companies/pearl/html /pearl_hp.html

Zoot Hawaii Zoot had modest beginnings. An Ironman groupie started custom-tailoring triathlon apparel and developed a business that blossomed into one of the most successful companies in this specialized industry. With that underdog spirit still intact, this site banters casually with the customer, while offering a small catalog of transitional clothing for runners, walkers, boaters, and bikers. Also included is a store locator, an amusing company bio, and a FAQ-ish "Zoot factoid" on every page. Customers can order all the clothes over the phone, and in keeping with the spirit of the enterprise, are reminded to ask for

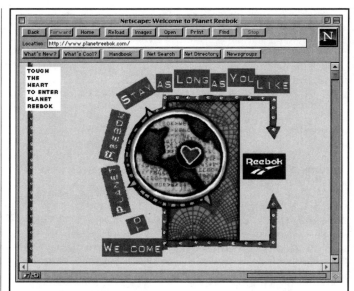

IN-SITE: Planet Reebok
http://www.planetreebok.com
One of the first non-computer companies to develop a presence—or should we say "planet"—on the Web, Reebok has turned its site into a hangout where sports and fitness enthusiasts gather to chat with each other, check in for fitness tips, browse features about the Olympics and women's sporting events, keep tabs on the causes that Reebok supports (including human rights and Project America), and get Reebok's guidance about other sites to explore on the Web ("We believe in life on other planets, so here are the places we like to visit"). The focal point of Planet Reebok is its Cyberbok, an area which Reebok uses to host live chats with well-known sports personalities like Roger Clemens, Frank Thomas, Rebecca Lobo, and Dominique Wilkins.

their Zoot tattoo, free with each purchase.
✓**www**→http://www.zoothawaii .com

Other

Arts of Avalon The slogan of this children's costumiere is "Valuing the Imagination," but while a towering image of a fantastical castle beckons parents to enter the Land of Avalon, the site is really all business. The straightforward catalog showcases medieval costumes on surreal wicker mannequins, and occasionally a live kid. Everything can be ordered online.
✓**www**→http://www.cruzio.com /~costumes

L'eggs L'eggs is taking the initiative in Cyberspace by giving a 20 percent discount to customers ordering online. But the real star of the L'eggs Website is the interactive online hose selection function, which lets customers select their pantyhose over the Web.
✓**www**→http://www.pantyhose .com

Peace Frogs Along with information about Peace Frogs' contests and promotions, the company provides an 800 number for ordering from a wide selection of its trademark merchandise.
✓**www**→http://www.peacefrogs .com

Consumer electronics

Buzz, whirr, click. The electronics industry is making a lot of noise on the Internet, as

major companies like **Eastman Kodak, Inc.** develop their digital powers with Web technology. The industry sports some hefty Websites—hefty on information, hefty on graphics, yet surprisingly light on hard sell. In addition, they are invariably crowded with hi-tech facts and digital trivia. **Sony Electronics** provides detailed information on every single Sony hardware product, from the Handycam to the Multiscan Graphic Display, from the Walkman to the Discman. **Magnavox** offers a similarly extensive guide to its products and services, and its site is smart. And **NEC** focuses on its sponsorship of computer events. If you want to use the Web to find tech facts, the electronic industry has positioned itself as a key source of product information. The consumer electronics industry is getting major exposure online.

On the Net

Casio Casio's site, which focuses on digital imaging, is straightforward, with product information, an archive of press releases, a list of trade shows, and a direct email link to the company. In addition, the site contains an Educational home page, which offers teachers tips for using Casio products in the classroom.
✓**www**→http://www.casio-usa.com

Eastman Kodak, Inc. Throughout this Website—peppered with Kodak's familiar red-and-yellow logo—the film pioneer positions itself as a company on the cutting edge of image-processing techniques. Along with an extensive company history and an online photography gallery, the Website includes a vast product information archive, which divides the company's products into conceptual categories such as "Capture," "Storage," "Manage," and "Share." In addition, there's a large databank of tips for both novice and professional photographers and a Customer Solutions section with summaries of Kodak's contributions to a number of fields, including motion picture production, printing, and medical imaging.
✓**www**→http://www.kodak.com

Fujifilm Bilingual and in full color, the Fuji site relies on space-age graphics to highlight the latest developments in image producing—

IN-SITE: **Canon USA**
http://www.usa.canon.com
Canon's Website positions the photo and copier company as a leader in creating high-quality color images featuring bios on leading photographers and pictures of their work. Canon also runs a number of promotions, with cameras for prizes, but the real prize of the site may be the bank of support software available to its customers, which lets Netsurfers download manuals for copies, spec sheets for cameras, and printer drivers.

cutting-edge film composition, electronic imaging systems, and new light-sensitive optics. But in Fuji's positioning strategy, science is counterweighed by art—the Fuji Square area contains an online photo gallery, as well as links to other galleries on the Internet.
✓**www**→http://www.fujifilm.co.jp

Hitachi With a space-age home page complete with animation, Hitachi's Website includes product information, news, and the ominous-sounding game, The Challenge. This graphic-intensive competition requires players to match products with the proper Hitachi division—and it's an especially fun way of driving home the company's brand name. In addition, the site also includes a unique feature which it has dubbed the Viewseum, a collection of online fine art images from U.S. museums created with Hitachi's digital imaging systems.
✓**www**→http://www.hitachi.com

Konica Overseen by Konica's trademark rainbow, this site uses bold icons to highlight Konica services such as the Advanced Photosystem and FlashDelivery, as well as providing press releases and basic product information. But the main attraction is the Konica Picture Show area. Devoted to software that lets home shutterbugs display their snapshots on their PCs, the Picture Show section of Konica's site includes a list of local dealers, a mail-order form, and a set of promotional offers. Konica has chosen not to highlight one of its strongest features—the Internet gateway, which collects a set of business and general-interest links for Netsurfers.
✓**www**→http://www.konica.com

Minolta The front of Minolta's site is divided into areas representing Europe, the U.S., Asia, and Japan. At present, only the American section of the site is up, and it's devoted primarily to the new Advanced Photo System. Minolta also uses the site to reiterate its commitment to beauty and cultural enrichment with the Magical Tour, an online photo essay that tours Netsurfers through the Herb Gardens of Japan's Mt. Kaimondake.
✓**www**→http://www.minolta.com

NEC What's new at NEC? Well, not just products. Although the NEC site does include information on its products, it also furnishes detailed information on upcoming events the company is sponsoring, including the New Jersey Programming Languages and Systems Seminar and the NECI Computer Vision Workshop.
✓**www**→http://www.nec.com

Panasonic Online With an image of the company's U.S. Headquarters and a header that links Panasonic to its parent company (the Matsushita Electric Industrial Co. Ltd) back in Japan, this is a site that is proud of its internationalism. Bursting with information about the American R&D laboratories and advanced technology products, the site doesn't quite forget about its consumer-oriented offerings; for those wanting to buy, there is a list of consumer product information phone numbers on the site.
✓**www**→http://www.panasonic.com

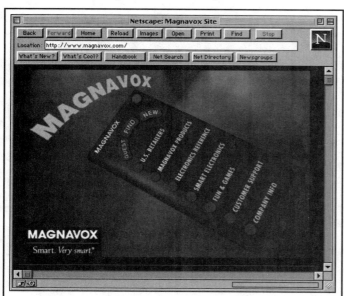

IN-SITE: Magnavox
http://www.magnavox.com
With the help of innovative navigational graphics—an online remote control and console buttons—Magnavox has created an elegant guide to its products and customer support. What's here? A reference area that includes a glossary of all electronics terms mentioned on the site, a store locator, a steady stream of TV giveaways, and links to entertainment sites. And, of course, there are specs for each product in Magnavox's catalog with hypertext links that explain some of the features.

Pentax Branded with Pentax's consumer-friendly slogan ("Life is Fun. You've Got the Pictures to Prove It"), this large site focuses on products, not only offering specs on cameras and binoculars but also helping Pentax customers select the models best-suited to their needs. Netsurfers can visit the Pentax University, with its history of the company and a list of photo tips, subscribe to either of two Pentax mailing lists, or consult the online explanation of the company's warranty policy, all the while marveling at the almost total absence of images.
✓**www**→http://www.pentax.com

Ricoh Ricoh's streamlined site includes product information for copiers, printers, and scanners, all marked by icons containing the company's stylized capital-R logo.
✓**www**→http://www.ricoh.co.jp

Sharp Electronics Sharp's Website is overseen by Nano, an electronic man in the shape of a lightning bolt who serves as a navigational aid for Netsurfers visiting the site. The site provides product-information, divided into Presentation Tools, Consumer Electronics, and Appliances.
✓**www**→http://www.sharp-usa
.com

Sony Electronics Sony's elegant Website includes a section for business and professional applications, as well as a direct email link to corporate headquarters. But the gem of the site is the Consumer Products section, a comprehensive virtual catalog complete with detailed information on every piece of stereo, video, telephone, and television equipment manufactured by Sony. In addition, the site includes special features on new products such as the digital Handycam, and there's even a

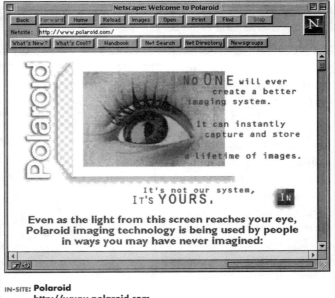

IN-SITE: **Polaroid**
http://www.polaroid.com
Polaroid's site focuses on Polaroid's contributions to science and art. With an online gallery, a detailed treatment of professional applications of Land camera technology, and even a section devoted to the museum-replica service Replica.com (complete with art history essays), Polaroid wants its customers to know that there is more to the company than just instant snapshots on public holidays and birthdays.

sweepstakes that gives Netsurfers a chance to win a Vision Touch home entertainment system.
✓**www**→http://www.sel.sony.com

Tandy Primarily a corporate site, this site covers all the companies under the Tandy umbrella—Radio Shack, Computer City, and Incredible Universe—with a company history, press releases, and even an "Investor Relations Page." What's here for consumers? Store locators, a chance to order catalogs online, and the occasional contest.
✓**www**→http://www.tandy.com

Texas Instruments An instrumental part of the calculator field, Texas Instruments uses its Website to furnish product information, list employment opportunities, and detail new findings in corpo-

rate research and development. But the site is most noteworthy for TI&ME, Texas Instruments' Internet service, which offers Netsurfers the chance to create a customized version of the TI site.
✓**www**→http://www.ti.com

Toshiba Toshiba uses this Website to continue to establish itself as a leader in futuristic technology and high-tech products. Helping to sustain the company's reputation are illustrated specs on everything from CD-ROM drives to fax machines to Liquid Crystal Displays. Updated monthly, the site indicates that Toshiba will soon offer additional customer services, including a "Club Toshiba" membership that carries special consumer privileges.
✓**www**→http://www.toshiba.com

Health & beauty

Cosmetics and pharmaceutical products are essentially very personal items, and selling

them online requires an understanding of both the potential consumer and the Net environment. Using authoritative evidence as its point of difference, **Advil** has filled its site with medical and health advice, ensuring the customer will think of the company first when worried and in pain. Makers of intimate products like the hair regrower **Rogaine** and **Trojan** condoms are making the most of the anonymity of the Net, offering blush-free purchases and information. Some companies create an ambiance that appeals to personal values or fantasies. **In@veda**, an environmentally friendly cosmetic maker, creates a whole, well-linked, green cyberuniverse in which to sell its product and philosophy. **Ralph Lauren**, on the other hand, appeals to those who dream of the lifestyles of the rich and famous. A final, daring, refinement of this strategy can be seen at **Women's Link**, a virtual environment with a wide variety of online resources for the modern woman—and only a tiny mention of its corporate sponsor, Bristol-Meyers Squibb.

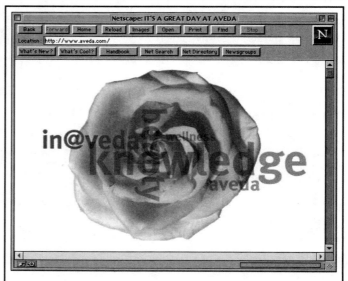

IN-SITE: **In@veda**
http://www.aveda.com

The holistic cosmetics company Aveda has turned its Website into far more than a product-information resource, focusing instead on its customers' lives and lifestyles. In@veda publishes a Web magazine with articles on topics such as ecotourism, the scents of mother nature, and organic cooking. It offers several resource guides to herbs; and maintains a long list of links, including sites about wellness and alternative medicine. Though a store locator is also available, the magazine and guide here are the real attraction.

On the Net
Health Products

Advil Online, Advil positions itself as a health-education instructor, with a dense and informative Forum on Health Education that gives treatment tips on everything from lower back pain to those splitting, pounding, searing, please-kill-me-now headaches.
✓**www**→http://www.ahpc.com

Ciba-Geigy The international pharmaceutical concern, best-known for its contact lenses, has a straightforward site filled with contact lens-sized graphics that highlight different aspects of the company—its financial reports, history, and product research. In addition, Ciba includes a special section on its environmental policy (the company acknowledges its "duty to dispose safely of all unavoidable waste using state-of-the-art technology").
✓**www**→http://www.ciba.com/

Oxyfresh The front door of this hygiene product manufacturer's site carries a huge image map of a tree, divided into three sections—

What's New, Extraordinary Products, and Vision. Why a tree? Presumably because trees connote cleanliness, purity, and integrity. Netsurfers visiting Oxyfresh's site can collect product information on dental care, skin care, hair care, nutritional care, weight management, home care, and pet care—Oxyfresh, apparently, wants to let consumers know that it cares a lot. Site visitors can also view an online catalog.
✓**www**→http://www.oxyfresh.com/Oxyfresh/home.html

Pfizer Pfizer continues its "Putting People First" campaign online with pictures of common citizens helped by Pfizer products. There's Johnny Moore, Lina Taskovich, and Helen Yates, all of whom suffered from a number of afflictions including arthritis, hypertension, and depression. Apart from the Putting People First area, this is primarily a corporate site, with financial reports and sales bulletins.
✓**www**→http://fdncenter.org/pfizer

Rogaine The Upjohn Company, which manufactures the topically applied hair-replacement drug Rogaine, uses the Web to good effect. Jointly targeting men and women with basic information about the hair regrowth process, the Rogaine Website includes a doctor locator that finds dermatologists nationwide. And for those balding Netsurfers who need an extra incentive, Rogaine includes this offer—any visitor who fills out an online questionnaire receives a $10 gift certificate for an initial hair-loss consultation.
✓**www**→http://www.igroup.com/rogaine

Tampax Targeted primarily at teens, Tampax's site provides ad-

vice and information to parents and teachers—like Body Matters, a health index with links to common gynecological issues, and classroom guides that help teach girls (and boys) about the perceived terrors of puberty. The real star of Tampax's site, though, is the Troom, a 12-year-old girl's virtual bedroom complete with dirty clothes and sports equipment. The bedroom—which belongs to Tampax's online spokesteen Tina—contains more than a dozen links to interactive pages, like the Top Drawer (which includes things like free samples and instructions for using the product) and Tina's Diary (where she confesses her homework fears and best-friend anxieties). With the Tampax Pen Pal club and Tinanet, an online feature devoted to embarrassing stories about that time of the month, the Troom promotes a sense of community, and there's even an interactive online calendar that helps girls keep track of monthly periods.
✓**www**→http://www.tampax.com

Warner-Lambert If you've ever been sick, or shaved, or chewed gum, you've probably used one of Warner-Lambert's products, although you may not know that Warner-Lambert manufactured it. Makers of Schick, Dentyne, Rolaids, Neosporin, Bubblicious, the e.p.t. home pregnancy test, and a full line of aquarium products, the manufacturing giant has a Website that unifies all its divisions. Netsurfers can click on thematic links—shaving, women's health, chewing gum and candy, skin care, etc.—to visit Warner-Lambert's many content areas, which not only include product information but also connect to related sites across the Net. The allergy/cold area includes a valuable program that recommends products based

on symptoms the user inputs through an online questionnaire. This large site is also fitted with a search engine, so that customers lost in the jungle of hygiene can find their way out.
✓**www**→http://www.warner-lambert.com

Women's Link (Bristol-Meyers Squibb) For its lavish, high-production Website, the large manufacturer of beauty and health products has chosen to minimize its corporate identity (a tiny logo appears at the bottom of the window) and instead target women. Bristol-Meyers touts Women's Link—which contains information on skin care, hair care, and even career management for the distaff side—as "the place for women-in-the-know...a library, a cafe, a wellness center, and a spa—all in one." The company ends its welcome message with the observation that "Cyberspace isn't a men's club anymore."
✓**www**→http://www.womenslink.com

Beauty products

Estee Don't get fooled—there's no Estee Lauder here. But Estee, The Natural Home Skin Care Program, is selling its line of products on the Internet. Customers can email in their orders, and the site even runs monthly specials for cybersurfers.
✓**www**→http://www.estee.com

Ralph Lauren Fragrances The front door of Ralph Lauren's Website is a virtual mansion, with large, clickable hypertext windows. Mr. Lauren has filled his sprawling home with beauty hints, style tips, and information about his line of fragrances. What's inside is not just product information about Polo, Safari, Lauren, and the company's other fragrances. Clicking on the kitchen window, for example, links to the Bridget Hall calendar and juice recipes while clicking on the garage window leads the visitor to sports profiles and skincare tips for harsh weather.

✓**www**→http://www.ralphlauren fragrance.com

Revlon Revlon shows off its star qualities by teaming up with the Academy Awards to launch it presence on the Web. At Revlon's site, the cosmetically driven can link to a hefty Oscar contest where choices for Best Actor, Best Director and so on can be made and submitted. Since Revlon's site is still in its infancy, the company solicits a comprehensive feedback section, garnering advice from cybercosmeticians about what the site could contain. Currently, there are coupons for free make-up, a veritable dissertation on the eye-catching colors for Spring, and, of course, pictures of the Revlon pin-up girl of the '90s, Cindy Crawford.

✓**www**→http://www.revlon.com

Shiseido Shiseido, the sleek international cosmetics company, was one of the first makeup companies to go online. This Australian-based company spices up its Website with monthly quizzes (winners get free make-up) and hypertext links to skincare tips. Shiseido even enhances their high-end products by offering application tips and advice on color choices.

✓**www**→http://www.world.net /shiseido

Condoms

Durex With slick graphics and a number of online features (How to Use a Condom, 10 Good Reasons to Use a Condom, 10 Lame

IN-SITE: **Helene Curtis**
http://www.yoursalon.com/salon/default.html
Helene Curtis, the makers of that totally perky and bouncy shampoo, Salon Selectives, has created a totally perky and bouncy home page to accommodate its cybergal friends. The Website concentrates on matching product to hair type and personal style to personal coiffure. There are contests, quizzes, product information and a little experiment in interactive fiction called "Your Personal Story," which is like a Mad-Lib for twentysomethings.

Reasons For Not Using a Condom, etc.), a Romantic Story Contest, a romance I.Q. test, and an advice column written by Dr. Dilemma, this British condom manufacturer has positioned itself as an expert in sex and romance. There's very little downer info here, like disease statistics or AIDS etiology. In addition, the site contains equally slick corporate features, including com.munique (press releases) and Durexcetera (financial reports and a corporate history).

✓**www**→http://www.durex.com

Lifestyles At its Website, Lifestyles offers a Safer Sex in the '90s video contest, where Netsurfers can watch and vote on which videos they prefer. As an extra incentive, Lifestyles also randomly gives away free T-shirts to visitors who offer feedback on the videos. Though it's not giving away free

condoms, Lifestyles does let customers write for discount samplers of contraceptives.

✓**www**→http://www.lifestyles .com/ls

Trojans Mentor, Magnum, or NaturaLamb; Assortment, Extra Strength, or Very Thin. Trojans is here to educate the world at large about the birth control and health benefits of contraceptives. The Trojans Website links to information on more than a dozen Sexually Transmitted Diseases, taking every opportunity to remind its sexually active audience that the use of a latex condom greatly reduces the risk of transmission. Trojans will even send the Netsurfer a free sample (mailed in a plain envelope for the sake of discretion).

✓**www**→http://www.linkmag.com /trojan

Food

How do food companies get the consumer to buy their products from an aisle that

stretches from New Jersey to Paraguay? Two words: exposure and temptation. Food companies have hit the Web with guns a-blazin'—almost all the major manufacturers have elaborate Web presences. These companies want visitors to spend a long time at their sites, and they want them to come back, often. Thus rich, multi-featured pages filled with contests, recipes, games, factory tours, mouth-watering images, and even online soap operas are *de rigueur*. Whether the home pages are cybervillages like the **The Nabisco Neighborhood**, or theme sites such as Ragu's **Mama Cucina**, interaction plays a big part. Among myriad superstore delights, visitors can write odes to discontinued ice cream flavors, and get psychoanalysis from an animated Freud: "Your Oedipal complex is easily solved, eat a bag of Chee-tos and call me in the morning."

On the Net

BeechNut This site is sure to be bookmarked by new parents. BeechNut uses it not only to showcase its products, but to build the image of BeechNut as a company that cares about all aspects of family life. It gives a great deal of advice from pre-natal care to general medical advice to college planning, and links to newspaper articles about everything from fluoride to pesticide. The site also features an Internet birth announcement service and a playpen where the parents get to have some fun with games and baby humor.
✓**www**→http://www.beechnut.com

Ben and Jerry's Marketing with a social conscience. Sure, customers can play games and visit the Flavor Graveyard to bemoan the loss of their favorite B&J ice

IN-SITE: **Godiva**
http://www.godiva.com
How do you get a customer craving chocolate? Godiva puts up a Website with descriptions of Godiva chocolates and mouth-watering pictures, chocolatier and liquor recipes, and an ongoing soap opera ("A Tale of Two Hearts") about romance in Manhattan, with chocolates worked not-so-subtly into each episode's plot. How do you get a customer to buy chocolate? Godiva advertises specials, offers a store locator where customers can track down the nearest Godiva store, and features a service whereby Website visitors can request that Godiva email them a reminder to send chocolates before a gift-giving occasion. The site also offers the chocoholics' dream promotion—by filling out a survey they are entered in a sweepstakes where they can win a year's supply of Godiva chocolates.

Food **Household Names**

cream (no tears!), but Ben & Jerry's is also using its Website to take a stand on important issues, with a left-leaning celebrity quote and a healthy dose of liberalism on every page.
✓**www**→http://www.benjerry.com

Campbell Soup This site does one thing and does it well—recipes. Campbell offers Website visitors recipes for every occasion—from parties to holidays to hectic days. Diet tips are also available. And guess what consumers get when they fill out the online survey? A calendar with... recipes.
✓**www**→http://www.campbellsoups.com

Dole 5-A-Day Homepage Dole has turned its Website into a campaign to get kids to eat five servings of fruits and vegetables a day. While the Fun section is aimed at young children (Play the 5-A-Day Game!), the rest of the site is for teachers willing to preach the 5-A-Day gospel. Great URL.
✓**www**→http://www.dole5aday.com

Frito-Lay Frito-Lay's site has contests, recipes, and company and product info (the company has enlivened product descriptions by including product histories which chronicle all the advertising campaigns associated with each product), but the site takes a captivating and unusual twist with the section known as the "Dream Site." Building on the association between snack foods and relaxation, Frito-Lay—makers of Doritos, Chee-tos, Fritos, Tostitos, and Lays—has included in this area a virtual dream house with multimedia treats and links to other mulitmedia sites on the Net, a dream vacation page with links to travel sites, a daily dream days calendar reminding Netsurfers of not-so-important dates such as Bill Gates' wedding anniversary, a dream analysis program that features a virtual shrink who talks back, and a dream date program that builds a goofy cartoon version of the visitor's fantasy man or woman.
✓**www**→http://www.fritolay.com

Gerber Aimed at the media and the health professional community—not new parents—Gerber's site offers Gerber press releases, pediatric and food product news, company background, technical and legal information, and online ordering of corollary patient materials.
✓**www**→http://www.gerber.com

Healthy Choice Who wouldn't click the "free stuff" button on the opening screen of the Healthy Choice Website? Customers who do get $1.00 off coupons, as well as other incentives (a free magazine, a free demo of personal health management software, etc.). Set up to look like an online magazine, the site also publishes recipes using Healthy Choice products, health and fitness tips, and health and food-related news.
✓**www**→http://www.healthychoice.com

Hershey Foods Corporation Hershey's Website uses several behind-the-scenes features to make customers feel at home. Customers can take a "Chocolate Tour" which walks them through different parts of the Hershey chocolate factory, visit Hershey's kitchen for baking tips and recipes, or head out to Chocolate Town, U.S.A., to explore the sweet town of Hershey, Pennsylvania. The site also includes the history of chocolate, an amusing bio of founder Milton S. Hershey, nutritional information, Fun Facts about the company, promotions for new products, and company fi-

nancial data.
✓**www**→http://www.hersheys.com
/~hershey

Kelloggs Cereal is for kids, and
so is the Kelloggs' Website, which
uses a clubhouse motif to guide
young breakfast-eaters through a
series of interactive games and coloring exercises with the help of
puffed-rice pixies Snap, Crackle,
and Pop.
✓**www**→http://www.kelloggs.com

M&M's Mars uses its animated
M&Ms to lead kids and bakers
through an FAQ, a history of the
candy, and other chocolate links.
A short factory tour, recipes, and
baking hints are also onsite.
✓**www**→http://www.baking.m-ms
.com

Mama's Cucina (Ragu) This
award-winning Ragu Website mixes the best of the old country and
the new country with a virtual
tour of Manhattan's Little Italy,
city guides for Italy's hot spots,
lessons on Italian art and architecture, family stories gathered from
visiting Netsurfers, handy phrases
translated into Italian, a kitschy
Italian-American soap opera called
"As the Lasagna Bakes," and, of
course, a huge cookbook with all
of Mama's favorite recipes. There's
even a contest where pasta fans
can win an all-expense-paid family
reunion in the U.S. city of their
choice. Ragu has done everything
humanly possible to position itself
as an ethnically-flavored company.
✓**www**→http://www.ragu.com

NutraSweet Netsurfers are invited to walk around the virtual
NutraSweet village with their tour
guide, that lovable old Mr. Magoo
(who'd you expect, Cher?). Upon
entering each building, Mr. Magoo promotes the nutritional value
and versatility of NutraSweet. The

Market contains product info and
recipes, the Library serves as a NutraSweet FAQ, the Gazette
promises press releases, and the
Fitness Center provides fitness
tips, a calorie calculator, and a
health questionnaire.
✓**www**→http://www.nutrasweet
.com

Pillsbury Bake-Off For almost
50 years, Pillsbury has sponsored

the Pillsbury Bake-Off Contest. In
1996, Pillsbury for the first time
promoted the event on a Website,
announcing finalists and winners.
It also featured a nostalgic look
back at contestants and hosts
(Ronald Reagan, the Duchess of
Windsor, etc.) of the bake-off contests of the past. The site is packed
year-round with recipes and Pillsbury merchandise.
✓**www**→http://www.bakeoff.com

IN-SITE: The Nabisco Neighborhood
http://www.nabisco.com
Nabisco has created an extensive, engaging neighborhood. Tips for healthy living, company info, merchandise, games, product histories, recipes, screensavers, and the multimedia histories of Oreos, Barnum's Animal Crackers, Cream of Wheat, and Grey Poupon are
packed into areas of the Website known as the kitchen, the museum, the store, and the
town hall. Visitors can even take a guided tour of the neighborhood. Nabisco also has an
extensive survey that it invites consumers to fill out in order to receive updates on new
products and new developments.

Soft drinks

Extensive competition has led beverage companies to create some of the most inter-

esting sites on the Web. **Coke** and **Pepsi** are online, of course, but so are other companies with name recognition not quite on the same scale as these two industry giants. If you're a sports fan, however, you've heard of **Gatorade**, which keeps its head up in a sea of fizzy drinks by creating a sports hubsite around spokestar Michael Jordan and filling it with copy that suggests one sip will have consumers leaping tall buildings in a single bound. And the flavored-tea favorite **Snapple** has settled an entire online village to reinforce its friendly image.

On the Net

Celestial Seasonings Celestial Seasonings has created a quiet, cozy Website that's as soothing as a cup of Sleepytime. The company offers customers a list of the ingredients in each tea, a catalog of gift baskets with tea and other products, brand apparel, and the opportunity to order products online. Netbuyers who spend over $39 are also sent a "special gift."
✓**www**→http://www.usa.net/celestial/seasonings.html

The Coca-Cola Company Coke is it, and now it's it on the Web, with an enormous site effervescing with interactive fun. Fans can sound off on topics of the week, download Coke screensavers or clips from TV and radio ads, email Coca-Cola postcards to friends, use the onsite classifieds to trade Coca-Cola merchandise, explore a virtual historical museum, link to the Diet Coke site, play a game where they can match one of the 150 other drinks Coca-Cola makes with its country of origin, pick a category (someplace cool, someplace refreshing, someplace fun, someplace else) and tour the Web with a random link generator, or spend some time in a huge section that Coke has set up to cover the Olympics. Well designed, the site includes a navigational button at the bottom of each page that links to a site index or tree, and a button that links to a site survey.
✓**www**→http://www.cocacola.com

Jolt Jolt has twice as much caffeine as Coke or Pepsi and its graphic-happy, hyper-color Website is touting the message to Gen-Xers who want to bounce off the walls. There's a section comparing the caffeine contents of Jolt to chocolate, tea, coffee, and other

IN-SITE: **Gatorade**
http://www.gatorade.com/

Gatorade has always advertised its product in the context of sports, and the Website stays true to form. Sure, there's an icon customers can click for information about the drink, but other icons lead to reports and features about big sporting events, a sports cartoon archive, and a splashy section devoted to Michael Jordan (Bulls game reports, Jordan stats, Jordan photos, and a different Jordan-related question each week). Gatorade's focus, as always, is on the game.

IN-SITE: **Perrier**
http://www.perrier.com

Seeking to make the connection between art and Perrier, the Website features galleries of bottle art, sells apparel and art-ad prints designed by everyone from Cassandre to Warhol, runs bottle art contests, and even showcases the slogan—"where The Art of Refreshment comes to life!" But it's Gayot's extensive restaurant guides for New York City, Los Angeles, Chicago, and Washington, D.C. that are likely to get the site bookmarked by visitors. Consumers are encouraged to fill out a cybersurvey with the chance to win a year's supply of the bubbly beverage. The refreshingly tasteful site also carries company and product information.

sodas. A locator, playing on the product's image as a potent pick-me-up, tells consumers, store owners and ditributors where they can "score" some Jolt. Company bio, press releases, Jolt apparel merchandise, and product information are also resident.
✓**www**→http://www.joltcola.com

Lipton Product information, press releases, a proclamation of environmental responsibility, a company bio, contact information for Lipton-sponsored charities, and an offline 800 number are all here. The Lipton Website's heavy hitters are its recipe pages and contests (win an all-expense-paid weekend at a Country Inn!). Mmmmmmm good.
✓**www**→http://www.universe .digex.net/~lipton/index.html

Pepsi—The Fridge Where will the Pepsi refrigerator be today? The British Pepsi site opens with a graphic of a refrigerator appearing in the most unusual places. One day the Fridge might appear inside a Dali painting; another, on the lawn at Wimbledon; and another, at the Edinburgh Festival. To travel to these places (or to Websites about these places), visitors must choose to "defrost" the Fridge. But it's easier to open the fridge than to defrost it, and there are several interesting draws inside—a chance to take the Pepsi Challenge via the Web, a Top Ten List compiled by the British music magazine *Pulse* a contest to predict the hit song of the week, a showcase of Pepsi fans' electronic art, and "digital pin-ups" of Cindy Crawford, Jean-Claude Van Damme, Pamela Anderson, and Luke Perry.
✓**www**→http://www.pepsi.co.uk

Pepsi For months, Pepsi only had a British site; now the soda company has come home with a cy-baroque site that deals exclusively with image. Pepsi World's a cyber-planet aimed at teenage Webheads and it's so huge that the kids will never have to go anywhere else for their daily dose of entertainment. Each area of the planet—crammed full of intense multimedia and atomic graphics—is either a chore or an adventure, depending on the modem speeds of visitors. La La Land houses movies and television, Adreneline is devoted to gaming, Backstreet features music, Mainframe runs rotating contests, and the Tower of Power is all about *Pop* Culture. Appealing to a wide range of teenage subcultures, from hip-hop to alternateen to white bread, the site is bound to win over every kid on the market.
✓**www**→http://www.pepsi.com

Snapple As campy and catchy as its TV counterpart? Snapple launched its Website without the presence of the well-known Snapple Lady, opting instead for an illustrated "Land of Snapple," but like its offline ads, Snapple's colorful site focuses on the consumer's relationship with the product. Dedicated to making its customers the center of attention, the site leads off by linking to unofficial Snapple fan pages. Featured throughout the site are archives of fan letters, the Letter of the Week, multimedia clips from famous fan-letter commercials, a Battle of the Flavors contest where fans can win a case of Snapple by defending their favorite flavor, archives of Snapple anecdotes, and even a personals service that matches sweethearts based on flavor choice. Two words: brand loyalty.
✓**www**→http://www.snapple .com

Alcoholic beverages

The alcoholic beverages industry has always followed a wide variety of strategies, and

the Web continues this trend. **Zima**'s site snags Gen-Xers with an anti-hero host that reminds every visitor of their junior-year roommate. **Stoli Central** links to pages that focus on spirits around the world and artistic activities that appeal to the highly cultured. **Guinness** focuses on cultivating community spirit at a virtual version of what those from across the Atlantic usually refer to as "The Local." And **Cuevo**, in a marketing coup of glamorous proportion, intends to create an actual country, and uses its site to promote the island it has just bought off the West Indies (and for which it is petitioning the United Nation to get a seat). But even in these distinct markets, extensive competition mandates further distinctions, and much energy is devoted to creating unique product identities. **Bass Ale** determinedly identifies itself with English pubs, while **Jack Daniel's** sets up shop in a virtual frontiertown (Lynchburg, Tennessee). And **Molson** associates its beer and its extensive Web site with all things Canadian.

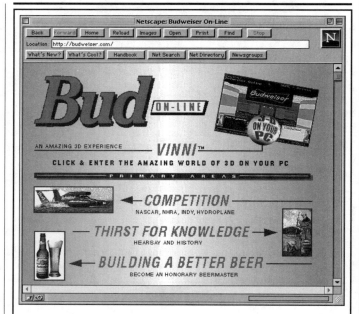

IN-SITE: **Bud On-line**
http://budweiser.com

Not for a virtual moment will Netsurfers visiting the Bud On-line site forget where they are—or forget about beer. This is Budweiser territory and it's branded on every page. Budweiser merchandise is on display. There are features (and video clips) for sports events sponsored by Budweiser, descriptions of conservation and environmental organizations financially supported by Anheuser-Busch, explanations of the beer brewing and tasting experiences, video clips and schedules of Clydesdale appearances, and history and trivia about beer. Bud pulls off an impressive site for a one-time visit, but it's clearly trying to draw visitors back too. That's where the Pad (named for the frogs used in Budweiser TV commercials) comes in. The Pad has a living room, a VR bar, a music room, a closet, a kitchen, a mailbox, and a shed. In this area, visitors can access rules for barroom games, chat live with other Bud drinkers, join bulletin board discussions, get RealAudio clips and bios of Bud-sponsored bands that are touring, and even get bios of the frogs. There's a lot going on, and if customers can run the 3-D software available here for PCs, it can be quite a—ribbit—experience.

On the Net

Bass Ale Set up like a homey English pub, a place with cherry oak bars and a bartender named Robert, this refined site complements the offline ad campaign promoting Bass's "pivotal role" in cultural and political history. The Website includes a gallery of famous paintings that "feature" Bass Ale, an archive of old advertisements, and a long hypertext history of Bass Ale's involvement in great historical moments. The site also offers a chance to tour the brewery, purchase Bass merchandise, and enter a contest to win a trip to Bass pubs worldwide.

✓**www**→http://www.guinness importco.com

Cuervo Gold Cuervo's site gets lots of points for interactivity. Website visitors are immediately challenged to a game of roulette (click the blenders: three matching monsters win the visitor a T-shirt) and then invited into Cuervo-World, a place with links to volleyball updates, concert reviews and music sites, drinking games, recipes, Tequila myths, and FAQs. For the adventurous, the site features the J.C. Road Hog Adventure, a 3-D cartoon experience where Netsurfers can virtually fly, cycle, and swim their way to winning all kinds of Cuervo merchandise. In addition, the site is promoting its whimsical campaign to create the Republic of Cuervo Gold, an actual plot of land in the West Indies (perfect for beach parties) that is going to petition the UN for a seat this year!

✓**www**→http://www.cuervo.com

Finlandia Vodka Finlandia offers fans of its Scandinavian vodka a set of well-designed Web pages full of recipes and mixer instructions.

✓**www**→http://www.compart.fi /finlandia

Goldschlager This site showcases Goldschlager merchandise, a Goldschlager FAQ, and a "World Wild" directory listing party announcements for bars hosting Goldschlager events in the U.S. and Canada.

✓**www**→http://www.schlager.com/

Guinness Think neighborhood bar. Think community. Think Ireland. Think Net. The Guinness Website is designed around the idea of a virtual bar called "The Local." Customers are invited to listen to some Blarney (facts about Guinness), take home some goodies (screensavers, Net applications, etc.), or join the Net equivalent of the local bar's betting pool (fill out a survey and maybe win a trip to Ireland). To appeal to its Net patrons, Guinness has also set up a section on its Website which solicits its favorite URLs from its customers and then randomly generates a connection to these sites for other adventurous explorers.

✓**www**→http://www.itl.net/guinness

Heineken The Dutch Heineken site takes an old hospitality strategy—have visitors sign a guest book—and reupholsters it for Cyberspace, letting visitors leave messages and home page URLs for other drinking buddies to browse on their way through the site, and it's a phenomenal success. The rest of the site isn't too shabby either. There's the Heineken Quest, an interactive game which, as part of its basic rules, requires players to check their email daily and make moves; pages devoted to major Heineken promotions (for instance, the site features dozens of videoclips of artists performing in Heineken-sponsored concerts); a

IN-SITE: **Jack Daniel's**
        http://www.infi.net/jackdaniels

Jack Daniel's, with tongue in cheek, uses this interactive Website to promote its image as a coupla good ol' boys making whisky in their shed. Jack drinkers can explore the homey virtual community of Lynchburg, Tennessee (minors are asked to stop at the town limits), take a virtual tour of the distillery, read Jack's hypertext bio, play a game of blackjack, swap a story, pick up some recipes, enter the Faux Faulkner writing contest, and even listen to the town dog bark. And when the sun sets, they can order a virtual drink for the road (sound clips are on tap).

history of Heineken; and a program that lets vistors email an illustrated postcard to a friend.
✓**www**→http://www.Heineken.nl

Molson Customers are going to want to stay and play on this Website for a while. Molson goes all out promoting its Canadian heritage with sections dedicated to Canadian culture, Canadian hockey, Canadian humor, and Canadian music. The site hosts a virtual Canada MUSH where Molson drinkers can chat with each other; a section called "The Word" with interviews, poetry, and humor; a Molson Fantasy Hockey pool; a Canadian Concert Calendar; and a Cooler with software and utilities. A recent addition to the site—the *Brewmaster's Circle*—is a quarterly newsletter dedicated to the art of brewing beer. The Molson site celebrates not just a product, but its position on the electronic frontier.
✓**www**→http://www.molson.com

ShyMongrel's Homepage (Grolsch Lager) From all appearances, this is some Netsurfer's brilliant home page, but the Website claims to be the official site for Grolsch Lager. The contest giving away tickets to Grolsch-sponsored concerts smacks of legitimacy, but the all-sensory Net tour linking to everything from Le Web Louvre to the Clinton Sex Scandals to the cyberfeminist e-zine GEEKGIRL is curiously beer-free and daring. So how many marketing points does a company get for coming off as super-hip, non-commerical, and Netsavvy?
✓**www**→http://www.intervid.co.uk /intervid/esp

Southern Comfort Living in Austin and looking for a music club, restaurant, or new radio station? Or maybe you're from Buffa-

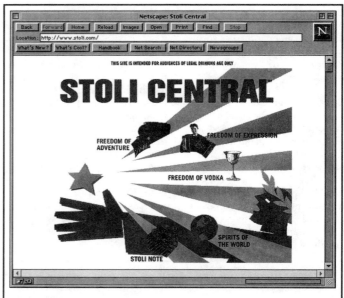

IN-SITE: **Stoli Central**
        http://www.stoli.com
At Stoli Central, Stolichnaya Vodka reinvents revolutionary propaganda art to fuel a campaign heralding post-Communist freedoms. The vodka promotes itself, and its customers, as jet-setting and cultured—consumers can link-hop around the globe, tour the world's spirits, translate any phrase into 16 languages, take part in artistic activities from ciphers to cybercanvases, or invent their own cocktails. And before they leave, they can order Stoli online—capitalism wins again.

lo, Philadelphia, Boston, Chicago, or San Francisco? The folks at Southern Comfort are trying to create the ultimate online city guides for young people across the country, and they're using their Website to survey 20-somethings "who really do the things and go to the places named." The site is enthusiastic (if not comprehensive) about its city guides, the only product information available is recipes for drinks using Southern Comfort, other visitors would likely benefit from more information about the product itself.
✓**www**→http://www.southerncomfort.com

Zima Zima's doing a little bit of everything on its Gen-X-cellent site: contests; links to other cool

Internet sites through the continuing adventures of the site's faceless, hapless, and Zima-drinking antihero Duncan; product information; and merchandising. Zima's made its fridge-full-of-goodies the site's centerpiece. Visitors can click on the bucket of Leftovers for old Duncan adventures, the Diversions container for shareware games, the jar called Icons for packets of icons (all with discreet Zima markings), and continue to click until they find something that satisfies. Any Netsurfer who wants access to even more areas of the Zima Website can join Tribe Z by filling out a questionnaire (ahh, those marketing ploys). All in all an innovative and hypnotic site for fans of clear malt liquor.
✓**www**→http://www.zima.com

Automobiles

In some ways, you could say that the Web is the mass medium most like a car—individ-

ual Websurfers, like drivers, navigate a series of highways and byways, stopping to see the sights whenever their interest is piqued. And car manufacturers are among the most interesting sights online. With stratospheric production values and no shortage of multimedia flash, the car industry has shifted gears effortlessly to accommodate the Web. **Pontiac**'s virtual showroom puts Websurfers in the driver's seat with complete spec sheets. **Lexus** focuses on another kind of drive, furnishing an extensive golf database. And then there's **Toyota**, which has turned away from simple auto info to offer its visitors a set of online magazines that cover everything from entertainment to home life to sports.

On the Net

Manufacturers

BMW USA "BMW the Ultimate Driving Machine." Giving new meaning to the phrase "click stream," visitors are invited to click each of the words in the slogan for access to different parts of the BMW Website. Click "BMW" for corporate information, dealership locations, and news; click "Ultimate" for award info, a link

to the Olympics site (sponsored by BMW), and a profile of the BMW driven in the latest James Bond flick; click "Driving" for links to online BMW car clubs and mailing lists, safety info, and a form to let BMW know about your driving experiences; and "Machine" for profiles of each of the BMW models.

✓**www**→http://www.bmwusa.com

Buick In Buick's online show-room, a visitor can pick a car model, customize it, and get a picture and price tag for his/her dream car. Car buyers can also tour the virtual showroom for car information, take a spin on selected models (using the site's Quick-Time VR technology), or email Buick for a brochure which is delivered via traditional mail. But a trip to the Buick showroom is only one of the roads that a customer can take at this Website.

IN-SITE: **Chrysler Technology Center**
http://www.chryslercorp.com/ctc.html
Chrysler's site makes visitors feel as if they're getting an insider's look at the operation. Everything here creates the impression of getting a hand-held, behind-the-scenes tour of the company and its products—from a site index that looks like a factory floor plan to a feature that inserts the visitor's name into the Website's narrative.

IN-SITE: **Ford Motor Company**
http://www.ford.com

Ford's site includes spec information, purchasing options, and a searchable database of dealerships. Ford offers detailed product information for its different divisions (which include Ford, Mercury, Lincoln, and Jaguar). Customers who register online with the Ford Customer Link are eligible to be chosen to test market Ford products and are emailed when Ford produces a new product or offers a special incentive.

Buick also entertains its guests with PGA golf tour results and a schedule of car shows.
✓**www**→http://www.buick.com

Cadillac Cadillac vies heavily for the sports fan market at its Website with links to sites on harness racing, golf, auto racing, and the Olympics. The site also features information on various Cadillac models, instructions on ordering a catalog, and a searchable database of Cadillac dealers.
✓**www**→http://www.cadillac.com

Chrysler's Home Page It may be a bit confusing to car-shopping Netsurfers, but Chrysler the car manufactor also carries a flagship line of cars called Chryslers, and this home page is where they're showcased. Each car is displayed with an image and extensive descriptions of features. Links to this page, as well as the pages for Plymouth, Dodge, Jeep, and Eagle, can also be accessed through the Chrysler Technology Center Tour site.
✓**www**→http://www.chrysler cars.com

Dodge The company's straightforward Website is filled with news, articles, and spec sheets for this year's cars.
✓**www**→http://www.4adodge .com

Eagle Eagle offers its customers car buying tips, purchase option plans, detailed model descriptions, special incentives, and rebate offers on its Website. But what Eagle really wants its customers to do is test-drive Eagle cars—either on the Internet through sound and video downloads or at a local dealer—and the Website explains how.
✓**www**→http://www.eaglecars .com/eagle.html

Ferrari With content in both Italian and English, the Website of the famous sports car manufacturer capitalizes on the rearing stallion trademark and the legend of founder Enzo Ferrari.
✓**www**→http://www.ferrari.it

Honda Honda draws car enthusiasts to its site with exciting graphics, articles on auto-related topics, screensavers, monthly car incentives, virtual tours of specific models (called a "walkaround" on this Website), a section devoted to road tripping, a dealer locator, a feature on Indy cars, and, of course, information on all the Honda models.
✓**www**→http://www.honda.com

Hyundai Hyundai's high-res pictures of cars, detailed spec info, and company press releases are aimed at the serious car buyer. For pleasure, however, the site includes video clips of Hyundai TV commercials and links to Korean cultural sites.
✓**www**→http://www.hmc.co.kr

Jeep Unpaved Featuring a getaway-from-it-all-in-the-country-with-a-Jeep message, Jeep sets the scene at its Website with nature pictures, audio clips of the sounds of nature, letters from Jeep owners who've discovered "the true potential of their Jeep vehicle," and even a survey that lets visitors check off vacation criteria and then recommends a particular trip. Jeep Unpaved, however, is more than a vacation planner. Customers can use the dealer locator, explore pages for each Jeep model, and check for Jeep events in their area.

✓**www**→http://www.jeepunpaved.com

Lexus Delivering more golf content than most sports sites online, Lexus draws visitors to its Website with tournament schedules, a golf course locator, a golf equipment shop, links to golf-related sites online, golfing news, putting advice, and contests. It also shows off its cars—rather elegantly. The entire site speaks to a wealthy, male audience. Lexus is also planning a site at http://www.lexususa.com.

✓**www**→http://www.lexuscar.com

Mercedes Net Luxuriously colored photographs and car descriptions are the centerpieces of this Website, which broadens its functionality with a searchable database of dealers.

✓**www**→http://www.Mercedes-Net.com

The Nissan Pathfinder Created by Chiat Day, The Nissan Pathfinder site offers customers a dealer locator, links to separate Websites for Nissan in Japan and Italy (each with a different look and features), and a form to request a brochure. The centerpiece of the site, however, is the Practical Guide to Outdoor Adventure. Using a series of outdoor adventure stories and outdoorsman tips, Nissan shows off the features of the car and links to a seemingly endless number of Internet resources for the outdoorsman—from scuba diving sites to mountain biking discussions to sled dog racing FAQs. In 1996, Nissan promises to incorporate a test driving fea-

ture into the site.

✓**www**→http://www.nissanmotors.com

Plymouth Plymouth's brochure-like Website features sharp pictures and detailed spec sheets for Plymouth models. The Website targets recent college graduates with special offers. It also offers a dealer locator, contests, and a schedule for Plymouth's nationwide tour through malls. What's Plymouth doing at the mall? The car manufacturer has set up kiosks that let customers sit down at computers, create a customized Plymouth car, and print out the spec sheet to bring to a local dealer. But Netsurfers don't have to go to the mall. They can build their

ideal Plymouth right here at the Website.

✓**www**→http://www.plymouthcars.com

Pontiac In TV and magazine ads, Pontiac has built a campaign around the idea of "driving excitement," and its Website carries over the theme by highlighting the car company's involvement with auto shows, car races (customers can access schedules and news), and other major sporting events. Taking advantage of the interactivity of the Net, Pontiac also prominently features a suggestion box—a form which solicits customer feedback—and runs an ongoing online soap opera dubbed "Backseat Drivers" about the adventures of a

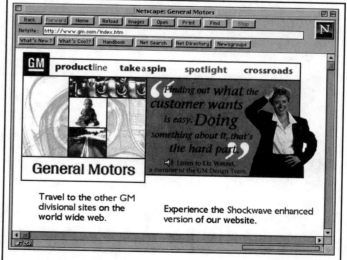

IN-SITE: General Motors
http://www.gm.com
Audio clips from designers and factory workers, a GM quiz and a section devoted to subsidiary services and social programs introduce customers to the General Motors corporation, but the cars are still the stars of this homepage. A number of models are showcased with QuickTime VR movies giving visitors a 360° view of both the interior and exterior of the vehicles. There are also sections devoted to each specific car line—from Chevys to Saturns—with images and descriptions of features. And if the customer needs even more detailed product info on a particular line, the site links to elaborate, independent home pages for each division. To keep visitors coming back, a rotating spotlight section offers fun features such as "Concept Studio," which previews the cars of the future, and no, they don't fly—yet.

group of young road trippers heading down Route 66. Customers are encouraged in a variety of ways to help steer the story (email a character a haiku, send in suggestions about what should happen next, etc.). Even the Cyber Showroom promises a high level of interactivity: customers can locate a local dealer or design a car online.

✓**www**→http://www.pontiac.com

Saab Saab ties the Website in with its already popular print and TV advertising. The vibrant watercolor illustrations that decorate Saab's other media promotions show up on the Website along with rules for a Win-a-Lease contest, company news, and a virtual showroom.

✓**www**→http://www.saabusa.com

Saturn Some car companies associate their products with sports, some with the pleasures of the open road. Saturn uses its Website to reinforce the messages of quality, commitment to customers, and community involvement that mark its offline promotions. The site features letters from happy Saturn customers, a database of "Extended Family" members (Saturn owners), an online magazine with news about Saturn, a dealer locator, updates on the progress of the Saturn Cycling Team, and information about the Saturn CarClub (an organization with local chapters that Saturn owners can join to stay in touch with each other). It's like one big happy family.

✓**www**→http://www.saturncars .com

@Toyota When you think of cars, you probably think of engines, brakes, and tires—not restaurants, women's health, or opera. If Toyota has its way, you may soon be associating all of these topics with the Japanese automaker of Tercels, Camrys, and Corollas. The site maintains several regularly-updated Web-based e-zines based on the interests (Sportszine, Car Culture, Living Arts) and demographics (A Man's Life, Women's Web Weekly) of its customers. Cars aren't getting the short shrift here, though. Toyota creates a friendly Web environment for customers to explore its products, get assistance in choosing a car, find a local dealer, and keep on top of news about Toyota products. The superbly designed @Toyota site seamlessly blends coverage of a wide range of life and leisure topics and information about Toyota's cars.

✓**www**→http://www.toyota.com

Toyota Internet Drive "Go ahead, you drive!" Toyota's Website in Japan invites customers to cruise through the Toyota landscape—from the Community Plaza to the Museums to Toyota University—for company news, information about new models, and even a virtual showroom. This interactive extravaganza turns the customer's mouse into a steering wheel that navigates him or her

IN-SITE: Isuzu Motors
        http://www.isuzu.com

Isuzu has not just set up shop in Cyberspace; it's built a whole town there, and called it Isuzuville. It's a quaint little town with a visitor's center, its own newspaper (The Isuzuville Times), and even a Road Kill Cafe, a joint with roadkill recipes (Winshield Wabbit, anyone?). The site also delivers car maintenance tips, a dealer locator, finance option information, and road trip suggestions. For travelers passing through Isuzuville, Isuzu has created a good annotated directory of outdoor/sports links called WWW Trails to guide Isuzu customers to other online spots, and probably get them to return to the quaint, helpful town. Customers who answer the online survey before they leave will be sent car brochures in the mail.

around sections of the Website.
✓**www**→http://www.toyota.co.jp

Volkswagen Volkswagen's site puts visitors on a map of a highway where they can head to the spot marked Dealer Showroom for the name of a dealership near them, to the Newsstand for company press releases, or to the Technology Center for updates on new Volkswagen technology. But this being Volkswagen, there are also plenty of cultural pit stops, including the Museum of VW History with photos of VW's from the past and Shakedown Street where Jerry Garcia is memorialized.
✓**www**→http://www.vw.com

Volvo Safety is job one at Volvo, and the company's Website reinforces the safety maker image with pictures of crash test dummies and children strapped into car seats. An entire section of the site is devoted to outlining the safety options available for each model.
✓**www**→http://www.volvocars.com

Dealerships

Burt Automotive Network The huge Colorado dealership tries to make shopping for a car at Burt's a little more convenient. Customers can actually search online Burt's entire inventory by make, model, year, and other desired features with the Website's Vehicle Locator. If customers register with the notification service at the site, Burt lets them know when the dealership is running special car promotions. Standard fare such as a directory of dealerships and company information are also available, and the site is starting to link to other interesting auto sites in Cyberspace.
✓**www**→http://www.burt.com

Culver City The site is essentially

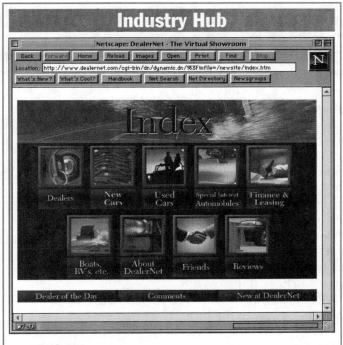

IN-SITE: DealerNet
http://www.dealernet.com
Car dealerships from all over the country list information about their businesses and inventories with DealerNet, and the large number of companies promoting their services on the site attracts car buyers. Customers use DealerNet to check their credit histories, apply for credit, read car reviews, search for information on new car models, locate dealerships selling the type of car they want to buy, and even search the inventories of dealerships for used or new cars. The Website offers the convienience of many services to car buyers and guarantees traffic for dealerships. It's an easy way for even small-town dealers to establish a Web presence.

a simple dealership text advertisement, except for the online business card with the sound clip of a salesman saying, "Hi! I'm John. Please give me a call!"
✓**www**→http://www.kaiwan.com /~lfyang/jpark

Reeves Import Autocar For each of the cars that Reeves sells— Porsche, Audi, Volkswagen, etc.— the dealership has created a Web page with profiles of this year's models, a link to the manufacturer's home page, and, when available, pictures and reviews.
✓**www**→http://www.allworld.com /reeves

Sierra Motors The California family of dealerships uses a panda bear icon on its feel-good Website, because "The simple truth is we like them, and did you ever meet anyone who got mad looking at one? Don't they make most people feel good?" More than cutesy, the site offers a car buying guide, car buying tips, and a list of the company's dealerships.
✓**www**→http://www.geninc.com /sierra

Auto aftermarket

The online auto aftermarket is like a souped-up version of the offline auto aftermarket—

the players are the same, but they have a few more surprises under the hood. The Italian tire manufacturer **Pirelli** has uploaded its famous auto-garage calendar, which has 12 months of lovely ladies to keep cyber-savvy grease monkeys warm on those those long, grimy winter days. **Dunlop**'s Fitment Guide uses state-of-the-art interactive technology to help customers with retirement. And a number of sites, including the high-output **Valvoline's Indy 500**, target men by linking to other auto racing and auto enthusiast sites online.

On the Net

Tires

Bridgestone/Firestone Inc. This tire manufacturer's home page is all about company identity. Half the Website is devoted to an illustrated history, press releases, and articles on the company's tire technology. The rest of the site builds on Firestone's connection to the Indy Racing community, with a History of Indy Car Racing, profiles of the drivers and teams, as well as this year's racing schedule and links to related sites. In the near future, however, the site will be changing its focus to service—a store locator and tire selector are coming soon.

✓**www**→http://www.bridgestone-firestone.com

Dunlop Dunlop has built a tire reference center on the Web for its customers. The site includes a guide for first-time tire buyers, a dealer locator, a library full of articles on tire maintenance and technology, and even a handy "Fitment Guide" which returns a list of tires with specs when a customer enters a car's make, model, and year.

✓**www**→http://www.dunloptire.com

Goodyear It wouldn't be a Goodyear advertisement without a picture of the blimp. Guess what adorns the opening of this Web page? But Goodyear's promoting more than hot air. Goodyear knows its tires, and they've created a "Tire School" that walks consumers through caring for, choosing, and buying a tire. Customers can then use the store locator to find out who's selling Goodyear tires. Goodyear rounds out the site with driving tips, a calendar of racing events, and a collection of links to other auto-related sites.

IN-SITE: **Pirelli Tires**
http://www.pirelli.com/home.htm
Tires and cables aren't usually seen as glamorous, but the graphics on this Website suggest otherwise. Although the site offers an extensive FAQ about tire topics (conversion, maintenance, marking, terminology, etc.), Pirelli, an Italian company, delivers company and product information without getting its hands dirty.

You'll want to spin your tires here for a while.

✓**www**→http://www.goodyear.com

Other

Apex Audio and Electronics

Apex has set up an online store where shoppers can browse through catalogs of auto stereo equipment, enter contests to win free merchandise, learn about new products, and order merchandise. The only thing missing is the overbearing salesperson!

✓**www**→http://www.bright.net/~apex

Exide Batteries Exide Batteries wants to be perceived as the battery company that cares. It's gone online with tips on helping batteries weather the winter, reports on recycling lead batteries, and a helpful order form for its products.

✓**www**→http://www.exideworld.com

Hammond Audio Hammond wants to construct and maintain Websites for car audio companies. To attract companies, Hammond has tried to generate traffic on its Website (if there are customers, the companies will follow) by linking it to an extensive collection of audio-technical information on the Web. It may be the most extensive collection of such links in Cyberspace.

✓**www**→http://islander.whidbey.net/~hammonda/stereo.html

Jiffylube When visitors leave the Jiffylube site, they'll know more about car maintenance than the technicians! This info-packed site takes the customer through each service Jiffylube offers, from air conditioning to gearboxes to wiper blades, with diagrams and step-by-

IN-SITE: **Valvoline's Indy 500**
http://www.valvoline.com

Vroom, vroom! At first link, the customer is faced with a 3-D image of a racecar in a garage. Valvoline, which produces car oils, fluids, and lubricants, has created a virtual garage of greasy stuff for the car-lover. Signs on the garage wall link to a Mechanics Only section where an automotive expert answers car-related questions; a Racing Store, with Valvoline-branded merchandise; and a Product Catalog, with information on all of Valvoline's products to get the old jalopy running again. The site also takes advantage of the Web's resources by linking to auto newsgroups, manufacturers, magazines, racetracks, and auto-related associations. Car-racing buffs will appreciate Valvoline's racing section, which offers Indy and NASCAR updates.

step descriptions under the titles "what we do" and "why we do it." The site also provides a store locator, a company profile, franchising and employment info, and links to related sites.

✓**www**→http://www.jiffylube.com

Mother's Polishers By adding an auto classifieds and car-care guide to its site, this manufacturer of car wax ensures that its site will come up in browser searches other than "car wax" and "old dust rag." Check out the URL!

✓**www**→http://www.mothers.com

Chemicals & fuels

You might not need high octane to drive the information superhighway, but that hasn't

stopped gas stations from setting up shop on the Net. **Chevron**'s Website, layered like the planet's strata, emphasizes the company's history as a mover of man and earth. **Texaco** chooses to play up the fun side of fuel, and adds a world of really fast cars to its offerings. Not many consumers head out cybershopping for new polymer blends, but chemical companies are networking with other companies in Cyberspace. Stockholders appear to be **Dow Chemical**'s target audience—Dow fills its site with information on profits and promising programs. **Dupont**, on the other hand, positions itself not as a corporate entity but as a consumer-oriented one, stressing its commitment to "improve everyday life."

On the Net

Chemical companies

Ciba Home Page This worldwide biological and chemical company offers a clean, simple home page aimed at familiarizing the public and the company's potential business partners with Ciba's products and employees. The company profile covers each department, furnishing reports, press releases and short articles on fi-

nance, development, and corporate identity—including illustrated profiles of each member of the executive committee and the board of directors.
✓**www**→http://www.ciba.com

Dow Chemical A company profile that kicks off with a map showing every Dow office, plant, and subsidiary worldwide drives home the size and scope of Dow. The profile addresses company financial projections, charitable campaigns, employment opportu-

nities, and department overviews, and then reassures visitors that sound business judgment underlies every project—even environmental improvements are shown to "provide a competitive advantage." The language used for product information is less layman-friendly—there is an entire home page dedicated to liquid separation. If not consumer-oriented, Dow's site still serves to attract client and business partners and gives investors confidence.
✓**www**→http://www.dow.com

IN-SITE: **DuPont**
http://www.dupont.com
With the tagline "Better things for better living," DuPont's site is targeted at the average consumer. The front page features inviting graphics of cyclists and laughing babies, with a single hypertext sentence—"We're a science and technology based global company of people who make products that make a difference in every day life." Each highlighted word leads to a page showcasing services, products, and campaigns. Features run the gamut from articles on development awards and employment diversity to entire home pages on environmental advocacy and product information. While the site's size and scope reflect the company's scale, the eye-catching graphics and friendly tone keep the site from being intimidating.

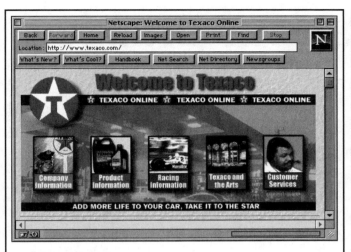

```
[Netscape: Welcome to Texaco Online]
Back  Forward  Home  Reload  Images  Open  Print  Find  Stop     N
Location: http://www.texaco.com/
What's New?  What's Cool?  Handbook  Net Search  Net Directory  Newsgroups

            Welcome to Texaco
     ☆ TEXACO ONLINE ☆ TEXACO ONLINE ☆ TEXACO ONLINE

  Company      Product      Racing      Texaco and    Customer
  Information   Information   Information   the Arts     Services

      ADD MORE LIFE TO YOUR CAR, TAKE IT TO THE STAR
```

IN-SITE: Texaco Online
http://www.texaco.com

Texaco, the manufacturer and retailer of coolant, antifreeze, gasoline, and lubricants, has created a Website that appeals to the mechanic, the sports fan, and even the opera lover. How? Well, for the mechanically minded, there are descriptions and suggestions for all of Texaco's products—motor oil to hydraulic fluid. For racing fans, Texaco's Website covers the three racing circuits (Indy, NASCAR, and NHRA), with schedules and driver trivia. And finally, there is information about arts programs supported by Texaco, a longtime sponsor of the arts, and a current contributor to the Metropolitan Opera (radio) and various PBS specials.

Monsanto World Wide Web Server Do you know Monsanto? You're probably standing on a Monsanto product right now, or ingesting Monsanto's handiwork as you read. The maker of Wear-Dated Carpet and NutraSweet, Monsanto has produced a straightforward, unassuming site with high-quality graphics and plenty of information. In addition to press releases and a company bio, there is a range of articles on financial data, company products, environmental campaigns, and helpline services. The site provides an overview of Monsanto to familiarize the visitor with the company and its products.
✓**www**→http://www.monsanto.com

Sumitomo The home page for this leading Japanese chemical corporation is oriented toward businesses, focusing on financial and developmental information in the form of reports, articles, and organizational charts. Little product information exists on the site, but a comprehensive company profile picks up the slack.
✓**www**→http://www.sumitomo-chem.co.jp

Gasoline companies

Amoco The site may include a black background, but the message Amoco is sending is all green. The simple site features an online magazine called *Onstream* which reports on Amoco's environmental efforts in addition to the company's stock prices and job openings.
✓**www**→http://www.amoco.com

Chevron Chevron takes the Earth and its resources very seriously—so seriously, in fact, that it has designed its Website to look like a cross-section of the Earth's layers. Click on the top layer of soil for news about company operations; click near the groundwater for info on how refineries and gas stations work.
✓**www**→http://www.chevron.com

Mobil Corporation Mobil has put its huge database of service stations and lubricant distributors online to help customers locate a station. Customers can even specify if they want a station to be a convenience store, have a service bay, offer a car wash, or sell diesel. Mobil also encourages customers to use its Website to apply for a Mobil credit card onlin or check Mobil stock prices. There's even a unique political feature that enables visitors to email Congress—Mobil maintains an archive of company editorials on topics ranging from trade with Vietnam to the balanced budget amendment and invites its customers to speak out on the issues. Links to other standard corporate information adorn the site's home page, but Mobil apparently has more on its mind than business and politics. The Mobil site includes information on arts programs the company partially funds, such as *Masterpiece Theatre*, *Mystery!*, and the Pegasus Prize for Literature.
✓**www**→http://www.mobil.com

Shell Oil On the Web, Shell doesn't sell gasoline. In addition to company and product information, Shell's Website promotes its new Interactive Marketplace—an online mall that currently sells Shell collectibles and golf gear, but has plans to include other merchandise.
✓**www**→http://www.shellus.com

Miscellaneous brands

High-value, trusted brand names are vital to the growth of the Web as a marketing and

shopping medium, since they legitimize Cyberspace as a place where consumers can reliably research and purchase products. The arrival on the Web of many of America's most well-known and trusted brands, from **Maytag** to **Black & Decker** to **Frigidaire**, serves notice that the Net is no longer a medium so young that traditional marketing powers can afford to ignore it, and it also suggests that the Web is likely to grow as a place for marketers. Many companies are not yet selling their own products directly to consumers online, in part, no doubt, because these manufacturers are sensitive to the concerns of their existing retailers. For now, a store locator will have to do.

On the Net

Greeting cards

American Greetings American Greetings' Website is exclusively a business-to-business endeavor, offering a variety of services to AmGreetings retailers, including Electronic Data Interchange and the Automated Direct Store Delivery program. In addition, American Greetings highlights its Consulting Services, which are geared to-

ward installing new technologies in retail outlets.
✓**www**→http://www.amgreetings .com

Hallmark Connections Card Studio Though this site is really an advertisement and virtual tour for a greeting-card creation software package that lets consumers customize their hellos, goodbyes, good wishes, and apologies, it lives or dies by the Hallmark brand. A whimsical "Top Ten Reasons To Try Hallmark Connections Card Studio," in fact, makes this point

bluntly: "#1: Hallmark Quality: Need we say more?" Apparently not.
✓**www**→http://www.micrografx .com/imagine/hallmark.html

Home & garden

Electrolux Electrolux, the manufacturer of home appliances from vacuum cleaners to washers, positions itself at its Website as the "old-timer with a new face." Its Web page contains the same kinds of information typically found in corporate brochures, like stock

IN-SITE: **BDHome (Black & Decker)**
http://www.bdhome.com
Black & Decker's Website, which uses as its graphic theme the blueprint of a house, positions the company as a valuable source of domestic information, with dozens of articles on home improvement, household maintenance, and related topics. In addition, B&D runs contests and provides an illustrated Web history of the company.

trends and product descriptions. However, Electrolux has also dedicated a large portion of its site to company history, including a timeline of company developments running parallel to the past 75 years of world history. Electrolux more than amply proves that even though it's been around awhile, it's not going to be left behind in the age of cybertech.
✓**www**→http://www.electrolux.se

Frigidaire Think service and dependability—think Frigidaire. On the Internet, Frigidaire has provided consumers with product descriptions, equipment specs, and everything else required to select the best range, refrigerator, or washer. Frigidaire even offers a repairs and service database where buyers can input their addresses and Frigidaire will locate the closest outlets.
✓**www**→http://www.frigidaire.com

General Electric General Electric's site isn't much for multimedia—in fact, the site has no pictures, only a long list of links that connect to corporate and consumer resources. Why? Well, it seems as though GE has decided to position itself as an old-fashioned company that knows that corporate value lies in earnings and holdings (GE links to subsidiaries like NBC). Still, consumers will see a lot of the familiar GE logo, and they can also download the new "We Bring Good Things to Life" jingle and video.
✓**www**→http://www.ge.com

Hamilton Beach Proctor-Silex Hamilton Beach, the home appliance manufacturer, has created a highly interactive site that matches the customer with a virtual dwelling most like the one he or she currently occupies—apartment, brownstone, etc. (The dwelling can be upgraded if the customer aspires to better digs.) Once inside, Hamilton Beach offers contests, product information, and suggestions for filling your virtual (and actual) home with appliances.
✓**www**→http://www.hambeach.com

Maytag Remember the lonely Maytag repairman? He and his basset hound Newton were always bored because Maytags were never broken? Well, Ol' Lonely is back, and this time he's a friendly tour guide working Maytag's graphically pleasing Website. Click on any window in the Maytag virtual house for information on its trusty appliances. Ol' Lonely even points out incentives to keep customers returning to the site, like a scavenger-hunt contest to win a free appliance and a shareware game of Solitaire for other loners.
✓**www**→http://www.maytag.com

Simmons For all those interested in the subconscious, this will keep your eyes open! Simmons has put together several extra content pages about the science of sleep disorders, including home remedies for insomnia and a Sleep Debt Analyzer that rates sleeping habits. There's also information about dream interpretation and even links to dream newsgroups on the Internet.
✓**www**→http://www.simmonsco.com

The Toro Company Toro knows that the average person doesn't buy a snow blower, lawn mower, or tractor often, so its Website is set up to give customers the guidance they'll need. Customers can select a type of product, answer a few simple questions, and Toro will recommend particular products. The site also runs a Dealer Locator to track down the products and offers an extensive searchable database of lawn-care information. Discolored grass? Insects? Just ask Earl The Yard-Care Answer Guy.
✓**www**→http://www.toro.com

Jewelry

Wry Art Wry Art's home page is the antithesis of the hard sell—using an amusing, conversational tone, it presents its unusual handmade jewelry with images and lots of text, describing not only the production process, but also the concept behind the piece. Online ordering is quick and easy, with no sales tax or "silly" shipping and handling costs, and, ever user-friendly, the site insists that the ordering info won't be added to a list because Wry Art "protect[s] our customers from junk mail."
✓**www**→http://www.wry-art.com

Office supplies

3M It's simple, really—companies want customers to try their products; they also want customers to complete their online surveys. 3M rewards customers who fill out their online surveys with free samples of its products (Post-It Notes, transparency film, etc.). Customers can also save money with this site by printing out Internet Rebate Coupons to redeem for cash upon purchase of spotlighted items.
✓**www**→http://www.3m.com/market/omc/index.html

DeskTop Online Selling paper products over an electronic medium presents a challenge—"tactile" is one thing the Web is not...yet. DeskTop Online sidesteps this issue by emphasizing its colorful stationery designs, with hundreds of thumbnail sketches linked to

product descriptions. Customers can stay on top of DeskTop's latest offerings or find a local dealer by submitting an electronic form.
✓**www**→http://www.esselte.com /desktop

Eagle Envelope Company
While the service descriptions at this Website are simple and the designs sparse, Eagle Envelope makes efficient use of the Web's capabilites. Customers can email Eagle for price quotes; send envelope designs created in QuarkX-Press, PageMaker, or other common desktop publishing programs (both Windows and Mac) to the companies for estimates; and link to the U.S. Postal Service Website to look up ZIP codes or check postal rates.
✓**www**→http://www.eagleprint .com

GRC This image supplies manufacturer offers a unique, handy service at its Website. GRC has created a Guide to Ribbons & Cartridges (tm), a cross-reference database of manufacturers' part numbers for over 3,300 laser, ink jet, or dot-matrix printer cartridges. Where applicable, GRC offers its own money-saving remanufactured toner cartridges as an alternatative to name brands. GRC's remanufacturing processes are described at length, along with the company's other recycling and environmental efforts. Customers can use the handy store directory to find their nearest GRC reseller.
✓**www**→http://www.printgrc.com /grcguide.html

Micro Format With the Imagination Gallery, this paper supplier has gone online creatively. But then that's a necessity when the products it markets are "interactive involvement" papers. The site devotes considerable space to de-

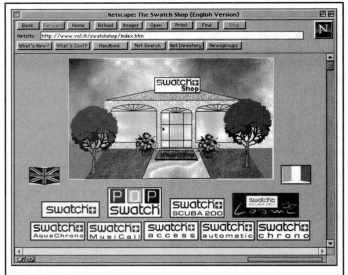

IN-SITE: **Swatch**
http://www.vol.it/swatchshop
From the Space Dog of the Russian Inspiration line to the Klirr of The Big Cold line, Swatch brings its entire catalog of watches to the Net with this stylish Italian site. Dozens of models are showcased with images and dramatic descriptions, reinforcing the brilliant marketing notion that each Swatch model has a distinctive story to tell. Everything is available for online ordering.

scribing the applications of—and providing instructions for—its Color-Change paper (the pulp equivalent of a mood ring, changing color with the application of body heat) and its 3-D/Virtual Reality paper (used with a red/blue viewer like those 3-D movies). Customers sufficiently awed by the products can obtain a special discount code at the Website; and win even bigger discounts by locating a hidden 3-D image.
✓**www**→http://www.sendit.com /mformat/home.html

On Paper Since the product it sells—high quality paper—is designed to give users an air of distinction, it's no surprise that On Paper uses electronic backgrounds to simulate a distinctive effect online. To supplement its illustrated online catalog, On Paper provides a detailed guide which explains

terms like "basis weight" and "opacity" to customers. Those ready to order can do so online—at a 20% discount—while those still not sold can purchase their Big Help Sample Kit, or sample up to five styles free!
✓**www**→http://www.onpaper.com

Planet Xerox How big is Xerox? Big enough to have its own planet—Planet Xerox, that is, a collection of corporate-oriented links, from investor information and stock prices to the company's sponsorship activities (including a great collection of official and fan pages for the '96 Olympics) and environmental efforts. Xerox's hefty research division gets its fair share of the Web spotlight. Xerox's line of copiers, fax machines, and other office equipment receive detailed descriptions. In fact, the company's entire product catalog

is published online.
✓**www**→ http://www.xerox.com

Pets

Iams At its Website, Iams proudly lists every ingredient in the company's popular products. The company also helps pet owners select the best food for their pets, gives them the scoop on serving suggestions and pet digestion, and sponsors the Veterinarians' Corner (an advice column where a real vet answers questions about those little bundles of domesticated fur). The pet food company has also set up a customer service outpost on the Web—customers can use the email form to ask Iams product-related questions.
✓**www**→http://www.iamsco.com

Sunglasses

Gargoyles This site is visually appealing, but beyond the nice graphics it's all business. Gargoyles has three lines of sunglasses to get off the shelves, and it showcases them in a well produced catalog with images, clear descriptions, and easy access to online ordering.
✓**www**→http://www.gargoyles .com/index.html

John Lennon Glasses With the world's revived interest in the Beatles, John Lennon is in style again. And as a result, the John Lennon line of frames and sunglasses, all exacting Italian replicas licensed by the Lennon estate, positions itself as a company carrying on the legacy of the late Beatle. Seperated into "The Walrus," "Imagine," and "Revolution," the catalog features a large image of each pair of glasses. While the site is a little under-designed, it does offer an extensive list of Beatles links.
✓**www**→http://www.synapse.net /~neuron

IN-SITE: **Crayola**
http://www.crayola.com
Crayons and contests everywhere! While Crayola packs its Website with coloring contests and promotions (e.g., Crayola's big "find the 100 billionth crayon" promotion had an online component as well) for kids and adults alike, the site also includes stain removal tips for parents, trivia, product information, and even a history of the crayon.

Kirk Originals Hard to believe these ultra-hip shades come from a country where it rains most of the time—that's England, in case you were lunging for the Almanac of Precipitation—but they do. Kirk cashes in on London's pop life with contests that associate the glasses with Britcelebs like Simply Red's Mick Huxnall and Sir Cliff Richard, an e-zine on up-and-coming artists and musicians, and pictures of prog-rockers and club kids sporting the sunglasses. A rotating catalog showcases a couple of designs every month, available for online ordering, and a world-wide store locator is available so the kids can buy the rest of the line offline.

✓**www**→http://www.kirkorig.co.uk /jason/index.html

Toys

Gund What is Gunderland? It's a place where stuffed animals are the citizens and the rulers, and the humans only servants who do their bidding. And it's also an un-bearably cutesy virtual community for teddy bear buffs that offers product information (a bear family tree), a program to find the nearest Gund retailer, games and activities with teddy bear themes, and even a live chat channel for teddy bear talk.
✓**www**→http://www.gund.com

Chapter 7

Arts
&
Entertainment

Entertainment giants

It's not just Hollywood anymore. It's not even just TV and movies anymore. There's a

great, big burgeoning world of entertainment out there, but only a few media companies can be top dogs. As a result of the immense competition, industry biggies are rushing to take advantage of the Net, and especially the Web, constructing ever larger and ever more impressive sites. Almost as soon as Web developments in multimedia occur, they are showcased on these pages. **MGM/ United Artists— The Lion's Den** relies on its signature lion and granddaddy position in the movie market to create an online movie palace complete with clips of its Academy Award crop and plush virtual seats. **Sony**'s site explodes with masses of material on far more than just the Walkman. And then there is **Warner Bros.**, which plays up its wacky history with a fun-filled site that any Daffy Duck fan would declare "T'riffic."

On the Net

MGM/United Artists—The Lion's Den The Lion's Den home page integrates MGM/UA's motion picture, home video, TV, and interactive entertainment arms

with a studio. At this classy multimedia site, top billing goes to the studio's current Academy Award nominees, linking to home pages for each of these movies. The home video section features a complete index of MGM/UA titles (over 2,400) and a For Retailers Only link, where store-owners can get a first look at coming titles and download trailers. The TV area houses the a Website for the new *Outer Limits*—fans who dare can chat about the show at the "Inner Eye," download video clips, and win T-shirts. Also on the darker fringe is a promotion for the H. R. Giger screensaver, available via the interactive area. Through the store, customers can purchase videos, games, and other MGM/UA merchandise…though they'll have to buy the popcorn somewhere else.
✓**www**→http://www.mgmua.com

Sony Online What do Ozzy Osbourne, *Party of Five*, and the Walkman have in common? They're all part of the Sony corporation, of course, and all part of its virtual hub, Sony Online. This site's home page provides links to eight divisions of Sony, putting music labels, movie studios, electronic gear, and more at surfers' fingertips. A "What's New" menu links to the latest developments in each division, such as a viewer poll to select a college for a certain TV character, or a special on a digital camera. Areas within the larger site provide visitors with a high degree of functionality; customers can compare features on electronic products, locate the nearest Sony theater, check programming

schedules, and shop for Sony merchandise.
✓**www**→http://www.sony.com

Viacom Within Macmillan Publishing's Website is the Viacom Cyberspace page, which summarizes and links to the notable Websites of other divisions of the Viacom empire. Viacom's cable TV channels are well-represented; Showtime, MTV, VH-1, Nickelodeon's Nick at Nite, and Comedy Central all have links. Movies, whether on the big screen (Paramount Pictures) or the small one (Blockbuster Entertainment), get their share of the spotlight. Viacom's publishing companies and their "new media" divisions are on the Web as well—Simon & Schuster Interactive, Macmillan's Information SuperLibrary, and even Viacom New Media.
✓**www**→http://www.mcp.com /general/news4/webw.html

Warner Bros. People come here to play in the six arenas of the Warner Bros. domain: television, music, movies, the studio stores, D.C. Comics, and Kids. This is a Website designed to entertain fans of all ages with Warner Brothers comics, cartoons, musicians, and shows. Thanks to tons of real-audio soundclips (Looney Tunes, Madonna, etc.), video clips (*Animaniacs, Babylon 5*, etc.), and even a program that lets you send Warner Bros. postcards electronically to friends, the site is all about feel-good fun—and it works like a charm.
✓**www**→http://www.warnerbros .com

Movie studios

Movie studios were among the first businesses to recognize the marketing potential

of the Web, and their efforts have led to some spectacular results. A studio's best offline tactic reaches its full potential on the Net when sound bites, screenshots, QuickTime clips, synopses, cast profiles, production notes, and more can create a completely new atmosphere of anticipation. Trailers can be as much fun as the movies they are advertising, and with the Net, customers can download favorites and watch them whenever they want. As one would expect, coverage varies. Some movies receive only sparse attention, and others—particularly those with cyberthemes—are the basis for entire virtual worlds.

On the Net

Fine Line Features The producers of such art house blockbusters as *Hoop Dreams*, *The Player*, and *The Incredibly True Adventures of Two Girls In Love* offer sound clips, screenshots, bios and synopses of their latest releases; features for archived classics; and a national listing of release dates.
✓**www**→http://www.flf.com

Gramercy Pictures The makers of such hits and misses as *Shallow Grave* and *Panther* also hit and miss here—some successful films

get nothing more than a synopsis and a few pictures, while bombs targeted for the Nethead generation get entire cyberworlds built to promote them.
✓**www**→http://www.polygram .com/polygram/film.html

MGM Home Video The leading role on this Website belongs to MGM's searchable directory of more than 2,400 movies on videocassette. Customers can search for favorites, add them to virtual shopping carts, and buy them online. The site's supporting cast includes features on new releases, movie trivia, and movie-related games and puzzles.
✓**www**→http://www.mgmhome video.com

Miramar Productions For animation films such as *Into the Minds Eye* and *Anima Mundi*, Miramar has produced downloadable interactive previews complete with images, music, biographies, liner notes, and more.
✓**www**→http://useattle.uspan.com /miramar

Miramax Films Known for its successful art house films, Miramax has also produced one of the best movie studio sites on the Net, with fantastic graphics, movie news, celebrity gossip and interviews, multimedia grab-bags for its entire archive of films (not just

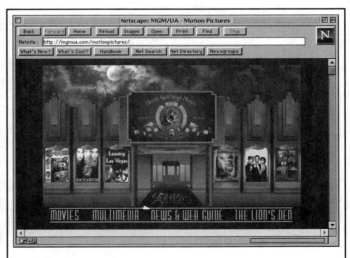

IN-SITE: **MGM/UA**
http://www.mgmua.com/motionpictures
Most of MGM's current releases get the star treatment on this sleek and sexy Website. MGM builds huge interactive promotions for each movie, linking to stunning pictures, movie downloads, character profiles, and other gimmicks (sometimes even an email address for a movie's leading actors). The site also features links to MGM's enormous video collection, CD-ROM game demos, and a list of ten Websites related to the themes of one of its movies.

current releases), stores to purchase merchandise, access to its entire video catalog, weekly features focusing on specific filmmakers or movie-related issues, and monthly contests offering prizes such as a walk-on part in a new flick.
✓**www**→http://www.miramax .com

Paramount Pictures Like many movie studios, Paramount's movie pages vary from film to film, with little more than a synopsis for sleepers; the requisite screenshots, bios, and synopses for the runaway hits; and sleek, interactive pages for movies with Gen-X appeal or cyberthemes. The page also connects to Movielink, a directory of movie theaters and movie listings in big cities across the country.
✓**www**→http://www.paramount .com/

Sony Classics Sony's Website is just about as good as it gets. Movie features include multimedia downloads, plus production info, reviews, interviews, contests, and hypertext summaries that link to other Internet sites related to a movie's themes.
✓**www**→http://www.spe.sony.com /Pictures/SonyClassics/index.html

Sony Pictures Entertainment This big budget Website for blockbuster Sony movies includes virtual tours of movie worlds, interviews with screenwriters, and links to related Web pages.
✓**www**→http://www.spe.sony.com /Pictures/SonyMovies/index.html

Tromaville Troma makes hilarious, anti-authoritarian and proudly vulgar movies like *The Toxic Avenger* series and *Nuke 'Em High*, and has been cultivating a very specific audience for years. Here the company offers an object les-

son in how to please your target market. So long as the Net remains a democratic medium in which a catholic range of tastes can be indulged, the guys at Troma will continue to focus on truly tasteless links, fanzines for cult films, and beauty contests for men, women, and mutants.
✓**www**→http://www.troma.com

United International Pictures United International Pictures— worldwide distributors of MGM/ UA, Paramount, and Universal films—provides poster GIFs, synopses, cast and production info, and screenshots for the latest U.S. flicks to hit the international market.
✓**www**→http://www.uip.com

Universal CyberWalk Some of the most appealing virtual worlds on the Net—fast loading, multimedia presentations—have been created for Universal films. Not every film was so lucky; some were

barely mentioned.
✓**www**→http://www.mca.com /universal_pictures/index.html

Walt Disney Pictures Only a few movies are featured at a time, but the site is impressive and highly interactive. Includes all the usual multimedia stuff, plus games and contests for the kiddies.
✓**www**→http://www.disney.com /DisneyPictures/index.html

Warner Bros. Pictures Warner Bros. has developed some of the most talked about movie sites on the Web, pages that use high-gloss graphics and interactive features to make virtual worlds based on their runaway hits. In fact, the site occasionally continues to feature films long gone from the theaters—*Batman Forever* and *Ace Ventura*, for instance—because of the Websites' popularity.
✓**www**→http://www.movies.warn erbros.com/

IN-SITE: **Twentieth Century Fox Home Entertainment**
http://www.tcfhe.com
Twentieth Century Fox uses multimedia downloads and contests to advertise new video releases and games. The movie studio has also created an online discount club— ClubFox—which gives customers discounts on the entertainment company's merchandise, videos, and games.

TV networks

These days TV networks are as busy broadcasting their hits in Cyberspace as they are

looking for the next big hit. **ABC**'s online strategy rings out the old and rings in the new with special features on shows like *Murder One*—and the site links to their email address to encourage online fandom. Likewise **CBS** leads, and therefore identifies the network, with Letterman, setting a self-mocking tone bound to appeal to younger fans. **CNN** builds on its reputation as the source for news by emphasizing the immediacy of Net delivery, and at **Fox**, character counts in a world of interactivity and exploration that Bart, Mulder, and Scully would love. But these channels aren't the real discovery of the online world. What is? **The Discovery Channel**, of course, which has revolutionized the medium by creating a whole new network in Cyberspace with its own interactive features and links to the distant corners of the Web.

On the Net

A&E A&E's front door is dense with graphics that link Netsurfers to eight different sections of the Website, including program list-

ings, features on specials, and an area devoted to the network's popular Biography series. The network spotlights its contribution to education with study guides on historical and cultural topics.
✓**www**→http://www.aetv.com

ABC ABC's Website provides lists of images, sound clips, and video files from new prime-time sitcoms. Leaving out on-air classics like *Roseanne*, ABC also leans on cast bios and weekly plot summaries for the season's newcomers. Fans can also email their comments

about the show to ABC.
✓**www**→http://www.abctelevision.com

Bravo! The arty Website for the venerable Canadian arts channel includes synopses, schedules, and video samples from the network's programs.
✓**www**→http://www.muchmusic.com/bravo.html

C-Span The C-Span Website has a formal design, with helpful icons and graphics that reinforce the reputation of quality news report-

IN-SITE: **CBS Eye on the Net**
http://www.cbs.com
The CBS site is updated daily and opens with network news briefs. A grid of mini-television screens offers a FAQ, scheduling info, videos, and images of CBS shows. CBS chose to enter the online medium with its most popular show outfront—David Letterman is the site's main attraction.

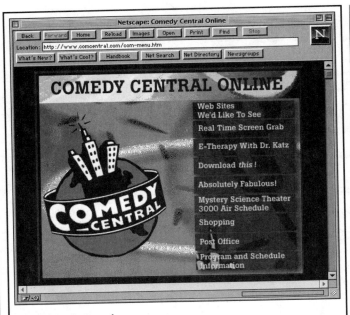

Netscape: Comedy Central Online

Back | Forward | Home | Reload | Images | Open | Print | Find | Stop

Location: http://www.comcentral.com/com-menu.htm

What's New? | What's Cool? | Handbook | Net Search | Net Directory | Newsgroups

COMEDY CENTRAL ONLINE

Web Sites
We'd Like To See

Real Time Screen Grab

E-Therapy With Dr. Katz

Download *this*!

Absolutely Fabulous!

Mystery Science Theater
3000 Air Schedule

Shopping

Post Office

Program and Schedule
Information

IN-SITE: **Comedy Central**
http://www.comcentral.com
Comedy Central pays special attention to its cybersavvy audience, providing hefty doses of Internet humor on its Web page (Web Sites We'd Like To See, or the Disgruntled Postal Workers page, for instance). The site also offers online versions of popular network jokes like E(mail)-Therapy with Dr. Katz, and QuickTime videos and soundclips from *Ab Fab*. Customers can order merchandise with the 800 number listed in the Totally Not Free Shopping area.

ing. It provides news coverage of what's happening in the government, with RealAudio clips from the previous day's speeches, and announcements from the capital.
✓**www**→http://www.c-span.org

CBN—The Christian Broadcasting Network Now a Webevangelist, Pat Robertson has taken the Word to a new medium. The Website for the CBN includes news and press releases about special events within the organization as well as information about the history and practices of the ministry. But interactive prayer is the real draw here. Followers can email prayer requests or ask questions on the site's forum.
✓**www** ...→http://www.cbn.org

...→ http://www.the700club

CNN Though James Earl Jones doesn't introduce CNN's Website in his *basso profundo*, Ted Turner's news-around-the-clock network is doing far more than promoting its television network; it's creating an online news service. Visitors get a Hot Link of the Day, a search engine for exploring the thousands of archived news stories, a NewsQuiz, and even QuickTime videos of on-location, round-the-clock reporting.
✓**www**→http://www.cnn.com

Court TV Court TV viewers can't get enough courtroom drama, and the Website feeds this thirst. Weekly contests, Menendez trial

transcripts, the hottest courtroom news of the week, online legal help, and a searchable database of law files are featured. Court TV even sells key chains and various other memorabilia from its site.
✓**www**→http://www.courttv.com

ESPNet On this Web-based sports news service, Netsurfers can participate in polls, surveys, and contests to win ESPNet T-shirts, read daily sports coverage, and listen RealAudio game broadcasts. Subscribers to ESPNet can receive video clips, player profiles, and articles. The site also accepts advertisers.
✓**www**→http://espnet.sportszone.com

Fox Entertainment On television, Fox relies on the wit of Homer and Bart to entertain; on the Web, it's counting on a series of interactive games based on the network's programming. Get ready to play. For kids, Fox provides several interactive activities, like editing the *Totally Kids* newsletter. Fox's *Sunday Night Football* fans are invited to play fantasy football on the site. And everyone else can head to the Entertainment section for games that bring you closer to the network, like the *Dating Game*—type in a description of your perfect mate and you'll be paired with a Fox-y mate.
✓**www**→http://www.foxnetwork.com

HBO Home Video Online Home Box Office uses this Website to promote the video releases of movies produced by the network. The site includes video clips, images, and reviews.
✓**www**→http://www.hbohomevideo.com

International Channel Network The International Channel

provides programming in more than 23 languages. The Website offers visitors updated programming information (click your language of choice for a list of programs in a foreign tongue) and, perhaps more impressively, links to Internet resources that will help students learn languages and educators teach them.

✓**www**→http://www.i-channel.com

MCA/Universal Television Group Plot summaries for the current week's line-up, chat forums for each show, and bios of cast members. MCA isn't stingy with its multimedia additions either—there are lots of GIFs, audio clips, and video clips for each series.

✓**www**→http://www.mca.com/tv

MTV MTV's putting on quite a show on the Web with regularly updated music news briefs, music industry gossip and rumors, album reviews, music charts, and a multimedia fest of soundclips and videos. And that's just the Music section! The Animation section goes all out promoting network stars like *Beavis & Butthead*, *Aeon Flux*, *The Maxx*, and *The Head*. Enough changing content here to keep music and popular culture fans coming back regularly.

✓**www**→http://www.mtv.com

NBC HTTV NBC teamed up with Microsoft and put together a site that not only promotes the network's shows—show synopses and schedules—but also delivers news, interactive games, and even online chat sessions with stars like Quincy Jones and John Laroquette.

✓**www**→http://www.nbc.com

NewsTalk Television NewsTalk is all about updates. The cable channel promises the hottest, the quickest, and the latest news stories—and their Website follows close behind! News addicts will return daily to this site for news discussions and daily polls. NewsTalk also provides additional editorial content, in the form of *Position Paper* magazine. The magazine carries news-related articles of interest like "Would Thomas Jefferson Think We're Free?" and "Punishment by Education Deprivation: It's Gonna Cost Ya."

✓**www**→http://www.newstalk.com

Nick at Nite Low-key on the Web, the classic TV network has wacky Nick at Nite commercials, a schedule of this week's classic TV shows, and an essay about the bonuses of preservation. Where would we be without Mary, Dick, and Lucy?

✓**www**→http://nick-at-nite.com

Playboy TV *Playboy* sells sex, but online it's not using any "dramatic photos" to promote its cable channel—just a program guide for the current and following month.

✓**www**→http://www.playboy.com/PlayboyTV/PlayboyTV.html

QVC Currently, host bios are the main attraction at the shopping channel's Website. For actual online shopping, see the Internet Shopping Network (http://www.isn.net).

✓**www**→http://www.qvc.com

Sci-Fi Channel: The Dominion This far-out channel offers video clips, stills, and audio files at its

IN-SITE: **Discovery Channel**
http://www.discovery.com
The Discovery Channel's Website was designed to be participatory—there's far more for the Netsurfer to do here than check program listings. Visitors can head to topics such as Science, Nature, People, History, Exploration, and Technology for news stories and discussion boards. Netsurfers with real-life adventures to tell can submit a 700-word essay to the Your Story page; selected essays will be posted online and the site will provide related links. The Discovery Channel also accepts outside advertising.

Website, which is advertised frequently on the air. A program guide for the Sci-Fi Channel and a bulletin board for comments and questions are also provided.
✓**www**→http://www.scifi.com

Showtime Online Aside from a programming schedule and movie news, Showtime lets you order its home cable service online.
✓**www**→http://showtimeonline.com

Sony Pictures Entertainment The Sony site features a visually charming selection of icons to click for video clips, sound clips, cast bios, trivia, and plot summaries for shows sponsored by Sony like *Matt Waters*, *Party of Five*, and *Ned and Stacey*.
✓**www**→http://www.spe.sony.com/Pictures/tv/cttv.html

TBN The Trinity Broadcasting Network has a very user-friendly home page, with easy to interpret icons and a well designed table of contents. The faithful can access a weekly program schedule, flip through the rolodex for information on a host or guest star, and submit a prayer request via email.
✓**www**→http://www.tbn.org

The Travel Channel The Travel Channel has created a Website that is an online travel resource as well as a promotion for a cable channel. The site runs weekly travel features and columns, holds message-based and live travel discussions, carries a huge gallery of travel photos uploaded by visitors, offers travel advice and info, maintains a searchable database of more than 26,000 electronic travel brochures, and links to other travel sites. Cable customers can use the Website for programming and schedule information.

✓**www**→http://www.travelchannel.com

Turner Classic Movies With press releases and programming schedules for Turner's epics, this site is most noteworthy for its live chat room. Fans choose from a handful of icons (one that represents a star persona) and then enter the chat room to talk about movies.
✓**www**→http://www.turner.com/tcm/index.htm

VC Interactive The channel that brings you Pay-Per-View now lets you watch QuickTime video clips of those tempting movies online. More than 40 movies a month are previewed here, along with a movie schedule for six elective channels. Weekly contests keep the couch potato coming back.
✓**www**→http://www.ppv.com

VH-1 VH-1's Website features artist bios, a multimedia music library, and weekly program guides for fans of adult contemporary artists such as Joan Osborne, Sting, and Bonnie Raitt. A section called Chatter provides discussion boards for viewer feedback.
✓**www**→http://vh1.com

The Weather Channel If you were promoting The Weather Channel, what would you have on your Website? Weather forecasts, perhaps? The Weather Channel offers a clickable map of the U.S. that connects to forecasts for each city in the country. The site also features video clips from weather programs, meteorology shareware, weather definitions, and other interactive features that help visitors keep up with their atmosphere. Oh, and there's a program schedule as well.
✓**www**→http://www.weather.com

IN-SITE: PBS Online
http://www.pbs.org
Includes a "daily program trivia challenge," guides to educational programming, a quilt-like clickable map of the U.S. that serves as a directory of local PBS stations, home pages for many PBS programs, and up-to-date features on current events. The site's online news hour moves beyond promotion and offers essays, news, transcriptions of interviews on PBS shows, and online events.

Radio stations

Sound is probably not the first thing people think of when they think of the Internet,

but in Cyberspace everyone can hear your scream, shout or make whatever noise you want—if you want them to. Nevertheless, radio stations still have to work hard to get people to tune into their sites. Some use the tried-and-tested strategy of playing up the celebrity status of stars like Rush Limbaugh or Howard Stern. Others provide useful Net services like **NPR**'s topical news links, or **WNZW**'s tailored list for senior surfers, or even recast themselves as online gateways, like the WMMS **BuzzardWeb**. Because it's not their primary medium, stations must convey their identity with well-crafted sites, and none does this better than the **BBC**, whose Deco Webstyling recalls the halcyon days of the 1930s, when the radio networks were the only information superhighway.

On the Net

Networks

Bloomberg Information News Radio Bloomberg markets itself as a source for 24-hour world news and financial analysis and a staple of any businessperson's daily info-diet. How does a radio sta-

tion enhance its product? Bloomberg turned to the Net. Listeners can broadcast a Bloomberg radio feed directly to their desktops using software available from the site This page also links to other areas of Bloomberg Online's massive information offerings.
✓**www**→http://www.bloomberg.com

BBC (British Broadcasting Corporation Is it the 1990s or the 1930s? On its retro-looking Web page, the British broadcasting giant offers programming schedules, regularly updated home pages for its shows and documentaries,

and even program email addresses. Taking advantage of RealAudio technology, the BBC broadcasts some of its radio shows live on the Internet, and, capitalizing on the resources of the Net, links to sites related to many of the network's programs. The BBC Website has also set itself up as a guide to the online world. "Babbage's Guide to the World Wide Web" links to Web browsers, several search engines, and a hotlist with hundreds of categorized links.
✓**www**→http://www.bbc.co.uk

Capitol Radio Networks Targeted towards true news-addicted

IN-SITE: National Public Radio
http://www.npr.org
The simply designed NPR Website leads with the news and promotes the radio network with programming schedules, previews of upcoming shows, and samples of the day's top stories via RealAudio clips. Other valuable features include a catalog of tapes and transcripts available for online ordering, and a clickable locator map to help visitors find local affiliates. NPR even augments on-air content with links to related topical sites.

Tar Heels—this Raleigh, North Carolina-based network offers RealAudio sound capsules of hourly news broadcasts for its listeners straight from the Research Triangle. And so as not to exclude its financial supporters, there's information on its corporate background planed specifically to interest potential advertisers.
✓**www**→http://www.capitolnet .com

Stations

104.7 Buzz Radio Like the Websites of many radio stations, 104.7 in Richmond, Virginia, is encouraging listeners to send in online music requests. No more busy lines and frustrated customers! The station also invites listeners to log on to its Website to chat, check for information on local concerts, get descriptions of on-air promotions, and use its links to music sites. Visitors might just want to hang out here for a while.
✓**www**→http://www.buzzradio .com/

KALL 910 Go with the stars! This Salt Lake City talk radio station dedicates the lion's share of space on its Website to high-profile syndicated personalities like Rush Limbaugh, G. Gordon Liddy, and Oliver North. The station also links to a variety of radio-specific resources, including the National Association of Broadcasters, the Talk Radio Guide, and the AM/ FM FCC Database.
✓**www**→http://www.aros.net /KALL/Welcome.html

KBNP-AM 1410 The Website of "Oregon's only all-business news and financial information radio station" serves its finance-oriented audience with links to news and stock quote services as well as lists of business-class recreational sites (e.g., skiing, golf courses). The site also features information for potential advertisers—listener demographic profiles, for instance.
✓**www**→http://www.teleport.com /~kbnp

KIAK-FM "Alaska's number one country radio station" is online advertising its programming. How does KIAK-FM draw traffic to the site? The station offers local news reports, weather forecasts, and special features such as a link that encourages visitors to email troops in Bosnia. Links to sister stations in the local market serve potential sponsors.
✓**www**→http://www.polarnet.com /Users/COMCO/KIAK.HTM

KING FM 98.1 Laying claim to being "the first in the world to broadcast classical music live on the Internet 24 hours a day, 7 days a week," this Seattle station blurs the line between using the Web to market a product and using it to deliver a new product.
✓**www**→http://www.king.org

KLSX If listeners didn't know that Howard Stern was syndicated on KLSX before they visited the Website, they will by the time they leave. This Los Angeles station primarily uses its Website to promote its affiliation with the big-mouth radio personality. An email address for Stern is listed at the site.
✓**www**→http://www.realradio .com

WBAI Working to ensure the continued success of this listener-sponsored community station (located in New York City), WBAI solicits online donations and extensively details the company's mission on its Website. Its activist-oriented Web content summarizes the station's award-winning coverage of controversial topics, and provides links to related resources.
✓**www**→http://www.dorsai.org /~wbai

WFMU The oldest freeform radio station in the country, New York City's WFMU, has a strong Web presence that is as eclectically entertaining as its on-air broadcasts. WFMU takes advantage of the interactivity of the Net, and entertains visitors with soundbites, interactive polls, and even an online catalog.
✓**www**→http://wfmu.org

WMMS—BuzzardWeb This Cleveland alternative-music station is reborn online as Buzzard-Web, a launch pad for its listeners to interesting sites on the Internet. BuzzardWeb features many links to news, sports, entertainment, and local-interest sites. Although the site solicits online song requests and features several promotional soundbites, station-related content takes a back seat to Internet content.
✓**www**→http://www.wmms.com /wmms

WNEW How does a site get added to a customer's hotlist? WNEW, a New York City radio station, offers an extensive collection of links to Internet sites, including large lists of links to music, television, movie, weather, and New York City sites. It also links its weekly playlist to artist sites on the Web.
✓**www**→http://www.wnew.com

WNZW 1430 AM Memphis This Memphis AM station with a retirement-aged audience, has created a guide to online resources for seniors.
✓**www**→http://www.flinn.com /1430.html

Music labels

Judging from the number of music-related fan pages and newsgroups, and from the gen-

eral demographics of the Internet, music labels would be foolish not to construct state-of-the art sites—the fans are certainly out there, and so is some tough competition. **American Recordings** chooses to let the Net sell its site, providing thousands of music links and squarely positioning itself as the premier online music hub. High-tech attractions are **Capitol**'s strength, while **Atlantic Records** prefers to create an online community through live chat and fan newsletters. **Hollywood Records** has delved even further into the culture of the Internet, creating a dark cartoon world that requires visitors to navigate hazards to reach their rewards. Then there is the **Smithsonian**, where the venerable museum curates a site on music history to accompany its online catalog of roots music and tuneful Americana.

On the Net

American Recordings American Recordings' home page positions itself as the preeminent launching pad for the music-loving Netsurfer. The Website contains the Ultimate Band List, a guide—updated by users—to

thousands of music-related Web pages, the Ultimate Chat List, and the Free For All, where visitors can post links to their own home pages (or leave snail mail addresses). There's also the American roster, which includes artists like Johnny Cash, Devo, and Slayer.
✓**www**→http://american.record ings.com

Atlantic Records The newsletter posted on this home page informs fans about free giveaways with album purchases, artists' TV appearances, contests, tours, live chat, and the launch of *Stereo-Type*—a gay and lesbian newsletter. In addition, the page links to informa-

tion about Spew+, Atlantic's enhanced CD-product, which places the label at the cutting edge of interactive technology.
✓**www**→http://www.atlantic-rec ords.com

Capitol Though Capitol directs visitors towards its artists' pages, what sells this page are its downloadable goodies. From a Beastie Boys screen saver to Adam Ant's Interactive Ant Farm—which samples the Antman's latest album while viewers revel in animated silliness—Capitol offers memorable promos for its artists.
✓**www**→http://www.hollywood andvine.com

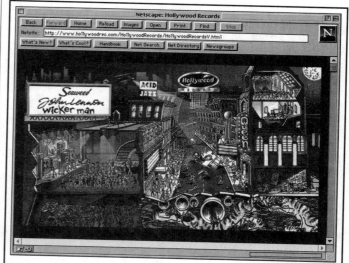

IN-SITE: Hollywood Records
http://www.hollywoodrec.com
Hollywood Records has designed a dark cartoon world to promote its artists—Acid Jazz, Queen, Wickerman, etc. Music fans touring the "city" will bump into sound clips, videos, pictures, and concert schedules for bands playing on the label. If they aren't disturbed by the imagery, vistors can hop down into a sewer where they can link to other big rock sites online. Rock and Roll's a dirty business!

EMI EMI's home page offers an inviting target for would-be music bizzers by advertising openings for internships and paid college representatives. Links to fan pages devoted to EMI artists are spotlighted, along with those to official band Websites.
✓**www**→http://www.emirec.com

Geffen/DGC From its artists' home pages, users can link to Pollstar, "the Concert Hotwire," to get current tour information for Geffen artists, or visit CDNow to purchase albums. In either case, the user arrives at the site with the current artist's relevant information already loaded.
✓**www**→http://geffen.com

Grand Royal The hip home page for hip-hop pioneers the Beastie Boys contains an online boutique with a catalog for the band's imprint, print fanzine, and X-Large clothing line. Previews of the 'zine (including an electronic version of the long-out-of-print first issue), samples of the tunes, and label news are all here.
✓**www**→http://www.nando.net /GrandRoyal

I.R.S. Records No tax returns here. The preeminent new wave label of the early '80s offers old fans an audio Hall of Fame to relive their memories, while new fans can sample digitized stacks of the label's current wax on the I.R.S. RealAudio Jukebox.
✓**www**→http://rocktropolis.com /IRS

Rhino The independent label's Website offers an online catalog, with album cover thumbnails and track listings. Buying still requires a phone call, though the full Website (now in the works) may offer online purchase.

✓**www**→http://cybertimes.com /Rhino/Welcome.html

Smithsonian This venerable American institution's recordings (on the Smithsonian Collection Recordings and the Folkways Collection) are the places to start for anyone interested in the bountiful history of American music, from folk to jazz to American Indian (not to mention their classical and world music catalogs). This multimedia catalog is just one part of the museum's extensive Website.
✓**www**→http://www.si.sgi.com /products/shopmall/records/start .htm

Sony Music The site for Sony's musical holdings is predictably multimedia:-heavy, with audio and video samples of Sony products, promotional screen savers, and electronic press kits. There's no shortage of catalog information—from an advance schedule of new releases to a massive list of every Sony album in print—as well as the requisite artist and tour content.
✓**www**→http://www.music.sony .com/Music/MusicIndex.html

Warner Bros. Records This home page offers users access to several tentacles of this entertainment company: TV, movies, stores, and DC Comics, as well as affiliated record labels (Warner, Elektra, Atlantic, Reprise, Luaka Bop, and so on), and artist home pages. The artists' pages use various promotional tactics—one band's site offers phone numbers and applicable email addresses for local radio stations so that users can request their favorite songs, while another includes a downloadable Macromedia Director application.
✓**www**→http://www.music.warner bros.com

IN-SITE: Sub Pop
http://www.subpop.com
While the email address of the label that made grunge a household world remains "loser @subpop.com," Sub Pop's Website is considerably more upscale. Monthly columns written in gossipy tones give readers an "in-crowd" feel; downloadable music samples and online purchase facilities make Sub Pop a one-stop shop.

Performing arts

Without the budgets of their cinematic counterparts, live theater and other performing

arts can't mount huge multimedia sites. Nevertheless, theater and dance companies have gone on the Web, often with innovative marketing strategies. With big hits few and far between (the Toronto-based **Tommy: The Home Page** is an exception), smaller musical productions like **Pope Joan** can shine with online previews and songbooks. When it comes to dance, national companies like the **American Ballet Theater** and renowned regional companies like **The Washington Ballet** have choreographed elegant, media-rich sites that showcase both performers and performances. And finally, there's Web opera—companies from the **New York City Opera** and the **Royal Swedish Opera** furnish schedules, plot summaries, and even online ticket ordering capabilities.

On the Net

Theater

Jekyll and Hyde Home Page
Don't be afraid—this page is definitely more Jekyll than Hyde. With a newsletter, a tour schedule, a mailing list, essays on the performers and production staff, mer-

chandising and shopping opportunities, and a fan club, this site is very helpful for anyone interested in the show.
✓**www**→http://reedycreek.stanford.edu/RecArtsJH

Nosferatu, The Vampire Dark colors and gothic graphics set the mood at this page, which promotes the Bernard Taylor musical (which is, in turn, based on the famous F. W. Murnau film). If visitors have the courage to face the monster, they can sample sound clips from the show, read about

show news, and even link to other related sites (including the *Phantom of the Opera* page).
✓**www**→http://www.webzone1.co.uk/www/phantom/nosfera2.htm

Pope Joan The show's creator, Christopher Moore, promotes his new show (and himself) as vigorously as a cult member worships its leader. At the Website, sample scenes, lyrics to entire songs, and a history of the production are included. Netsurfers can even read a weekly newsletter on the *Pope Joan* phenomenon. And finally, the

IN-SITE: **Tommy—The Home Page**
http://www.mirvish.com/tommy
This page does a lot of name-dropping in its first few lines (Jimi Hendrix, the Rolling Stones, Bob Dylan, and The Beatles) to associate the bastard Broadway-flavored child of Pete Townshend's rock opera with the revolutionary spirit of sixties rock. The rest of the site includes information on The Who, as well as offering fans a chance to email the show's Toronto producers.

page offers a little practical info about actually acquiring tickets to the production.

✓**www**→http://orlok.com

Dance

Boston Ballet Though the images are washed-out and the targeting somewhat unclear (is the page aimed at dance students or dance fans?), the Boston Ballet makes good use of the Web in one respect—information. With data on volunteer fundraising programs and dance education, dancer profiles, tour schedules, and even phone and fax numbers to contact the company, this is a comprehensive online guide to ballet in Beantown.

✓**www**→http://www.arts-online .com/bballet.htm

New York City Ballet It's worth a visit to this page just to see the amount of merchandise available in the NYC Ballet's online store. New York City Ballet stationery, toys, calendars, and posters, and even trading cards are available for purchase, so that fans never have to be too far from their pliés.

✓**www**→http://www.nycballet .com

Paul Taylor Dance Company There's only very general info about the company here, which indicates that the page is meant for new arrivals to the company's fan base rather than longtime vets. In fact, the only real resource at the site for diehard Taylor followers is an email response form.

✓**www**→http://soho.ios.com /~ptdc

The Washington Ballet The Washington Ballet's elegant home page has an image of a dancer and a sound clip of a radio advertisement. Throughout the site, sophisticated and compelling images introduce sections on touring, performances, the Washington Ballet school, and more.

✓**www**→http://home.worldweb.net /washingtonballet

Opera

New York City Opera The New York City Opera has a terrific site that works as a real tool, helping patrons and subscribers buy tickets and keep on top of upcoming events. The site also sponsors regular contests, where coveted prizes like NYCO caps and sweatshirts are given away. Too bad coveted seats in the orchestra section aren't part of the booty.

✓**www**→http://plaza.interport.net /nycopera/index.html

Royal Swedish Opera House The Royal Swede promotes its opera company in full regalia. At its site there's an essay about the famous opera house, information on this season's performances and a handy seating and ticket chart for opera lovers.

✓**www**→http://soho.ios.com /~gberkson/operan

Santa Fe Opera The Santa Fe Opera's Website jumps off the page with colorful graphics that make opera fun and accessible. The Santa Fe Opera highlights some of its additional endeavors, like the Enchantments program, which organizes special events at the opera house like picnics and lectures. Santa Fe Opera fans will also be pleased to know that tickets as well as libretti can be ordered online.

✓**www**→http://www.walpole.com /walpole/Santa_Fe_Opera

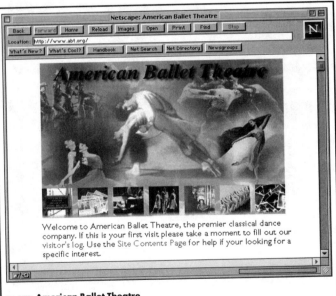

Welcome to American Ballet Theatre, the premier classical dance company. If this is your first visit please take a moment to fill out our visitor's log. Use the Site Contents Page for help if your looking for a specific interest.

IN-SITE: American Ballet Theatre
http://www.abt.org

Besides providing the requisite tour and show information, this site offers extensive profiles of all the principals and soloists, including a To The Point feature that gets up-close-and-personal with a new dancer every week (typical questions are "Who's your favorite Beatle?" and "Brady Bunch or Partridge Family?"). But the real star of the site is the section devoted to the ballets themselves, which lets visitors unfamiliar with ballet revel in plot summaries, images, and even multimedia excerpts.

Museums

Museums must walk a fine line online—they want to sustain the interest of Netsurfers

with online exhibitions and activities, yet still inspire actual museum visits. Marketers have attempted several strategies to interest the public in museum-going, virtual and otherwise. **The Canadian Museum of Civilization** walks the visitor through the museum exhibit by exhibit. The living museum **Old Sturbridge Village** relies on the glories of Net technology, filling its sites with sounds, movies, and information. And one of America's grandest museums, New York's venerable **Metropolitan Museum of Art**, chooses to bring visitors in with a glimpse of a masterpiece or two, and keep them coming back with an email notification service that keeps taps on new exhibits at the Web site—and at the big building on Fifth Avenue too.

On the Net

Andy Warhol Museum This site features a virtual tour of the museum, devoted to Pop Art's godfather. The site provides images of Warhol's works, screening and exhibition schedules, a bio, and an FAQ for the museum.
✓**www**→http://www.warhol.org /warhol

The Franklin Institute Science Museum The Franklin Institute invites people to get struck by lightning, tour a human heart, travel to a future earth, ride in one of the first steam engines ever built, lift 500 pounds with their bare hands, see a 60-foot-high movie, and visit the stars. Visitors are encouraged to use the Website for scheduling information and summaries of current exhibits, and the museum runs a few online exhibits to attract attention to the site. Appealing to parents and educators, the museum also maintains an excellent collection of teaching materials and instructions for experiments.
✓**www**→http://sln.fi.edu

Jorvik Viking Center This site offers more than a cybervisit to a museum located in York, England; it's the virtual home of red-haired, plundering seafarers worldwide. Anyone with sea salt in his/her blood and romance in his/her heart will enjoy the online offerings collected on the links page— from rune casting programs to the electronic Beowulf to a cybernetwork of Viking world schools. After grabbing the attention of lovers of all things Viking, the Jorvik pushes for a real visit, offering bargain prices to other York-area attractions and descriptions of upcoming festivals.
✓**www**→http://www.demon.co.uk /tourism/jvc

IN-SITE: **Canadian Museum of Civilization**
http://www.cmcc.muse.digital.ca/cmc/cmceng/welcmeng.html
One way to promote your product is to just give it away. The Canadian Museum of Civilization uses a similar strategy. Online visitors can virtually enjoy the whole museum experience (except the sore feet) by walking from gallery to gallery via a clickable floor map. The museum makes a concerted effort to keep the attention of the little ones by providing fun activities in the Children's Museum section. The Website maintains a schedule of museum events, lists movie showings in the Imax theater, and offers general information about the museum and its hours.

Los Angeles County Museum of Art The LACMA attract new visitors with a mixed program of music, movies, exhibitions, education, and, of course, fine art. All are previewed on the Website. The site profiles current exhibits, sometimes including artist interviews, art history perspectives, and curatorial insights.
✓**www**→http://www.lacma.org

Le Louvre If you've never been to Paris, then you haven't been to the Louvre—until now. With the power of the Web, you can visit Europe's most renowned museum, checking out the da Vincis, the Michelangelos, and the Delacroixs. For now, the site is only in French, but plans to add English, Spanish, and Portugese are in the works. And even if you can't read the words, you can look at the masterpieces, from El Greco's *Le Christ en croix adoré par deux donateurs* to Gericault's *Le Radeau de la Méduse*.
✓**www**→http://mistral.culture.fr/louvre

Metropolitan Museum of Art How does the Met convey the sheer immensity of its collection? Through a clickable floor map the museum allows virtual visitors to wander from archaic Greek sculpture to 19th-century American home furnishings. The Met also offers visitors the option to register their email address with the site. Those who do are notified when areas are added to the Website or when the actual museum runs a new exhibit.
✓**www**→http://www.metmuseum.org

Museum Moderner Kunst Stiftung Ludwig Wein A Viennese café scene welcomes visitors to this museum's site, which is presented in both German and English. The museum features online exhibits of modern art and, for visitors planning a trip to the offline museum, links to other Austrian tourist sites.
✓**www**→http://www.mmkslw.or.at/MMKSLW

Old Sturbridge Village Sturbridge Village in Massachusetts is in the business of recreating the past with a group of 19th century buildings and costumed interpreters living as if it were still 1835. The Website of the for-profit enterprise takes visitors on a virtual tour of the village, whetting their appetites for the real thing. Here visitors can walk village streets, watching blacksmiths hammer horseshoes and listening to the bleats of sheep, or they can read a Hornbook in the schoolhouse. Sturbridge runs several contests based on the 19th-century theme and sponsors a resident cyberhistorian to answer questions and entice frequent stops to its Website.
✓**www**→http://www.osv.org

Smithsonian The Smithsonian delivers directions, links to exhibit pages, and even provides staff notes on several topics—Far Eastern Art, Natural History, Air and Space, among others. To supplement information about the museum's galleries and to encourage an actual visit, the Smithsonian has constructed a travel planning service that includes lodging, dining, and transportation suggestions.
✓**www**→http://www.si.edu

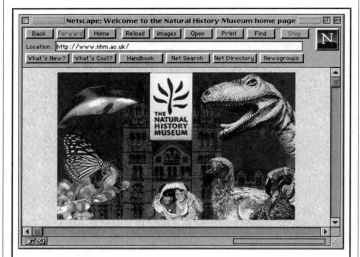

IN-SITE: **Natural History Museum**
http://www.nhm.ac.uk

If marketing a museum is solely intended to draw visitors to the real-world version, then London's Natural History Museum isn't really using the Web to "market" itself. But if it's about promoting and even distributing the museum experience in some form—whether through an actual trip to the building or to a virtual exploration of its galleries—then the Natural History Museum is way ahead of everyone else. This famous monument to the vision of Prince Albert presents samples of its collections in elegant and animated online galleries—but that's not all. The Museum is boldly creating a new virtual network that will allow "home owners in Belgium to access the virtual museum via a cable TV network." A sneak preview, complete with viewing software, is already online so that visitors can download virtual fossils. If only other fossils could mesh so gracefully with the future.

Book publishers

Once the publishing industry decided *en masse* that "if you can't beat 'em you might

as well join 'em," it leapt online with wit and elan. Traditional publishing houses have used the online world to market their books. Who's doing what online? **The Bookstore at Houghton Mifflin** has online previews of its CD-ROMs for kids. **Penguin Books** has crafted clever online contests that send visitors scavenging the entire Website for literary trivia. **Random House** enhances its upcoming titles with related features. There is also an entirely new industry comprised of companies who *only* publish online. **The Automated Pen**, for example, sells both novelty and immediate gratification with its e-texts.

On the Net

Academic Press Know your audience is basic marketing wisdom, and the high-tech sorts who are likely to pick out one of Academic Press's programming tomes probably won't be swayed by run-of-the-mill Net tricks. So in addition to offering an online catalog and ordering facility, this site houses extra special attractions, such as "Fuzzy Logic Fun Facts" and a sound file of the "Fuzzy Logic Love Song."
✓**www**→http://www.book.uci.edu

/Books/Academic/index.html

Atomic Books—Literary Finds for Mutated Minds Calling all self-consciously twisted Gen-X'ers and aging downtown types! Atomic Books has made several Net top-ten lists for its potent combination of Web technology and bizarre subjects. Visitors can link to performance artist Annie Spinkle's collection of porn goddess playing cards (featured on an HBO *Real Sex* special), or to visit Lobster Boy, the online freak show gallery promoting a recent Atomic publication: James Taylor's *Shocked and Amazed*. They'll stay to take part in the cool monthly contests like "Net Lingo A-Go-Go" and to purchase adult comics, tattoo manuals, and the latest J. Edgar Hoover meets Shirley MacLaine conspiracy screed. There's even an Atomic BBS— with a Baltimore number— where

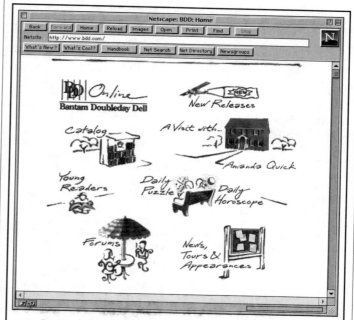

IN-SITE: **Bantam/Doubleday/Dell**
http://www.bdd.com

Pen and ink sketches signify Bantam's online offerings, and create an attractive artsy ambiance. The author-of-the-week feature pursues this literary focus by profiling writers and new works, linking related Websites, and offering email connections. Past features are archived for those who wish to go back and read about literary lights like Carolyn Heilbrun and John Grisham. Authors' publicity schedules are also included for serious fans who want to see their authors in the real world. Bantam seeks to foster an online literary community with a few forums, currently focusing on science fiction and business. Further fun comes in the form of a daily puzzle.

piercing aficionados can meet C.I.A. buffs.

✓**www**→http://www.atomicbooks .com

The Automated Pen What about the much touted notion that Cyberspace will be the death of the printed word? The Automated Pen solicits fiction from cyberwriters and sells it online, as well as providing tantalizing excerpts and many links to reading-related Websites.

✓**www**→http://www.quake.net /~autopen/autopen.html

Blackwell Publishers This famous academic publisher focuses its might on colorful online catalogs with long descriptions of every title. Blackwell sells its books online, but also provides an international list of retailers for those who prefer to shop in person.

✓**www**→http://www.bookshop.co .uk/blackwellpublishers

The Bob Book: A Celebration of the Ultimate Okay Guy One trick ponies aren't always busts—just ask the guy who invented the Pet Rock. But the guys who market *The Bob Book* (no, neither is named Bob) are playing this idea for all they can get. Consumers can email them to let them know which products they would like to see—a Bob mousepad, a Bob coffee mug, a Bob towel. They've even set up a Bob mailing list for Bobs and friends of Bobs. Who's on it? Bob Dylan, Bob Keeshan (Captain Kangaroo), and Bob Dole. If nothing else, *The Bob Book* stands as a perfect example of target marketing—can books for other popular names be far behind?

✓**www**→http://www.gigaplex .com/wow/books/bob/index.htm

Books That Work How-to

books conjure up images of uninspiring line drawings of drywalling and kitchens in avocado green. No longer. After a visit to this excellent, interactive site, everyone can feel as competent as Bob Villa. Much of Books That Work's material is on CD-ROM and the multimedia used on the Website is very effective as promotional material. Visitors sample the plant encyclopedia by choosing a type, color, blooming season, and available light, and 30 options in full color will bloom on the screen along with sound files for pronunciation assistant. Remodelers can wander through the 3-D kitchen with a free download of Shockwave. Then there are QuickTime movies of common home-repair problems like replacing a light socket. A cooperative program with *Popular Mechanics* lets customers search for new car reviews. And that's not all. A paint calculator provides exact gallon counts for the salmon gloss for the breakfast nook, and a kitchen counterspace program makes sure the microwave won't end up on top of the fridge. Best of all, these folks keep adding more all the time! Online assistance and a list of useful 800 numbers make customers feel cared for, and able to do it themselves, as long as Books That Work are at their side.

✓**www**→http://www.btw.com

The Bookstore at Houghton-Mifflin Houghton-Mifflin really has a handle on selling new technology. Two of a planned eight interactive pages demonstrating the charms of their CD-ROM titles are already operational. There kids can create goofy monsters that dance and blow bubbles, and aspiring Houdinis of all ages can pick up a few magic tricks. Each site also has an associated mailing list and encourages visitor involve-

ment in unique ways. An online discussion moderated by a real magician is a weekly event, and kids can upload their monster creation to an online archive where other tots who have the Monster CD can use their creations. Even the regular old textbooks published by HM are rendered more attractive to online readers through a number of moderated discussion groups, and links to related Websites and newsgroups. This is a state of the art site bound to make kids and adults long for a CD-ROM player and unlimited Net access.

✓**www**→http://www.hmnco.com /trade

Bookworks Bookworks is the online home of Warner Books and Little, Brown and Company. The site regularly runs author interviews and excerpts. It has also mastered the medium, offering live chats with favorite authors and frequently linking to related sites—the Mysterious Press Homepage, for instance, might link to the Sherlock Holmes Page.

✓**www**→http://pathfinder.com /twep/Library/Library.html

Bookzone Joining a group of small businesses is a good strategy for those who'd like to build a large innovative site, but can't do it alone. Bookzone offers small publishers the chance to electronically publish their catalogs, as well as creating an online publishing community for sharing resources and advice. There is a bulletin board for chat, links to many reading-related sites, and pointers to online bookshops. Bookzone also fosters industry interest by providing suggestions on how to promote a small press, on the Net and off.

✓**www**→http://ttx.com/bookzone /homepage.html

Britannica Online Britannica, the encyclopedia publisher, offers customers a free seven-day trial subscription (customers must register with a password) to the on-line version of the product, as well as a brief interactive demo of the encyclopedia's features.
✓**www**→http://www.eb.com

Grolier Electronic Publishing Grolier's interactive CDs are, unfortunately, only available in French for the time being. For now, this site does an interesting job presenting the joys of interactivity through several online crossword puzzles. But the true attraction of the site is its weekly live video sports show. People from all over the world log on to watch the week's highlights and chat with the pros, all in glorious movement and full color. In addition, "Link Madness" selects and reviews interesting Websites on a weekly basis, providing visitors a reason to return.
✓**www**→http://www.grolier.com

HarperCollins HarperCollins gathers together the catalogs of its many imprints here, presenting new titles, best-sellers, and press releases attractively. The publisher's smartest feature, however, is an online users survey, which collects consumer response on a variety of questions and then promises to tailor the Website to meet those needs.
✓**www**→http://www.harpercollins.com

Macmillan Information Superlibrary—Viacom Although a visitor to this site's need for an Internet Starter Kit (after all, they're already there) is questionable, Macmillan's commitment to the new mediium is admirable. In addition to the starter kit (downloads, advice, workshops), this site

IN-SITE: **IDG Books**
http://www.idg.com
Blam! Zowee! Pow! The colorful cartoon graphics here exude energy, and highlight the company's image as a hip techno/human connection. Every one of their popular tech titles is on sale here with free excerpts and hypertext links to related sites and information. The giveaways don't stop there—free downloads of everything from spreadsheets to "Kaboom" sounds go further in making computing with IDG fun. These guys are also intent on fostering a sense of security through online tech help for any computer-related problem. Email links to the authors of IDG how-to publications are also provided. IDG strives to go even further with chat events and an industry news service.

includes a good searchable computer reference desk, a learning lab for those who want to master the ins and outs of MUDs (a form of online gaming), an Internet guide, and loads of free software and shareware downloads. As for Macmillan's own publications, new offerings are excerpted and linked to related pages. Macmillan's staff is even accessible through an email link called "Talk to Us."
✓**www**→http://www.mcp.com

McGraw-Hill Publishing McGraw-Hill wisely chooses to lead with its Internet books catalog (the site also houses engineering, computers, business, and science texts). The wide array of titles is destined to make any Internet traveler consider dropping some cash.

✓**www**→http://www.bookshop.co.uk/mcgraw

Penguin U.K. The flightless waterfowl has done it—bringing literature to the people both through affordable paperbacks and through Cyberspace. In addition to listing thousands of classics, popular novels, and electronic texts, Penguin wants people to read. Each week the members of its online community can post their own reviews of talked-about tomes, with the best critic winning a free book. Other contests are subtly constructed, sending participants hunting for answers in the Website itself. It's a fun place to be, and if one learns the names of the three Brontë sisters along the way, all the better. (That's Charlotte, Anne, and Emily, in case you don't make it to the site.)

✓**www**→http://www.penguin.co.uk

Random House One of the largest book publishers in the world, Random House has also become a major presence online. Knopf, Del Rey, and House of Collectibles are using the Internet to advertise upcoming books, publicize book tours, distribute newsletters, and publish book excerpts. But more than that, Random House is putting Web technology to use by creating intriguing features that keep visitors clicking their way to new titles. Random House's online book promotions are often as good as movie trailers, and the house also reports on interesting publishing news. The site also includes a catalog search of their many imprints

and online book-ordering capability.

✓**www**→http://www.randomhouse.com

Routledge Online This is undoubtedly the only publishing site (nay, only site at all) online which features a Who's Who in Nazi Germany. Routledge's marketing staff has gone to great lengths to make their academic books interesting, and their Web page dynamic. Along with a complete catalog, visitors will find monthly featured titles (technoscience and "cross-gendered verse" two recent profiles). Routledge's online journal, *The Cultural Studies Times,* is well worth a peek. Knowing that lifelong academics are often low on funds, Routledge also offers sample journal copies and sample texts, thus endearing themselves to penniless (but curious) scholars everywhere.

✓**www**→http://www.thomson.com/routledge.html

Salon Salon is a hip online magazine and virtual, well, salon, where visitors can find everything from book and music reviews by well-known print journalists (even Joyce Carol Oates), monthly humor columns, interviews with big-name authors like Salman Rushdie, features by Camille Paglia on Hillary Clinton, and other cultural insights from the glitterati. Package this with games, trivia contests (with prizes) and lots of graphics, and you've got a winner. But what's unique about this online magazine? Well, it's teamed up with Borders Books and Music to invent a unique little book and music sale for each issue. Every book and CD referred to, and many works by featured authors, are available for immediate gratification online purchase—at a discount, no less!

✓**www**→http://www.salon1999.com

Wolff New Media Where can online newcomers get comprehensive coverage of the World Wide Web, Usenet groups, gophers, FTP sites, and bulletin boards, as well as all major commercial services? Detailed entries organized by subject? There's only one series (and Website) that fits the bill, and that's the NetBooks series published by Wolff New Media (formerly Michael Wolff & Company). To market the book series, the Net-Books team has chosen to do more than simply sample its product. In fact, it has published to the Web the full text of all its guidebooks—*NetGuide, NetGames, NetChat, NetMoney, NetTrek, NetSports, NetTech, NetMusic, NetTravel, NetTaxes, NetVote, NetJobs,* and even parts of *NetMarketing.* In addition, the company is developing a powerful Web presence that combines editorial know-how with new software applications; the Resume-O-Matic, for example, helps visitors create a resume and post it online.

✓**www**→http://www.ypn.com

W.W. Norton Norton's clean, easy-to-navigate Website features a different part of the publishing house each month—the college textbook publications, the fine art books, the New Directions poetry and literature paperbacks, and so on. In addition to showcasing its authors and most recent titles, the Website celebrates Norton's corporate history, concentrating on the fact that the company is the oldest employee-owned publishing house in the world. While there is not yet online ordering, Norton furnishes a toll-free number and downloadable order form.

✓**www**→http://www.wwnorton.com

Game companies

Few computer game companies have the budget to afford the kind of extensive (and ex-

pensive) advertising available offline to organizations accustomed to factoring significant adspending into their strategic planning. A Website, then, is often a gamemaker's strongest play, and there is perhaps no product better placed to exploit the Net as a marketing medium. The strategy used to promote game companies and software, in keeping with the nature of the product, generally focus on demos and multimedia presentations of products. **Sega Online** has tried to break the mold by offering live chat and a range of contests, but free demos still snag the most surfers. That the formidable success of **id Software**'s Doom is now an Internet legend proves that while "play before you pay" seems like a magnanimous gesture, it is also the surest way to get a gamehead hooked on your software.

On the Net

Across the board

3DO Home Page Give 'em more, more, more. 3DO's cluttered site quite clearly takes the approach that more is better. Potential customers are regaled in the hardware section with detailed info, demos, and pictures of the Interactive Multiplayer System and 3DO accessories. In the expansive software area, 3DO offers the entire 3DO catalog with a description and screenshots for each game. A handful of spotlighted games get press releases, behind the scenes info, contests, trivia, reviews, and more.

✓**www**→http://www.3do.com

Nintendo Some gaming companies have created huge Websites packed with content (magazines, discussion boards, etc.) and full of nooks and crannies that will take most Netheads half a dozen visits to fully explore. Nintendo has taken a very different approach. The fast, easily navigable Website keeps visitors focused on the product: the site features an extensive assortment of product information

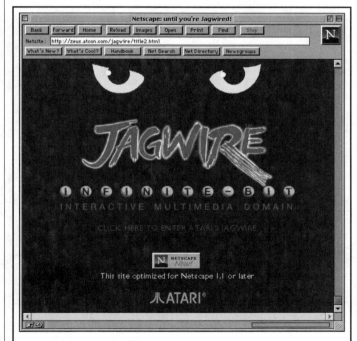

IN-SITE: **Atari Interactive/Jaguar**
http://www.atari.com

Atari may give top billing to its newest home-gaming system, Atari Interactive, on its Website's home page, but inside the site Atari goes all out promoting its highly popular Jaguar system. Atari not only sells Jaguar products online, it also does everything it can to engage potential buyers. The company gives away game demos and video clips, carries an extensive store of product information, and, to generate even more interest, maintains links to other Jaguar-related Internet sites. To keep customers aware of upcoming game releases, Atari maintains a mailing list that customers can sign onto at the Website.

and company news. For newly released games, Nintendo creates special spotlight pages with multimedia presentation, extensive overviews, and demos. The only digression Nintendo takes from its delivery of product information is its page of links to other gaming sites on the Internet.

✓**www**→http://www.nintendo.com

Sega Online Sega, a leader in the interactive gaming industry, couldn't exactly go online with a simple, low-key Website—and it didn't. The sophisticated Website holds live chat sessions for gamers, sponsors message boards to encourage customer feedback to game developers, runs contests, links to other gaming sites on the Net, and even maintains a place for gamers to upload their own add-ons and patches. And that's just the Sega Live! section—one of four sections on the Website. The others, all of which are highly interactive, include a product info area (Sega offers excellent multimedia presentations of dozens of hardware products and software games), a company info area, and a section devoted exclusively to Sega sports games. Moving some of its customer support services to the Web, Sega included a Customer Service Link which lets gamers email Sega with a question; Sega promises to try to email back a response within five days.

✓**www**→http://www.segaoa.com

Software companies

Bullfrog This British software company showcases its most popular new titles and upcoming releases with extensive hypertext game descriptions, lush screenshots, and demos. But Bullfrog mixes the sale orientation with a softer approach, and also offers gamers hints and tips, a walkthrough of one of its more complicated virtual environments, an interview with a Bullfrog designer, info on beta testing, and a contest where Netheads can win free software if they fill out the online survey. Pages can take a long time to download, however, and consumers may lose patience. Surfers may move on to other pages before Bullfrog has a chance to complete its pitch.

✓**www**→http://www.bullfrog.co.uk

Bungie Software Marathon and its successor are headlining at the Bungie Software site. The gaming company is drawing Marathon fans to the Website with long synopses of the storylines of popular games, screenshots, cheats, hints, patches, and demos, plus links to Webchat, fan pages, and FTP sites. What more could Bungie do to attract a crowd to its Web advertisement? The site even runs a contest that gives Marathoners the chance to win computer hardware.

✓**www**→http://www.bungie.com

Epic Megagames Epic's spread-

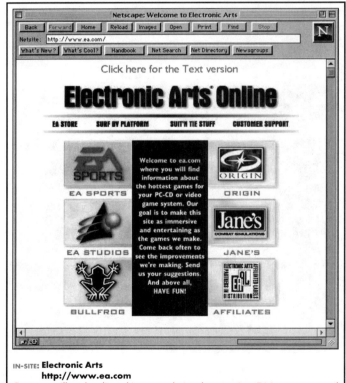

IN-SITE: **Electronic Arts**
http://www.ea.com
Customers will need to digest this mammoth site a byte at a time. EA is parent to several multimedia companies and software lines including EA Sports, EA Studios (film production), Origin, Jane's Combat Simulation, and the Bullfrog—all of which have a presence at this site. The gaming giant promotes its visually compelling games with screenshots, sound files, demos, contests, interviews with designers, technical specs, official guides and reviews, and links to other relevant Net sites. Electronic Arts also uses its Website to sell its products directly to consumers.

ing the word. The game developer wants everyone in Cyberspace to know where they can get the shareware versions of Epic's biggest games. For each big game, Epic links to several places on the Internet and lists sites on America Online, CompuServe, and the company's BBS where gamers can download them. Epic seems sure that if customers download the games, they'll be back to buy the commercial versions, and Epic's ready to take orders online. Epic, however, is giving away more than the games; it's offering gamers screenshots, game descriptions, lists of system requirements, press releases, FAQs, tech support, and links to other Internet gaming sites.

✓**www**→http://www.epicgames .com

GT Web The makers of Doom and Mortal Kombat 3 take the requisite home page features and kick them into overdrive. The site offers not just screenshots, but QuickTime clips of its games; not just synopses, but links to forums, FAQs, and FTP sites; not just online ordering, but online delivery of games; not just tech support, but interactive tech support and shareware; and not just a company bio, but an extensive company profile with personal email addresses for management. To keep in touch with its customers, GT Interactive Software offers customers the opportunity to sign up for its Web-Flash bulletins, which notify customers by email when new products become available or developments occur with popular games.

✓**www**→http://www.gtinteractive .com

I-Motion I-Motion uses film imaging to create hyperrealistic live-action games starring actors

IN-SITE: Psygnosis Online (Sony Interactive)
http://www.sepc.sony.com/SEPC/Psygnosis/sisdex.htm
In-your-face graphics draw surfers in, and Psygnosis—a European software publisher owned by Sony—expects the pre-loaded (no waiting!) game demos to hook them. Customers are encouraged to try the demos—travel in a man's head to distant lands in search of a lost soul, virtually smash a car to bits with various tools, explore a 3D cyberworld with a VRML browser. The site also features information about upcoming and current releases, carries a company bio, and offers software support.

IN-SITE: Viacom New Media
http://www.viacomnewmedia.com

Viacom is heavily involved in film and television, and its software line reaps the benefits. *Congo, Deep Space Nine*, and *Beavis & Butt-Head* are hot properties with audiences captured by their TV and movie equivalents. Offering more than the usual multimedia grab bag, the company makes sure every game gets different, but equally intense treatment, including walkthroughs of virtual worlds, screenshots, sound clips, QuickTime movies, demos, hypertext overviews, press releases, and bulletin boards. Viacom also offers gaming news, a company profile, a search engine, and tech support on its site.

that would otherwise have ended up on *Fantasy Island* or *The Love Boat*. On its Website, I-Motion offers customers basic synopses and screenshots to give them a taste of the product. Hints and rotating contests keep gamers coming back.
✓**www**→http://www.swcp.com /~coach/i-motion

id Software How does a company get its game on almost every PC in the known universe? It creates texture-mapped, animated, morphed, open-architecture shoot-em-up games like Doom and Heretic, and then uses the Net to give away the first few, fully functioning levels of the games. As id suspected, the games were addictive. Gamers wanted more, and they were willing to pay for it. Not a bad strategy.
✓**www**→http://www.idsoftware .com

MacPlay Demos, demos, demos! MacPlay has produced some of the most successful Mac games on the market, from Descent to Monopoly. The gaming company is trying to engage consumers by leaving demos for them to download on its Website. The site has a dozen other features—coming attractions, company and designer bios, sales and ordering services, press releases, tech support, gaming links, online registration, Web navigation help, job opportunities, a message board, a fantastic gaming 'zine, and even a random generator that leads Netsurfers to an arbitrary MacPlay link—but it's the demos that drive the company's marketing effort online.
✓**www**→http://www.macplay.com

Rocket Scientist Rocket Scientist—the maker of award-winning live-action games—has produced a fantastic Website that manages to excite but not smother the consumer. The incredible graphics are the icing on the cake for this site which delivers stills, movies, tips and hints, behind the scenes info, demos, cheats, and tech support for its products. Weekly contests add to the excitement.
✓**www**→http://www.rocketsci.com

Spectrum Holobyte Spectrum Holobyte leads with a live chat area and a bulletin board and follows up with a company bio, press releases, and gaming news. But the real draws here are the games which Spectrum Holobyte promotes with huge screenshots, hypertext overviews, synopses, and, in some cases, video clips, demos, press releases, FAQs, and contests. With all this and links to affiliate companies like Domark, Inverse Ink, Animatek, and PositronicBio, Spectrum Holobyte wants gamers to flit around its virtual universe for a while, stopping occasionally, perhaps, to make a purchase.
✓**www**→http://www.holobyte.com

Sports business

The baseball strike, high ticket prices, migrating franchises...pro sports teams have

had to hustle to win back disillusioned fans and their entertainment dollars. On-line, the strategy is simple—call in your stars. The **Seattle Mariners** have created a Web page devoted to super-star Ken Griffey, Jr., and the Mariners and other teams are also trying to whip up fan enthusiasm by linking their pages to fan-chat newsgroups. The **National Basketball Association**'s site, packed with live chat, video clips, expert basketball columns, and an astounding 400+ player home pages. The **Professional Golfers Association Online**'s home has a less exuberant feel, as befits the sport's nature. There's an online clubhouse for pro golfers and their deeply reverent fans that provides chat sessions and expert advice. Simply, a hole in one.

On the Net

Auto racing

Indy Racing League—Official Home Page Looking to mend a schism within the sport's ranks, this page offers itself as a service to the auto racing community and a news source for professional journalists. An archive of press releases

details the happenings of this league, while pages entitled "Fiction and Fact," "Fact Sheet," and "Q&A" further clarify its mission. In the near future, the page plans to bring fans complete statistical coverage of races.
✓**www**→http://www.brickyard.com/irl

Baseball

Major League Baseball: @Bat
This baseball site is overseen and operated by InternetMCI, and de-livered with the fan's daily bread of scores, schedules, stats, and standings. Users are only one click away from MCI's daily news feeds, a

high-powered search engine, and the brand-name stores within MarketplaceMCI.
✓**www**→http://www2.pcy.mci.net/mlb/index.html

Seattle Mariners Home Plate
The Mariners team, baseball's Cinderella story during the strike-addled 1995 season, has developed one of the game's most marketable commodities. This official site capitalizes on the Mariners' suc-cess, providing fans and media with access to a wide array of products and services. Superstar Ken Griffey, Jr. has both his own home page and an official fan club page. The innovative Kingdome

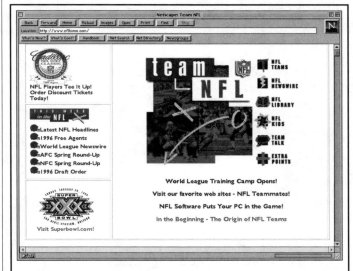

IN-SITE: **National Football League**
http://www.nflhome.com
Within the entries for each of the league's 30 teams is a "Hometown Huddle" page, which provides a collection of links to official organization home pages, local media, and city guides. A "Team Talk" area gives fans the option of subscribing to team mailing lists, chatting live with other fans, or posting messages to the NFL Chalkboard—card collectors even have their own section.

Seating Viewer lets ticket buyers sample their seats via a clickable map (although a phone call is required for actual purchase). One page summarizes the team's community service efforts, another brings users a QuickTime movie preview of the team's new stadium, and yet another links them to alt.sports.baseball.sea-mariners, where they can spread the Mariners gospel over Usenet.
✓**www**→http://www.mariners.org

Basketball

1996 Southeastern Conference Men's Basketball Tournament This Web-savvy NCAA basketball conference not only has its own page (at http://www.sec.org) but also has a dazzling multimedia site devoted to its post season tournament. High-profile sponsors get the high-tech treatment, with animated buttons that scroll through corporate logos every few seconds. A special sponsor page features graphic links to company Websites. And finally, a high-resolution map of New Orleans (the tournament site) accompanies restaurant, hotel, and transportation info, with additional links to weather services.
✓**www**→http://www.secevent.com

National Basketball Association Long the most successfully marketed professional sports league, it's no surprise to find that the NBA's official Website is of championship caliber. Maximum content, from last night's scores to home pages for every player (almost 400 in all!), to ticket, stadi-um, and TV schedules for every team, assures this site a spot on any fan's bookmark list. Weekly live chat with stars, online All-Star voting, and audio and video clips make the site highly interactive. The league's gala All-Star weekend draws in high-profile sponsors, while Schick's "Rookie Report" tracks the next generation of Jordans and Shaqs.
✓**www**→http://www.nba.com

Football

Superbowl.com This splashy multimedia site added a new twist to the most heavily marketed (and widely viewed) yearly sporting event. In addition to a wealth of content about the game's history, the co-sponsors of the 1996 Superbowl, NBC and Microsoft, promoted their high-profile products: NBC's 1996 Olympic coverage, and Microsoft's Windows 95 and Internet Explorer.
✓**www**→http://www.superbowl.com

Tostitos Fiesta Bowl In an era when college football's national championship game is itself a corporate advertisement, it's fitting that the game's Website devotes plenty of space to sponsor Frito Lay's product line. Users can download recipes to fuel their big game experience, sample Chester Cheetah's bookmarks, participate in product giveaways, or check out career opportunities with the snack-food giant.
✓**www**→http://www.fiestabowlxxv.com

Golf

The 1995 Masters Tournament The Website for golf's most storied tournament remains relevant year-round, providing up-to-date golf news from high-profile

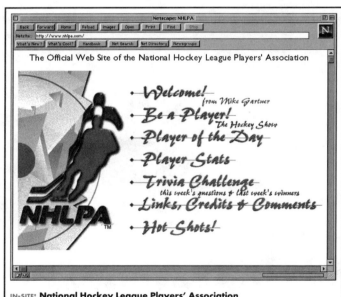

IN-SITE: **National Hockey League Players' Association**
http://www.nhlpa.com
Spotlighting players both past and present, this highly interactive site was designed to appeal to the full spectrum of hockey followers, from casual fans to the corporate community. A press release archive keeps journalists current on the league's labor happenings. A tough trivia challenge yields prizes for the studious. And a downloadable multimedia schedule lets users check the daily skate slate at their own convenience.

sponsors *The Augusta Chronicle* and *Sports Illustrated*, as well as comprehensive listings of local hotels, restaurants, golf courses, and related shops. The *Chronicle* emphasizes its historical tie-in with the Masters by archiving post-tournament lead stories back to the 1934 inaugural.
✓**www**→http://www.masters96.com

Professional Golfers Association Online This Website serves as a communications hub for members of the association, which is "dedicated to nurturing and maintaining the quality of the game for the 25 million golfers nationwide." Non-members can cull info about the PGA's rigorous 3-year qualifying program, read about the organization's extensive grassroots efforts, or use the local search engine to comb PGA publications.
✓**www**→http://www.pgaonline.com

Olympics

1996 Centennial Olympic Games Home Page Counting down the days to the 1996 Summer Games in Atlanta, this site—which went online almost a year before the torch was lit—keeps visitors abreast of the latest Olympic developments, with an emphasis on those athletes who will journey to the mecca of sport and sportsmanship. Potential spectators can search for available tickets, download a ticket request form, and then link to WorldTravel Partners' Olympic Games Travel Network, a one-stop lodging and transportation service. All, in all, a gold-medal performance in the marketing Olympics.
✓**www**→http://www.atlanta.olympic.org

IN-SITE: Sprint US Ski Team Stop
http://www.imworks.com/sprintsports/ski
This informative site spotlight's Sprint's sponsorship of the U.S. Ski Team, the U.S. Snowboard Team, and several ski events. The Ski Poll lets users vote on their favorite U.S. team member, with a chance to win a collectible calling card.

The Games of the XXIV Olympiad NBC Sports' Olympic site trumpets the record-breaking amount of exclusive coverage the network is slated to offer (168.5 hours, "estimated to be seen by 9 out of 10 Americans"!). Targeted at the home viewer, this site steers clear of logistics and instead promotes the pomp and pageantry of the Games with coverage of the cross-country Olympic Torch Relay, a multimedia "A Day in the Life of an Olympic Hopeful" page, and an Athlete of the Week profile, which leans towards established stars.
✓**www**→http://www.olympic.nbc.com

Soccer

Fédération Internationale de Football Association Staying abreast of the latest soccer developments worldwide is no small task. At this site, the governing body of the world's most popular sport—which represents almost 200 national associations—offers an extensive library of media releases, newsletters, and magazines. Frequent updates on World Cup and Olympic qualifying are provided, while a hypertext FIFA handbook lays down the "Laws of the Game."
✓**www**→http://www.fifa.com

Tennis

IBM at Wimbledon This site showcases the IBM technology used to cover the tennis tournament. Whether it's courtside data entry, a commentators application, television captions and graphics, or the server and network that bring the information to the Internet, IBM products are the focus.
✓**www**→http://www.ibm.com/Features/Wimbledon

Chapter 8

High-Tech

Telecommunications

One would have to be a media-free ascetic not to have been aware of the battle of the

telecommunications giants over the past few years. With recent legislation, even more competitive activity is likely—and much of it will take place on the Web, as companies scramble to provide consumers with the flashiest, most entertaining, and most sophisticated Websites. **NYNEX**, both online and on television, positions itself as the vanguard of the revolution, packing its site with visions of a thrilling high-tech future. **AT&T** stresses that it provides solutions for a wide range of markets: "At Home, At Work, Around the Globe & On the Net." **Sprint** has also mastered the medium, creating a quartet of virtual worlds for exploring the joys of the Internet. Can a telecommunications company's site be eye-catching and fun? See for yourself.

On the Net

AT&T AT&T is a leader in communications technology the world over, so it only follows that the company would arrive online with a sophisticated and Net-savvy site that does almost everything a corporate site should do. From the opening page, which serves as an introduction to both business-to-business and consumer services, AT&T positions itself as a communications company capable of meeting a wide variety of needs. Visitors can view online demonstrations of products, read FAQs, link to sites across the Web, download business-themed games in the edutainment center, or learn about AT&T's active sponsorship of cultural and educational activities.

Marketers should pay special attention to the telecommuting section, which speculates how the offices of the near future might work—and how they might work better with AT&T. Not planning on staying awhile at the site? You will.

✓**www**→http://www.att.com

Bell Atlantic The telecommunications giant of the D.C. area

IN-SITE: **Sprint**
   http://www.sprint.com

How does a telecommunications company make sure it reaches out to all its constituencies? Well, if that company is Sprint, it creates four distinct online areas. Sprint Stop brings a 1950's nostalgia to the information superhighway with a cute Gas Station attendant guide, a Cyberdiner for Net chatting and netiquette tips, a Sports Stop, rec room of games, and an excellent highway guide packed with fun links and surfing advice. A filing cabinet holds business-related offerings—from travel links to stock quotes to online classified ads—made manageable through an excellent search function. There is so much here that Sprint"s "Fridays are Free" for business-customers promotion goes almost unnoticed. Druper's House is directed at college students, offering goofy advice from an ex-hippie, college links, and, of course, phone cards to call home for more money. Sprint City resembles a neo-Gotham cartoon world where government links can be found on Main Street, and teen music hangouts in Cyburbia. There are also excellent online Yellow Pages, and plenty of soundfiles from Candice Bergen, famous not only for playing Murphy Brown but also for being "the dime lady."

starts its customers off in a cozy library room. Visitors can then click on sections of the room tagged with such broad labels as business, information center, and technology for information about the company's products. The site's only concession to its non-business customers is its searchable yellow pages for the D.C., Baltimore, and Maryland areas.
✓**www**→http://www.bell-atl.com

British Telecommunications
The days of red callboxes and "pip-pip" phones seem far in the past after a visit to this corporate home. British Telecom places great emphasis on its technological achievement with a link to its laboratories, online technical journals, and networking resources for telecommunications professionals worldwide. A highlight of the site is the Global Challenge, a round-the-world sailing race tracked by satellite technology followed and wave by wave on the Web. BT also targets the specific communities with a cheerful "bargain hunting" guide for online businesses, a beta testing program of new computer games for consumers, and a disability resources guide.
✓**www**→http://www.bt.net

GTE GTE reinforces its corporate identity with a site that is essentially an online annual report. Stockholders and big business network planners are likely to appreciate this approach, which goes heavy on statistics, figures, and an objective presentation of telecommunications options. Evolutions is the one section that should appeal to more general consumers, providing easily understandable articles on the "new" technology and a number of fun links to introduce Net surfing and even Web design.
✓**www**→http://www.gte.com/Home

IBM Telecommunications and Media International Business Machines divides its extensive services into separate sites—this page offers descriptions of its telecommunications services and technology ranging from online consulting to a definition of wirelines. BM has also placed a good examination of the new Telecommunications Act online and offers an email update service aimed at the technology professional that reports on industry developments. The Media offerings are a bit more flashy and less starkly utilitarian, portraying all the good that IBM is doing through its Digital Library—one month, for example, highlights of the Vatican Library might be shown in all their glory.
✓**www**→http://webster.ibmlink.ibm.com:80/telmedia

MCI Telecommunications, Inc.
MCI is intent on selling its Net service by displaying the charms, and uses, of modern technology. So what's on display? MCI shows visitors how to use a Skytel pager and invites them to visit an MCI-sponsored online mall to purchase laser printers or boxer shorts. There are also explanations of MCI's services for home and office, with emphasis on their affordability. Another constant theme of the site is the uncharted fabulous future of online business; news briefs keep visitors hip to Net news, from online giveaways to MCI's spamming policy. This site is clearly directed at a Net audience, and works harder on selling MCI's Net access than MCI's phone service.
✓**www**→http://www.mci.com

NYNEX Connection NYNEX's television campaign places the company in the forefront of the brave new world of telecommunications, and its Website continues the theme. Wired Words serves up high-tech articles and interviews, and the Digital Datebook holds the names and locations of cyberevents worldwide. Even though this feature thinks globally, NYNEX also emphasizes its local nature with brief but useful and searchable guides to New York and New England travel and tourism, and its local loan programs for small-business users. The NYNEX Internet Yellow Pages cleverly merge basic business information with Net resources. For example, a search for the famous Pink Adobe restaurant in Santa Fe, New Mexico not only yields the name and address of the establishment, but links to online restaurant reviews, the Chili Heads hot cooking page, and more. And familiar TV spokeswoman Mary Alice Williams is an everpresent search-engine icon on the site, offering guidance for those Netsurfers who have lost their way.
✓**www**→http://www.nynex.com

Southwestern Bell Filled with animated graphics of international flags, friendly operators, and people of all ages and races talking to each other on the phone, Southwestern Bell's site positions the utility as a friendly company with an interest in its customers. At the site, SBC offers detailed overviews of each of its service, from Cable Television to Messaging to Interactive Video, as well as financial/investor information, press releases and telecommunications news. Special online features include an electronic form that lets customers request a second phone line, and a page showcasing SBC's PC Phone Manager—a special feature that allows customers to make phone calls from a virtual phone on their computer!
✓**www**→http://ww.sbc.com

The online world

If you are in the business of providing an online service you had better have a terrific

Website—but you had also better make sure that you give customers a good reason to pay for your services. Otherwise your company will become yet another struggling access provider fighting for market share in an increasingly crowded industry. **America Online** attracts visitors with an extensive excursion through the Web which segues into a tour of its own offerings. **CompuServe** provides an extensive preview of its proprietary content, and makes signing up easy with a quick download of the connection software. Internet providers, on the other hand, are selling the rather vague notion of "access." **BBN Planet** focuses on the corporate market, detailing state-of-the-art security measures, while **Earthlink** appeals to the individual user, suggesting that those who remain unwired are left out of the excitement.

On the Net

Commercial services

America Online AOL spends as much time selling the idea of the Web (it even offers its customers tours) as it does enticing visitors to

subscribe to its popular online service. From special features on member home pages and charitable organizations to hundreds of categorized Weblinks, AOL highlights the Web branch of its services by providing a great resource for surfers. But while the meat of the site is Internet-related, AOL makes it clear that the Web is only the tip of the glacier that is its vast online service. Visitors can get a glimpse of AOL-only services by taking an online tour from the Website. Clicking on a mockup of the AOL "Welcome Page" retrieves descriptions of categories

and spotlights services and areas such as Parental Control and Tower Records. Visitors can also download the necessary software from this Website and use their ten free hours to experience the service first-hand.

✓**www**→http://www.aol.com

GEnie GEnie's online site wants visitors to have a good time exploring the Web. To that end, it offers an interesting collection of with their hotlinks and the Fingertip Guide to the Internet. But GEnie also want to get its visitors to subscribe to its commercial ser-

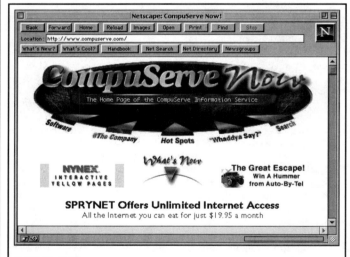

IN-SITE: CompuServe
   http://www.compuserve.com
CompuServe's Website does more than just give Netsurfers a taste of its online services—it gives them a full seven-course meal with all the trimmings. The home page contains more than a dozen CompuServe "headlines" that highlight the service's entertainment, sports, news, and business offerings; other areas of the site spotlight corporate history, a search engine (Web and CompuServe both), and an online poll on current topics that returns its results immediately. In addition, CompuServe has used the Web to display its content, not only linking to the CompuServe Usenet newsgroup, but also recreating certain forums on the Web—most notably the Software Forum, which includes subscription software for new CompuServants.

vice, and the company does this in three ways—by answering direct questions through email, by providing links to a gopher that outlines everything from front-end navigation software to RoundTables and services, and by giving Netsurfers a taste of GEnie by providing samples of RoundTable transcripts and GEnie magazines previously available to subscribers only.
✓**www**→http://www.genie.com

Prodigy Prodigy's Website is short on graphics, but long on corporate identity, positioning the venerable online network as a place where Net newcomers can do their one-stop shopping. But rather than point outward towards the Web, Prodigy's site points in-ward, toward the service itself. The Website offers a brief review of Prodigy's contents ("Glide and Go Seek"), press testimonials (including one from Howard Stern), a tech support line for bewildered Prodigy users, and a history of the company. Prodigy's Web-only product, Prodigy.Net, is buried in the site, but committed visitors can find it. And there's even a ten-free-hours offer that lets Windows users download their start-up software from the Web.
✓**www**→http://www.prodigy.com

Internet providers

AT&T WorldNet Announced in February 1996, WorldNet is likely to change the face of the online-access-provider industry. By offer-ing special Internet-access rates (including five hours free per month) to its 90 million long-distance customers, AT&T made its mark. As *NetMarketing* goes to press, AT&T expects to give WorldNet subscribers a free version of the Netscape Web browser branded with AT&T's logo, link to a large database of Website reviews, and even offer a complete Internet content guide for online newcomers.
✓**www**→http://www.att.com /worldnet/wis

BBN Planet Security comes first at BBN Planet. Because corporate Internet accounts are vulnerable to information sabotage, BBN's Website stresses the airtight security of its Internet access. It even goes so far as to illustrate its Firewall Technique (literally, with an easy-to-follow graphic), a system devised to keep company information top secret. BBN also details its services and rates.
✓**www**→http://www.bbnplanet .com

Concentric Network Concentric Network, an Internet provider, has devised a unique way to distinguish itself from the thousands of other companies on the Net. They will award $5,000 to a lucky new subscriber—just for making a home page! Aside from the possibility of winning, Concentric's Website offers hook-up service within the hour and access to its private Internet search engine.
✓**www**→http://www.cris.com

Earthlink Earthlink's Website proves there is a place for everybody on the Information Superhighway, making its Website seem more like a commercial for the World Wide Web than for an Internet service provider. With links to newsgroups, tutorials, and cre-

IN-SITE: **Microsoft**
http://www.msn.com
The 1950's Winnebago on the front door of Microsoft's Website is there to comfort the not-so-cybersavvy as they take their first voyage into Cyberspace, and to position Microsoft as a reliable and friendly guide to the riches of the online world. Essentially an advertisement for Microsoft Net, the Website is most useful for Windows 95 users, who can sample the bulk of the services, which include regularly updated news and forums.

ative lifestyle sites (like the Indian Marriage Center), Earthlink has gone out of its way to show the expansive nature of the Net. The Website links to some of the best and the brightest sites on the Web, giving the potential customer a taste of what the Internet has to offer and indirectly marketing itself as well.

✓**www**→http://www.earthlink.net

IBM Internet Connection IBM will hold your hand in Cyberspace! Its Website is designed as a help tool for new users, with links to handpicked sites covering business, shopping, news, sports, etc. The site even goes so far as to create an Internet Schoolhouse, where such subjects as modems, HTML codes, and megabytes are explained. Dial-up service is also described on the IBM Internet Connection site.

✓**www**→http://www.ibm.net

Internet MCIaccess MCI's internet-provider division relies on an easy-to-navigate Website and a wealth of technical information to convince consumers that the telecommunications company is their best bet for getting (or staying) online.

✓**www**→http://www.mci.com/for net/access/indexacc.shtml

Netcom Netcom opens its site with the innocent question, "Why choose Netcom?," and then amply answers with a number of reasons: low rates, unlimited weekend access, free software, and nationwide local access numbers, to name a few. "Club Netcom," effectively a sample of all the good things users get if they sign up, is the key tool in this strategy. Among membership benefits are up-to-date news articles from Reuters, Web tech support, and a search engine. For added convenience, Netcom pro-

IN-SITE: **Pipeline**
http://www.usa.pipeline.com
Pipeline, like other Internet service providers, posts a healthy list of links to incite those who resist the online world in the "not-so-convinced about this computer junk" position. The site links to national museums, NPR, sports leagues, MTV, and even SeniorCom (hoping to tap a new demographic?). Aside from providing a general idea of what's on the Internet, Pipeline's Website includes start-up fees, rates, and software—everything the beginner will need.

vides a clickable map of the U.S., so potential Netheads can find the phone number of their closest provider's office.

✓**www**→http://www.netcom.com

Walrus With an enigmatic URL and a wonderful opening graphic of a flying pig, Walrus introduces customers to the Internet in style, with detailed product descriptions and links to some of the best sites across the Net.

✓**www**→http://www.walrus.com

The World @ Software Tool & Die The World, the Internet access service from Software Tool &

Die, introduces itself as one of the oldest and largest providers available—and does it live up to such credentials? Well, despite the bold selling point, frankly, it's hard to say. The site has so deeply buried samples of its services that the average Netsurfer will be unlikely to find them without extraordinary persistence. The site showcases some of The World's membership benefits, including the World Kiosk, a general directory of companies with World accounts; and Govline; a database of Congressional transcripts.

✓**www**→http://world.std.com

Computer hardware

Computer companies have an edge in the Internet selling market, but they also face

greater competition than any other industry. Companies must strive to show with ever more exciting sites that they have command of the technology, and cater to an audience of both techies and beginners. **IBM**'s home page is a good example of this dual presentation, offering silver platter service to the business and programming community and user groups and providing tech support for lone PC owners. **Apple**'s creation of a complete virtual world is a great strategy; in this world, where mice and icons replace buildings and bridges, users explore and have access to a virtual support group for discussing Apple-related issues. And **Silicon Graphics** sells consumers on the prospect of an entire virtual experience, loading its Website with so many technological thrills that it makes the prospect of living without SGI technology unthinkable.

On the Net

Platforms

IBM "Oy, more hardware?" The digital download of IBM's latest

"Solutions for a Small Planet" TV ad, which features Yiddish subtitles, is one of this immense Website's highlights. The site's focus throughout is squarely on Big Blue and its corporate customers, starting with a hefty dose of IBM-related business news and moving on to features about its new "network-centric" products. The "Industry Solutions" section offers a directory of sector-specific consultants and their information technology recommendations, as well as links to IBM business customers within the field. Browsable hardware and software catalogs detail the full IBM product line, from mainframes to laptops, and let customers prepare an order. The site's support area covers the product line and links to user groups and IBM publications. For a break from the biz-talk, the "Stretch" area invites visitors to solve puzzles at the Electric Origami shop.

✓**www**→http://www.ibm.com

IN-SITE: **Apple Computer**
http://www.apple.com

More than just a simple choice of platforms or products, Apple presents users with an alternative way of life and provides a Website to promote that alternative. Its employees have created the Always Apple site to give loyal customers a place to communicate more openly with Apple, and to debunk the rumors that swirl around the company. The Apple Website itself contains plentiful links to the company's hardware and software divisions, with specialized areas for developers, business, and education users. The site is strongly focused on Apple's latest technology innovations like QuickTime VR and OpenDoc. There are links to just about all the resources a user could expect, from product intros to authorized service providers to Apple-specific newsgroups and mailing lists. And the Tech Info Library contains a searchable database of over 5,000 articles for the answers to all things Apple.

Power This manufacturer of Macintosh clones greets its online visitors with the favorable ratings its products have garnered from industry trade publications. Those still not convinced can check the site's veritable library of press reviews and customer testimonials. Since one of the clone's main selling points is the variety of configurations offered, Power provides customers with an "Online Configurator." Potential customers fill out a form—which takes into account everything from RAM size to expansion slots to warranty plans—and receive a price quote and a phone number for ordering. The site cultivates a high degree of customer feedback, from online computer registration and customer satisfaction surveys to future product wish lists. There's also plenty of online tech support, and any visitor who signs the guest book is eligible to win a free computer.
✓**www**→http://www.powercc.com

Silicon Graphics This high-end graphics company operates in a different dimension than most computer users—the third dimension, that is. Laypeople can salivate as they read the site's feature on VRML, the coming standard for 3-D Web design, but it's Silicon Graphics workstation users and developers who will get the most mileage—and fun—out of this spot. The site features a comprehensive guide to third-party software for SG workstations and servers, "extreme tech" support, and downloads for registered users. But the real spotlight is on the Surf Zone, where those with the IRIX operating system (they get all the fun) can download WebSpace Navigator, the 3-D browser for the World Wide Web, and begin charting a new dimension. The rest of us can download *Surf Zone: The Movie*, and dream....
✓**www**→http://www.sgi.com

Peripherals

Global Village Global Village Communication's colorful and homey Website is called The Village; not surprisingly, it's also organized in that way. The Visitor's Center offers company background and a chance to sign the Guest Book, while the Newsstand delivers an archive of press releases and investor information. The Solution Center is the customer-oriented heart of the site. It houses the product catalog and tech support facilities; customers can get detailed specs and a retail price list for the company's fax/modems, servers, and software. Also within the Solution Center is "The Business User's Guide to the Internet," a lengthy, well-organized primer. The Internet Depot links to search engines, shareware sites, and several business and pleasure spots, and offers a "Day on the Internet" tour, which walks browsers through tasks like checking the stock market, researching a vendor, hiring a graphic designer, and sending birthday flowers.
✓**www**→http://www.globalcenter.com

Hewlett-Packard Although it manufactures and supports everything from calculators to chemical analysis equipment, Hewlett-Packard reserves plenty of Web space for its computers and components. Its Peripherals Directory features an easy-to-use graphic menu, and the "Helping You Choose" section lets customers fill out a brief product requirements form and receive a table which lets them compare HP product specs and relative prices. Users can also call up product info on HP's PCs, servers, and storage devices, and browse the HP SupportLine for a directory of technical and training services. On the lighter side is the playful Computer Graphics FUNdamentals section, which instructs users to "plant tongue firmly in cheek" as they link to cartoon illustrations that define graphics terms.
✓**www**→http://www.hp.com

Iomega Iomega uses its Website to promote and support its popular removable-media portable storage devices. The detailed product descriptions plant storage-related ideas in the minds of potential customers ("Use one Jaz disk to...save over eight hours of CD-quality sound...") while running down the specifics. The technical support area provides installation FAQs, troubleshooting guides, and accessory price lists. Drivers and utility packages for Iomega products are available via free downloads, and a checklist helps customers prepare fax orders.
✓**www**→http://www.iomega.com

MicroSpeed, Inc. "It all starts with input" reads the slogan here. For work or pleasure, MicroSpeed has the input device—keyboard, mouse, trackball, or joystick—and the Website to deliver it. The site offers detailed intros to its new products; several screenshots illustrate the set-up options for its task-saving WINtelligent Keyboard. Customers can order the peripherals online (or print out a form for fax/mail orders), register their MicroSpeed products, and download driver updates and joystick tests. The site's fun page links to clnet's Virtual Software Library, shopping sites, and JobNet. Visitors should check out the animated clip.
✓**www**→http://www.microspeed.com

Computer software

A surplus of software? There's certainly a lot of it, so much of it that manufacturers

must struggle to make their code stand out from the rest. **Netscape** and **Macromedia** rely on their technical expertise to impress visitors, **Lotus** provides a LotusNotes test drive at its site, and **Quark, Inc.** is confidently direct, asking and answering the basic question "Why should I use QuarkXPress?" **Adobe Systems** employs an interesting variation on these themes, linking visitors to elegant Websites created with its software. And **Intuit—The Quicken Financial Network** chooses not to build on its technology, but rather to appeal to its constituency, providing a wealth of general financial information that reinforces the need for its money-managing programs. Most pervasive, though, and most effective, is the strategy of giving away samples or demos.

On the Net

Business

Claris Claris uses its Website to demonstrate its high-profile products—one promo lets site visitors send Cybervalentines to their loved ones, storing the letters in FileMaker Pro and informing recipients via Claris Emailer. The company's popular products get their own home pages, with downloadable demos in some cases. Elsewhere on the site, Claris lets customers download templates and collect software updates, as well as detailing several technical support options, such as the site's searchable TechInfo database, FAQs, and a CD-ROM with articles on the latest products.
✓**www**→http://www.claris.com

Finance

Intuit—The Quicken Financial

Network Intuit's Website isn't just named after its flagship personal finance software—its Quicken Financial Network provides users with a gateway to a wealth of financial tools, as well as supporting Intuit's product line. In addition to detailed Quicken tips, the site posts informative articles such as "Avoiding Debt Hangover" and a "Portfolio of the Month" profile, which explain how customers can improve their money management. The site's Financial Directory provides links to free online stock quotes and financial institu-

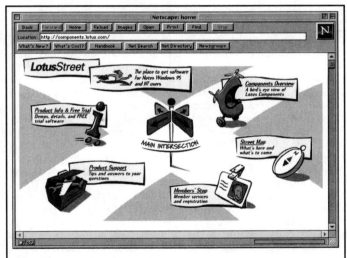

IN-SITE: **Lotus**
  http://www.lotus.com
Lotus devotes the bulk of its site to promoting the latest version of its workgroup software Lotus Notes. The site announces forthcoming features like the Lotus Notes:Newsstand (which brings industry and trade publications such as "Phillips Multimedia Week" to the Web), offers free trials of Notes Components at an area called Lotus Street, and links to Notes@Work, a site devoted to the business culture surrounding the product. Updates and enhancements of the full Lotus line are available via the Lotus Selects Catalog. The International Informational Kiosk combines store location resources with an index of products by language (for those who need 1-2-3 in Arabic). Multimedia coverage of the Lotusphere '96 convention is on-site, and links to new parent company IBM (including automatic stock updates) are also provided.

tions which provide special services to Quicken users. At the Product Marketplace customers can buy the software online—those still not convinced can check the testimonials from critics and real users.
✓**www**→http://www.intuit.com

TurboTax Online Intuit's highly successful tax program may make preparing taxes easier, but the Website tries to make tax time a little more fun. A Fun On the Net section links customers to sites they might want to explore when they "want to avoid even thinking about taxes." Intuit also uses the Website to deliver a wide range of tax tips and technical support.
✓**www**→http://www.intuit.com/turbotax

Graphics

Adobe Systems The underlying theme of Adobe's Website is demonstrating its Acrobat software, a publishing tool available for free at the site (all site contents are available both in online HTML format and as downloadable Acrobat Personal Document Format [PDF] files). The site's content, in addition to detailing its products and online customer service info, focuses on how customers use Adobe software. The Customer Spotlight area provides visitors with links to Websites built with its products, while the Tips & Techniques page offers users helpful hints for applications such as PageMaker, Illustrator, and Photoshop. Adobe even provides links to product-related newsgroups and mailing lists, so customers can compare notes.
✓**www**→http://www.adobe.com

Corel Windows-oriented software companies must support a wide range of user capabilities and con-

figurations (don't even mention operating systems!). Corel uses its large Website to stay on top of things by selling and supporting several versions of its programs (e.g., CorelDRAW 6, 5, 4, 3; and 3 for UNIX) at once. Along with detailing its product line, the site offers several tech-support FAQs and tip sheets. The site also links to Corel-sponsored sites (such as the Women's Tennis Association site and the Internet 1996 World Expo) and CorelNet, the independent online site for Corel users. The ever-expanding company's corporate doings, such as its recent acquisition of WordPerfect, are also spotlighted.
✓**www**→http://www.corel.ca

Quark, Inc. Quark's elegant site focuses on its flagship product, QuarkXPress, the "killer app" of desktop publishing. It provides extensive online support for XPress, with a library of tips and troubleshooting documents, and an FTP address where customers can download free XTensions (plug-ins for XPress), updates, printer drivers, and product demos. The company also posts links to join the QuarkXPress mailing list, check related newsgroups, or reach third-party XTension vendors. The lengthy "Why should I use QuarkXPress?" page walks the unconverted through the program's features, while the upgrade page and the new product descriptions should "XCite" XPress vets.
✓**www**→http://www.quark.com

Online

Netscape If any one company is responsible for the recent popularity boom of the World Wide Web, it's Netscape. No small part of that is the seamless way its Web browser—Netscape Navigator, the killer app on the Web—integrates links

to Netscape's home, or the quality of the site itself. It's a gateway which points users toward new and cool sites, and offers a powerful search engine hotlinked to other search services. It's a tech support and upgrade center for Netscape users. It's an instruction center for anyone looking to program for the Web. It's a Net-industry newswire. It's the corporate headquarters and investor relations center for what is so far the most successful software startup venture of all time, with up-to-the-minute stock quotes. Most of all, it's a resourceful site with something to offer every Internet user.
✓**www**→http://home.netscape.com

Qualcomm The maker of Eudora, the leading electronic mail application, offers far more than just an email address here. The site provides detailed product literature, including a comparison between the commercial version, Eudora Pro, and the freeware, Eudora Light (available for download). Those with a server can download the appropriate mail host to match their hardware, thanks to a convenient table. The site contains plenty of Eudora-related press releases, a trade show calendar, and links to Eudora newsgroups. Visitors can win a copy of Eudora Pro or a T-shirt for their "Why I Love Eudora" submissions.
✓**www**→http://www.qualcomm.com

Operating systems

Microsoft Other software companies devote the bulk of their Websites to pushing their biggest or newest product. Microsoft has an entire network to sell, as well as a huge product line, including its Windows operating systems. Its home page offers the latest Microsoft press releases and product announcements and provides colorful links to the site's tech support, search, and feedback facilities. A pull-down menu brings visitors instant access to descriptions of roughly 100 Microsoft products. Windows 95 users can download free accessories; Net novices can get an Internet tutorial; and developers and businesses also have specialized areas. Visotirs who click on the Microsoft Network page are treated to membership information and the weekly picks at Link Central—users can even customize the msn.com home page to provide sports scores and stock updates at every visit.

✓**www**→http://www.microsoft.com

Utilities

Aladdin Systems, Inc. Aladdin has become an important player in the online world, thanks to its industry-standard StuffIt compression programs, which scompact files for faster electronic transmission. From its Website, Aladdin offers freeware essentials like DropStuff and StuffIt Expander, and a shareware version of its commercial StuffIt Deluxe. One page includes a printable order form which lets customers save-money on Aladdin's commercial software bundle. The Aladdin site also features new product demos, customer service and tech-support email addresses (including an infobot which provides more detailed info about the programs), and current job listings within the company.

✓**www**→http://www.aladdinsys.com

Berkeley The maker of the popular After Dark screensaver calls its site "Toasted," after those ubiquitous, ridiculously fun flying toast-

ers which have become the company's signature. The entire site has a humorous feel. The Café Slack section features a risqué downloadable serial, "Toast Opera," and lets visitors obtain fashion and romance advice from Miss Hane, the resident beauty queen. Along with its product info and tech-support FAQs, Berkeley offers free After Dark modules from the site, and merchandises its toasters like there's no tomorrow, with Flying Toaster T-shirts, hats, and even ties. Finally, visitors are encouraged to keep abreast of the site by subscribing to the Toasted-News mailing list.

✓**www**→http://www.berksys.com

Symantec Virus alert! Symantec uses its Website to deliver the latest information on those pesky, potentially problematic computer contagions. Its AntiVirus Research Center raises awareness to the viral menace, defining the basics of infection and providing a full virus database, a list of the Top Ten most frequent infections, instructions for submitting samples, and downloadable updates to its bug-combating software. Symantec's site isn't all virally oriented; the company offers product info and support for its whole line of utilities, applications, and development tools.

✓**www**→http://www.symantec.com

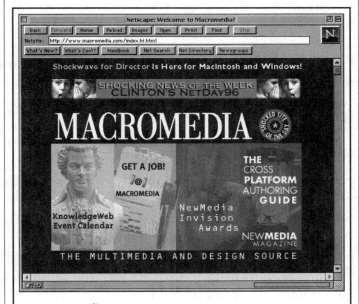

IN-SITE: **Macromedia**
http://www.macromedia.com

A multimedia company had better have a multimedia Website. Macromedia's up to the challenge, using graphics, sound, and video to demonstrate its product line. QuickTime movie overviews accompany descriptions and data for Director, FreeHand, Extreme 3D, and other programs, while the Gallery offers samples of Macromedia-aided works. Overall, the site has a distinct orientation toward designers and developers, the power users already on the Macromedia bus—then again, its software isn't for the faint of heart. The company solicits users' wish lists for future software upgrades. And along with its healthy serving of industry news, it offers those looking for work a place to post at their "position wanted" page, as well a chance to browse the current job openings.

Going to Market: Business to Business

One of the most important areas of Web marketing is business-to-business marketing. Because so many of the early users of the Internet are businesspeople (in-office connections are responsible for a significant fraction of all online use), the Web has immense potential for assisting businesses that sell goods or services to other businesses. Not only can the Web serve as an effective sales and marketing mechanism for a business, it can also serve as a means of bringing buyers and sellers together through improved information delivery. Grey Poupon's Website (**http://www.menunet.com/sn /greypoupon**), which is located on an online hospitalty network named Restaurant SupplySite, markets its famous Dijon mustard to restaurant and hotel owners—a classic business-to-business strategy and one that harmonizes with the goals of the larger site (**http://www.menu-net.com /supplysite**). Federal Express (**http://www.fedex.com**) lets customers, including other businesses, track packages at its site. And dozens of other companies have started to build business-to-business features into their Websites.

The best way for a business to approach creating a business-to-business Website is to think of it as a living example of how the company's top salesperson would sell the company and its products. In other words, the site should include a clear overview of what the company does and an explanation of why it is superior or unique as compared to competing companies, a vision of what the company hopes to accomplish for its customers, detailed product descriptions, case studies of satisfied customers, and several places for potential prospects to interact with the business marketer and volunteer their names. While most of these are self-explanatory, the last two—case studies and interaction areas—merit more detailed discussion.

Case studies. A company can illustrate its capabilities and build trust for potential clients by showcasing successful case studies. A case study works well when it includes a clear summary of the business problem and an explanation of how the services or products provided by the business marketer solved that problem—but it works best when it uses the name of a well-known customer. If appropriate, the ability to describe several case studies, involving different types of customers, is particularly persuasive to potential customers: it shows flexibility in the event that the visitor to the business Website is looking for something unique. A particularly effective example of how to use case studies is incorporated in the Internet Solutions area of the Hewlett-Packard Website (**http://www.hp.com**), which describes how Hewlett-Packard created new Internet-based businessess for companies from a wide range of industries.

Interaction areas. A company should view its Website as a powerful tool for making a sale or building a relationship with a prospective customer. How? Well, a company could either create an area where visitors could indicate if they wanted to be on a product-related email mailing list or develop a corner of the site for customers to ask questions about the company's products. Sending customized email to anyone who responds to these areas will build loyalty among exiiting customers and respect among prospective customers.

Once a company builds the business-to-business element of its site, it must promote its site. Chapter Four of this book discusses the issues involved in promoting Websites to consumers and building consumer traffic. All of the techniques descibed in that chapter can be applied to a business-to-business environment as well. There are also a few more specific ways that business-to-business sites can promote themselves:

- Include the URL on sales materials and the business cards of salespeople.
- Include the URL and a description of the Website in targeted trade advertising, promotional materials, and even on product packaging.
- List the site in appropriate commercial indexes, such as the Commercial Site Index (**http://www.directory.net**) and other industry-specific indexes on the Web.

In addition to positioning companies as reliable sources of information, the Web can help individual businesses create low-cost secure networks that link them with their customers and their suppliers. These "Enterprise Networks" use the Web's secure communications capability to efficiently link customers and suppliers. To date, Enterprise Networks have been both company-specific and industry-specific; the second type, so-called Industry

Directories or Master Sites, provide listings and information on a geographic basis for companies looking to buy or sell specific types of products. For example, Industry.Net (**http://www.industry.net**) includes immense amounts of information on the wholesale supply of thousands of products, including a comprehensive list of trade shows nationwide and 250,000 listings for suppliers of virtually every product and service used by industry.

As a communications (and community-enhancing system), the Internet also has the ability to diversify the kinds of buyers and sellers it unites. Several new sales mechanisms are likely to emerge in the age of the Web, including various forms of barter and auctions. All of these new techniques recalibrate the relationship between supply and demand, and aspire toward a more perfect match between production and consumption. Barter sites, for example, allow users to post items they want to barter, what they will accept in exchange, and a mechanism for contacting the business that posted the offering. As the number of companies doing business on the Web increases, the overall barter business is likely to grow, and it may well emerge as a significant arena in which sellers derive value from merchandise that they cannot sell at full price. Auctions, which are discussed at the conclusion of this Chapter Five, are a variation on this selling mechanism in which goods are offered for sale to the highest bidder. And the National Materials Exchange Network (**http://www.earthcycle.com/g/p/earthcycle/index.html**) gives new teeth to the old saw "one man's trash is another man's treasure" by allowing companies to sell or trade, on a global basis, used and surplus materials. The NMEN has already accumulated 10,000 listings. Business-to-business networks can also streamline the bidding process, the process by which companies make their services available to other companies. The General Electric Company, for example, has established the GE Trading Process Network (**http://www.ge.com/tpn/index.html**), which "enables suppliers to bid for GE contracts from their desktop computers, reducing the time and cost associated with business-to-business transactions." GE expects TPN to handle $1 billion dollars of transactions in 1996.

Intranets, Web-based networks that connect a company's employees with World Wide Web technology, are becoming increasingly popular for business-to-business marketing. Most Intranets are private, restricting access to a company's employees. To prevent nonemployees from accessing the information available on these internal networks, companies have created "firewalls," or security gates. Intranets allow companies to continuously post the most up-to-date information and avoid the costs of printing and distributing employee handbooks and other materials. For companies with salespeople spread across a large geographic area, an Intranet can be a particularly valuable tool. Salespeople can use this Network to access current pricing information, technical data, and position papers. This eliminates the need for salespeople to travel with heavy manuals, and for headquarters to update the information that their salespeople have in a swiftly evolving, competitive environment. In addition, an Intranet can be an efficient mechanism for salespeople from around the globe to report new orders to the "home office," and begin the shipping or manufacturing process.

Chapter 9

Financial Services

Personal finance

Many of the large financial service firms are already online, with Websites that not only

position them as dependable sources of financial advice, but also employ Web technology to tailor that advice to the needs of individual consumers. **Merrill Lynch's Internet Center** uses a virtual village to map its customers' various concerns (paying for college, buying a home, investing in stocks). **FinaCenter's Home Loan Department** and **SallieMae Online** attempt to combat those middle of the night monetary worries by providing online calculators that show exactly how much a bungalow or a B.A. is going to cost, using their financial services, of course. And **MarketNet** furnishes financial advice for our European friends, linking investment and planning resources to related industries such as travel and law.

On the Net

Across the board

MarketNet This Internet-based electronic marketplace site—which greets visitors with a choice of 12 languages and 8 currencies—offers a menu of legal, travel, florist, brokerage, banking, and other services. Though customers do not have to be U.K. residents, all of the services and vendors linked are British or Continental. Most of the financial transactions can occur online, although signature requirements may necessitate some offline contact. Customers who register as MarketNet clients can open InvestNet accounts, display their portfolios online, and trade securities through their brokerage houses. BankNet account-holders can view their accounts on the Web, and write electronic checks "using Public/Key/Private/Key cryptographic techniques." The site posts the bank's interest rates and fees. Through MarketWeb, registered customers can even post their own free Web pages and offer services; currently posted pages run the gamut from finance to travel to Web consultants.

✓**www**→http://mkn.co.uk

Merrill Lynch's Internet Center The opening graphic of a road running by buildings in suburbs, financial districts, colleges, and high-tech centers evokes places and themes that customers understand. Merrill Lynch invites its customers to these places—the Investor Learning Center, the Personal Finance Center, the Business Planning Center, or the Financial News & Research Center—to explain financial concepts and learn about opportunities with the investment company. Each "building" includes a RealAudio clip that welcomes visitors and describes its resources (stock quotes, advice on retirement planning, tips for writing a business plan). The site is easy to navigate and offers a series of guides and interactive exercises which can help focus customers' financial and business concerns or illustrate the types of services the company provides.

✓**www**→http://www.ml.com

FinaCenter's Home Loan Department While this comprehensive site offers the day's best rates, real estate glossaries, and reports on the market, the most useful services are the calculators for home buying, refinancing, and calculating home equity lines of credit. The calculators help customers find the perfect loan for each borrower. The visitor enters information into certain fields, and the calculators suggest which particular type of loan is best for a given financial situation, estimating everything from down payment to closing costs. FinaCenter is also partnered with a lender, so customers can apply and get preapproved online. Visitors can also ask more detailed questions which a loan representative from the site will answer by email.

✓**www**→http://www.financenter.com/homeloan/AFI/index.htm

SallieMae Homepage One of the largest financial services companies in the U.S., SallieMae, delivers a Website packed with financial aid advice, worksheets, and calculators for students, parents, and college financial aid advisors. In addition, there's an extensive glossary of financial aid and educational terms to help customers differentiate their default from their deferment.

✓**www**→http://www.salliemae.com

Banks

Despite, or perhaps because of, all the publicity about the dangers and benefits of

virtual banking, most established financial institutions have focused their Net presence on other attractions. Breaking down the marble edifice of corporate disinterest is a common tactic—**Bankers Trust**, with its "Build Your Own Bank" feature, strives to personalize its presence for each and every home; while **Meridian**'s site highlights its community activities. Other banks rely on added content to direct traffic to their more traditional services. **NationsBank** promotes its sponsorship of the upcoming Atlanta Olympics, while **Barclay**'s talks about travel insurance along the sidelines of its travel resource links. Banks also use Net technology to create virtual communities of interest—**BayBank**, which caters to Boston's immense student population, has filled its site with college hijinks. **First Hawaiian** has created a virtual paradise complete with the local surf forecast. Marketing history has also shown the value of playing on name recognition—**Wells Fargo**'s Wild West motif speaks volumes about familiarity.

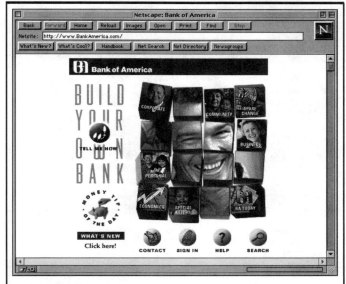

IN-SITE: **Bank of America**
http://www.BankAmerica.com
http://www.bofa.com

With an opening image-map composed of average American faces (of all races) and a home-page graphic of a piggy bank that links to a Money Tip of The Day, Bank of America positions itself as a friendly institution with an interest in both whimsy and the interactivity of the Web. Areas on personal finance, business banking, corporate banking, and more are packed with information about the bank's services. But Bank of America really gets creative with its "Build Your Own Bank" feature that lets visitors customize their "dream bank"; in return, Bank of America emails them daily doses of personalized financial advice. Hooked yet? And then there are the added-value applications—customers can apply for a credit card online in the credit card area, calculate car payments with a loan calculator in the auto loan section, and use the student budget calculator to create a realistic student budget in the student union.

On the Net

Bank of Boston Despite the odd and unexpected URL (boston$ .com is still unregistered, as are bankbos.com and—incredibly—bankboston.com), this straightforward page positions the Bank of Boston as a leader in financial news, with more than 20 categories ranging from New England economic news to updates on the Bank's holdings. In addition, the page has large areas devoted to personal banking, corporate banking, and global banking. The bank asks its visitors to comment on the site with an online form.
✓**www**→http://www.bkb.com

Bankers Trust Bankers Trust not only reinforces its offline brand, with a large home-page graphic of

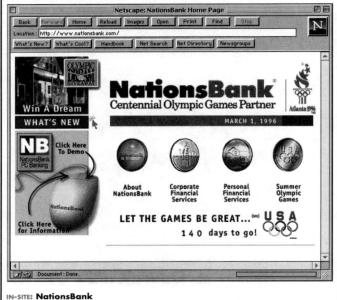

IN-SITE: NationsBank
http://www.nationsbank.com

NationsBank has many large clients, and its primary service is assisting them in filing their taxes electronically. And while its home page spotlights this service, it also offers links to other sites (IBM and CityLink), and even features an online store which sells merchandise targeting active accountholders (including NationsBank T-Shirts, shorts, golf umbrellas, and tote bags). Cashing in on its sponsorship of the 1996 Olympics, the site provides a searchable calendar of Olympic-related events nationwide.

a bridge made up of shaking hands, but also uses its Website to dispense more than wisdom—the software section includes a set of financial downloads, including demo versions of auditing and capital management programs.
✓ www→http://www.bankers trust.com

Banque National du Paris This modest site includes a direct email link, a bank locator, and a section called BNP editorial that delivers sporadically-updated editorial content.
✓ www→http://www.calvacom.fr /BNP/ukindex.html

Barclays The financial giant lives up to its larger-than-life reputation in Cyberspace, with a page that

collects resources on banking, trading, and the company's credit card (the BarclayCard). To draw visitors to its Travel Insurance section, Barclays has built a travel resources area, and Barclays also offers the BarclaySquare shopping mall, a large online environment that includes consumer news, a magazine, and more.
✓ www→http://www.barclays .co.uk

BayBank Online BayBank has built an interactive extravaganza on the Web for the next generation of serious bankers and bank customers—college students. But BayBank isn't preaching the value of saving early; instead, it's entertaining its visitors, positioning itself as a bank with a sense of fun,

making it seem like the kind of place where college kids would be comfortable banking. So what's here? The site runs an interactive online mystery where college students try to find a missing chicken, links to sites about the annual Head of the Charles races (including a link to a virtual version), and includes an ATM locator so that New England undergrads know where to get their cash. The Press Box makes press releases available in three forms (Web text, email, or RealAudio recordings of press conferences). And since March 1, the site has included a demo of Bay-Bank's HomeLink, one of the nation's first real-time home banking services.
✓ www→http://www.baybank .com

Chemical Bank Banks publish many glossy brochures each year describing their mortgage, credit card, business financing, and other services. Chemical uses its Website to deliver the same information, albeit with the aid of Web graphics. In addition, the site includes an ATM locator.
✓ www→http://fstc.poly.edu /Chemical/Chemhp20.html

CitiBank/CitiCorp CitiBank/ CitiCorp thinks on a global scale, presenting consumer-oriented banking information for CitiCorp and its various branches worldwide on its Website. Despite the site's incredible level of detail—a series of maps identify various ATM locations in a shopping mall in Singapore, for instance—it takes only a few clicks for visitors to get to any information on the site.
✓ www→http://www.citicorp.com

First Hawaiian Bank Flashing lights! Stars! Prizes! Celebrity host Pat Morita! Is it *Karate Kid* theme week on *Jeopardy*? No, it's the home page of First Hawaiian's Website, which includes both entertainment and local color. Besides the inevitable surfing and Don Ho jokes, the site also offers online contests (with offline prizes) for those who bank with First Hawaiian, as well as pages full of puzzles. Bank information is limited.

✓**www**→http://www.fhb.com/fhb

First Union First Union, the "original Cyberbank," here promotes its online banking features. The site lets new and existing customers apply for a consumer loan, a home equity loan, or a customized MasterCard (with a choice of 20 picture-postcard images) through its Applications Online area. By using the site's inter-

active Retirement Services, customers can open an Individual Retirement Account, check the status of an existing account, and even project their earnings. In addition to some general corporate background and press releases, First Union provides its Web visitors with a library of free investment advice, including links to economic forecasts, credit information, and industry articles. A creditable effort.

✓**www**→http://www.firstunion .com

Merchant's National Bank
Merchant's leads with its strongest feature—a calculator that lets customers figure out what they would save by using the Merchant's Bank Visa card instead of their current card. The page continues in this

consumer-oriented vein by offering essays on banking services for individuals; commercial banking resources are relegated to the bottom of the page.

✓**www**→http://www.bnt.com /~mnb

Meridian Meridian uses this simple, well-designed site to build its reputation as a bank that is not only reponsive to its customers, but a true member of the community. There's the usual company profile and press releases, but the rest of the site offers a branch/ATM locator, a personal finance quiz, a community section offering calendars of local events sponsored by the bank, and a "Talk to Us!" feature that encourages customer feedback.

✓**www**→http://www.meridian bank.com

People's Bank Home Page
More than just information about the bank's assets and services, this Website positions People's Bank as a bank for, well, people—not only does the software area provide downloadable programs for PC users, but the site also includes a hypertext schedule of cultural events in Connecticut and links to helpful sites like the IRS publications page.

✓**www**→http://www.peoples.com

TransAmerica An image of the company's famous building greets visitors, inviting them to click on different floors to move through the site. From its virtual bird's eye view of the financial world, TransAmerica delivers information about the company's services—specialized financial and life insurance products—and its corporate history.

✓**www**→http://www.transamerica .com

IN-SITE: **Wells Fargo**
http://www.wellsfargo.com
Wells Fargo positions itself as an historical bank and a gateway to the Old West—witness the large picture archive of frontier settlers. The frontier motif continues throughout the site, as Wells Fargo demonstrates how it is conquering new territory in banking and online services. With an online search engine guide and quick-loading graphics, this is one of the most engaging bank sites online.

Credit cards

The credit card industry uses one of two strategies when it comes to Web marketing.

Sites such as **American Express** devote their energies to providing industry-specific services and selling their products to target markets. Other pages, such as **Visa Expo** and **MasterCard International Pointers**, act as Web indexes by taking visitors site-hopping around the globe, thereby promoting the idea that credit cards are doorways to the world.

On the Net

American Express Company news, financial reports, and a "Connecting to Us" section all let customers check out what's up at AmEx. The site incorporates a variety of valuable worldwide services including an ATM locator, a Travel Services Office locator, and American Express University—a Web resource for college students that covers everything from budgets to job hunting to travel
✓**www**→http://www.american express.com

AT&T Universal Card Services The Universal Card is truly universal—it can be used as a credit card, a bank card, a calling card, and a frequent-flyer mileage card (with USAir)—and AT&T has targeted the card (and its Website) toward college students, devoting an entire section of its site to those with their lives and credit histories ahead of them. In addition, the site includes product and service information and a feedback link.

✓**www**→http://www.att.com/ucs

BarclayCard This credit card supplier has created a masterpiece of interactivity and service. Visitors can check out product info for six different credit cards, enter a contest to win 12 bottles of red wine, choose which free gift (travel bag, CD player, or atlas) they might want if their credit application is accepted, or talk directly to customer service reps online about their existing cards.
✓**www**→http://www.barclaycard .co.uk

Edvance MasterCard This version of MasterCard is offered online by the Advanta National Bank, and it's targeted toward new parents. How? Well, Edvance users earn points toward free U.S. Savings Bonds, which they will presumably use toward their children's education. To enhance its card's value, Advanta includes an online calculator so that parents can calculate savings.
✓**www**→http://www.edvance.com

MasterCard International Pointers MasterCard has created a site for the citizens of the Net. It offers extensive Web tutorials and tours, pointers (hence, the name) to "cultural treasures" online, fiction for the cybermedium, and directories of online shopping sites accepting MasterCard. MasterCard's Website also offers an ATM locator service, talent contests, information about job hunting for college students, and more.
✓**www**→http://www.mastercard .com

IN-SITE: **Visa Expo**
http://www.visa.com
Visa positions itself as the starting line for Web exploration, elegantly integrating links to other relevant and reliable Websites, using the Net to entertain and inform its customers. In its Visa Worldwide section, customers can link to "Visa-friendly" banks in countries all over the world. In addition, Visa often features spectacular Web pages for the many sporting- and entertainment-related events which it sponsors.

Investment

Wall Street has long been using computers to track the ups and downs of the market.

Now that Cyberspace gives investors control of their portfolios, a number of businesses have stepped in to assist moguls at home. Among the online stock market quote servers, **PC-Quote** draws the penny conscious, pound wise, by offering five free quotes up front. **Nest Egg** associates its investment advice with increased wealth for its customers—articles about overseas homes and golf vacations reinforce the idea that *Nest Egg*'s counsel will fatten the wallets of its customers. **Charles Schwab** offers investment software for online portfolio management. Personalized service has always been a key to effective selling. And **Fidelity**, with its many interactive financial planning features, makes visitors feel like they are on the track to a perfectly tailored investment plan.

On the Net

Investment counsel

Nest Egg Recalling the exquisite jeweled Fabergé creation, this site's logo is a neo-Palladian mansion perched atop a mound of cash. The investment advice magazine *Nest Egg* builds on this "lifestyles of the rich and famous" image with online articles about real estate, living abroad, and golf getaways. *Nest Egg* also builds online associations with well-respected names on "the street." It offers a Smith Barney Wall Street Watch, news from the editors of *Investment Dealers Digest*, and Dow Jones performance information. *Nest Egg* appeals to those who not only have (or want) the money, but are serious about managing it. Don't miss the IRA calculator from Smith Barney.
✓**www**→http://nestegg.iddis.com

Security APL Marble edifices symbolizing stability and capital are prominent features of this site's design and its very name is a potent counterweight to images of Black Friday. A member of the PAWWS financial network, Security relies on information to sell its online trading functions. A quote function allows customers to follow their investments and a well-endowed market watch keeps them up to date on industry trends. An online forum links visitors to investment advisors who assist prospective clients in making the right trade.
✓**www**→http://www.secapl.com/secapl/Welcome.html

Online brokers

AGS Financial Services AGS

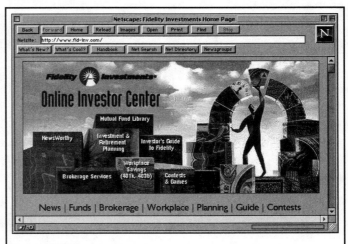

IN-SITE: **Fidelity Investments**
http://www.fid-inv.com
Fidelity has a long, trustworthy reputation in the financial world, and its information-packed site builds on that reputation while establishing Fidelity as a company that offers a wide range of financial services. The site covers every facet of its business, from brokerage services to mutual funds to retirement planning. In each section, Fidelity offers guides, glossaries, and even interactive quizzes to help customers find the best plans for them, making each visitor feel special and well cared for. And its online magazine reports on investment topics ranging from college costs to market trends in easy-to-understand prose.

has set itself the difficult talk of playing both the small investor's advocate and insider's information source. A section entitled "What discount brokers don't want you to know" tells amateurs how to avoid large fees (by using AGS, of course). But the group that just placed itself squarely on the side of the consumer follows up with a "for stockbrokers only" description of how to get the "best payout package in the industry." Aside from this mixed message, AGS does serve up some perks—a weekly $10 contest, and free trade for first-timers with accounts over $25,000. All in all, AGS's most potent lure is probably its "one price" brokerage fee, lost somewhere in the translation.

✓**www**→http://ags-financial-services.com

Baker & Co., Inc. The company is concerned with one thing and one thing only—making your money grow. That's the message here. The background displays the familiar visage of George Washington, there's an animation of growing dollar signs, and the page's headline promises dollar savings on each order. Baker relies on both incentives and security to clinch its sale. An S&P stock guide is free with any new account, and securities up to $25 million dollars are protected. Baker also offers an email comparison of its rates on any recent trade with other brokers, to reassure customers that they're getting the best deal.

✓**www**→http://www.coolsite.com/baker1.html

Charles Schwab Online With a tag line of "Helping Investors Help Themselves," this comprehensive site promotes the idea that investors should stay, well, invested in their financial life. The site provides the means whereby clients can stay informed about and active in their investment decisions, with extensive information on Schwab's mutual funds, brokerage accounts, and investment services, as well as offline guides, investor tools, and software programs that support online investment.

✓**www**→http://www.schwab.com

National Discount Brokers Having "discount" in the title never hurts when the business at hand is money. National Discount Brokers sells its bang for the buck in a clever retooling of the ever-popular "our prices can't be beat" claim. In fact, it offers a calculator to allow customers to see how much cheaper National's fees are than its competitors. These folks alsotake care of newbie online investors, providing a comprehensive, calming, FAQ; simple online ordering forms; and an upfront price list.

✓**www**→http://pawws.secapl.com/ndb

NetInvestor Leading with its "Best on the Net" award, this online brokerage follows up its kudos with an emphasis on cheapness and control. The word "free" is scattered all over the site, always in bold type (a potent attraction even when not technically true—these "free" services come with a fee-based package). NetInvestor also focuses on the empowering aspect of Net investing—portraying its cash management (checking, Visa, money markets), and brokerage services as the very best way to keep a 24-hour watch on matters that once resided exclusively in the

IN-SITE: NETWorth
http://networth.galt.com/www/home

This investment service for mutual funds, equities, and college and retirement planning has a ready-made audience courtesy of its place in the online universe of the popular money management software Quicken. NETWorth, like Quicken, lets consumers take control of their finances—in this case their investments. The site enables visitors manage their investments through a combination of features including "Atlas," a mutual fund, free 15-minute delayed stock quotes, company research, and Net links. Once lured into online dollar watching, visitors are pointed towards NETWorth's fee services. These include crack investment advisors, a life insurance company, and a group of "tax-conscious" managers who promise to minimize IRS "success" penalties. There's also a link to Quicken's online store for purchase of financial software.

hands of unknown Wall Street professionals.

✓**www**→http://pawws.com/tni

Stock quote services

CNNfn Though it's part of a larger network, the Website of CNN's new financial network merits mention for the way it handles stock quotes, offering unlimited quote information at no cost all day. The quote service, prominently displayed on the site's front page, also links to a ticker-symbol lookup service.

✓**www**→http://www.cnnfn.com

DBC Online A ticker-tape headline greets each visitor to this virtual trading floor, along with a headline proclaiming DBC the leading provider of real-time market data. DBC brings in would-be bulls with a deal-making, 30-day free trial and a promise of exceptional profits.

✓**www**→http://www.dbc.com

Lombard Lombard trades on exclusivity, promising unique online graphs charting each stock's performance and custom research tools unavailable to the masses. Lombard also practices a Hansel and Gretel type lure—offering free delayed-time quotes on 7,000 companies for those who register, from which position it's a simple electronic jump to the fee-based real-time service. Links to the site of respected names in the financial industry add to Lombard's credibility; visitors are linked to the SEC, Dow Jones info, and the Federal Reserve Bank.

✓**www**→http://www.lombard.com /PACenter/index.html

MoneyQuick Quotes *Money* magazine sponsors this free quote service not necessarily to profit directly from online trading but in-

IN-SITE: **Closing Bell**
http://www.merc.com/cbell2.html
This service posits itself not as the trader's tool with the fastest real-time quotes, but rather as the email alternative to the newspaper where the average investor can track his five shares of IBM. There is a daily sample online of the report which augments the numbers with news briefs on the companies concerned. The free two-week trial will undoubtedly appeal to the small investors that make up Closing Bell's market.

stead to bring habitual market watchers to its personal finance site. In combination with selected *Money* articles, a news search function, and Hoover's Company Profiles, this service provides a more informated quote than other services.

✓**www**→http://quote.pathfinder .com/money/quote/qc

PCQuote This quote service aims to recreate a little of the ambiance of a trading floor with digital ticker displays and a Reuters board. The sell is simple: In bold type the site proclaims "maximum data, with minimum fees...quite simply the best." After exuding such confidence, PCQuote sweetens the of-

fering with a sample of its wares— five free quotes. This online ad campaign is then capped by hypertext links to favorable press releases.

✓**www**→http://www.pcquote.com

Stockmaster In addition to providing the previous day's close for all New York Stock Exchange companies, this service, which is run on the MIT experimental server, also creates graphs of the past year's stock prices and graphs comparing individual stock performances against the market's trading volume.

✓**www**→http://ww.ai.mit.edu /stocks

Tax & accounting

Cheap and easy—it's what all Americans want in a tax system, isn't it? That's certainly

the pitch that online services are making. **Nelco Inc.** has a big, bright site which not only presents a user-friendly ambiance, but uses the word "easy" with comforting frequency. The **NetTax** page touches on April anxieties with constant references to the firm's low, low fees. **Ernst & Young** has leveraged its reputation and provided a safe haven full of trustworthy tips and an aura of impeccable, i.e. "audit-proof," services to soothe frightened taxpayers

On the Net

Ernst & Young LLP Ernst & Young has the benefit of name recognition, and the company's Website plays on this trustworthy image, enhanced by informative articles that promise to deliver the taxpayer's dream—saving money. People love concrete lists to guide them through life's troubles, and Ernst and & Young's "25 common errors" and "10 smart tax planning tips" are a sure sell. The business community will be lured in by expert advice, and both sets of consumers are encouraged to turn to actual Ernst & Young offices with promises of even greater savings and peace of mind.
✓**www**→http://www.ey.com/us /tax/eyustax.htm

H&R Block Not only is H&R Block the world's largest tax preparer, it is also a major force in the online industry—it owns CompuServe. Though the main H&R Block site links to CompuServe and Block's general financial services, the tax section of the Website focuses on the April blues, offering customers a tax preparer locator, information about H&R Block's tax school, and a regularly updated tax tip.
✓**www**→http://www.handrblock .com/tax/index.html

Jackson Hewitt Jackson Hewitt's site is built around a balloon theme, perhaps to suggest the possibility of floating through life, unencumbered by tax worries. Jackson Hewitt's lists of common mistakes are guaranteed to bring crowds of Netsurfers, and the "tax tip of the day" strategy will presumably keep them coming back. With the wealth of tax-cutting info presented here, Jackson Hewitt comes off as a useful expert to have around.
✓**www**→http://www.infi.net/~jhe witt

Nelco Inc. Nelco's site opens with a glorious soft-focus montage of the bald eagle, a waving flag, and the Capitol building—although why anyone would want to remind people of the government at tax time is an open question. Patriotic citizens then choose a red, white, or blue button in order to discover what Nelco offers. The words "inexpensive" and "easy" are repeated many times. After describing its services and software, Nelco plays the immediate-gratification cybercard, placing very large email buttons at the top of every page.
✓**www**→http://www.nelcoinc .com

NetTax Though the Courier typeface used at this site gives it a low-tech ambiance, the flashing price line certainly drags every visitor's eye immediately to NetTax's low, low fees. Key tax-time lures like "inexpensive" and "easy" stand proud in bold. NetTax also calms the fears of those who worry about trusting their auditability to an unknown. There are the expected helpful tax hints to prove expertise, but also a novel enticement of $7.50 in cold, hard, tax-free cash for every referral a client can make. NetTax obviously has tremendous faith in the Internet community.
✓**www**→http://rampages.onramp .net/~daywa/taxintro.htm

Pace Tax and Accounting Online Pace pushes all the right buttons at its tax site—specifically locating a "free stuff" link at the bottom of every page. In addition to stressing the ease and low costs of online filing, Pace hands out free IRS publications and tax tips online. Pace personalizes its pitch too, documenting the success of its specialized tax-law research service with the tale of a woman, the IRS, and the profit she made from selling trees on inherited land! Pace makes the complexity of filing seem surmountable, as long as you have the company on your side.
✓**www**→http://www.pacetax .com

Insurance

Not everyone understands insurance—the complicated architecture of premiums and

deductibles, the difference between whole life and term life. At least that's the assumption of the insurance firms online, who concentrate on answering questions about the industry's products while furnishing customers with "agent locators" that point clients to insurance agents in the offline world. While many of the largest insurance providers, like **Prudential** and **Aetna**, place their insurance business in their context of their overall financial services, other firms like **State Farm** and **Canada Life** exclusively emphasize their insurance business. Positioning strategies vary—**Great-West Life and Annuity Insurance Company** opts for a corporate home page, while **The New England** serves as a guide to other insurance and financial planning services across the Web—but product information, usually in the form of customer-policy matching, dominates.

On the Net

Aetna Life Insurance Aetna's crisp, clean home page relies on monochromatic graphics to deliver information about the company's

various financial services, including life insurance, investment planning, and college aid. With a direct email link to Aetna's corporate headquarters and the Aetna News Center—which strives to demonstrate the myriad ways insurance coverage can improve policy holders' quality of life.
✓**www**→http://www.aetna.com

MassMutual MassMutual's Website prominently displays the company's slogan, "We help you keep your promises," and then delivers on a number of modest goals, offering insurance con-

sumers a description of the company, a list of offices, and specific information on pension and investment management packages.
✓**www**→http://www.massmutual.com

Metropolitan Life The Peanuts gang has arrived in Cyberspace, and instead of reminding viewers about blockheads, 5¢ psychiatric fees, or the Red Baron, Charlie Brown and friends are holding forth on life insurance. At the MetLife Website, Charles Schultz's cartoon creations take Netsurfers to a whimsical Art Gallery (check

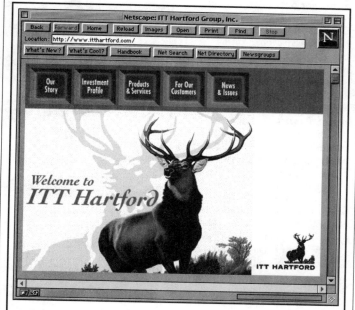

IN-SITE: **ITT Hartford**
http://www.itthartford.com
With a home page that emphasizes the company's long tradition of insurance and financial services—clients have included Abraham Lincoln and Robert E. Lee—ITT Hartford's site is most noteworthy for its interactive financial-service features, such as the Retirement Time Machine which helps Netsurfers plan for a secure future.

out the Mona Snoopy), show them where to find insurance rates, and provide general financial advice for basic life matters like children, marriage, college, moving, retirement, etc. But that's not even half of what's covered at this site! Snoopy explains MetLife's history, Franklin introduces job opportunities, and Woodstock tallies up the bill as the first winged accountant. And if following the cartoon characters gets too difficult, MetLife has created a specialized search engine good for both casual inquiries and directed questions.
✓**www**→http://www.metlife.com

The New England This Northeastern insurance company offers more than just the traditional policy information and mission statement, not only providing an extensive glossary of insurance terms from AD&D to zero-coupon securities, but also positioning New England as a guide to financial planning resources across the Web.
✓**www**→http://www.tne.com

Prudential Insurance Company of America Prudential has designed an innovative Website that invites its visitors to help seven real-life customers make a series of life decisions, and then publishes online forums about those decisions, complete with images, transcripts of conversations, and more. Brian and Simone Cook of San Inez, California, talk about buying their first home. David Springer of Livingston, New Jersey, debates leaving his job to start his own business. With the help of questionnaires, visitors advise the subjects; Prudential then asks for basic demographic information from new visitors. All in all, a wonderfully interactive way to position Prudential as a customer-oriented organization and collect informa-

IN-SITE: **Plaza Insurance, Inc.**
http://pwr.com/blo
With a large opening image of a stylish young man thinking, "I need insurance but who can I turn to?" and a well-designed home page with six insurance divisions (automobile, home, motorcycle, boat, life, and other insurance), Plaza Insurance is a full-service online insurance provider, with extensive Web forms that let visitors obtain initial quote information for insurance plans.

tion on prospective customers.
✓**www**→http://www.prudential.com

State Farm The Website of State Farm's auto insurance division provides customers with an agent locator, information on claims and policies, and a brief review of the company's commitment to the community and the environment.
✓**www**→http://www.statefarm.com

Real estate

Who would buy a thatched cottage in Devonshire, sight unseen from someone ten thou-

sand miles away in Fargo, North Dakota? You might, especially if you see the property listed and illustrated in all its glory on the Web. Thanks to its graphic capabilities, the Internet can sometimes make a place as real as though you were actually there. **Coldwell Banker** has a virtual real estate agent, as well as a search engine, which allows house hunters to plug in location, features, and price range and responds with a listing for a white-picket-fenced bungalow. **Homes Internet Magazine** goes a step further in selling the global village by profiling neighborhoods, facilitating mortgages, and finding every Mr. Blandings a dream house. Creating an interactive relationship is **Imark**'s tactic. This company has augmented its house registry with bulletin boards where sellers and buyers can discuss specific homes on the market, and provides an online expert to field property questions.

On the Net

Better Homes and Gardens
While several of the site's features are still under construction, it is still a competent matchmaker for those interested in finding properties in Toronto or Florida. The property search engine not only matches the visitor with the perfect residential or commercial property in their price range, but also includes a mortgage calculator to show how it can be financed.
✓**www**→http://www.betterhomes re.com

Century 21 A clickable map links to a list of cities in each state that Century 21 serves. From the list, visitors can access a general order form for Century 21's offline "Newcomer Package," which includes community profiles, maps, and sample homes for the desired location. There is no online information for the properties, however.
✓**www**→http://www.century21pro .com

Coldwell Banker Finding the right home is complicated, but Coldwell Banker helps the frustrated home buyer by providing a virtual real estate agent. A specialized search engine, now common on real estate sites, lets customers enter the city and state in which they are looking to buy a home, enter their price range and minimum number of bedrooms, and the program responds with a list of

IN-SITE: CB Commercial
http://www.cbcommercial.com
CB Commercial cultivates a prestigious air, and promises it will be "Delivering Solutions Through Local Knowledge Worldwide," if not through its Website just yet. Although a commercial properties database is in the works, and there are a few useful features such as a 1996 market forecast, the site is more of a company profile that also offers extensive offline services overviews.

Real Estate **Financial Services**

Dream Home Real Estate Network This is a fairly comprehensive index of real estate sites covers all aspects of the home-buying process, from selling to relocation to mortgage. At the moment, the actual cache of properties and realtors is severely limited, but the complex search engines will become very useful when the rosters grow. More useful at this stage in the site's development are the loan calculators and the "create-a-page" services for realtors and home sellers that let them put an ad online, for a fee.
✓**www**→http://www.islandsd.com/island/dreamhm

Global Real Estate Registry Much of this tremendous site is still under construction, and while it promises to have several new features up and running soon (New Homes, Rental Properties, Commercial Properties, Financial District, Guided Tour), for now the site is limited to an extremely competent residential properties section. Offering estate tours of properties valued at over $1,000,000, an international listings search utilizing clickable maps, specifying dozens of property features, and linking to real estate firms & agents, the site makes good on the company's tagline, "Neighborhood Focus & Global Exposure."
✓**www**→http://www.goglobal.com

Home Buyer's Fair The selection of real estate resources here, as at any fair, is varied and widespread. Each substantial section links to a dozen different resources, some original and some collected from around the Web. Sections for buyers, sellers, home financing, relocation services, and property brokers offer everything from internal classifieds to links to other hubsites and companies on the Net to calculators, articles, charts, and tables. The eclecticism sometimes leads to disorganization or inconsistency (e.g., the buyers' section, while sizable, doesn't offer concrete listings for a large range of cities), but if the visitor takes the time to dig through the site, she's sure to find some gems.
✓**www**→http://www.homefair.com

Homes Internet Magazine This multi-frame site wants to be a home for the homeless, a one-stop shop where the home buyer can do everything from profile a neighborhood to locate a mortgage broker. There are many special features here, both general (a highlighted house of the week, a mortgage calculator, a chat room) and local (regional home-buying statistics, a map library, even collections of regional links that help buyers get a sense of communities in a growing number of states). The best resources here are the search engines that match visitors to their dream houses by location (urban, rural, etc.) or other specifications (such as ski-slope accessibility). Regional agent and broker listings are also available at this page, offering contact information and email forms that direct the visitor's query to the appropriate party.
✓**www**→http://www.homesmag.odc.com

properties—illustrated with lavish photos.
✓**www**→http://www.coldwellbanker.com

Electronic Reality Service Don't be fooled by the name—the "electronic" in Electronic Reality Service doesn't refer to the Internet, but to the company's internal computer network. ERS spans the globe and encompasses hundreds of offline real estate offices. The offline services are described on the home page, but ERS also has set up a Website where property sellers can advertise. The site's powerful search engines help match clients with properties and agents.
✓**www**→http://www.teamera.com

Imark Imark follows the Teddy Roosevelt rule of real estate sales: speak softly, and carry a big stick. While the spotlight is on a simple clickable map with a small but consistent number of properties listed for each U.S. state and some international locations, the features at the bottom of the page are deeper than they appear. The on-line mortgage calculator links to free software, other calculators, and licensing info; the services resource links to mortgage brokers, agents, and consumer reports; the bulletin board provides a space where home buyers, sellers, and professionals can post their ads free of charge; and a link with the unassuming title of "Three Big Questions to Ask" is actually a showcase for software based on the T.V. show *Your New House*, with almost a dozen features including hundreds of excerpted tips on home buying, as well as detailed advice on refurbishing
✓**www**→http://www.imrk.com/imark/realest

Chapter 10

Travel
&
Hospitality

Travel guides & services

In a business as old as commerce and as competitive as boxing, marketing is less an

option than a prerequisite, and online travel industry marketing effectively duplicates its offline antecedent. Big, bold, expensive branding is the key to maintaining the status of major players like **Fodor's** and **Lonely Planet**. Car-rental services, locked in constant combat for a finite number of customers, have also geared up for online marketing. **Alamo Rent-A-Car: Freeways**, for instance, has filled its site with infotainment features, including U.S. city maps and children's travel games, while **Avis** invites visitors to Ask the Magic Car travel questions. Finally, there's **Amtrak**, the venerable national rail company, which has gone online with schedules and travel tips.

On the Net

Guides

Aer Travel Although Aer attempts to target both business and luxury travelers, it favors business travelers. All of the links to weather info, restaurant reviews, and special events info are located under the business section. An online form for making travel reservations through Aer is available for both types of travelers.
✓**www**→http://www.aertravel .com/browse

Beachcomber Tours If Beachcomber believes that a picture is worth a thousand words, its Website would be worth many words, indeed. This site offers very limited text about the company's specialty—the African island of Mauritius—and focuses its sell instead on pictures of the island.

✓**www**→http://www.tcp.co.uk /~holidays/beach.html

Changes in L'attitudes, Inc. This travel agency has established itself as the place on the Web to plan a Caribbean holiday. It features links to the Come to Jamaica and Feel All Right, SuperClubs, and Poinciana Beach Resort pages plus rate-inquiry and reservations

IN-SITE: **Lonely Planet**
http://www.lonelyplanet.com.au/lp.htm
Lonely Planet's Website is peppered with phrases like "jumpstart your travel plans" and "In a hurry?" and offers text-only access for those who want their info the quickest way possible. In addition, the site offers guides for most destinations around the globe.

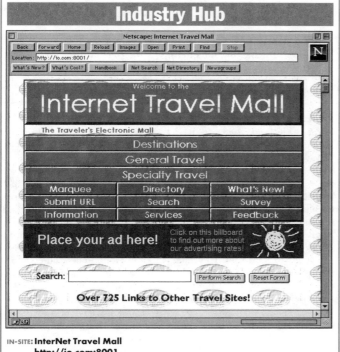

Industry Hub

Netscape: Internet Travel Mall

Welcome to the
Internet Travel Mall
The Traveler's Electronic Mall

Destinations

General Travel!

Specialty Travel

Marquee	Directory	What's New!
Submit URL	Search	Survey
Information	Services	Feedback

Place your ad here! · Click on this billboard to find out more about our advertising rates!

Search: [ ] Perform Search · Reset Form

Over 725 Links to Other Travel Sites!

IN-SITE: **InterNet Travel Mall**
http://io.com:8001

"Definitive" is the operative word at ITM, which is the Net's answer to a Yellow Pages for travel. Hotels, agents, and clubs add their URLs by the thousands to this collection of links making it a place for travel-related businesses to see and be seen.

telephone numbers.
✓**www**→http://www.changes.com/Changes

Council Travel Council continues its established reputation as a budget and student travel agency with to the point information for all of those kids doing "the backpacking thing." This down-to-business page doesn't offer fancy pics of beaches or jumbo airliners—just a brief intro to the agency (which includes links to the addresses of its 40 U.S. offices) and links to tips on low-cost hotels, airfares, restaurants, rail passes, tours, and general travel advice.
✓**www**→http://www.ciee.org/cts/ctshome.htm

Fodor's The first name in published travel guides volleys to become the first name in online travel guidance. Just like the company's offline guides, the Fodor's Website strives to be comprehensive and authoritative, with thousands of listings for restaurants, hotels, and recommended activities in cities worldwide, as well as a wealth of practical travel info that ranges from the general to the witheringly specific.
✓**www**→http://www.fodors.com

Grand Travel Grand Travel, an agency which promotes tours to Zambia, was developed in conjunction with the Zambian National Tourist Board, lending Grand's Website the clout of

an official name and an air of authority.
✓**www**→http://www.zamnet.zm/zamnet/zntb.html

Great Escapes Travel In large flashing letters, this company announces that "Latin America is Our Specialty." Great Escapes lists fares and discount deals to Mexico. But that's not all—the Website offers reservations, telephone numbers, weather reports, and an online exhibition of Mexican art.
✓**www**→http://www.tai-travel.com

Instant Travel Instant Travel's page provides travel agency info like discount fare info, contests, and suggested tours. But the real draw to this Website is the E-Z Quote Form, a service that provides fare quotes for a visitor's selected itinerary.
✓**www**→http://www.cgl.com/~it

Preview Vacations One of the leaders in designing innovative online travel promotions, Preview runs contests, matches travelers with their ideal vacations, auctions off travel packages, and provides details on a number of travel options. Sponsored by MCI, the site is quick, clean, and easy to use.
✓**www**→http://www.vacations.com

STA Travel The self-proclaimed leader in student travel makes a plug for every one of its services at its Website, going into great detail about its insurance plans, (for parents shipping off their children), the International Student Identification Card (which entitles the holder to discounts on everything from movies to airplane tickets), and contact info for hundreds of STA branches worldwide.
✓**www**→http://www.sta-travel.com

Vacation Station The Site makes interesting use of a number of travel-related incentives, offering suggested itineraries, discount coupons for participating airlines, and tips on frequent flyer programs with different airlines. Appropriately named the Station—Nettravellers will want to stop here before their next vacation.
✓**www**→http://www.castles.com/vs/vacation_station.html

Clubs

Association of Business Travelers ABT advertises its membership services at its text-only Website. Interested parties can also utilize the reservations quotes and query service here to "secure the cheapest rates online within 24 hours."
✓**www**→http://www.hk.linkage.net/markets/abt

Car rental

Abel In harmony with this Australian company's slogan ("Keeping it simple since 1979") this page is well-organized, attractive, and informative. The Preview section, updated daily, offers pics, specs, and even price info for a variety of rentals.
✓**www**→http://www.squirrel.com.au/abel

Alamo Rent A Car: Freeways Booking a car may lead the list of things to do on the Alamo Website, but Alamo doesn't just hand travelers the keys. The site delivers travel tips, information on destinations across the U.S., games for "cooped-up kids," an Alamo locator, directions for getting around popular U.S. cities, coupons for tourist sites, and even links to other travel, map, and weather sites. Knowing that travelers like to talk about their trips, Alamo offers a

---

forum for customers to give advice on road-side food, hotels, restaurants, and sightseeing.
✓**www**→http://www.freeways.com

AutoRent Although the bulk of the information here is presented in non-interactive, tabular form, AutoRent's site still offers easy access to detailed rental info. Its informative table displays daily rate info, pictures, and specs for each of the company's rental models. (Does he car have a cassette player? automatic or manual? air conditioning? power windows?) Links lead to online reservations forms and a page on the locations of the company's various offices.
✓**www**→http://www.macom.co.il/Tourism/AutoRent/index.html

Avis The Avis Galaxy home page situates the car company in the midst of a huge nebula of rates, car descriptions, maps, and special information on business accounts. In addition, Avis includes a Fun section that lets you Ask the Magic Car; enter a question and a cartoon of an anthropomorphic red sedan will deliver a one-word answer.
✓**www**→http://www.avis.com

Eurodollar Europe Eurodollar UK shows how a simple, brief, compact, and well-organized page can make researching and reserving a car easy and fast. Even though the page is low on panache, its high on practicality—delivering everything a car rental

---

Website should.
✓**www**→http://www.eurodollar.co.uk

Hertz Asia Hertz Asia's Website opens with a large, cheerful picture of a cheerful customer closing a rental agreement with a cheerful Hertz employee. Get the picture? In case you don't, this site emphasizes the efficiency, convenience, and all-around cheerfulness of the company. By providing the names, locations, and phone numbers of Hertz offices in seven Asian countries, this site reinforces the notion of service and reliability found at Hertz. There is even an email link provided for reservations and pricing inquiries, however, a time-zone converter would be more helpful for those who still use the telphone.
✓**www**→http://www.singapore.com/companies/hertz

Rail

Amtrak Up until now, terminal has meant something different to train companies. On the Website, Amtrak's president is waiting at the platform to meet all the cyber-travellers. After a brief introduction, Netsurfers can visit one of the many links covering Amtrak's travel packages. There's also information on all of Amtrak's routes and a number of maps for further inquiries. Aside from ticketing info, Amtrak provides extra content in the form of travel tips and vacation advice.
✓**www**→http://www.amtrak.com

Airlines

As a rule, the more established an airline, the higher the production values of its Web-

site. But online even a sharp-thinking short-hop specialist can compete. All in all, dozens of airlines have taken to the cyberskies, trying to attract new customers, build loyalty among old customers, and set up services that let all customers check on flight schedules and track routes. **Lufthansa** effortlessly adapts its sleek corporate style for the Web. **Cathay Pacific** has jetted onto the Web in style by offering innovative promotions, including frequent-flyer mile giveaways. And **Mexicana Airlines** does double duty, functioning not only as an airlines but as a full-service travel agency that books hotel rooms, reviews restaurants, and describes a number vacation destinations.

On the Net

U.S. & Canada

Air Canada Flyers who want to read an Air Canada company profile can find one in the in-flight magazine; if they go to the Website, on the other hand, they can expect service. After a mission statement heralding new routes and an Open-Skies agreement between the U.S. and Canada, the site delivers an exhaustive list of phone numbers for reservations, a downloadable, searchable flight schedule, and daily press releases on expanded/revised services. All AC info in Cyberspace is available in both French and English.
✓**www**→http://www.aircanada.ca

America West Airlines A straightforward site that gets straight to business with flight schedules, prices, and conditions (information is updated every six months). A contact number for reservations is also provided.
✓**www**→http://www.cucruising.com/cu/amwest.html

American Airlines Although its airline pages are within a large corporate site, American Airlines has established one of the strongest airline Web presences. Opening with a glossy graphic that puts the visitor behind the wing of a jumbo jet, the site offers dozens of services designed to make planning and travel trouble-free. These include a full, searchable database of American Airlines flight schedules a list of all U.S. American Airlines ticket offices and toll-free reservations numbers to use around the world. Flyers can also research specifics like baggage restrictions, find out which in-flight movie is playing, track their frequent flyer

Southwest Airlines Home Gate

IN-SITE: **Southwest Airlines**
   http://www.iflyswa.com
Southwest has gone out of its way to make this site informative and fun. The opening graphic of a boarding gate is actually an interactive map which leads to ticketing and boarding info, as well as company news, and an online version of SA's *Spirit* magazine. Visitors can scan down the page for daily updates on special fares and for lighter items such as packing tips and an archive of video and print clips from SA's previous advertising campaigns.

miles, and even download recipes so they can enjoy those airline meals at home!

✓**www**→http://www.amrcorp.com/aa_home/aa_home.htm

Canadian Airlines International Just the facts on this page. Flight schedules, prices, and weather a phone number for making reservations, but no graphics.

✓**www**→http://www.cucruising.com/cu/cp.html

Carnival Airlines This visually appealing page gives as much space to a profile of the company (info on the fleet, training programs and executives) as it does to service details (flight schedules, tour packages, online frequent flyer program enrollment, and contact info for charters).

✓**www**→http://www.carnivalair.com

Delta Air Lines Delta Airline's site offers a mix of business and pleasure. Practical features include a searchable database of flight schedules, reservations numbers, descriptions of special deals and services, an FAQ with company stats, maps of airports and diagrams of airlines. On the entertainment side, there are cool contests, a downloadable video game demo, and an ongoing travelogue that gives a virtual tour of a new destination each week.

✓**www**→http://www.delta-air.com/index.html

Mexicana Airlines Chosen by Net.Value as one of the most interesting sites of January 1996, Mexicana Airlines is an all-out travel agent. It offers flyers a schedule and price database, info on frequent flyer programs, and the opportunity to make online reservations—there's even a page on the company mascot, Capitàn

Turbina! And it doesn't stop there. Visitors can browse through illustrated profiles of destinations and hotels, link to other travel sites, and study online maps of each region. Smartly identifying itself with the new medium, Mexicana Airlines also offers the online "Amigos in Travel" program. The airline provides hypertext "spotlights" on hotels, guidebooks, commuter airlines, tour operators, restaurants, and other tourism companies, which it will build and display on its own pages.

✓**www**→http://www.mexicana.com

Presidential Airlines An eclectic site offering some very useful resources (flight schedules and fares, an email address and a telephone number for making reservations), as well as some curious extras (an operator-participant contract and a report on performance specifications). PA keeps a mailing list and sends fare and schedule updates directly to the customers.

✓**www**→http://www.presair.com

Western Pacific Airlines What this site lacks in beauty it compensates for in functionality—visitors can get an online reservations request form or pick up a reservations phone number. The fare info listed shows prices in tiers, at one-day, one-week, and one-month's notice. The price info is worked into the route info, so the flyer can get everything he or she needs to know in one fell swoop.

✓**www**→http://www.cucruising.com/cu/wpair.html

Africa

Chartair A simple Web presence offering a highly stylized overview of the airline's services. There is an online form visitors can fill out to receive flight information.

✓**www**→http://www.aztec.co.za/biz/africa/chartair.htm

South African Airways While the site's flight information is presently limited to an overview of its frequent flyer program, a fun, multimedia teaser for upcoming Real Audio/Virtual Tours will ensure the return of curious Netsurfers.

✓**www**→http://www.saa.co.za/saa

Asia

All Nippon Airways All Nippon's service doesn't begin and end on the plane. This company wants to help travelers with all aspects of their trip as well. Featuring an interactive travel guide for ANA and other East Asian airlines, the page offers text and photos of China, Hong Kong, and Japan as well as links to the home pages of hotels and restaurants in each region.

✓**www**→http://metrotel.co.uk/travlog/ana.html

Cathay Pacific Cathay's Website has been one of the most revolutionary in these early years of online marketing. The airline's original objective was to use the Web to build a mailing list, and to do so it ran a contest offering 1,000,000 frequent flyer redeemable at American Airlines. As a result of this promotion—and the high market value of American miles—the page was swamped by visitors, and Cathay began soliciting sponsors for its site. The site is fun to visit for consumers as well, many Web-only incentives and price discounts as well as great graphics, the million miles contest, seat auctions, and the inevitable company profile.

✓**www**→http://www.cathay-usa.com

Sempati Airlines Sempati Airlines' home page leads off with a huge image of an Airbus A-30—the plane that's "extra wide for extra comfort"—at sunrise. But the company's attitude when it comes to Websites seems to be that size doesn't matter. This tiny page holds its own against much larger competition, offering basic route and timetable information.
✓**www**→http://ios.com/~asia net/Asia_Trade/Travel -leisure/Sin/Preair/Sempati/index .html

Central America

Aero Costa Rica Aero Costa Rica gets the flyer up and about in no time with well-produced, straightforward information—flight schedules, details on the airline's frequent flyer plan, telephone numbers, and an email link for further info and reservations.
✓**www**→http://www.centralamer ica.com/cr/tran/aero.htm

Down Under

Air New Zealand ANZ entices visitors by providing links to companies offering entertainment possibilities all over the country—everything from kayaking to paragliding. How to get to the places where it all happens is less apparent, as no flight info is provided.
✓**www**→http://www.clearfield.co .nz/hotpac/hotpac.htm

Ansett Australia This airline also operates a limo and car service in Australia and uses the Website to promote all of its service, offering info on how to apply frequent-flyer miles to car and limo rentals. Visitors are enticed with pictures and lengthy descriptions of some Ansett destinations (Bali and Norfolk Island, for example), a down-loadable Ansett screensaver, and even special deals on theater tickets and theme park admittance. All in all, a rich site, and one that balances utility and content skillfully.
✓**www**→http://www.ansett.com .au

Mount Cook Airlines This tiny fleet only services itineraries between NZ and Australia, but it has a surprisingly large cyberpresence. Visitors can learn about their flights (where to, how much, and when) and choose from three booking options—phone, fax, or email.
✓**www**→http://www.clearfield.co .nz/mount_cook/

Qantas Airways While the Qantas page showcases the Aussie airline's services—the page includes an air-route map, illustrated stats, a company profile, special (offline) offers and programs, and detailed info on services from advance seat assignments to in-flight movie listings to smoking policy—brand identity is developed using the popular, offline "I Hate Qantas" advertising campaign, which features a comically disgruntled Koala Bear. And Qantas doesn't skimp on tradition either, mentioning the airline's 75-year history and long tradition of safe flight prominently.
✓**www**→http://www.anzac.com /qantas/qantas.htm

IN-SITE: **SwissAir**
http://www.swissair.ch
This site is full of media-rich features. Practical info is plentiful, overviews of services are comprehensive, the searchable database allows visitors to check on just the flights they're interested in, and visitors have easy access to the latest discounted fares and new or revised flight services. But the real draw here are the monthly destination profiles which are full of pics and descriptive text.

Europe

Aer Lingus Fresh Shamrock! The opening tag line may not actually mean anything, but it certainly screams "Ireland," as does the rest of this green, friendly, service-packed site. Visitors can click on a departure city and destination, and they'll get a current flight schedule with prices. Special promotions and offers are updated every month, and Lingus also suggests vacation itineraries in Ireland, featuring special deals for those traveling to the country on business. A table of reservations telephone numbers worldwide rounds out the site.
✓**www**→http://www.aerlingus.ie

Aeroflot The detailed fare info and timetable of flights between various U.S. cities and Moscow are helpful, but what makes this site shine are its descriptions of Aeroflot's aircraft.
✓**www**→http://www.aeroflot.org/Aeroflot.html

Air France At its link on the Cannes home page, black-and-white photographs of stars like Alfred Hitchcock and Anouk Aimée aboard Air France flights, lend this airline a sense of established elegance. The official home page, on the other hand, exchanges élan for information. While the page pays equal attention to it's "catalog of products" and its health tips for travelers, most flyers will concentrate on the catalog of flight services the airline provides. Feature-filled pages—intriguingly organized by airplane model, including the supersonic Concorde—offer detailed information on every step of the journey from airport to air.
✓**www** …→http://www.airfrance.fr …→http://cannes.cyber.ad.jp/~cannes/sponsors/airfrance/index2.html

AirUK Featuring news articles and flight info updated every week AirUK has an exhaustive database that allows visitors to obtain the information they need. Select a destination city, an approximate time of arrival, and a departure day, and the site provides a range of appropriate itineraries. Visitors can also register for an Executive Card online and be eligible for discounts at restaurants and hotels in their destination cities. The brand can even be hot-wired into your monitor via a downloadable AirUK screensaver.
✓**www**→http://www.airuk.co.uk

Austrian Airlines MORE AA delivers a searchable database of flight itineraries, a Hot News section that outlines promotions and special deals, travel info (baggage restrictions, customs and boarding info, etc.), and some pictures of Austria.
✓**www**→http://www.aua.co.at/aua

British Airways With a tone reminiscent of its offline ads, British Airways has created nothing short of an online encyclopedia of services. If the visitor knows what to look for, he or she are directed to the index which, for each letter in the alphabet, lists between two and ten multimedia features, under such headings as Air Miles, Fleet Maintenance, Luggage Allowance, and Video Clips. If the flyer would rather take a more casual trip through the site, the choice of surfing by category— Business, Leisure, or Culture. Either way, the time that it would take to experience each link on British Airways' enormous home page would fill a flight from London to Sydney.
✓**www**→http://www.british-airways.com

Lauda Air This unusual site is aimed straight at students and casual corporate travelers. A strange rodent-in-boxers mascot pops up on the pages, which are filled with multimedia presentations of on the company's history, flight schedules, rotating student specials, and even a poem describing the cabin crews' uniforms. Another neat feature assures visitors will check out each area on the site— Lauda has hidden an angel icon on an unspecified page, and those who find the angel can win prizes. The deeper the visitors go into the links, the more German they'll find, but English speakers can still navigate with ease.
✓**www**→http://www.laudaair.com/engl/indexe.htm

Lufthansa A near-perfect mix of style and utility. Comprehensive flight and fare schedules for itineraries to Asia, South America, and the U.S., and info on special promotions including ticket discounts and giveaways and price breaks are all showcased with excellent graphics, giving the company a pristine and elegant online identity with virtually no effort.
✓**www**→http://www.Lufthansa.ch

Virgin Atlantic Virgin Atlantic's lavish home page doesn't mirror its offline campaigns of celebrity endorsements or sixties nostalgia, opting instead for a service-oriented site with a great deal of interactivity. Punchy graphics and conversational copy balance the weightiness of Virgin's content, which includes a flight-plan database, a devilishly difficult trivia quiz with prizes, holiday packages, service overviews, and even brief city guides with links to local home pages.
✓**www**→http://www.fly.virgin.com/atlantic

Vacations

Having absorbed the advice of travel agents and worked out the most cost-effective

routes anywhere in the world, the digital traveller must eventually decide where to go. The Net does not disappoint. All four corners of the world have pages that disport themselves with the passion of market traders yet offer depth and density of information far beyond the ambitions of most capital cities' tourist offices. **Asia Travel** and **Hong Kong Wonder Net** score huge points for the East. But it's not only nations that are putting their best feet forward. Cruise companies like **Carnival** and **Royal Caribbean Cruise Lines** attempt to convey the ambiance of the islands and the majesty of the big ships. And **Disney** is online as well, with a site that details the myriad joys of the Magic Kingdom.

On the Net

Countries

Asia Online This Website is intended to promote Asian businesses, but does a great job meeting the needs and inspiring the dreams of travelers. Planning a trip to Asia is a hefty task, and Asia One wants to be the one-stop-shop for the overwhelmed. The site offers a regional newsfeed, a mammoth index of Asian Websites, a guide to

corporations in Asia, and, most significantly, a cyberguide to traveling in Asia. The cyberguide links to hotel listings for each Asian country, country profiles, and an interesting collection of Asian travel resources. The resources are broken down by country. If a visitor chooses Malaysia, for instance, she is rewarded with a clickable map of Malaysia, popular Malaysian recipes, a guide to student traveling in Penang, and even a currency converter.
✓**www**→http://asiatravel.com/index.html

Asia Travel Asia Travel's Website with literally thousands of hotels, restaurants, and travel agencies,

makes planning a trip to the continent easy. At this page, major travel industry players from all over Asia join forces and the result is a massive advertisement for all the services a traveler would ever need for exploring Asia.
✓**www**→http://www.asia-online.com

Barbados Home Page Pictures of couples snorkeling and white-clad men playing cricket promote the idea that Barbados is an elite paradise. The images are the stars of this site—there is little else here except a short list of hotels, restaurants, and bars.
✓**www**→http://www.bajan.com/barbados

IN-SITE: **Hong Kong Wonder Net**
http://www.hkta.org
The Hong Kong Tourist Authority effectively recreates the rapid pace of the business capital of the east at this action-packed site with QuickTime movies, bold graphics, and diverse services. Potential visitors imbibe some of the ambiance of Hong Kong through virtual presentations on culture, food, and fesitvals. But the site is also interested in selling Hong Kong's economy to business and vacation travelers alike, and offers tips on doing business the Hong Kong way and where to find a bargain on fur.

Bavarian Alpine Net The official tourist organization of Bavaria steers away from a stiff, official presence by offering a personal, insider view of Munich; the city's attractions are profiled with the testimonials of people who have already visited.
✓**www**→http://www.bavaria.com

British Virgin Islands Bright colors and a large opening banner that shouts "Welcome" establish a friendly, make yourself-at-home atmosphere at the British Virgin Islands Website. Its online comments and response form at the bottom of each section also enhances the impression that visitors are valued and welcome.
✓**www**→http://www.caribweb .com/caribweb/bvi

Discover Spain There's a world of resources packed into this international page. Everything here, from the graphics (like Spain's globe-like national logo) to the diversity and depth of tourist info (hotels listed by province and price range) is geared towards persuading travelers from around the world to visit Spain (the site even provides info in Korean and Japanese in addition to English and Spanish).
✓**www**→http://www.spaintour .com/

France's Cafe Maybe it's the bright, primary colors, or maybe it's the map of France that opens the site, but the feel of this page is reminiscent of a grade-school text book. Visitors can access rudimentary essays and a few pictures of the various regions of France, and there's also a writing contest that lets online travelers try their hand at conveying the beauty of the City of Lights.
✓**www**→http://www.france.com /francescape/top.html

Hungary Online The modern type in the site's logo and the enormous picture of Budapest's Parliament make Hungary seem like a successful blend of ultra modern-chic and old-world charm. To underscore that effect, the Hungarian Tourist Board offers QuickTime videos of some of the oldest markets in Europe and online schedules for one of the world's most respected operas.
✓**www**→http://www.hungary.com /tourinform

India Tourist Office The info at the India Tourist Office is easy to access and detailed, which will surely count as a valued travel aid to any visitor. The Office's Website offers an info-packed page including clickable maps of the country, and lists with addresses of hotels and "other accommodations." There are descriptions of attractions (the Taj, etc.), calendars of special events, and even temperature and rainfall charts for every month of the year.
✓**www**→http://interhealth.com /india

Jamaica Come to this page and feel all right. The famous slogan, beautiful photographs, and copious amounts of tourist info work together to get Netsurfers in the mood to visit the island.
✓**www**→http://www.jamaica-tours .com/Jamaica

Japan Travel Updates Sponsored by the Japan National Tourist Organization, this page doesn't just push travel in Japan—it practically shoves travelers on the plane! Laden down with maps of the country, travel tips, explanations of traditional Japanese hotels and food, suggested itineraries and activities, the site is guaranteed to put thoughts of Japan in a traveler's head. There's even a message

board at the page, and guess what—it's packed with tips and tales from travelers.
✓**www**→http://www.jnto.go.jp

Latvian Tourist Board With nothing but links to essays on typical tourists' topics, this page is like a straight shot of Stoli—it takes potential travelers where they need ot go, but not very smoothly.
✓**www**→http://latvia.vernet.lv /travel

Samoan Government Tourist Pages This is a government-sponsored page with hotel listings, pictures, and statistics on the local population.
✓**www**→http://www.interwebinc .com/samoa

Sawaddee Thailand Sawaddee Thailand floods its site with colorful pictures of temples, sound clips of Thai lessons, and links to addresses for hotels and restaurants. Sawaddee's use of complex graphics and sounds promotes Thailand's commercial outlets like hotels, restaurants, and shopping without excluding its most precious assets—the culture and people.
✓**www**→http://www.cs.ait.ac.th /tat/index.html

Scottish Tourist Board It's hard to take this page seriously. It's supposed to be an official page promoting vacations to Scotland, but it opens with a picture of a flying tartan boot logo and offers links to the *Braveheart* and *Rob Roy* movie pages. It couldn't get any more fun than that—not on the Web or in Scotland, either!
✓**www**→http://www.scotourist.org .uk/stb

The Singapore Online Guide The Singapore Tourist Promotion Board is using the Web to attract visitors with a searchable guide to

Singapore that offers information about shopping, restaurants, festivals, hotels, and island nightlife. The real draw to the site, however, may be the interactive tour guide which prompts travelers to nail down their elusive travel plans. The tour guide asks a series of questions about destination and interests. With that done, Singapore's Website will generate a customized itinerary for each day of the proposed trip. No more headaches!

✓ **www**→http://www.travel.com.sg/sog

Welcome to Austria This page creates the impression that the Austria seen in movies actually exists and is waiting for tourists, by displaying pictures of typically Austrian attractions—ski villages, Sigmund Freud, and blonde-haired Mädels.

✓ **www**→http://austria-info.at

Travel attractions

Alcatraz The National Park Service markets one of its more unusual attractions, with a great interactive site that allows Web visitors to undertake a "self-guided" tour of the prison (something inmates never get to do!). Links lead to essays and sound clips that are both fun and educational, and there's practical info on visiting the island. Alcatraz's Website only leaves one thing out—an escape route.

✓ **www**→http://www.nps.gov/alcatraz

Australian National Botanic Gardens The Garden's Website is an excellent example of how smaller and more specialized tourist attractions market themselves on the Web. There's standard fare here like pictures, directions for reaching the Gardens, and links to other botanical sites.

✓ **www**→http://155.187.10.12/anbg.html

Disney Disney's Website may be a little too expansive for the average Netsurfer to handle—but then again DisneyWorld is not your average amusement park. Inside of Disney's large site, there's advice on everything that makes up the Magic Kingdom—from movies, to the parks, to the Mickey Mouse watch that turns Mickey into a double jointed time-keeper. There's also plenty to do like daily puzzles and contests that bring some of that Disney magic to your computer.

✓ **www**→http://www2.disney.com/DisneyWorld/index.html

Everglades Alligator Farm The site matches the spirit of the attraction—pics of people sitting on gators and an ad for dried alligator heads advertise this unusual tourist attraction.

✓ **www**→http://florida.com/gatorfarmer/index.html

Mammoth Mountain Conditions have to be right for a ski resort to be operable, so this page offers daily snow reports with a unique use of Web technology: the MammothCam, which yields a picture of the resort's slopes every morning at 8:00 am.

✓ **www**→http://www.cccd.edu/~markb/ski/mj/mammoth

Sea World/Busch Gardens Informative essays on around 20 different animals form the core of the site (the somewhat technical language of the essays requires that most children be accompanied by adults when learning about their feathered, furred, and scaled friends). The only actual commercial plug for the park is a list of addresses buried at the bottom of the site.

✓ **www**→http://www.bev.net/education/SeaWorld/homepage.html

Singapore Zoo The Singapore Zoo tries to make its page as fun as actually being there with a QuickTime movie of the zoo's animals at play, descriptions of the zoo's programs, and an invitation to "have breakfast with the orangutans." Admissions info is also provided for those lucky enough to actually visit the offline facility.

✓ **www**→http://www.ncb.gov.sg/sog/att/abal/zoo

Cruise lines

Carnival Carnival's page is the flagship site of cruise ship advertising online. Its page establishes the identity of the various cruise lines that now fly under the Carnival flag (Windstar and Seabourne are now among them) and encourages booking by offering special deals for Internet users.

✓ **www**→http://mmink.com/mmink/carnival/carnival.html

Dolphin A clear, sharp design and blue everywhere on the page evoke thoughts of sailing in smooth waters on a beautiful and efficiently-run ship. And talk about efficiency...a link just below the site's stunning opening graphic invites visitors to submit an online form to receive a full-color brochure.

✓ **www**→http://mmink.com/dolphincl/dolphinhome.html

Royal Caribbean Cruise Line No fancy pictures of ships or ports of call here—just a listing of RC's latest specials and a cruising FAQ. The stripped down-look and feel of the page go a long way to underscoring the budget fares offered by the cruise line.

✓ **www**→http://mmink.com/rccl.html

Hotels & resorts

Imagine a hotel where the staff gives you more than just a clean room and a smile.

Imagine a hotel where every desk clerk, elevator operator, and housekeeper showers you with gifts ranging from travel tips to frequent-flyer miles to rental cars. You've just imagined an online hotel. Although most major hotel chains offer room-availability checks and rate cards, extra features are the rule in this business, from **Marriott**'s air miles offer to the **Holiday Inn**'s fun-and-games site. As they learn interactive technologies, hotel and resort sites are also oriented toward helping vacationers choose the appropriate destination; **Club Med**, for example, offers a Village Locator service that helps visitors find the antidote to civilization best suited to their particular character.

On the Net

Hotel chains

Best Western International
Best Western International, Inc., the world's largest hotel chain with 3,400 properties worldwide, stresses its universal presence with a massive searchable database of hotels.
✓**www**→http://www.travelweb .com/bw.html

Continental Plaza Hotels &

Resorts Continental offers a unique blend of commercial practicality and cultural information at its Website. There is a clickable map for information on its hotels in Mexico City, Cancun, and Veracruz, as well as essays on archaeological digs and ecotourism.
✓**www**→http://www.wotw.com /wow/situr/cpl-main.html

Embassy Suites Embassy Suites, the expansive hotel chain, works

the Net to full advantage with descriptions of, and reservations for, its hundreds of hotels. A convenient destination map helps travelers choose a hotel, and its online reservations form makes securing a room fast and simple.
✓**www**→http://www.embassy -suites.com

Hilton Hilton's Website is hosted by a cartoon concierge that makes navigation easy. It's a good thing

IN-SITE: **ClubMed**
http://www.clubmed.com/cm/pages/homepage
ClubMed, the well-known resort chain, knows that "destination" is the name of the game in travel, and its Website provides a clickable map customers can use to find a resort in their destination area. The pitch for each resort includes photographs, videos, daily weather reports, and online reservations capabilities.

Industry Hub

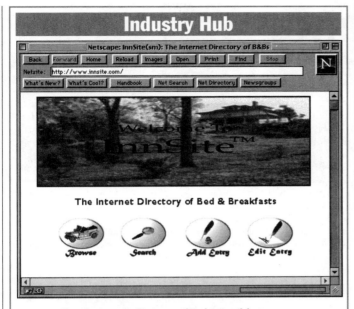

IN-SITE: **InnSite: The Internet Directory of Bed & Breakfasts**
http://www.innsite.com/

Many smaller hotels and inns across the country are marketing their lodging services online at large, free directory sites like this one. Entries typically include a photo of the establishment, simple text descriptions of its location, and reservations numbers. InnSite, which has one of the best URLs in the travel industry, is an excellent example of how lodgings with a small marketing/advertising budget can create a Web presence.

---

too, because Hilton's Website is brimming with extra content and active links. There's a detailed reservations system, a directory of its hotels nationwide, info on its mileage programs, special promotions, the HHonors program, and even contests!

✓**www**→http://www.hilton.com

Holiday Inn Along with its directory of Holiday Inn hotels worldwide and online reservation system, the site challenges its visitors to compete in an Internet version of the trivia travel board game, Travel Buff. Players choose regions and levels of difficulty and are then asked questions ("The Aleutian Islands can be found in: Alaska, California, Georgia, or Florida?") which they must answer

within a fixed period of time. The goal is to get your name on the site's high score list. Visitors may also download versions of the game to play offline.

✓**www**→http://www.holiday-inn.com

Marriott Marriott believes in the personal touch—its site opens with a greeting by Bill, Jr., the head of the luxury hotel chain. The site offers detailed information on the whole line of Marriott chain hotels, which include The Courtyard, The Residence Inn, and The Fairfield Inn. As an extra boon, Nettravelers can enroll in the Marriott Miles Club, which enables them to earn free airline mileage as an incentive to lodge with the chain in the future.

✓**www**→http://www.marriott.com

Novotel Novotel's page takes a different approach to the Web. With over 300 locations worldwide, the company highlights only ten of its North American properties with color photos and informative guides. These ten highlights don't serve as a complete guide to Novotels, but they do give customers a sense of the hotel's style and philosophy, as well as a detailed look at a few properties.

✓**www**→http://www.novotel.com/welcome

Radisson Hotels Radisson's Website is a service-oriented and international enterprise fluent in four languages: English, French, Spanish, and German. The site provides travel tips for business travelers and vacationers and reservations capabilities for most Radisson properties worldwide.

✓**www**→http://www2.pcy.mci.net/marketplace/radisson

Resorts

Australian Resorts Home Page Five luxury hotels find strength in numbers by combining their info online in a brochure featuring a clickable map, text descriptions, and photographs of each hotel. Online reservation capability is an added bonus.

✓**www**→http://peg.apc.org/~austresorts

SuperClubs What's a SuperClub and what does it look like? This Website answers these questions and more with photographs of each of the SuperClub hotels (Boscobel Beach, Grand Lido, Hedonism II, Sans Souci Lido, and Jamaica Jamaica) and full descriptions of each of the resorts.

✓**www**→http://www.IntNet.net/SuperClubs

Restaurants

Most restaurants have missed the first course when it comes to Web marketing. Re-

nowned franchises have yet to make an appearence on-line, while obscure outfits like **Bagel Oasis** are happily chowing down on the new medium. The large chains, while generating dozens of fan pages, have almost no official sites, although in early 1996, **KFC** (formerly known as Kentucky Fried Chicken) opened a site. The pages that currently exist are Jack Spratt-spare at best, with a menu, link lists, and coupons; but some sites, such as **Little Caesars** and the **Philadelphia Pretzel Company**, have make a real effort to create a moveable online feast.

On the Net

Bagel Oasis It's not a hallucination! It's New York City's Bagel Oasis online with lots of fun graphics (palm trees, a smelly laboratory where the "others" make their bagels, etc.), a company history, and an order form that projects an image of health, established quality, and service.
✓**www**→http://www.bageloasis .com

Bravo Restaurants The parent company of theme restaurants like Gino's East of Chicago and Ed Debevic posts standard info—locations, menus, coupons—for its establishments.

✓**www**→http://www.GinosEast .com

The Fish Market With a graphic of a lobster flashing itself and a tagline that reads "Expose Yourself to a Great Seafood Dinner," The Fish Market uses its Website to send the message that its seven California restaurants are fun, relaxed places. The Website includes descriptions of each location, complete with sample menus, prices, and pictures.
✓**www**→http://www.thefishmarket .com

Hooters The company's bio heralds the Hooters restaurant chain as "the place to go for families." Maybe if the kids haven't been

weaned yet. People come to Hooters for one reason, and it isn't the clam chowder. The site offers franchise information, a restaurant locator, a *Playboy*-like calendar, and sports coverage.
✓**www**→http://www.hooters.com

Il Fornaio How do you create the impression that yours is a restaurant for the elite? Il Fornaio, an Italian restaurant in California, runs a newletter that reads like a gossip column and offers customers an online menu with an elegant design.
✓**www**→http://www.ilfornaio.com

KFC The KFC page started off with a blow against it—at the time of the site's birth in 1996, the do-

IN-SITE: **Bagel World**
   http://www.bagelworld.com/index.html
Why would a tiny bagel restaurant in Cape Canaveral, Florida, hawks its ware on the Net? Because it ships its delectable bread rings anywhere in the United States. Coupons encourage bagel eaters from Maryland to San Francisco to order from Bagel World.

Industry Hub

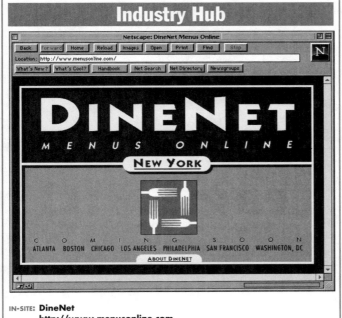

IN-SITE: **DineNet**
http://www.menusonline.com

DineNet is a directory of menus for thousands of restaurants in major cities across the U.S. It's a good place to advertise—at no cost—even the tiniest, most intimate of eateries.

main name "KFC.COM" belonged to a small computer tech service in Albuquerque, New Mexico, and the chain was forced to revert to the original recipe in cooking up a domain name. Apart from the What's New section, which features announcements of special meals and mouth-watering pics of new dishes, the site opts for company information over human interest. One man, however, stands tall—the founder and spokesman for the famous fried chicken, Colonel Harlan Sanders. Not only is there a complete biography of the Colonel at the site, but almost every feature—from the company history to the FAQ—is filled with references to him, and his face on the KFC icon adorns each page. The site also features a branch locator which showcases the mega-chain's new home delivery service.
✓ **www**→www.kentuckyfried chicken.com

Little Caesars Pizza! Pizza! Coupons! Coupons! Buried among links to charities, an article on the effectiveness of commercials, a catering menu, and corporate information are coupons and downloads of the singing baby and the Little Caesars "dude" quipping "pizza, pizza."
✓ **www**→http://pages.prodigy.com /LittleCaesars

McDonald's Austria McDonald's Austria takes the mystery out of fast food with nutritional information, news about employment opportunities, lists of restaurant locations in Austria, and the names of companies that supply the chain food. The site is in German.

✓ **www**→http://www.mcdonalds .co.at/mcdonalds

OinkExpress Featuring sound clips of oinking pigs, a lengthy essay on the restaurant's service style known as "pig picking," and an order form that lets adventurous eaters sample OE's hushpuppies anywhere in the continental U.S., the Website isn't exactly striving for an aura of refinement, but refinement isn't what the pork-loving, bacon-crunching OinkExpress customers are actively looking for.
✓ **www**→http://www.eastnc.coast alnet.com/business/food/kings /kings.htm

Philadelphia Pretzel Company Appealing to a combination of old-world romanticism and value, the Philadelphia Pretzel Company uses the word "tradition" three times in the first two lines of text at its Website and features pictures of the Liberty Bell and City Hall. Online discounts, coupons, and giveaway contests are offered.
✓ **www**→http://amsquare.com /pretzel

Pizza Hut Although delivering to only a small area in Santa Cruz, California, the Pizza Hut Website lets customers in the area order pizza from a virtual menu and have it delivered to their homes.
✓ **www**→http://www.pizzahut.com

Round Table Pizza Round Table Pizza, which has several locations in Northern California, offers customers 10 percent off if they order online. In addition, the site links to an extensive guidebook to dining and entertainment in the Bay Area. The guidebook also carries an advertisement for the restaurant's Website.
✓ **www**→http://www.round-table .com/home.htm

Chapter 11

Services

Professional services

It was not so long ago that the idea of professionals advertising in print raised a few

eyebrows, and the idea of doctors and lawyers selling their services on television was unthinkable. But the world has taken another turn, and now professionals ply their trade across all media, including Cyberspace. Some, like **Nichols, Kaster & Anderson** recognize the vastness of the Net community and provide an unmatched drunk-driving defense database. The good doctor at **Naples Plastic Surgery** can convince shy patients with online before-and-after photos. **The Credit Department** attracts those drowning in debt with a free email credit analysis. And in this virtual world there is also more room for oddities—**Sherlock Bones,** a pet detective agency that would give Ace Ventura a run for his money, maintains a large site, full of advice and praise from customers worldwide.

On the Net

Accounting

American Business Services
This online credit manager has little interest in attracting the all-American family with its day-to-day financial niggles; instead its

site targets troubled small businesses. ABS "shouts" its promises of up to 80 percent off original amounts owed in all caps. Avoiding unpleasant words like "bankruptcy," their colorful business pitch promises potential clients that they will never see a legal document or encounter the "grief and aggravation of dealing with creditors." A no-strings-attached email evaluation attempts to seal the bargain.
✓ **www**→http://public.navisoft.com /a/a/aambussvcs/index2.htm

Credi-Care There is no one to contradict this site's headline proclaiming it "the largest and most experienced credit management organization in the nation." Their pitch is directed at beleaguered consumers, down to the cartoons of families sweating over a pile of bills. Even their phone number touts their almost magical credit expertise—1-800-last-bill. The final selling point is a free debt consolidation analysis by email. Potential customers just fill out a email form and await the pro-

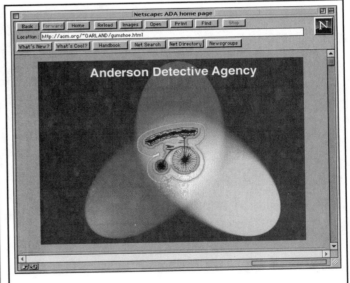

IN-SITE: **Anderson Detective Agency**
http://acm.org/~GARLAND/gumshoe.html
Everyone has an image of the perfect private detective, whether in the form of Sam Spade, Sherlock Holmes, or Magnum, P.I. Each of these masters knew that probing into other people's business often has a shady side, but the need to know is practically congenital. The Anderson page certainly has a sense of panache and uses pop culture references aptly. While The Prisoner stares at visitors from behind virtual bars, Anderson describes its services, and discusses its philosophy of right and wrong. The prominent placement of the logo of *The X-Files* suggests that all is not absconding accountants, adulterous spouses, or even potential son-in-laws here. Ed Anderson also investigates "unexplained abductions and occult" incidents. The truth is out there…

mised good life.
✓ **www**→http://www.starnetinc
.com/credi-care/home.html

The Credit Department The creator of this page is playing on the belief that groups know more than individuals, calling his service the credit department when he is really selling individual services. The hook is a free email analysis. Businesses are invited to send in their problem and if they like the solution, to negotiate further services. The no-obligation promise is a great incentive with tried and tested appeal.
✓ **www**→http://www.iquest.net
/~rfluecki/

Pace Tax and Accounting Online Pace Accounting is hoping that the extra-simple flat tax favored by former Presidential candidate Steve Forbes won't be approved by the new administration. Why? Because Pace is online, offering tax help in a variety of forms. Pace Tax already gives freebies—tax tips and IRS news ready for downloading. But they they also take it for granted that even with the 1040s at their fingertips, many taxpayers will still feel helpless. Where better to turn than to the helpful folks at the end of the modem?
✓ **www**→http://www.pacetax.com

Tax/Accounting Services Over the Internet Michael Sklar has created an impressive presence on the Net, offering lots of free info and the realization of a universal dream—lower taxes come April. Offering a free tax tip every week and a newsletter full of financial planning guidance is bound to attract the tax-paying multitude. But Sklar's most potent sales pitch is the magic of the Internet and the promise of near-immediate access, day and night, to a personal ac-

countant.
✓ **www**→http://pages.prodigy.com
/CA/internetcpa/

Architects

Klein Dytham Architects Mark Dytham and Astrid Klein have constructed their architectural home page to appeal to the hip young people who live (and spend) in Tokyo. Cheerfully labeling themselves "gaijin" and their site "blatant PR," they present a stylish site with clean lines on the page and in their buildings—one combines a petrol station, fast-food take-out, and office building in a gleaming tower of glass. Their trendy self-parody extends to their own ezine, where they choose their favorite Japanese oddities like a "gumtoro" machine for removing wads of Juicy Fruit from subway platforms. All in all an effective presentation for people whose business is style.
✓ **www**→http://www2.gol.com
/users/zapkdarc/index.html

Doctors

Family Fertility Center Every one of the fertility treatments presented here is accompanied by a fuzzy pink heart. The Family Fertility Center attempts to create a nurturing environment for wishful parents, stressing their case by case management, donor matching, emotional support, and follow-up programs.
✓ **www**→http://www.ihr.com/fam
fert/index.html

Jacqueline Gail Gorton— Ovum Donorship Services Jacqueline Gail Gorton's site leaves visitors with a sense that she is pretty much a virtual panderer. Directed at both desperate childless couples looking for fertile eggs and potential egg donors, she ap-

pears to believe brevity is the soul of salesmanship.
✓ **www**→http://www.ihr.com/gorton/index.html

Louis C. Herring and Co. Each of the selections at the home page of "the recognized world leader in stone analysis" is topped by a picture (in all their glory) of a type of kidney stone—visitors simply click on a stone to retrieve in-depth information. Each analytic technique from X-ray diffractometry and infrared spectrophotometry is described in full. In this cornucopia of kidney stone information are facts about kidney stones, references, and lots more photographs. Assured of making their sale, Herring & Co. provides instructions for mailing kidney stones in for their special touch.
✓ **www**→http://www.herringlab
.com

Naples Plastic Surgery Dr. Mogelvang's goal is for people "to realize that plastic surgery is for everyone"—not just Cher. The good doctor strives to make visitors feel secure, describing his log-cabin Kentucky background and medical education. But it is the before-and-after shots and testimonials that will sell his services— ecstatic recipients of new ears, breasts, and noses in full color.
✓ **www**→http://www.plas-surg
-naples.com

R. Kennon Boyden Dental Practice Dr. Boyden is one of the reasons why everyone in California seems to have gleaming white teeth. This friendly, yet professional page introduces the dentists and staff (cutting down on the dread factor) and offers lots of practical information for home teeth care. There are articles by experts, case studies on porcelain veneers, and "family tips for a better smile."

These helpful hints include an electric toothbrush review, and a fluoride Q&A.

✓**www**→http://www.catalog.com/cgibin/var/dentist/index.html

Schine On-Line Services, Inc.

Gary Schine has the ultimate advantage of a seller of a service; he knows whereof he speaks. This is especially important given what he is selling—a cure for cancer. Schine is a cancer survivor who researched his own treatment—and now he does the same for other sufferers. The presentation is simple—with headlines designed to hit home—"Is the Second Best Treatment Good Enough for You?" and "Can Information Cure Cancer?" His answers are unambiguous and he can present himself as living proof that intelligent research pays off in a big way.

✓**www**→http://www.findcure.com

The Virtual Dentist

This site is just about the farthest thing from the Lawrence Olivier-with-a-drill scene from *Marathon Man* as one can get—and that's its charm. The cyberdentist is a very funny guy— "Watch out plaque, this guy's got a mouth mirror with your name on it!!!" His special brand of whimsy makes a visit to the dentist a lot less frightening—as does his good collection of easy-to-read information about everything from root canal to dental insurance. Although the Virtual Dentist is not looking for business here, his warm and informative site is still a marketing model. Where else can you link to Tooth Fairy's Home Page?

✓**www**→http://www.virtual-dentist.com

Investigators

InPhoto Surveillance

InPhoto is making the most of its recent exposure on *Dateline NBC*, a salient

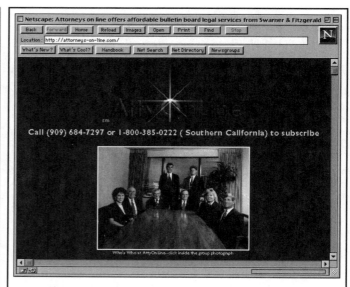

IN-SITE: Attorneys OnLine
http://attorneys-on-line.com

Not just a law firm online, but an online law firm, Attorneys OnLine revolutionizes the notion of legal counsel. With a minimal fee for four hours of legal advice each month (only $15) and the benefit of near-instant gratification (answers are promised within 72 hours), these virtual lawyers also hold public chat sessions on topics from probate to property liability, so subscribers will feel their legal welfare is being guarded from all angles.

example of the ongoing American fascination with cheaters and malingerers of all stripes (InPhoto catches insurance frauds). Along with the full color GIFS of Jane Pauley, InPhoto makes its case to the insurance community with lists of signs of fraud, surveillance laws, and how-to-use video evidence. It's a simple one-step process to order surveillance online, and for the consumer's ease, this page is cross-linked to all the major insurance Web sites. Smart move.

✓**www**→http://www.interaccess.com/inphotowww/

Sherlock Bones

Sherlock Bones is a winsome appellation chosen to convey the rather singular profession of John Keane—he is a real "pet detective." Realizing that pet loss is a trauma that touches American homes up and down the social scale, Keane altruistically offers search tips online, as well as chapters from his upcoming book, and even a lost pet bulletin board—all for free. His phone consultation service is presented as easy and effective—there's a whole page of glowing testimonials to make his personal services indispensable. Remarks one satisfied customer "My dog was found—and I thank God and SHERLOCK BONES— simple as that." Who wouldn't want Sherlock Bones on the case when beloved Fluffy is nowhere to be found?

✓**www**→http://www.sherlock.com/home/sherlock/

Lawyers

Albright & Associates

In attempting to attract aspiring Thomas Edisons, this patent firm

offers some self-help along with the promise of expertise. Albright & Associates has provided inventive Netsurfers with a large database of patent phone and fax numbers, fees, and even hotels near the National Patent and Trademark headquarters. In addition, the firm offers information on the thousands of patents and trademarks they've obtained for budding geniuses.
✓**www**→http://www.worldpat .com/albright.html

Craig and Macauley Home Page
This Boston firm positions itself as a quality source of legal advice with a banner proclaiming that it offers "the Best Lawyers in America." This strategy not only increases client satisfaction, but may result in Craig and Macauley showing up in online searches for "best" and "lawyers." Once they've attracted potential clients, Craig and Macauley woo them by offering an overview of firm services, cases won, and even parking instructions.
✓**www**→http://prospex.com/craig -macauley/Welcome.html

Nichols, Kaster & Anderson
This Minneapolis firm uses a homey approach, local color, and a unique online service to make itself Minneapolis's legal choice. Prospective customers can take a virtual tour of the offices (everything from the conference room to family photos) and link to a number of local news resources (including *The Minneapolis Star Tribune* and local TV listings)—features that both position the firm as customer-oriented and create reasons for Minnesotans to return to the site. But it is the national listing of DWI lawyers that stands as the site's biggest draw; thanks to the clickable U.S. map, drunk drivers from Anchorage to Key West

IN-SITE: Rosenman
http://www.rosenman.com
This large full-service firm has created a large, full-service Website with a detailed practice area (descriptions of the firm's legal work in corporate law, environmental law, employment law, etc.) and news of the firm's accomplishments. But Rosenman's main strength is in its awareness of online context—the excellent collection of law links allows Netsurfers access to a wide variety of legal resources across the Web.

can find, and email, lawyers willing and able to "vigorously challenge Intoximiter and Breathalyzer test results."
✓**www**→http://www.nka.com /index.html

Writers

Internet Screenwriters Network
This network is a virtual community for the screenwriting profession. A multitude of services are provided for free for anyone who has written at least one screenplay. These include several bulletin boards, dozens of topical chat groups hosted by well-known writers, job counseling, professional advice, legal counsel, and an exchange for synopsis and scripts. How does all this goodwill and fellowship pay off? Interspersed among the free features are plugs for books, videos, and

services to help people "make it" in the cold world of Hollywood. And who wouldn't take all the advice they could buy from the script doctor of *Ed Wood* or the writer of *Murder in the First*?
✓**www**→http://www.screenwriters .com/screennet.html

Robert V. Ausura Writing
Robert V. Ausura belongs to the school that believes talking about oneself in the third person makes theat person seem more important. So the bulk of the material at this site is third-person praise for the works of Mr. Ausura as an author, speechwriter, and text doctor, although the site also has a helpful newsletter. If winning two online writing awards from AOL is enough to sell his services, Robert must be a busy man.
✓**www**→http://members.aol.com /robertaus/writing.html

Going to Market: Professional Service Firms

Professionals of all stripes—lawyers, accountants, psychologists, architects, financial consultants, and more—are increasingly using the Web as a sophisticated marketing tool. Toward the end of 1995, it was estimated that there were more than 300 law firms with home pages on the Net, and the other disciplines are not far behind. Why are professionals flocking to the Web? How are they using the Web?

Professionals are coming to the Web because it serves their needs. A Website for a professional services firm is basically a specialized type of business-to-business site—the bulk of business for large law firms comes from their legal work for other companies. As a result, the principal guideline for business-to-business sites holds true for professional Websites: the site should reflect what the most effective salesperson (often called a "rainmaker" at these firms) would say to attract a new client. Like a rainmaker, the site should stress the firm's credentials, its accomplishments, its areas of expertise, its value per dollar spent, or its unique approach to analyzing and solving problems. In addition, a professional service firm can use the Web to demonstrate to existing and potential clients a "cutting-edge" image.

As they move onto the Web, professional firms should think about using some of the same strategies as consumer-oriented businesses, whether positioning themselves as reliable sources of information or as guides to the Internet. One of the most common strategies employs content links—law firms linking to legal resources online, financial consultants linking to stock market sites. There are two reasons why this is so effective. First, it demonstrates a firm's expertise, especially if the company offers a collection of its own working papers, analyses, discussion forums, and newsletters, along with links to other sites. Secondly, subject-oriented sites can be promoted in relevant trade publications and forums. For example, the Washington, D.C., law firm Arent Fox Kintner Plotkin and Kahn (**http://www.arentfox.com**) promoted its advertising law site in a Website listing area in the Interactive Section of *Ad Age*.

Companies placing content on their site or linking to other sites should remember the importance of regular updating—dead links or stale content are offputting. In addition, firms creating sites should remember this four-point checklist of must-have features:

Quality graphics. A surprisingly large number of professional service firm sites use almost no color or graphics. This gives the site a boring (and somewhat unprofessional) look. In general, a modern, but not ostentatious, look is preferable.

A guest book. In consumer sites, a guest book is sometimes intrusive, but a professional services firm has an obligation to offer visitors a place to sign in. Firms responding to sign-ins should remember that they should work through email, and that their responses should contain something of value to the recipient (an invitation to a firm seminar or a sample copy of the firm newsletter). In fact, if the firm already creates newsletters on specific topics, these can be distributed to a wider, interested audience—at almost no additional cost—by digitizing the content and sending the newletter via email to anyone who visits the site and requests it.

Forums on specialty topics. One way of interacting with potential customers and demonstrating expertise is to establish chat forums on specific topics at the site.

Descriptions of major accomplishments and lists of major clients. Nothing succeeds like success, and real-life examples involving well-known companies create tremendous credibility among potential customers. Without this list, potential clients have no yardstick by which they can measure your company. In addition, the newness of the online medium sometimes works against professional service firms that want to portray themselves as longtime establishment favorites; a list of past clients can offset this novelty effect.

Transport & delivery

Despite the speed and reach of the information superhighway, some things still don't

lend themselves to virtual transportation. The kings of the open road and open skies have roared onto the information superhighway, selling door-to-door transportation all over the cybermap. **FedEx** is intent on reinforcing its reputation for customer service and efficiency, and the company"s groundbreaking Website has enabled anxious mailroom workers everywhere to monitor package delivery with just an Internet connection and a tracking number. **Allied Van Lines, Inc.** allays fears about the moving process by offering visitors a moving guide packed with packing tips. In the online world of the big rigs, **Landstar Ligon** caters to the consumer, offering those anxiously awaiting the arrival of their antique harpsichord or their favorite teddy bear an interactive map of routes and road conditions. And the subscription-only **Internet Truckstop** provides a forum for speed-trap warnings, job exchange, and road humor—all that's lacking from this virtual truckers' community is a cup of Joe and a piece of cherry pie.

On the Net
Delivery

DHL Known offline for its flying van logo, DHL offers detailed online info about its delivery services to 217 countries worldwide. For each country, customers can check national holidays, operating hours, and local phone numbers to arrange for pickup. A list of handy information (address, weight, time of pickup, etc.) is repeated for every country.
✓**www**→http://www.dhl.com

FedEx With FedEx's online Express Menu, tracking a package or checking delivery options is just a click away. Any customer with a FedEx account can download free software to prep and print the proper paperwork for their package from their personal computer. Although the customer must still use the phone to schedule pickup or find out costs, a customer who

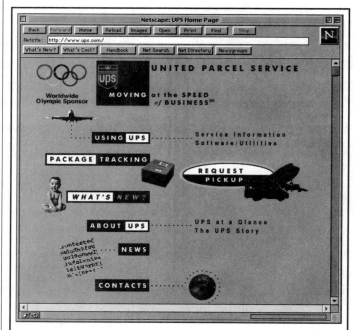

IN-SITE: United Parcel Service
http://www.ups.com

UPS's interactive Website serves as an elegant online customer-service hub. Detailed service descriptions, well-implemented forms and downloadable software let customers estimate cost-and-transfer times, and track their packages via the Web. Buying a roll of packing tape and a making a toll-free call the only things left for a customer to do—the "Browns" handle the rest (with care).

has already sent a package can check on its whereabouts on the Website with a tracking number.
✓**www**→http://www.fedex.com

Kitty Hawk Air Charter Kitty Hawk's multimedia Website plugs its same-day air cargo services, from on-demand charters to Next Flight Out shipping. It even places its 1-800 number on every page. The site illustrates its industry leadership with a news story—"Kitty Hawk Saves Big Blue Millions"—detailing its other corporate connections (including contracts with—and links to—several major shipping companies), and provides a page of aviation and transportation links.
✓**www**→http://www.onramp.net/kha

Mail Boxes, Etc. Mail Boxes, Etc.'s site attaches an interactive store locator to an online advertisement for its wide array of one-stop services; from package materials and UPS shipping to passport photos and styrofoam peanut recycling. Additional pages detail the company's corporate services.
✓**www**→http://www.mbe.com

United States Postal Service Reports of the death of snail mail amid the online revolution have been greatly exaggerated. With the interactive Zip Code Lookup alone, the U.S. Postal Service's Website illustrates its continuing relevance. This massive site has plenty of tips for consumers, a special section for businesses, extensive stamp images and info for collectors, and complete postal rates. Neither rain nor snow nor malfunctioning ISDN line...
✓**www**→http://www.usps.gov

Moving

Allied Van Lines, Inc. With its online "Guide to a Good Move," Allied's Website offers detailed step-by-step instructions which simplify the daunting task of relocation, including an eight-week "Countdown to Moving Day." The site provides a state-by-state directory of Allied agents and a section for international relocations. A special page touts the company's high customer satisfaction ratings and frequent awards.
✓**www**→http://www.alliedvan.net

Atlas Van Lines (Canada) The Website of this Canadian moving company (which does have U.S. offices) details its array of services, including storage and corporate moves, and provides a lengthy online form for price estimates. Special sections devoted to moving from Canada to the U.S., and the tax deductibility of moving expenses (Canadian only) include informative FAQs.
✓**www**→http://www.chch.com/atlas.htm

Galil This site makes heavy use of photos to illustrate Galil's "uniformed and highly skilled" workforce in action. Content is explicitly focused towards a demonstrative "what the company can do for you" angle, whether the consumer in question is residential or commercial, local or long-distance. A special page provides parents with helpful hints for preparing their children to face the move. The company's toll-free number and a button for email are at the bottom of every page.
✓**www**→http://www.galil.com

Global Van & Storage South While not exactly a household name in the moving industry, Global Van & Storage South is an innovator: its Website lets potential customers submit a quote request online via a detailed form.

The company takes direct aim at the competition here, offering maximum discounts for requests that include competitive quotes from at least two other "Major Movers." Several links to real estate, employment, and relocation resources make this site a potential one-stop shop for those on the move.
✓**www**→http://www.apms.com/global

U-Haul Plan "Designed to help you plan your do-it-yourself household move," the U-Haul Website describes its products in terms the average mover understands. Each box is described in terms of what kind of items the customer can pack into it, how heavy the items can be, and how many boxes are recommended for each room. How big a truck does the customer need? Each truck is described in terms of how many boxes it holds and in relation to the size of the customer's house. The site also features moving tips, and a customer service email address to which the DiY mover can addres a reservation inquiry.
✓**www**→http://www.uhaul.com

Trucking

Freightliner Corporation This truck manufacturer uses its attractive Website to deliver photos and specs of its product line, from severe-duty vehicles to stand-up right-hand drive systems (for those pesky curbside pickups). The site includes a calendar of Freightliner's exhibits at industry shows, as well as company news and an illustrated history.
✓**www**→http://www.freightlinertrucks.com

J.B. Hunt Transportation Services Having evolved from a regional carrier to a transportation

and logistics company, J.B. Hunt uses its site to discuss the specialized services of several company divisions. A page devoted to its on-board computer systems spotlights Hunt's leading-edge technology. The site's main draw for customers, however, is its online parcel tracking service, which lets customers use Cyberspace to locate their freight in real space.
✓ **www**→http://www.jbhunt.com

Landstar Ligon Landstar Ligon's Website stresses the company's commitment to safety, both on the home page and throughout the content. The easy-to-use site features an intuitive graphic menu and a clickable weather map, which itself comprises a convenient collection of links for road and traffic condition updates via several Departments of Transportation and highway patrols.
✓ **www**→http://www.landstar.com

Link Logistics Link Logistics Inc. creates and houses Web pages for trucking companies. Its site details its flat-fee services and the benefits to companies of going online. The home pages are fairly standardized, displaying logos and images, and providing basic service and contact information (including email addresses).
✓ **www**→http://www.linklogi.com

Roadway Express Online Roadway Express, one of the world's premier carriers, has gone online in style, with a well-designed Website rich in content and dashboard-themed graphics. While highlighting the company's carrier and technology services, the site works to personify Roadway Express for customers—its CEO provides a monthly column and his own hotlist. Extensive news and business links make this site a convenient resource for in-

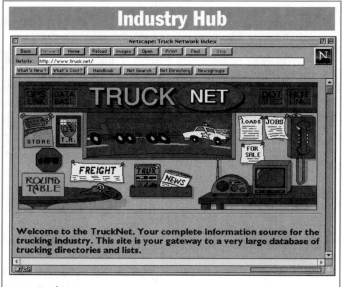

Industry Hub

IN-SITE: **TruckNet**
http://www.truck.net
TruckNet houses a fleet of lists and directories of interest to all areas of trucking industry, but drivers are the site's main focus. At the Driver's Roundtable, truckers can post messages, sounding off about speed limits or the hazards of fast food. They can also search (via form) for loads or link to several industry-related databases, like the Department of Transportation and the Hazardous Chemical Database.

dustry information. RexWorld, the site's entertainment area, offers visitors multimedia tours of the highways and byways of America. Anyone who signs the guest book can win a calendar or a replica truck.
✓ **www**→http://www.roadway.com

Truck services

Internet Truckstop With its slogan "Where the Information Super-Highway meets the REAL Road," this virtual truckstop is a BBS for the trucking industry. Paying subscribers can obtain load, truck, and bid postings via an interactive search engine. Advertisers can add links to their own sites from Internet Truckstop's home page or post pages in the

Corporate World section. And any user can use the site's email classifieds—those seeking jobs as well as those offering them.
✓ **www**→http://www.truckstop.com

The Truckers/Transportation Homepage Cruising for truck links? This site connects to dozens of them, from road conditions to job boards to NAFTA documents. With links to the AT&T 800 Information page, the Net Address Book of Transportation Professionals, and its own 300-strong Transportation Companies on the Net section, this site places the information necessary for contacting for a mind-boggling number of companies at the fingertips of the average Netsurfer.
✓ **www**→http://www.truckers.com

Personal services

The telephone book has limitations. There are things it doesn't do. It won't tell you the

differences between the psychologists it advertises; it is unlikely to list more than one toxic waste evaluator; and the heading "esoteric trance healer" just can't be found (except, of course, in Santa Fe). The Internet, on the other hand, is the first true people's directory. At least for now, every Brenda and Derek can advertise their services as astrologer, Cher impersonator, or therapist. Many such providers, like **Mystic Stars** and **Leonard Holmes, Ph.D., Therapist** offer a sample of their wares to win trade. Others, like, **Hypnosis.com** and **Randy Glassbergen, Cartoonist** rely on snappy presentations and interactive fun to sell their less than routine services. Still others, **The Wilhelmina Web** and **The Talent Network** market dreams—with a headshot reaching millions of users worldwide, everybody's a star.

On the Net

Astrology

Astrochat This virtual fortune-telling tent opens with reminders of the long history of astrology,

neo-classical decor, and the traditional Greek Zodiac wheel. The page header emphasizes the importance of astrology, because "All Life is Charted by the Heavens at the Time of Birth," is it not? Plenty is the selling point here, and Astrochat's seers provide a chart (with a separate fee) for almost any occasion that a visitor might experience. There are natal reports for parents and the self-absorbed, compatibility reports for the dating, relocation reports for travelers, career reports for workers, and even karmic reports for those who want to find out how often they

messed up in their past life. The more people want to be reassured the more appealing the site. Great marketing.

✓**www**→http://www.dgsys.com /~star

Astrological Spiritual Guidance Echoing the all-encompassing scope of the galaxies, this site offers readings according to several different systems—enough to suit all tastes. By asking deep, meaningful questions like "Who are you?" and then describing the specific chart that answers them, these purveyors of solace have de-

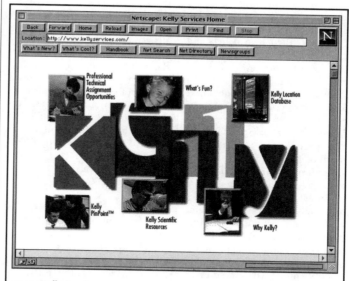

IN-SITE: **Kelly Services**
http://www.kellyservices.com

The once-famous Kelly Girl is nowhere to be seen at this technologically sophisticated promotional site. Instead, there is a wealth of well-presented information here for both prospective employers and temps. Many will undoubtedly be attracted by Kelly's online resumé assistance and database, holding out the very powerful promise of employment on the horizon, and adding to its "life-saving" image in the business community by providing a staffing need survey and a customized "productivity" enhancing software program. Wisely, Kelly also reiterates all its selling points in a wrap-up page entitled "Why Kelly?"

signed a site that sells itself. They hardly need their rather non-specific promise:"All work guaranteed to be Healing, Effective and more Instructive than current psychological methods."

✓**www**→http://www.sisna.com /users/rysa/astro1.htm

Astrology Alive! with Barbara Schermer Twinkling little stars welcome visitors to Astrology Alive, where friendly astrologer Barbara Schemer lays out her numerous qualifications. Barbara is almost unique among the online astrology community in offering free stuff on her Website. Every month she hosts guest astrologers, all of whom contribute articles on astrological phenomena Barbara also provides a "cheat sheet" (a printable astrological chart for beginners). In promoting good will Barbara goes even further, setting up a chat area where people can talk about their own beliefs and experiences, and perhaps decide they need further professional assistance from the host.

✓**www**→http://www.lightworks .com/Astrology/Alive

Buddhist Astrology This site attempts to add a respectable touch of spirituality to the slightly ridiculous business of fortune telling. Jhampa Shaneman (and why not?) compensates for his lack of resemblance to the Dali Lama with a long resumé of spiritual training and a discussion of his Tibetan monk-built Enlightenment Stupa.

✓**www**→http://www.mala.bc.ca /~shanemanj/wwwhome.htm

The Guru Welcomes You The Guru serves a selected clientele: the gay/lesbian/bi/transgendered seekers of psychic comfort. To that end, the Guru has created a page that is partly advertisement and partly community hangout, where visitors can link to hundreds of gay and lesbian links. The Guru also offers a free reading as a taste of the consultations and retreats that are the bulk of the Guru's spiritual business. "Lesbian Guidance from the Stars" is probably a unique headline; it also has the virtue of attracting cybertravelers who are searching for gay-related sites.

✓**www**→http://www.geocities .com/WestHollywood/1128

Mystic Stars Free weekly horoscopes are an unusual feature of online astrology sites, but Mystic Stars delivers what it promises, thus whetting the customer's appetite for more costly offerings. Lasha, the seer at this page, also offers several other unique attractions, including a special relationship hotline, an online PowWow (complete with software), dream analysis, and daily personal reading by email! Decorated with Pre-Raphaelite beauties and rich colors, Lasha's attractive site helps sell another of his one-of-a-kind products, daily mystical images. Personally selected by Lasha, the images can be e-mailed to you directly every morning as a kind of "cosmic wake up call" for a mere $19.95 per month.

✓**www**→http://www.nresults.com /mystic

Psychic Home Page This site bursts upon the screen with vivid purple rays emanating from that all-seeing eye familiar to Masons and owners of dollar bills. Although this site has the subtlety of a velvet bullfighter painting, the pitch is clearly not directed at George Will. Instead it effectively introduces a service that promises real interaction—video conferencing with a live psychic. Downloading the software enables visitors to sample the service for free. Once a piece of the future has been revealed—the charge rises to $4.95 per minute. So far, they're on their own in the online-psychic-head-to-head-hotline business.

✓**www**→http://www.mxol.com /~psychic

The Psychic Internet A bright flashing line insists that this is the "one source" site with a personal link to the psychic—virtually, of course. Much is made here of expertise. The psychics are "professional, experienced, and qualified" (whatever that means) and have lots of initials after their names. But the point of distinction here is a gift-certificate option—psychic readings as online presents.

✓**www**→http://www.wholarts.com /psychic

Children/education

Childcrest/Au Pair Program This soft pink page is adorned with a big heart and an abstract sketch of an adult cradling a small child—no psycho nannies here. Childcrest is selling security by showing calm images, and by making frequent references to certification and legal immigration programs (for prospective Presidential nominees). Snob value is a big selling point too; it is manifest in descriptions of board-certified British nannies and resumés of young European au pairs with knowledge of violin and French. The cap on this pitch to busy yuppies is a fast—no muss, no fuss—Internet service that promises a nanny within a week!

✓**www**→http://www.childcrest .com

Homework Help Hotline The red, turquoise, and black design here is attention grabbing, and the pitch concise and coherent. Ap-

pealing to both anxious parents hoping for a college scholarship and students wanting to get anxious parents off their back, the HHH promises qualified tutors at almost any hour of the day.
✓**www**→http://www.io.com /~qed

The Village Learning Center
Playing up the much touted educational aspects of the Internet proves to be an effective strategy for this small cyberschool. The tagline is "where the future begins." and flaws in the American school system are overtly mentioned. Further selling points include a "rigorous" study program to help kids keep pace with technology, a sample of which is provided. Stressing personal attention in the shape of an online Mentor is yet another call to anxious parents. Easy email enrollment probably catches a few more.
✓**www**→http://www.snowcrest.net /villcen/vlchp.html

Employment services

Ad-van-tage Staffing Services Inc. This woman-owned temp agency has a site with clean lines and bright colors, suggesting the temps for hire will be of professional appearance and demeanor. The site stresses flexibility, experience niche marketing to corporate and legal businesses.
✓**www**→http://www.advstaff.com

CompuTemp The use of computer-world lingo sets the tone for this specialty temp service which promises "realtime service, realtime people." CompuTemp clearly places itself at the high-tech end of the temp market. Great emphasis is laid on CompuTemp's extensive testing programs, an effective lure for businesses that rely on computer-literate employees. Com-

puTemp also lures in the job seeker by placing available positions on line—the value of a concrete job versus abstract promises is clear.
✓**www**→http://www.computemp .com

Temporary Resource Center
This New-York-City-based temp service focuses its appeal on the hordes of young college grads and aspiring actors who flood into the city every year. TRC attempts to create a friendly temp family, publishing an online newsletter, Tempted, which focuses on a different topic each month. Here businesses will find a company that is interested in its employees, a promise of heavily-vetted references, tough testing, and, of

course, careful recruiting.
✓**www**→http://www.panix.com /~nyctemps

Entertainment

CNI Cinema CNI Cinema's promotional site is attuned to the two principal currents of modern day hipness: independent films and cyberculture. Flashing titles highlight CNI's "award-winning" film, while graphics-heavy pages describe upcoming projects, including a live Website at the Cartagena International Film Festival. The purpose here is twofold: to attract new capital through "proven" success and technological savvy, and to capture the Cybermarket with appeals for Internet-related screenplays. CNI has

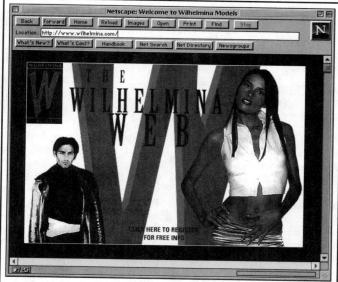

IN-SITE: **The Wilhelmina Web**
         http://www.wilhelmina.com
The Wilhelmina Web is selling a dream, and selling it very well. This site is the pinnacle of mod style—red, black, and white—decorated with beautiful people of both genders clad in spandex and vinyl. Ostensibly, advertisers and corporations come here to seek new spokesmodels, but the site also appears to be aimed at young girls who ache to be the next Kate Moss. The site features a newsletter full of chatty details of the exotic model life, as well as a new model contest, but to what end? There's also an online boutique where "authentic" professional model portfolios and other trademark products are sold.

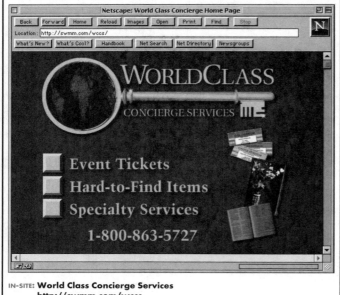

IN-SITE: World Class Concierge Services
http://swmm.com/wccs
The luxurious royal purple background with gold highlights represents everything this service is about: luxury and elitism. The pitch is simple, promising "finest personalized and professional attention in expediting your ordinary, extraordinary and challenging needs." (Tee times in Anguilla, tickets for the Summer Olympics, and a personalized shopper.) For busy executives, or aspirants to the lifestyles of the rich and famous, there is just enough here to tantalize — and spur them into emailing for more information.

situated itself as the film company of the future.
✓**www**→http://www.escape.com/~spyder/CNICINEMA.HTM

Fireworks America A fireworks firm has to labor to create that "Oooh, ahhh" feeling in potential entertainment clients who might otherwise go with mimes or a rock cover band. To sell their special effects, Fireworks America chooses to emphasize pyrotechnic expertise, peppering their page with the slogan, "the difference is quality." The rest of the site reads like a corporate business proposal, relying on the question-and-answer motif ("Why fireworks? What fireworks can do for you.") Their special feature—indoor fireworks—is probably guaranteed to perk up any convention.

✓**www**→http://www.electriciti.com/~firewkam

The Master's Image Productions Can you look up "One-Man Dramatic Presentations from a Christian Perspective" in the phone book? No, but thanks to the magic of the Web, no party need be without a religious dramatization to accompany the canapés. Chuck Neighbors' site is attractive, informative (including testimonials and a description of each reading) and, best of all, will pop up whenever the devout surfer searches for "Christian" on the Net. For vendors with less than traditional services, clever Web design can be a Godsend.
✓**www**→http://www.teleport.com/~chuckn

Molly Ann Leiken—Songwriting Consultant Melodious Molly Ann is selling a dream, ("You, too, can achieve fame,") and very effectively, too. Her Website is packed with examples of her expertise, in the form of a discography of her hits for stars like Anne Murray and Diana Ross. The effectiveness of her program is displayed by the fifty-two (nameless) clients who have gotten record contracts in the last year. But Molly-Ann goes a step further, providing free samples in the form of bi-weekly columns on the tricks of the trade, and a free email question-and-answer forum to get visitors hooked on her music doctoring skills.
✓**www**→http://home.earthlink.net/~songmd

Party Magic/Celebrity Lookalikes A colorful flying fairy introduces the reluctant hosts to party planning and the world of celebrity lookalikes of Elvis, Queen Elizabeth II, and Michael Jackson. Along with an extensive cast of celebrity impersonators, the regal trio are available for birthday parties and TV commercials. A listing of the parties the company throws (Mardi Gras to mimes) and other impersonators round out the site.
✓**www**→http://www.shadow.net/~party/index.html

The Raspyni Brothers The showmanship of this juggling act is evident in its Website which is full of bright colors, anecdotes (they once opened for Tom Jones), and lists of Fortune 500 companies and Television shows that have provided venues for their wondrous feats of tossing. But all is not flash and sparkle here: the Raspynis also make a play for corporate business by offering reasons why "custom tailored" juggling is

the perfect motivational entertainment for conventions. They support this claim with a list of satisfied clients ranging from State Farm Insurance to Nabisco. Critical praise is another crucial element in this online commercial, but it is the O.J. feature that may clinch the deal. That's right—the Raspynis were selected by Judge Ito to entertain the jurors.
✓**www**→http://www.raspyni.com

Shelby Danus Entertainment
Since there are a million hopefuls for every job, this site attempts to offer exposure for talent, and convenience for businesses, by constructing searchable databases of film technicians and actors, as well as a bulletin board for service exchanges. The databases are organized geographically, which should appeal to small businesses in Georgia that want to film their own commercials or, more rarely, film companies looking to cast a bit part. After paying the company's fee, individuals get a Web link and a place in the database. One day, hopefully, they'll also get to see their name in lights.
✓**www**→http://www.infi.net/~sdent

The Talent Network Right up front, the Talent Network expresses confidence in its services, reminding visitors to bookmark the page for easy return. Next, the company plays the professional card, and requests an extensive registration form for expediting the technical or talent needs of businesses, promising immediate 24-hour service through online databases. Since the company actually makes money from the talent itself, through registration and personal Web page development, it must practice dual marketing strategies. The hottest selling point here is the assurance that "Talent

Network members are just a click of a mouse button from being hired!"
✓**www**→http://www.talentnet.com

VCV Stunts VCV Stunts assures visitors that they have the right stuff "for your stunt actor needs." This Website advertisement features pictures of thirty foot falls by their star attraction, "Mad Dog." An email link provides immediate gratification for seekers of saloon brawls, but also comes with a warning against one of the drawbacks of promoting a rather glamorous business in millions of homes worldwide: VCV say they are not, repeat not, hiring any new stunt personnel.
✓**www**→http://www.procom.com/~daves/vcvstunt.html

The Virtual Headbook The Virtual Headbook is selling the future with lines like: "The Virtual Headbook revolutionizes the casting industry by bringing a Global talent pool to the Information Superhighway." This "free resource" for casting directors and talent scouts is well-constructed. All customers need to do is choose a locale and type (age, gender, race), and a bevy of airbrushed beauties pops up instantly—complete with resumé, video clip, and quicktime movie. As usual, it's the hopefuls who pay the bills. But with such nice presentation, two months free service, complimentary business cards with personal headshots, and an aura of professionalism, who can blame them?
✓**www**→http://www.xmission.com/~wintrnx/virtual.html

Funeral homes

Armstrong Funeral Home There is no black here, not even any gray. Instead this site is full of warm pinks and warm words

about "people who care about people." The content is pretty straightforward—advertising for this Niagara, New York business—but it is the only funeral home that is linked to The Cemetery Gate, a cyberspace where grieving people meet to mourn.
✓**www**→http://www.funeral.net/info

Pre-Need Funeral Arrangements The first selling-point listed here is a time-honored one—"Get substantial savings over at-need prices!" Of course that pitch demands that the buyers must first be interested in saving money for their nearest and dearest heirs. Other than great savings, this Tennessee funeral home site offers luscious GIFs of available plots and mausoleums, as well as a description of services. The site's sponsor, Oak Hill Cemetery, has a leg up on the local competition; it's part of a network offering pre-need sales in nineteen states.
✓**www**→http://www.tricon.net/Comm/preneed

Home/office

Bill's Pool Service A beautiful aqua background opens this California (of course) pool service. No pictures of beefy pool boys here — just a description of its 24-hour services, and phone numbers in bold listed over and over. It's the online equivalent of the local TV car dealership commercial—and probably every bit as effective.
✓**www**→http://www.fishnet.net/~rcman/home.htm

John's Town & Country Office & Carpet Care Systems This colorful promotional site makes its case to busy office administrators with a clear explanation of its income sharing program, but, more importantly, through a list of references and an email link for a free appraisal.

✓**www**→http://www.aardvarking.com/tc

Horseback riding

Vicki Wall Dressage Training

Gracing her pages with fine art backgrounds of equestriennes through the ages and a portrait of her slim, blonde self in full riding regalia Vicki presents herself well to her select audience,. This Website has Town and Country appeal aplenty for those who can afford her training on the Northern California gold coast. Subjects include fun facts about her illustrious ancestors (Wild Bill Hickock and Zachary Taylor), useful services like daily riding weather reports, and a horse barn offering the likes of Ben Hur, a 15-year-old Trakehner gelding by Condus, for $10,000.

✓**www**→http://www.wco.com/~kelley/wall.html

Psychological

Cybercounseling Interactive Network

Edvard Munch's famous expression of angst, The Scream, opens this virtual therapist's office—reflecting both the desperation of the prospective clientele and the basic strangeness of cybertherapy. These "licensed behavioral health professionals" offer treatment via the Internet for everything from anxiety to sexual dysfunction. In the near future, a group therapy chat room will also be installed! For those who shied away from the psychiatrist's office, this must be the biggest breakthrough since the late-night radio shrink.

✓**www**→http://www.netexpres.com/cybercounseling

HelpNet HelpNet's claim to offer

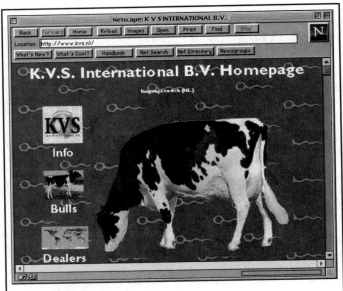

IN-SITE: **K.V.S International B.V. Homepage**
http://www.kvs.nl

If the service on sale is a bit out of the ordinary, why not make the most of the oddity factor? This homepage for a Dutch/American company that provides a stud service for Holstein cows opens with a blue background wallpapered with little sperm, upon which cows graze serenely. But all is not visual poetry here. Since this bovine dating service has a rather limited audience, its profiles of the studs themselves include plenty of information on farms they've already served. A studly presentation.

a quick hit, cheap fix step on the path to mental good health is reflected in its graphic-free, no-nonsense site. After all, as these people point out, you are getting hundreds of dollars worth of treatment for a mere twenty bucks. Taking it as given that you have done enough self-diagnosis to frame a question or two, the site offers "Accomplished psychologists and psychiatrists" who will explore a range of topics from Childhood Diosorders to Obsession. Replies are promised within seventy-two hours.

✓**www**→http://www.ottawa.net/~helpnet

Hypnosis.com Offering samples, and finding a good gimmick, are both tried-and-tested sales pitches, and the practition-

ers at Hypnosis.com have combined the two to market their rather esoteric services. At the opening page, tension-addled clients are invited to stare into a purple swirl and listen to an audio file of a calm authoritative voice telling them to take a deep breath and relax. Once visitors are hooked, further options get the hard sell—online brochures of training programs and hypnotherapy "doctorate at a distance," are offered. In another smart move, Hypnosis.com lets the Net do some of its selling through links to hypnosis-related newsgroups and FAQs where the already-converted are discussing the treatment's benefits at length.

✓**www**→http://www.hypnosis.com

Leonard Holmes, Ph.D. Dr.

Holmes doesn't believe in cybertheraphy—he can't see the patient's eyes or really build a personal relationship with a keyboard. From his flashing home page, however, he will make use of new technology—and new vocabulary—by providing "shareware" therapy. In other words, troubled souls email the Doctor to discuss a problem, and if they like his advice they negotiate a fee—if they don't it's free! Demurring to the fears of those who don't feel like sending details of their obsessive compulsive disorder around the world, encryption is included.

✓**www**→http://www.psychology .com/holmes.htm

Trance Esoteric Healer On a deep blue background, the bold words "Expect a Miracle" announce the presence of a magic power beaming through cyberspace. Miracle-selling has been an industry since history began, but it takes Elmer Gantry showmanship. Esoteric Trance Healer Barbara opts to fill her promotional page with testimonials and articles about her power from the "mainstream" press. She has also calculated that by mentioning a wide variety of problems—wandering eyes, cysts, and drug addiction—her page will pop up on many a troubled netters Web search.

✓**www**→http://www.healing-mira cles.com

Science/Agriculture

Chemical Accident Reconstruction Dr. Fox's Web appeal is based on two things—money and the modern awe of "experts." The Doctor stresses his experience in dealing with "accidents" ranging from nuclear power meltdowns (read Three Mile Island) to hot coffee burns (the notorious McDonald's case). Playing on the cor-

porate fear of large settlements and the public's desire to cash in, Fox points to his experience in "large (billions)" claims, and his "cost consciousness." An email link puts this expert witness literally at the client's fingertips.

✓**www**→http://www.Opus1.COM /interi/fox/index.html

Dick Wingassen, Consulting Chemist The title may sound like a failed televisions eries, but this Website demonstrates how any skill, no matter how obscure, can be marketed on the Web. Dick gives a quick précis of his life in the chemicistry set. He is "a person who has worked under pressure to stop field problems, particularly in mixing, foaming, emulsification, microbiological." Those interested can click to Dick's resumé, or just take a look at his other attraction—a free Science Fair help page for kids.

✓**www**→http://emporium.turnpike .net/R/rasberry/dad/dick.html

Eco-Rating International The dollar is green in more than one way these days—and Eco-Rating's appeal makes good use of both environmental ethics and financial concern. The argument is extremely well laid out, with bullets (in the shape of little green leaves) emphasizing Eco-Rating's philosophy of social and economic responsibility. Long but clearly-written pages cover all of Eco-Rating's many services, and there are two sample ratings online. Most effective of all is the subliminal salesmanship of hundreds of hypertext links to environmental-related Web pages—just think of all those potential customers who'd love to do business with a "green" company.

✓**www**→http://www.eco-rating .com

Other

Paul Frisbie "Renaissance Man" Mr. Frisbie admits up front that his "not very ulterior motive" is to attract some business (his Renaissance resumé admits to stand-up comedy, freelance writing, jingle writing, communications consulting and saloonkeeping) but his site is much more than a classified ad. Instead of touting his own skills, Paul offers an insider's view and helpful tips for each of his many careers. Accented with humorous cartoons, each little employment vignette is a comic gem—from advice on composing catchy jingles to writing software manuals. All in all, Mr. Frisbie has come up with a wonderful approach—what company wouldn't want to hire such a friendly, inventive man?

✓**www**→http://homepage.inter access.com/~frisbie/frisbie.html

Randy Glasbergen, Cartoonist It's no wonder that Randy Glasbergen's site has won praise from Net critics—it is a model combination of entertainment and advertising. Randy relies on his product to make his pitch, and studs the site with cartoons on everything from teenagers to corporate culture. Making plays for several different audiences—popular magazines, advertisers, computer companies, business interests, and more—Randy's pitches are individually tailored, and include a bulleted list of reasons why cartoons are a great idea. Randy also sells his instructional materials from this site; as a final push, he reminds visitors to the bookmark the page, so they're sure not to miss his daily cartoon treat. Funny and clever.

✓**www**→http://www.borg.com/~r jgtoons/aaa.html

Utilities

It's difficult to take the invisible entities that most Americans take for granted and

make them seem glamorous. Most people want simple things from their utilities—they want the lights to go on when they flip the switch, the heat to warm them in the dead of winter, and a nice hot shower every morning. Utilities online have chosen various routes to place their image more firmly in consumer's minds. The **Tennessee Valley Authority** relies on both name recognition and an interactive price calculator to win customers away from natural gas. **Brooklyn Union Gas**'s site builds on a consumer-friendly image, offering immediate contact with staff via email, and the implied promise of timely repairs. And **Consolidated Edison**, the venerable New York City utility offers a powerful lineup metropolitan tourism and entertainment resources that positions the company as the source of all things New York.

On the Net

Brooklyn Union Gas B.U.G. attempts to recreate the neighborhood feeling associated with the Brooklyn of the Dodgers, linguini,

and borscht through daily borough trivia, archive photos of its past, and a continuing commitment to the community. Ease of customer access is a key selling point here—the site includes email links to trouble-shooters, changing special offers, and public service information. There is some information for investors, presented in a typically low-key fashion, but it is B.U.G.'s links to local landmarks and its community activism that remain with visitors. Who wouldn't want a gas company that can boast that its Great Brooklyn Union Paper Race program saves 170 trees a month?
✓**www**→http://www.bug.com

Consolidated Edison The opening screen shot here is a view of the New York skyline and a familiar blue hard-hat, logo of the company known locally as ConEd. The emphasis here is to develop a warm image for ConEd by offering numerous plans, rebates, and business breaks with cute names like Project Appleseed and the Mega-watt Hour Store. There are also tips for saving electricity and money at every turn. In glamor-mode, ConEd plays up its cosmopolitan image by providing links to New York entertainment sites. After all, who supplies the lights on the Great White Way?
✓**www**→http://www.coned.com

East Bay Municipal Utility A surprisingly straightforward homepage for this publicly-owned water supplier to the Oakland, California, area conceals multiple levels of information and explains why the site was a Magellan Web

Award winner.
✓**www**→http://www.ebmud.com

Pacificorp Energy Planet This Portland, Oregon company appreciates the value of aesthetic associations—all the colors at this attractive site can be termed "electric." Pacificorp's appeal is overwhelmingly directed at investors—consumers will merely find information on new types of light bulbs and an email link. But for inveterate Monopoly players and Pacificorp stockholders there are 15-minute-delayed stock quotes and a wealth of financial reports showing the utility's glowing health.
✓**www**→http://www.pacificorp.com

Tennessee Valley Authority As the site proclaims, the Tennessee Valley Authority is the "largest power producer in the United States," but it is also one of the most famous legacies of the Great Depression and the New Deal. The TVA plays on its populist roots, emphasizing its role in the economic life of the southern mountains and the many people it employs (presented here are descriptions of business aids and a complete employee directory). A "dare to compare" form, an effective online tool, quickly compares the costs of heating with electricity versus gas. This friendly, consumer-oriented site also provides the name of the official in charge of every bit of TVA land from the Red River to Little Bear Creek—selling recreation and good feeling in addition to power.
✓**www**→http://www.tva.gov

Chapter 12

Shopping

General retailers

Retail stores have a vested interest in directing the growth of the online world, and en-

suring that the Web doesn't make traditional shopping obsolete. Thus, many of the large retail companies have chosen to construct Websites that enhance their corporate image rather than offer online sales. There are no fragrances wafting from **The Body Shop**'s homepage, but there is a good share of the green politics that has made its founder famous. Rather than allowing virtual purchase of lawn chairs, **Wal-Mart** and **Target** describe their savings plans, but still require a visit to the store to cash in. Retailers that don't rely on in-person purchasing are less conflicted, and have already begun to sell online. **Ticketmaster Online** promotes its virtual service effectively with a wealth of entertainment-related information nationwide.

On the Net

Department stores

May Department Stores The Website for the May department stores—which include Lord and Taylor, Hecht's, Pay Less Shoe Source, and Filene's— is used to publish financial reports about the company. More corporate infor-

mation is promised for the future.
✓**www**→http://www.lordandtaylor.com

Nordstrom Part of the MCI Marketplace, Nordstrom offers its customers intelligent-agent technology in the form of a free personal shopper. A customer can email Nordstrom with a product request (shoes in a size 12?) and his or her personal shopper will then email the customer back with suggestions. If the customer wants to buy, he or she can email an order to Nordstrom and the company will FedEx it. As a personal shopper gets to know the customer's taste (and as Nordstrom figures out the customer's buying patterns), the company will email the customer about special promotions or new items.
✓**www**→http://www2.pcy.mci.net

IN-SITE: **Egghead**
http://www.egghead.com

Egghead's online store is dedicated to helping its customers make educated choices when buying computer products. Its descriptions link to hundreds of industry reviews from a variety of sources, sorted by date and relevance. The site also offers linked summaries of industry articles, such as a comparison of commercial online services. The store includes special areas for corporate, government, and education customers, with services and features specific to their needs and interests. Cue Club membership entitles customers to discounts, specials, and access to proprietary information, such as Egghead customer feedback.

/marketplace/nordstrom

Service Merchandise Service Merchandise, the company that revolutionized retailing by actually providing less service to the customer (SM customers must search for desired items from a tome-sized catalog), continues its Spartan-like image on the Internet. The matter-of-fact Website has a zip-code locator for finding the closest store and a bevy of hyperlinks to warranty and return policies. Of special interest is the Bridal Registry, which soon-to-be-marrieds can join after downloading a registration form.
✓**www**→http://www.svcmerch

.com/service/svcmerch.html

Discount stores

KMart The discount department store presents a very corporate image on the Web, with stock reports and current market trends that appeal more to the analyst than to the homemaker.
✓**www**→http://www.kmart.com

Wal-Mart This company wants you to know that it has a heart. Wal-Mart's Website boasts of its many community endeavors, like support for the United Way and participation in Code: Adam, a program to decrease child abduc-

tions. For those who like to buy by bulk, there is also corporate information about Sam's Club, the members-only shopping center. On the lighter side, Wal-Mart's promotes its Country Music Tour with a section of links to country music sites and facts about the performers.
✓**www**→http://www.wal-mart.com

Computer & office

Boise Cascade Office Products This office supply retailer has an illustrated online catalog and a clickable distributor locator, but what sets Boise Cascade's site apart is its interactivity. The Office Products Interactive Bonanza solicits customers to submit their favorite uses for everything from paper clips (ejecting diskettes from disk drives) to tape flags ("small parades?"). Customers can even win a $500 shopping spree at the store for their Post-It Notes suggestions (although the small print stipulates that entrants must be employed by a company of "50 or more associates").
✓**www**→http://www.bcop.com

Computer City Though its inventory isn't online, Computer City's Website provides a request form for its Direct Catalog. The site also features a handy store locator; along with street address and phone number, the database includes a local map for each store. The site's Vendor's Hotline offers technical support, phone, fax, and BBS numbers, as well as URLs, for over 100 companies whose products it carries.
✓**www**→http://www.tandy.com/cc

Electronics Boutique Aimed primarily at the computer and playstation gaming market, Elec-

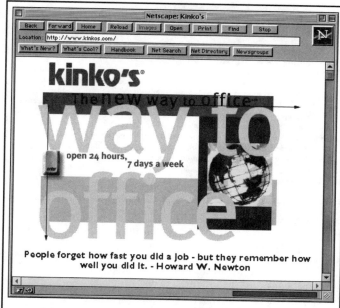

IN-SITE: **Kinko's**
   http://www.kinkos.com
Kinko's colorful Website presents an upscale image of the company—as not just a copy-maker, but a reflection of the ever-changing workplace. The site describes the range of products and services Kinko's provides, from copies to digital printing to video conferencing to Kinkonet, the company's new electronic transmitting, output, and delivery service. Lest anyone forget, Kinko's familiar "open 24 hours, 7 days a week" slogan is repeated on every page. Customers can locate stores by area code, ZIP code or state, or search for a particular service on-site. And those who complete the lengthy survey are eligible to win an Apple QuickTake digital camera.

tronics Boutique's Website informs customers when new products are being released, and when they'll hit the shelves. Its Buyers Notebook provides industry information, such as product and shipping date announcements. Customers can sign up for its software or video game mailing lists, which send out news updates and special offers several times a week. The site also provides a list of store locations so customers can snag those hot titles immediately, and links to several unofficial gaming sites for the latest hints.
✓**www**→http://www.eboutique .com

Office Max Part of the cybermall on MCI Net, Office Max Online is an enormously effective virtual store, with hundreds of products available for online ordering, showcased with descriptions, images, and price comparison between Office Max and other retailers. A handy search engine lets customers browse product lines or seek out specific brand-name items. Online customer service, attractive graphics, and all-around great organization make this site a mandatory bookmark for office managers and administrative assistants everywhere.
✓**www**→http://www2.pcy.mci.net /marketplace/ofcmax

Office Resources Office Resources doesn't just sell office furniture online—it uses its Website to highlight the company's commitment to creating ergonomically sound work environments. A special health and safety page raises customer awareness about the importance of ergonomics—designing a work environment which conforms to the physical and psychological needs of its workers. Any site visitor can sign up to receive free brochures on workplace

IN-SITE: **Target**
http://www.targetstores.com
Target, a huge discount store with over 600 locations (customers can use the online store locator to find a Target near them), hits the bull's eye for new parents with its energetic Web page that offers support and advice for beginning families. Target describes its popular Lullaby Club, a baby registry program that parents can sign up for at one of the stores, and follows up with helpful hints for first time moms and dads heading toward baby shower time. The site even includes a checklist of baby items that parents can use to figure out what they need. To assist parents with that all-important decision—what to name the little one—Target solicits favorite baby names from Website visitors and posts them online. Target isn't just selling baby supplies, though. The site runs a fashion column and other features to appeal to its single customers, but the site is in oriented toward positioning the chain as a family store.

safety along with the product catalog; Louisville-area visitors can even win an on-site Ergo Audit for their companies. And the online catalog offers healthy 50 percent discounts along with its product descriptions.
✓**www**→http://www.oriusa.com

Staples Staples' "Virtual Office Superstore" Website isn't really a store—it's more like a preview of a store. Each item in Staples' inventory receives its own page, with a picture, feature summary, product number, and price; with the printable order form, phone and fax,

purchases are a snap. Customers with the get-up-and-go impulse can use the store locator to business hours and driving directions for the nearest outlet.
✓**www**→http://www.staples.com /Welcome.html

Games & toys

FAO Schwarz Toys Curious about Curious George? FAO Schwarz has designed an illustrated Website using the toy store's trademark logo and colors. The store has placed its catalog of playthings online, along with informa-

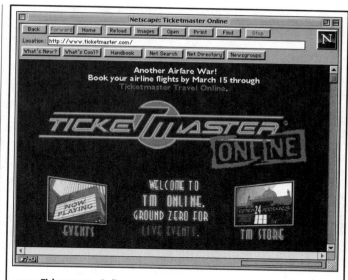

IN-SITE: **Ticketmaster Online**
http://www.ticketmaster.com

Where do you live and what do you want to see? Within seconds, Ticketmaster's Website can return the venue, the dates, and the price for an event. The site offers an extensive listing of arts, sports, family, and concert events in the U.S. by event and venue. It also highlights the most popular events nationwide in each category, offers special guides to events in New York City and Los Angeles, spotlights special Ticketmaster promotions, features its own entertainment magazine, and even offers customers a live chat area to discuss events and the entertainment industry.

tion about the store's special departments—like the Barbie Boutique, its cozy stuffed bears, and the recognizable clock towers.
✓**www**→http://faoschwarz.com

Game Factory "Download the shareware version. And remember this shareware version is only a taste of what awaits you in the FULL version of…" Game Factory promotes and distributes PC games for game developers. The company gets a cut from the sale of every game. How does it make the sale? The same way many other game companies do—Game Factory attracts customers with free downloads and excite them with screen shots from the full versions.
✓**www**→http://www.gamefactory .com

Toys R Us Toys R Us has divided its large selection of toys into categories, highlighting the bestselling products and showcasing educational toys. Appealing mostly to adults, Toys R Us also offers a telephone number for ordering PC software and promotes its new Toys R Us Visa card. Does Geoffrey carry plastic?
✓**www**→http://www.toysrus.com

Health & beauty

A-1 Fragrance This catalog showcases fragrances for women, men, even children, with images and short descriptions, all available for online ordering. But the most exceptional feature at this site is the request form—if the customer doesn't see a desired perfume or cologne online, he or she

can inquire about it and A-1 will respond with a competitive price.
✓**www**→http://www.webscope .com/a1

The Body Shop The environment, animal rights, social issues, and education get as much—if not more—play on the Body Shop's Website as its products do. In other words, Anita Roddick's company is marketing itself online exactly as it does offline. Visitors are also treated to a virtual tour of the Body Shop's U.K. plant which lets them track the manufacturing of a product from its conception to the shelves—total honesty, it's the only way.
✓**www**→http://www.The-Body -Shop.com

The Condom Shop The Condom Shop offers a huge catalog of brand name condoms, lubricants, and herbal products, outlining each line's special features in subdued language that still manages to be sensual. The site also provides articles about HIV and STD's, balancing its coverage of sex with a serious consideration of the issues.
✓**www**→http://geewiz.com

Walgreens The discount pharmacy has just what the doctor ordered—a store locator for the Walgreens nearest you, along with links to pharmacy related sites. These features, along with a no-nonsense design, position Walgreens as a quick and reliable source of pharmaceutical information.
✓**www**→http://www.walgreens .com

Home & garden

Dial-a-Mattress When it comes to bed purchasing and delivery, Dial-a-Mattress is an incredibly reliable service. At its Website, to ensure speed and efficiency, Dial-a-Mattress has employed whimsical icons (a comfy pillow and a delivery truck) to help Netsurfers (and Netsleepers) navigate through pages of bedding info and discounts.

✓**www**→http://www.sleep.com /DIAL-A-MATTRESS

Ethan Allen Home Interiors
Leading off with "Internet Promotions," which features pages canned from Ethan Allen's seasonal catalog, this site includes information on design services and financing and contact information for offline stores.

✓**www**→http://www.sermanco .com/Ethan_Allen

Home Depot The Home Depot phenomenon has swept America, with more than 400 of the giant hardware stores setting up shop in communities nationwide. Home Depot's Website offers customers a color-coded map that locates the store closest to them, along with links to related sites online.

✓**www**→http://www.homedepot .com

NC Furniture Online This furniture hubsite unites merchandise and resources from across Carolina, making the shopping process more convenient for the consumer. The page leads off with online furniture "galleries" that use images and descriptive copy to spotlight certain stores and manufacturers, even listing toll-free numbers for a handful of factory direct manufacturers. But the biggest resource here is a list of links to participatory retailers, whose home pages feature everything from contact info to full catalogs.

✓**www**→http://ncnet.com/ncnet works/furn-onl.html

Pier 1 The housewares and import company publishes stock reports, net sales figures, and a company overview on its site. As a result of the corporate orientation, there's very little here for consumers, with the exception of a store locator that lets customers locate the Pier 1 store nearest to them.

✓**www**→http://www.pierone.com

Shanti Bithi The Shanti Bithi site bills itself as a virtual nursery, albeit one in its infancy. Specializing in bonsai trees and Asian landscaping, the company has created a page that exudes spirituality, leading off with a poem by Sri Chinmoy and filling its catalog with esoteric copy—"Serenity is yours when you focus on this miniature PeaceGarden. An expression of balance and simplicity needed in our everyday life." Shanti hopes that its online specials and rotating monthly landscape images will keep visitors coming back to witness the site's growth and maturation.

✓**www**→http://www.webcom.com /~shanti

True Value What do customers expect from a hardware site? Utility, of course! This no-nonsense catalog offers a dozen "True Value" hardware bargains each month, supplementing the offers with an image and description, as well as a spotlight "gift" at a special price. All products shown at the site are available for online ordering.

✓**www**→http://www.wtp.net/bus -con/tv

Jewelry

Duncan & Boyd This Texas jeweler has designed an innovative way of delivering its information, inserting its product descriptions in a short hypertext mystery set at

a society party. Each step in the mystery links an object, a character, or a room to a product page where visitors can view and order merchandise—for instance, Netsurfers who stumble across a handprint on a bowl can link to another "clue" that is primarily a showcase page for Waterford Crystal. Some product pages have extensive descriptions and company bios, others provide a collection of photos.

✓**www**→http://www.dbaadv.com /duncan-boyd

Nomad Body Piercing Nomad does what any self-respecting piercing shop would do—positions itself within the tribal and piercing communities. Covered with photos of young men and women who've undergone rather *extreme* body modifications, this site gives Nomad street credibility at the same time that it filters out cruising preppies. While some accessories are available for ordering, the site's focus is on promoting the shop's services through an identification with the modern primitive movement—from a summary of tribal aesthetics to photos and QuickTime videos.

✓**www**→http://web.sirius.com /~stas/NOMAD/nmdhome.html

Pets

Pets Unlimited While this independent pet shop in Marietta, Georgia, provides contact information and a short company profile at this site, the real draw is the online coupon—after customers fill in the necessary information, they can print the coupon and bring it into the shop for a free gift for their Fido, Fluffy, or Winged Wonder.

✓**www**→http://www2.vivid.net /~petunltd

Clothing stores

For those busy modern types who aren't afraid of buying clothes without first trying

them on, Internet shopping is a valuable tool. For Net marketers, these people are even more valuable. At **Casual Male/Big & Tall** haberdashery, blinking dollars-off coupons work like bright neon shop signs and to draw in potential cybercustomers. Specialist cyberboutiques use other methods to enhance their Net presence. Over at **The Playing Field**, the footlocker crew offer a catalog for online ordering of their specialized footwear, a branch locator and, for customers of Lady Footlocker, a "fe-mail" address. **Prison Blues** focuses on the politically correct crowd, profiling its incarcerated labor force, and discussing prison reform while selling all-cotton clothing. Where there's a gap online, you can be sure an urbane outfitter will fill it.

On the Net

Across the board

Active Body This sports apparel shop, in Scottdale, AZ, sends out an open invitation to active ladies everywhere for a wardrobe consultation by owner Carmen Rosenblum. However, as a trip to Arizona is not on everyone's itinerary this vacation season, customers are welcome to order from its site garments made by their favorite designers like Aero Dynamics. Moda Prima, and Urban Flex.
✓**www**→http://www.primenet.com /~apfc

Body Pizazz Body Pizazz, with its home base in New Mexico, shows off its latest sports fashions for women (cozy anoraks, sexy work-out wear, and the indefatigable skort) at this form-fitting Website. Form-fitting because, the site provides just enough material to cover the basics—sizing, prices, and ordering information.
✓**www**→http://www.olworld.com /mall/mall_us/c_appare/m_body pi/index.html

Burlington Coat Factory Customers won't find any coats for sale at the Website, but the Burlington Coat Factory uses the site to encourage customer feedback, give away coupons for use at the company's Baby Depot stores, and feature a store locator to help customers find their outlets (over

IN-SITE: **Clothestime**
        http://www.clothestime.com
A very creative site. Clothestime's page promises to be particularly appealing to young, fashion-conscious women. Simple, artistic graphics and clearly presented fashion tips target a community of thoughtful—not trendy—consumers. Clothestime sponsors weekly promotions and provides a store locator.

150 locations nationwide). For businesses, the site also features corporate email addresses and home pages for retailers and manufacturers. Great URL!

✓**www**→http://www.coat.com

Casual Male/Big & Tall The store for big and tall men packs discounts and prizes onto its Website. Casual Male has made its Web page look like a print ad from the Sunday paper, using the familiar image of sales tags to attract customers and help them navigate the site. Click on one of Casual Male's recognizable black and yellow tags for big savings, big fun, and big clothes. Customers who click the blinking 25% off coupon are taken to a short registration form where the store surveys its customers. After filling out the survey, customers are registered in a monthly contest for a $100 gift certificate. Aside from the savings, Casual Male has made its site a fun place to be with "Mad-Libs" and extra links to "casual" sites for kids and adults. The Casual Male slogan—Think Big—is everywhere, even in the URL.

✓**www**→http://www.thinkbig.com

Prison Blues Prison Blues sells fashions made by incarcerated tailors, offers customers posters, and features discussions about the penal system at this captivating site.

✓**www**→http://www.teleport.com/~jailjean

Footwear

The Athlete's Foot The Athlete's Foot takes its shoe-shopping seriously—very seriously. Dedicated to helping Seekers of the Perfect Sneaker, this Website gives a profile of the Athlete's Foot research center, describes the process of type-fitting the customer's foot,

and even offers the customer lacing options. In addition, by providing a worldwide store locator, Athlete's Foot makes sure visitors don't wear out their old shoes looking for a new pair.

✓**www**→http://www.theathletesfoot.com

Florsheim Shoes Florsheim conveniently lets the male professional order shoes from the comfort of his own office. Whether ready to buy shoes or not, potential customers are encouraged to visit the site to ask the online podiatrist questions about foot problems or to consult with the Casual Day forum for advice on what's acceptable and what's not on those confusing Dress Down Fridays.

✓**www**→http://digimall.com/florsheim/i.html

The Playing Field (Foot Locker, Lady Foot Locker, & Champs) Part of Marketplace MCI, this site is devoted to the triple pillar of athletic footwear retailing. It is primarily a collection of catalogs for online ordering, although each store also has a branch locator and an email address. Marketers should also pay attention to clever targeting and positioning; Lady Footlocker, which sells activewear and shoes for women, has a "femail address."

✓**www**→http://www2.pcy.mci.net/marketplace/playingfield/index.html

Lingerie

House of Whacks With a name that is such a corny pun no one could possibly take offence. This sucssessful, Chicago-based lingerie shop exclusively targets those whose tastes in intimate apparel are less motivated by comfort and functionality than by, well, the very opposite. Establishing its cre-

dentials as central to the scene it so vividly costumes, HOW's Website advertises upcoming parties in the Chicago area, displays a latex-laden catalog, and posts a monthly newsletter for members of the HOW Club. As a tool for marketing to those who would prefer the rest of the world believed they had no idea such goods existed, the anonymity of Website purchasing should help HOW beat the competition.

✓**www**→http://www.whacks.com

La Senza With a sophisticated opening page that uses tasteful photography, this Canadian retail lingerie giant tries to reproduce the comfortable atmosphere of its stores. The site provides a store locator, a free classical-music CD contest (complete with online entry form), and gives customers plenty of reasons to return for more frilly things.

✓**www**→http://www.lasenza.com

The Lusty Love Shack The Love Shack, currently located in Florida, claims to be one of Orlando's hottest attractions. There's an online catalog for ordering underwear and a special incentive for Internet customers whose purchases total $100 or more (the shipping is free)

✓**www**→http://www.loveshack.com

Taboo At Taboo's Website, wearing PVC corsets and thigh-high boots is compared to mythological taboos like eating of the forbidden fruit and opening Pandora's Box. Taboo, a daring lingerie and apparel retailer, has an online catalog featuring its "taboo" attire, from fetish ensembles to revealing swimwear. All orders can be made by email.

✓**www**→http://www.taboo.com

Record stores

Cyberspace is like one big nightclub, or at least a really great record store for music

lovers. Making sales is a lot easier when consumers can actually hear a CD before plunking down their hard-earned dollars. On the Net, music retailers have tried several different approaches to attract business. **Allegro Corporation** employs personalized shopping with an email notification service that tells visitors every time the Purple Troglodytes have a new album. **Insomnia** targets the pre-screenagers of Generation X with band profiles and an appropriate attitude problem. But it is **CDNow** that has made the most of the technology. Not only can consumers select, sample, and read reviews for tens of thousands of CDs but the fantastic search engine means bets on who wrote that song about Jeremiah the Bullfrog can be settled instantly.

On the Net

1-800 Music Now This is an excellent way to sell music. Customers can sample a song from any album that they might be interested in (real audio or .au) and then order online if they like it.
✓**www**→http://www.1800music now.mci.com

Allegro Corporations The nation's largest distributor of classical music offers extensive jazz, world music, and miscellaneous (sound effects to blues to spoken-word) catalogs as well. Purchase automatically adds buyers to the New Release mailing list, though any visitor can browse back issues via an archive. Pages carrying soundbites and links to affiliated labels and artists are here as well.
✓**www**→http://www.teleport.com /~allegro

CD World The self-proclaimed "largest music discount store on the Net" (offering over 100,000 titles) reports its top selling albums in 15 genres, from classical to Tex-Mex. The powerful search engine lets users search by record label and catalog number, if known. Videos, headphones, blank tapes, and other music accessories are also available.
✓**www**→http://www.cdworld.com

EMusic This huge interactive site (over 100,000 titles) spotlights new releases and bestsellers, as well as "Essential Picks" in a dozen popular music genres. With the search engine, users can pull up

IN-SITE: **CDNow**
http://www.cdnow.com
This huge (165,000 product) music store is a veritable clinic in value-added online retail. For starters, CDNow offers an extensive search engine capable of providing the answer to "Who sings that song?" and where it can be found (including import and out-of-print albums). Shoppers looking for a critical perspective on the music can load ratings, reviews, and song listings from the All-Music Guide. The CDNow Lunchbox lets casual (lunchtime?) browsers save their shopping list for that next payday. Plus, there's one-price-fits-all shipping, no-hassle returns, inventory information, and Netscape-secure online purchase—a buyer could hardly ask for more.

IN-SITE: Sick & Tired
http://www.cafeliberty.com/sat

Sick & Tired is an independent online distributor that combines an indie-music mailing list with the means to obtain the (often obscure) discussion matter, rounding up the cream of the crop from dozens of smaller labels. A search engine that lets browsers distinguish between genres like "drone," "twang," and "kiwi" weeds out those more likely to find their product at a megastore. The "Tasty Thread" newsletter offers users a chance to submit show reviews and summarizes the latest chat on several indie-music mailing lists.

summaries, track listings, artwork, and availability info. Critics (everyone is a critic when it comes to music) can submit their individual reviews, while an "Own This" link lets them catalog their own collections to avoid duplication.
✓**www**→http://www.emusic.com

Insomnia With Frisky and Testy, the irrepressible Siamese mailmen mascot(s), guiding customers through the Website, this mail-order house has an attitude that harmonizes with with its punk-heavy catalog. Tart one-liners ("Great music for people who hate great music") call attention to recommended releases, and Insomnia even lets bargain-hunters browse the cut-out bins for overstocked product—just like the real stores.
✓**www**→http://www.insomnia.com

Music Boulevard Music Boulevard has positioned itself as one of the first retail stars of the new medium, a full-service online music store that lets visitors browse, preview, and buy any of more than 145,000 CDs and cassettes. With three versions—full graphics, slender graphics, and limited graphics—the store targets Net novices and high-speed cybercitizens alike. For those not in the purchasing mood, Music Boulevard offers online music publications (including *Spin*), contests, and superb additional content, such as lavish bios of rock stars—and Web-challenged Netsurfers can even download browsers.
✓**www**→http://www.musicblvd.com

Music Express This site works to build a strong relationship with customers based on frequency and feedback. Buyers who refer friends build credit towards free CDs; frequent buyers receive free T-shirts. The online order form solicits customers to add titles to the store's inventory, either to order themselves or to share a favorite with others. Additionally, the store promises that ten cents out of every purchase is donated "to furthering the advancement of the information highway."
✓**www**→http://branch.com/cd express/index.html

Newbury Comics The Boston-area alternative music store's online site boasts a recently-upgraded interactive interface. The whole lifestyle, not just music (though there's no shortage of that here), is for sale via secure online purchase, right down to T-shirts, lava lamps, and Doc Martens. The Boston Music Scene guide and the Underground Guide to Boston tell users what bands and clubs to check out, and where to get that nose pierced.
✓**www**→http://www.newbury.com

Soundwire Old-timey graphics, a wide selection of 7" vinyl records, and a focus on independent music should appeal to the most atavistic consumer, while the high quality (MPEG2) sound samples would impress a technophile. Color-coded catalogs, a search engine, and a record label index facilitate everyone's shopping experience.
✓**www**→http://soundwire.com

World Wide Music In advertising its huge catalog of records and tapes, World Wide Music emphasizes its sound clip capacity, claiming more than 200,000 online sound samples. In addition, the store permits online ordering and runs a recommendation service.
✓**www**→http://www.worldwide music.com

Bookstores

The vast number of bookstores online provides powerful evidence of the synergy be-

tween Cyberspace and the printed word. In fact, the Net may actually be encouraging readers, perhaps selling more copies of Chaucer and Jackie Collins, Douglas Adams and Shakespeare than even the local Barnes & Noble superstore. As wired as anyone, bookstores compete hard online and have developed a number of clearsighted and innovative tactics for attracting and keeping customers. **Amazon.com** continues to build a loyal constituency with an email service that announces the arrival of favored authors or topics; family-owned **Booksite** provides a personal librarian service guaranteed to enlarge its customer family. Other stores target specific market segments. **Betts Bookstore** serves Steven King fanatics, while **Books From Cyberspace** only deals in best-sellers. Added facilities at sites like **Blackwell's Bookshop**—packed with literary tidbits and online contests—ensure that reading, literature and the printed word will remain synonymous well into the next century.

IN-SITE: Borders on the Web
http://www.borders.com
Growing book chain Borders doesn't offer online catalog searches or ordering. At this site, daily reviews of books or CDs by eager staff members encourage more than one visit. But visitors still have to check the online list of stores if they want to purchase those recommendations.

On the Net

Abatijour Books Although small, this store is in the fast lane of Net selling—it takes the "First Virtual" Internet credit card. The technology enables consumers to purchase non-fiction books without ever resorting to concrete bank buildings or conventional plastic. For the time being, this is the site's main selling point.
✓**www**→http://www.corcom.com/vislink/books/index.html

Amazon.com "Earth's largest bookstore" has come up with a truly innovative way of making itself the one online bookstore to choose. "Eyes & Editors" is a personal notification service to keep avid readers apprised of new releases by favorite authors, new titles in any field, and any other book news by simply filling out a reading preference form—a most effective customer service feature. Once a visitor has read the Amazon email, it's simple to hop over and put in an online order from the company's huge stock. If that were not enough, a spotlight sale, which moves every day or so, keeps bargain hunters returning to the site—bestsellers are always discounted. There's even a choice of three types of gift wrap. A "boy-am-I-hard-to-please" email response form adds a final touch of consumer consciousness. Amazon has the art of cyberbookselling down cold.

✓**www**→http://www.amazon.com

Barnes & Noble—The Loci
With a B&N superstore now on every block in America, there might as well be a place in cyberspace to browse, chat, talk to authors, drink lattés, and even buy books. Having already established extraordinary brand penetration, selling books seems secondary to B&N's online, literary community-building activities. This site hosts a series of chat boards, and not all are book-related. Loci also sponsors frequent real-time discussions with authors and celebrities like Quincy Jones. B&N plays the public service angle well, too—offering excerpts from new texts on job searching, online counseling, and college info. There are games to be played, and just to make sure more than bookworms come by, B&N has weekly reviews of movies, TV listings, online artists, and music soundbites. In fact, you can't even buy books here—only magazines and posters. Guess they still want booklovers to visit the store where the scent of printed page mingled with the aroma of Starbucks' java can work its consumer magic.

✓**www**→http://www.loci.com

Best Books Online This online bookstore wants to appeal both to readers looking for the latest Jackie Collins and to cyberpals willing to discuss Proust's prose. Book business professionals (authors, publishers, and vendors) are also encouraged to look in. The power of interactivity is key here—readers can be critics by voting for favored titles, or post queries on a bulletin board and shop the online book store. Industry professionals have their own bulletin board, a classi-

fied section to advertise books, editors, typesetting services, etc. Its list of hints on getting good PR and marketing is an especially attractive lure for the small publishing community.

✓**www**→http://www.bestbooks .com

Betts Bookstore As Bangor, Maine's most famous resident is the ghoulmeister himself, Mr Stephen King, it's hardly surprising that this little bookstore, which also offers charming local interest books about lighthouses, blueberries, and moose, opens its site with the local superstar. King's name is prominently displayed near the top, and his home page is lavishly illustrated in black and blood red. The promise of autographed copies and works by the mistress of King manor, Tabitha, will probably keep fans checking back. Links to other King pages are another way of ensuring frequent travel through an otherwise standard small-town bookstore.

✓**www**→http://www.acadia.net /w95020/w95020aa.html

Blackwell's Bookshop Blackwell's Bookshop, celebrated Oxford purveyor of knowledge, adopts the "reading can be fun" strategy. Each month brings a literary quiz with truly fabulous prizes—how about all 900 Penguin Classics?—and new books are featured in detail. Aware that academic types have a tendency to be caught by almost any interesting looking book near the one they're looking for, Blackwell's provides wonderful browsing program that enables avid readers to salivate over all the books in a general topic area. Extra online sales undoubtedly ensue.

✓**www**→http://www.blackwell.co .uk/bookshops

Bonder Bookstore This Montreal-based bookstore plays on the novelty of cybershopping—constantly stressing the speed of service and providing a PGP (pretty good privacy) key for those fearful of ordering online. In addition Bonder keeps customers returning by offering quality reviews of new books by everyone from Bill Gates to Isabel Allende.

✓**www**→http://www.bonder.com

Book Finders Simplicity is the hallmark of this book search service—just four buttons send in a hard-to-find request. Up front about its minimum charge of $25, Book Finders also makes it clear there is no obligation to buy—a crucial added value to those seeking out-of-print publications.

✓**www**→http://www.aztech-cs .com/bookfinders/y-home.html

Book Finders Unlimited This site has several unique features bound to lure the literate. Every week all book reviews from the respectable British press are posted here, designed to inspire repeat visits and purchases of books not already on the shopping list. These generous souls also provide a wonderful email service—use the form provided, enter topics or authors of interest, and Book Finders' own librarian will email back a customized bibliography free of charge!

✓**www**→http://www.bookfinders .co.uk/bookfinders

Book Hunter Bare-bones search service for technical books, promising savings of both time and money. The best feature is the online request form which results in email quotes for searches far and wide.

✓**www**→http://www.i1.net/~bhun ter

Book Passage Bookstore Located in scenic Corte Madera, California, this bookstore broadens its appeal with clever use of cybertechnology. Known for attracting big name authors like Isabel Allende and *Washington Post* Editor Ben Bradlee, Book Passage attracts cyberconsumers with the promise of a direct email link to upcoming guests. Tailored reading lists are also a nice bonus, offering off-center topics like Sons of Sam Spade and Adventure Travel.
✓**www**→http://www.bookpassage .com

Book Stacks Unlimited Book Stacks is the granddaddy of online bookstores, and all that time and experience have led to a spectacular online venture. Access to a database of 400,000 titles is easy via the Web page, telnet and FTP options, but it is the Book Café that should win kudos for clever marketing. People will keep coming back for the sheer joy of the weekly author features, online discussions with living authors, tidbits from "Today in Literary History," and reviews of new releases. Playing on the immense popularity of the coffee bar, Book Stacks has created a series of forums for discussion groups, some chaired by actual genre writers. This participatory feeling is augmented by the open book review section where anyone and everyone can sound off about intriguing titles. The Lyric site has excerpts from popular audio titles. The Bookrack zips visitors out to magazine home pages all over the Net. Why not do as Book Stacks recommends: get a refreshing beverage and spend several hours in its carefully crafted literary haven.
✓**www**→http://www.books.com

Book TV It's a bookstore! It's a TV show! It's a Website! Not everyone has access to the TV show, so this page provides the products in interactive packets, including sound files of past interviews with Charlton Heston and Elmore Leonard. Beyond the TV schedule and multi-media entertainment here, there is also a staff who will take email orders and promise to find "any book, any time." Hard to categorize this business or its approach but it's probably safe to assume people who would watch a show about books would also buy them by email.
✓**www**→http://www.booktv.com /booktv

Booklink Booklink's site offers the incentives of a changing sale bin, and unusual subject matter—multiculturalism. But it's the site's use of Web links that is the real innovation here, constructed to channel a whole new clientele through the site. As well as selling politically correct books, Booklink links Web visitors to the famous Happy Puppy site for free downloads of demos and shareware games. Thus parents can get both a nice bedtime story about kids of all nations getting along together and a new version of Confirmed Kill.
✓**www**→http://www.intac.com /~booklink

The Bookpool An excerpt from *Teach Yourself Java in 21 Days* opens the presentation of this technical book house which offers 20-35 percent deductions and weekly specials. The Bookpool knows its clientele well and offers an email notification service to announce such arrivals as the new C+ programming text or a monograph on fuzzy logic.
✓**www**→http://www.bookpool .com

IN-SITE: **Beaconray**
http://jollyroger.com/beaconray.html
This publisher could well call itself the *Dartmouth Review* bookstore—marketing the wisdom of Limbaugh and the ages to young conservatives. It does so with price cuts—yes, 15 great conservative books for just $39.95. Beaconray also practices a bit of creative categorization by packaging *Catcher in the Rye* and the opium-induced wandering of Coleridge as classics of American conservative thinking for the "moral intellectual." Stock overrun perhaps?

Books From Cyberspace Part of the appeal of this online shop is that it offers 25 percent off the books listed in the *New York Times Book Review*. Each week there is a new selection of reductions. Reviews chosen from other arbiters of extremely popular opinion like *Time* magazine keep up the peer pressure. This company lives by the motto "if you do one thing, do it well, and cheaper."

✓**www**→http://www.bfcbooks.com

BookServe "A Million International Books!" proclaims this trilingual (English, German, and Dutch) site. Selling itself as a multinational megalith, Bookserve attracts with volume but clinches buyers with a user-friendly organization complete with charming icons. Books reviews and a virtual shopping basket to fill along the way are designed to promote long periods of window shopping. The site also offers links to publishers and even provides advice on making the most of online selling. This is a unique attempt to market both to book consumers and publishers.

✓**www**→http://www.bookserve.com

BookSite Conviviality and efficiency are the name of the game at this family-owned bookstore. The amazing speed of cyberbrowsing through 250,000 titles is mentioned more than once. It is Katie, however, family librarian, who strives to bring warmth to the customer's visit. Customers can email her their interests, she'll search two million books, and they will soon receive notification, via email again, of when the newest book on Gettysburg or molecular biology comes into print. In the big world of cyberspace, personal service like this is a nice hook.

✓**www**→http://www.booksite.com

The Booksmith This small bookstore on the Haight has several charming attractions. Along with the profiles of best sellers and an online catalog, the makers have created several special features. A science fiction ezine promises to attract hordes of passing fans, and the armchair traveler page utilizes Web links to their fullest. These folks also understand incentives and offer new sales and gift certificate contests monthly. In keeping with the locale, The Booksmith covers the quirk factor and offers author trading cards for favored writers.

✓**www**→http://www.sirius.com/~books

British Books@American Prices These folks play on the American belief that the old country is way more cultured than ours, stating, frankly, that "British books are consistently well-written, cultivated and literate." Effectively playing on national Anglophilia by prominently displaying the Union Jack on every page, BB@AP makes it easy to become as cultured as Alastair Cooke through online ordering of high-gloss coffee-table books. It's an effective strategy that targets a specific clientele.

✓**www**→http://british.books@american.prices.com/shop

Classics Illustrated Titles This bookstore sells comic book versions of classic literature, from Aesop to Kipling to Shakespeare. Jacket art, a large selection, and easy online ordering make this a great resource for consumers who want to get their kids interested in classic literature, students who think Cliff's Notes are a hard read, or busy adults who want to be able to spout off bits of Hawthorne or Dumas at cocktail parties.

✓**www**→http://ciei.com/1.html

Dillons Bookshop Already established as London's largest bookshop, Dillons here leads the field of online UK bookstores, with a site full of attractions for all ages. Adults get profiles of new releases and interviews with hot authors, while in a special kids section the little ones can post their own book reviews online, play games and even email favorite characters like the Jolly Pocket Postman and Winnie the Pooh. Dillons also links to interesting Web sites, provides search engines, and posts detailed reviews of computer books and programs like Windows 95. The site even links to hip Brit ezine Anorak (its name is derived from the British term for rainjacket, oft-used to describe those of a nerdy disposition). Combining technological reference with an established pedigree, this site has a uniquely successful spin.

✓**www**→http://www.dillons.co.uk

Internet Libri Bologna Esoteria is the overall enticement at this home for an Italian bookseller, which deals in everything from incunabula to CD-ROMs. The catalog of wares is supplemented by changing monthly exhibits clearly designed as stopping points on many Net museum tours.

✓**www**→http://www.ilb.it/ilb/books/welcomeE.html

Romance Authors Home Page Splashed with appropriately juicy red hearts, this hubsite for romance novels markets some of the world's most popular romance novelists, from Merline Lovelace to Carol Finch. Bios, cover photos, synopses, and online ordering for all their titles are resident here.

✓**www**→http://www.nettrends.com/romanceauthors

Food & drink

There aren't many supermarkets on the Web, but the online world is the province of

many smaller specialty stores that jumped online with their products as soon as they scented the possibility for profitable marketing. **Over the Coffee** specializes in the beverage of choice of the hyperactive '90s, enhancing its gourmet selection with bean trivia and a virtual coffee bar where cappuccino sippers can meet and talk Proust ("I find that his use of transgendered names is wonderful, as is this almond mocha decaf"). The bright graphics and brighter copy at **Hot Hot Hot** is also creating a Net culture, this time for those who like to test their fortitude by ingesting some of the hottest sauces known to mankind. And then there is the refined ambiance of the **Virtual Vineyards**, an online wine shop (and wine-recommending service) that sells its product with an equal measure of snobbery and salesmanship.

On the Net

Food stores

Hickory Farms Several regularly updated virtual catalogs reside here—California Cuisine, Mission

Orchard, Almond Plaza, Hickory Farms, Pfaelzer, and Brothers Ace Specialty Foods. Everything from Award Winning Beef Stick to Dolphin Safe Tuna to Very Berry White Chocolate Bark to Hickory Farms gift baskets can be ordered online, by phone, or by fax. The customer may also submit a form to receive a catalog by snail mail.
✓**WWW**→http://virtumall.com/Hick oryFarms

Hot Hot Hot This site, pushing hot sauces from around the world, is one of the coolest on the Net, pun intended. Eye-catching graphics lure unsuspecting Netsurfers in, and they stay for the catalog, which is organized by heat level, origin, and ingredients as well as brand name. The copy is witty and the products come with warning labels. Features such as sauce of the month, articles from *Chili*

IN-SITE: **Acme**
    http://AcmeMarkets.Com
Acme aims to broaden the consumer's image of the giant supermarket chain by pushing its corporate and party-catering services on the Website. The playfully illustrated site includes sections filled with entertaining ideas and food ideas for big sporting events (usually accompanied by coupons off the items and links to other big sports sites on the Net). The site also provides supermarket and pharmacy locators and lots of online coupons.

Pepper magazine and comments from rapturous chileheads, as well as frequent additions to the catalog, keep 'em coming back.
✓**www**→http://www.hot.presence.com/hot

Old World Venison Co. Old World Venison has made deer meat available for online ordering, and created a businesslike site in the process.
✓**www**→http://www.upstel.net/~pbingham/venison.html

The Original Cookie Company Customers can head to the site's coupon kiosk for a page full of cookie specials, print the page, and use the coupons at any Original Cookie Company store.
✓**www**→http://www.originalcookie.com

Over the Coffee As you might imagine, Over the Coffee's page is just a little caffeine happy, offering resources on every possible aspect of the little brown bean, and paying equal attention to the professional java hawkers and the regular ol' coffee achievers. The aficionado's best bet is the Reference Desk, which offers a huge collection of guides, works of art, and articles on coffee—from an article on the link between caffeine and cancer to an international guide to cyber-cafes to a collection of coffee folksongs—as well as collected searches for "coffee" from all the major Web browsers. The professionals have an equally large resource in the Business Section, which features indexes for retail and wholesale vendors and links to national coffee organizations. In addition, everyone can enjoy the classifieds section and the chat rooms, both a mixture of business and pleasure. A bookmark for caffeine achievers everywhere.
✓**www**→http://cappuccino.com

Wine shops

Berry Bros. & Rudd Leading off with an illustrated history of the company, this rather formal site gets down to business with virtual vintage charts recording the availability and quality of Vintage Port, Red Bordeaux, Red Burgundy, Red Rhône, Sauternes & Barsac, White Burgundy & Chablis, and Vintage Champagne. Each particular wine is presented with its own order form quoting both US dollar and yen prices, and every drop can be ordered online. One of the more promising sections on this page is "Great Estates." At the moment this feature offers short textual histories and order forms for the most famous vineyards in the world, and the site assures its visitors that it will grow into a virtual encyclopedia of wine-growing estates.
✓**www**→http://www.berry-bros.co.uk

IN-SITE: **Virtual Vineyards**
    http://www.virtualvin.com
Designed to sell wines to both practiced connoisseurs and wine novices, the Virtual Vineyards Website creates a comfortable environment for customers to learn about wines and Californian vineyards. Wine expert Peter Granoff guides customers with tasting charts, recommendations, brief descriptions of vineyards, an online column to send in wine questions, and a wine glossary. All features on the site lead to one thing—selling wine. The site actively promotes its Monthly Wine Program, which lets customers sign up for a wine plan in which Peter sends them a certain number of bottles of wine each month to sample with a tasting chart and his notes. Elegant but not intimidating, Virtual Vineyards has created a fun place to explore and buy wines.

Auctions & galleries

World renowned auction houses Christie's and Sotheby's demonstrate the versatility

of the Web as a marketing medium. How? By imparting some of the excitement and social cachet of the auction experience, and by filling their sites with interactive fun and photos of great treasures of the past (Catherine the Great's snuffbox) and the present (Jackie O's boudoir set). But not everyone can make purchases on that scale, and for those with less costly artistic needs, online galleries have numerous other products. Some, like **Art to Live With**, rely on artspeak to market "modernist masterpieces" in original prints. Others have created an online art viewing experience; most noticeably the excellent **Electric Gallery**, which enables its online visitors to wander through wing after wing of their virtual folk art gallery.

On the Net

Auction houses

Christie's International The venerable auction house decorates its home page with the signatories of its trade—gavels, bidders, and wealthy people. Although its page isn't as interactive as Sotheby's, Christie's has the distinction of be-

ing the first major auction house to host a cyberauction (December 1995 on America Online). The site is packed with information about the old auction house, including contact information, office locations, and, most impressively, profiles of upcoming auctions. Christie's also runs an email appraisal service on the site, thus building online relationships with

new customers curious about their own valuables.
✓**www**→http://www.christies.com /Christie.htm

Dorotheum This Viennese auction house has recreated an elegant Hapsburg environment on its maroon and black page. In addition to an auction calendar, selected catalogs, and links to other Net

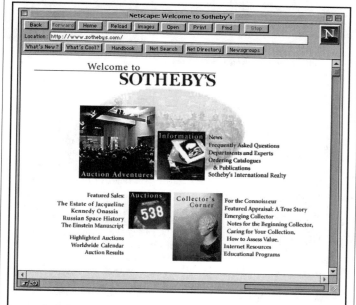

IN-SITE: **Sotheby's**
http://www.sothebys.com

Sotheby's, the renowned international art auction house, has moved into the cyberage with style. Not surprisingly, the site is elegantly designed, but it's also playful. Sotheby's has received a lot of attention for its Auction Adventures: three scenarios, each with a different level of difficulty, let customers research purchases, make tough choices, and even bid, while walking around cyberrooms full of antiques. In addition to using its Website to sell the excitement of an auction, Sotheby's sells its reputation, profiling upcoming sales (the estates of Jackie O. and Einstein), with high levels of interactivity. The site is primarily targeted at new collectors, offering advice on assessing the value of art objects and caring for collections. All visitors are encouraged to explore the world of art auctions through guides, glossaries, articles about auctioning, and even links to related Internet resources.

Industry Hub

Auctions On-Line is a comprehensive database of fine art, antiques and collectibles providing potential buyers with unrivalled access to auction information and catalogues worldwide.

IN-SITE: Auctions On-Line
http://www.auctions-on-line.com
While the name of this service is a bit confusing—the auctions in question don't actually take place online—the site, a boon to both collectors and auction houses, lists auctions around the world, links to the Websites covering them, and serves as a huge repository of catalogs for past and forthcoming auctions.

auction sources, Dorotheum provides potential customers with expert advice on the art of buying and selling valuables.
✓**www**→http://www.dorotheum.com

Art galleries

The Art Store The site's home page evokes a quaint small-town storefront. Customers are invited to browse through the store by artist or theme, and the site is designed to make browsing easy. Visitors can flip through an artist's portfolio, view large JPEGs of specific artworks, read bios of the artists and descriptions of each work, and order online.
✓**www**→http://www.gtp.com/art/index.html

Art to Live With Can a company capitalize on pretention and

snobbery to sell its products? Art to Live With certainly tries. The online gallery sells the mystique of fine art, headlining its site with promises of "verifiable collectibility and unconditionally guaranteed authentic" prints. Emphasis is placed on the difference between original prints (works of art) and offset prints (mere reproductions).
✓**www**→http://www.arttolivewith.com

The Electric Gallery The first commercial art gallery on the Web has certainly benefited from its experience, offering a visually exciting and intellectually stimulating site that actually feels like a real gallery. The bright yellow Electric Gallery, which showcases original art work found in galleries nationwide, is laid out in the form of a traditional gallery. Visitors interested in Haitian, Southwest, Ama-

zonian, and folk art walk between rooms and read small blurbs about the artists beneath their works. The gallery also takes advantage of the Net's technology—sound files of great jazz and blues musicians, for instance, accompany art works in the gallery's Blues and Jazz wing.
✓**www**→http://www.egallery.com

Galleries at the Canyon The 30 or so artists who have collected their wares on this Website attempt to recreate the feel of the famous gallery-lined thoroughfare of Canyon Road in Santa Fe. Each artist is pictured in appropriate neo-Western garb and allowed to express his or her artistic vision in a long essay. Visitors can also stroll through the studios of artists whose works they are considering purchasing.
✓**www**→http://www.interart.net/galleries/default.html

Gallerie Claude Lafitte This gallery, located in historic Quebéc City, has a cultured ambiance, intensified by its bilingual presentation. Visitors can imagine sipping white wine while wandering past the current exhibit of modern oils. Each thumbnail is accompanied by a biography, which includes as added selling value a list of the artist's collectors.
✓**www**→http://www.lafitte.com

The Salvador Dali Gallery A name like Dali has a certain bankability, and these dealers make the most of it, featuring a new Dali print each month and a retrospective catalog. For those who wish to move into the society of Andrew Mellon and Henry Frick, the site publishes a collectors' newsletter that lets buyers appreciate the master and watch their masterpieces appreciate.
✓**www**→http://daligallery.com

Direct selling

For those whose mail consists solely of catalogs, the advent of direct marketing on the

Internet may be an upsetting development. For those who remain resistant to junk mail, picking and choosing from glamorous online worlds may yet encourage latent consumerism. Retailers like **Lands' End** and **L.L. Bean** have moved to attract visitors via a cybertown and an outdoor recreation center, respectively. Others maintain that there is something comforting about our purchasing past, and allow visitors to thumb through **J.C. Penney's** catalog page by page or look through bargain bins at **Your Discount Product Store**.

On the Net

General merchandise

Lands' End Dodgeville is Lands' End's fictional hometown and home of the *Dodgeville Daily News*. The clothing catalog company uses the *Daily News* on the cozy Website as a vehicle to promote contests and company happenings. Lands' End is also selling its merchandise online.
✓**www**→http://www.landsend.com

Spiegel Spiegel has put its catalog online, and minimized loading speeds by showing images only when customers choose to view a specific product. Trying to get customers to return often, Spiegel offers more than just a catalog. It's running a magazine and an advice column focused on fitness, fashion, and nutrition.
✓**www**→http://www.spiegel.com/spiegel

Upscale Wholesale Buy a little or a lot! Of what? Of computer gadgets, pet accesories, automotive merchandise, personal professional security items, and outdoor and indoor recreation products. Customers can order one NV100 Night Vision Scope or 500 Australian Kuranda Trampoline Dog Beds, whatever their whim. Great presentation and a ridiculous array of products will keep visitors checking back for new oddities.
✓**www**→http://www.upscale.com

Your Discount Product Store The virtual equivalent of the local thrift store, with the merchandise—from computers to back support belts to wooden ducks—thrown haphazardly into special bins. Visitors will have fun browsing here, and practiced shoppers won't mind rifling through the

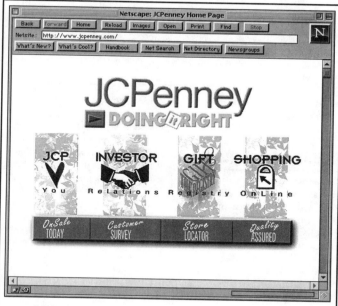

IN-SITE: **J.C. Penney**
http://www.jcpenney.com
J.C. Penney offers an extensive online catalog with pictures and descriptions for thousands of items for men, women, and the home. Currently, J.C. Penney provides an 800 number to purchase items. Like most companies online, J.C. Penney solicits feedback on its Website and stores through a survey.

IN-SITE: L.L.Bean
http://www.llbean.com

L.L. Bean's site is rugged and polished at once—rugged in its graphics and ambiance, which evoke rock-climbing and cross-country skiing, and polished in its execution, which uses state-of-the-art Web production techniques. In addition to Park Search, a database of more than 900 national forests and state parks, Bean provides links to sites on outdoor activities of all kinds. But the real draw is the online catalog, which not only describes products, but guides customers to related items—for instance, the Gore-Tex boots page links to a page on lightweight socks.

piles to find what they want.
✓**www**→http://www.opendoor.com/SevenHills/Home.html

Children's clothes

Cadema Industries High concept and low product, this fun site takes kids and parents on a little adventure through half a dozen punchy pages with enchanted houses and daisy diners filled with children in bright Magic Petals clothing. More of a commercial than a catalog, Cadema's site has no copy explaining the pieces and, for now, no way to order them. But the site promises online ordering will soon be available, and this enchanting presentation ensures that parents will check back to buy.
✓**www**→http://www.aztec.co.za

/biz/africa/cadema.htm

Golden Gate This catalog plays the cute approach almost to the point of toothache. The catalog of Ruff Raggs is separated into theme lines such as Puppy Dog Tails, Holiday Bears, Kitten in the Window, and Bear and Bees, and each item is showcased with an adorable illustration and heartwarming copy—"Oh....so many bears. Can you see me peep out of your pocket?" Aww!
✓**www**→http://www.best.com/~ggate/golden-gate.html

Lbow Mitten Here is a site that knows exactly what it is selling, at whom its sell is aimed, and how best to make purchasing as simple as possible. In the world of mit-

tens, few can claim to have made such technological leaps both online and off. For as the home page explains, there is more to a good pair of mittens than you might imagine—"Forget about idiot mittens; these are genius mittens!" The ordering system that follows is pretty smart too. As cute as a button, possibly cuter.
✓**www**→http://www.lbow.com

Computers

Creative Computers Creative Computers' Website places the MacMall and PC Mall catalogs online, with more than 12,000 products. In addition to its browsable product categories, the site spotlights a Deal of the Day (valid until 5 p.m. PST), a Bargain Basement, and other special deals and new products. While customers can't order online yet, each page repeats the superstore's toll-free number and a priority code to apply the online prices. Within the support area is a must-have bookmark—a manufacturers' page, which links directly to hundreds of computer company home pages. Visitors who sign up to receive the Malls' mail-order catalogs have a chance to win a limited edition Porsche 986/Boxster.
✓**www**→http://www.creativecomputers.com

MicroWarehouse, Inc. With the MicroWarehouse, MacWarehouse, and Data Comm Warehouse catalogs online here, this sophisticated site puts 14,000 products just an overnight delivery away. Customers can execute multicatalog searches from the home page, or narrow the search as they navigate a specific catalog's hierarchy. Each product is illustrated and summarized; Mac products even contain links to applicable *MacWorld* reviews. Weekly specials

are highlighted in each product category. Clicking an item code places the product in the customer's shopping basket; those with Secure Socket Layering-enabled browsers (e.g., Netscape Navigator 1.2 or later, Microsoft Internet Explorer) can complete the transaction online. The site's FTP server is a great resource in its own right, offering hundreds of product demos and an archive of PowerUser Toolkit shareware packs and updates.
✓**www**→http://www.warehouse.com

NECX Direct This online superstore provides two ways to shop: as a registered customer or as a member of its fee-based Buyers Club. In addition to the 20,000 products offered, Club members are eligible for lower prices and special offers—customers can apply online via a secure browser. The site's product descriptions are jam-packed with information, a specifications table, and links to recent reviews, applicable accessories, and similar products. In addition to the more common product/manufacturer/part number searches, customers can perform searches based on product specification forms— perfect for cross-comparison of items.
✓**www**→http://necxdirect.necx.com

RCSnet With more than 30,000 items in its catalog, RCS stakes its claim as the world's largest online computer store. Products are organized in a very "vendor-centric" manner, not only within each product category, but also in the site's product news section, which provides info on new and discontinued items as well as vendor price reductions. In addition, the technical support index links to vendors' tech support Web areas

(customers can also email RCS's own tech department via the "Ask the Specialist" link). A one-time fee of $10 lets customers create an account and make their purchases online.
✓**www**→http://www2.rcsnet.com/Rockwell/RCS

Jewelry

Better Than Sex While the names of the pieces are highly suggestive—"Bring Out the Tiger In Her," for example—Better Than Sex's jewelry is actually very tasteful. The marketing, however, is on a par with the nomenclature. The site's slogan is "You Have to Pay to Play," and the basic idea is that expensive trinkets are the way to a woman's…heart. This large catalog, divided into categories like Naughty Necklaces and Coax Her With Cables, offers images and retail price comparisons, and everything is available for online ordering. The site expands its inventory regularly, encouraging visitors to return for more persuasive purchases.
✓**www**→http://www.mja.net/better-than-sex

Diamond Advantage Buying a diamond is intimidating enough; buying one online without first-hand appraisal is downright forbidding. These L.A.-based direct importers allay consumers' fears by offering an extensive buying guide that uses layman's language and diagrams to explain cut, color, carat weight, and clarity. Filling in for a

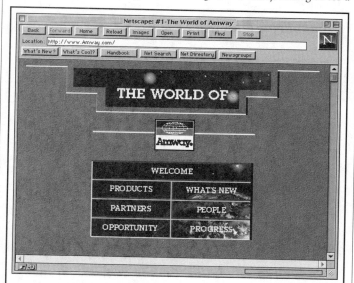

IN-SITE: World of Amway
http://www.Amway.com
Amway sells its products to a network of distributors who sell to friends, family, and co-workers. Amway's Website is targeted at entrepreneurs interested in signing up as distributors for its products. To inspire potential distributors, Amway features success stories from people who've sold Amway products, offers information on stock trends that support the Amway theory of business, and even features downloadable videos of greetings from Amway execs. Amway also maintains a searchable directory with information about its products—from face lotion to laundry detergent—and offers potential distributors, and anyone else who visits its Website, a tour of its plant in Ada, Michigan.

knowlegeable salesperson are photographs and rating charts for the entire catalog, and every item is available for online ordering.
✓**www**→http://www.diamond advantage.com

Zuni Traders Zuni Traders offers a large catalog of both Zuni and Navajo jewlery and objects d'art—all orderable online. A short illustrated bio precedes each of the artist's catalogs, and this grounding of the craftsperson in his/her tribe and region promotes the authenticity of the company and its products.
✓**www**→http://www.olworld.com /olworld/mall/mall_us/c_jewelr /m_zuni/index.html

Lingerie

2(x)ist Underwear Can consumers really be won over by big muscles and a little skin? 2(x)ist would argue yes, yes, yes! This daring site opens with an image of a prostrate man in just his underwear, and that's only the beginning. Targeting women and gay men, 2(x)ist sells underwear—and posters—online.
✓**www**→http://www.digex.net /2xist.html

Day's End Lingerie Catalog At the end of the day, people tend to wear lingerie more than at any other time of the day. Day's End know this, and to meet the demands of the crepuscular lingerie market, the online store has created a large site filled with underwear of various kinds. The Day's End Website is an extension of its print catalog, including photos, prices, and sizing charts. The Website also offers information on how to become an employee of the company—a sales rep, not a model.
✓**www**→http://cybershop.net/day send.html

International Male International Male has its entire catalog online. Customers can pick out a pair of chinos, dial the 800 number, and an operator will take their order. International Male is just beginning to do business on the Net, but it's open to suggestions by email.
✓**www**→http://www.intmale.com /intmale/intmale.htm

Lingerie Outlet This Website, targeted more toward women than men, is decorated with frills and lace and offers fast, convenient lingerie shopping. Owned and operated by a former NASA employee (?!), The Lingerie Outlet promises the best lingerie bargains anywhere in Cyberspace. The company also sponsors ongoing Website promotions that feature even more reduced merchandise.
✓**www**→http://www.loutlet.com

LingerieNet Opening with a cartoon of a voluptuous woman in her underwear, this is a site that knows exactly how to sell its product. Lingerie, it recognizes, appeals to a wide range of people and LingerieNet is there to provide all of them with all of what they need. And taking advantage of the technology, LingerieNet ensures that if visitors like what they see enough to buy it, they can order it, using email.
✓**www**→http://www.lingerienet .com

Playware, Ltd. This national lingerie catalog positions itself as a tasteful operation and on its home page superimposes a pseudo-Victorian pattern over a seductively-photographed woman. This is a site designed to appeal to the sophisticate and the would-be sophisticate. Clearly targeted at men, it offers a searchable catalog and a comprehensive index of its products.
✓**www**→http://www.playware .com

Steamed Heat Steamed Heat's Website tries to sell lingerie with neither literary ambiance nor fashion pretentions. It suspects that those who are looking to buy will find and in that respect, meets its objectives. As well as many shots of the range of products for men and women, there is also a gallery of risqué postcards that can be purchased.
✓**www**→http://www.steamed heat.com

Vega Lingerie Vega, the non-discriminatory women's lingerie company, welcomes both men and women to its world of intimate fashion. The Website offers a full-color brochure filled with high-quality photography and is divided into a number of departments including lace, leather, and swimwear. Given the market it aims to attract, the Vega site is clearly in favour of the subtle approach.
✓**www**→http://www.vega.com

T-shirts

Dream Builders This manufactuer of inspirational Ts uses star appeal to add glitz to its otherwise standard page. President Clinton ("I am dedicated to positive change and depend on the continued support of all Americans to achieve this goal") lends his official "endorsement" to the you-can-do-it shirts. Ordering info is also posted at the page.
✓**www**→http://www.Webmart .com/icc/dream.html

Gear Inc. To strengthen the tie with its market, this purveyor of

Ts with jazz musician motifs offers an Artist of the Month feature. Sound clips, discographies, and photographs of musicians like Robert Johnson and Miles Davis are provided each month in the spotlight section (alongside, unsurprisingly, T-shirt designs). It's an entertaining element that will bring music fans (and potential customers) back to the page on a regular basis.
✓**www**→http://iweb.www.com /gear

Hobies Sports Shirts It's not enough that hockey fans throw things at each other and exchange insults at the games. They have to compete at this page, too! Hobies divides its catalog into two sections, the Eastern Conference (Tampa Bay Lightening, Boston Bruins, Pittsburgh Penguins) and the Western Conference (St. Louis Blues, Chicago Blackhawks, Winnipeg Jets), creating the feeling of a match up and admirably capturing the game's unabashed spirit of competition.
✓**www**→http://www.oncomdis.on .ca/ccm.htm

I Survived Trivestiture A great example of how the smallest T-shirt manufacturer can use the Web to market her product. This very simple site gets the word on the Net about the "I Survived Trivestiture" shirt, which celebrates the division of AT&T into three sister companies.
✓**www**→http://mars.superlink.net /user/mholmes/tees.html

I Wear Tee Shirts A monthly T-shirt giveaway contest helps bring customers to this page, which also features graphics of the "Internet Surf Club" T-shirt, an online order form, and shipping info.
✓**www**→http://www.intcomm.net /~iwear

J. Dyer Animation This site gives people a reason to visit other than shopping for T-shirts. J. Dyer also offers a bi-monthly cartoon, called Bubba Bullmash, to get customers interested in the Website. This week: see how Buddy tapes his elderly G-ma to the wall so he can go fishing with his pal Peevy. Now that's entertainment!
✓**www**→http://www.com/bubba /index.html

Legalitees Maybe it's because the creator of this page is a busy law student that the page is so efficient. It cuts down on image load time by offering brief descriptions of the motifs (Coed Naked Law Enforcement, Counsel Approaching the Desk, Police Officer— Donuts, etc.) so visitors can choose the specific themes that interest them. The shirts are funny, the page name is clever, and most lawyers surely envy that URL!
✓**www**→http://attorneysatlaw .com

MINC.Home Page The page uses cryptic little quips to guide customers through its catalog, aka the hypertext link "The professor looked thoughtfully at the windshield, then upward, then turned towards me." 'European Starling' leads to a shirt that identifies 16 different types of bird droppings. A clever tactic—it draws visitors to look at shirts that might not interest them visually, and it cuts down on load time.
✓**www**→http://www.webcom.com /~minc/lt&b.html

IN-SITE: **In Your Face T-Shirts**
http://www.iyf.com/index.html
A site that's as straight to the point as the company's name. Visitors get three options at the page—they can either go directly to the catalog, to the order form, or to a form to sign up for a contest. (In fact the only thing that's not in your face at this site are the graphics showing the backside designs of the Ts which are accessed by clicking on the pics of the front designs in the catalog.)

DOOR TO DOOR

The Avon lady is calling, and she's not at the front door—she's on the Web. As the number of women on the Internet has grown, the number of commercial sites addressing traditionally female interests like fashion and cosmetics has also taken off. In fact, many direct-sales cosmetics companies—from giants like Avon and Mary Kay to smaller enterprises—have begun to market themselves on the Web, and home pages of sales representatives are sprinkled throughout Cyberspace. The sites are primarily online product brochures, with contact information for local reps; occasionally, pages include more advanced features like color charts, online order forms, copies of sales-rep newsletters like Avon Calling, and special offers for Internet buyers. Men are also making their mark in cosmetics sales—so don't be surprised if your Avon lady has a beard.

Avon

Avon by Amy
✓**www**→http://www.thepoint.net/~amy/avon.html

Avon by Anne-Marie
✓**www**→http://www.webrunners.com/resources/avonsele.html

Avon by Cyber Sandy
✓**www**→http://www.fastlane.net/homepages/meyer

Avon by Ken Lord
✓**www**→http://www.theriver.com/Avon_and_Other_Stuff

Avon by Jennie
✓**www**→http://homepage.interaccess.com/~smojo

Avon by Kerry
✓**www**→http://xpress.infinet.com/avon

BeautiControl

Julia Haskett's BeautiControl Brochure
✓**www**→http://www.webcom.com/bcontrol/catalog.html

Mary Kay

Christina Dalton
✓**www**→http://www.wwbcity.com/maryk.htm

Renia Johnson
✓**www**→http://rampages.onramp.net/%7Ernrinc

Mirror Image Mirror avoids getting lost in the slew of T-shirt sites by distinguishing itself in many ways. Right off the bat, it does something unusual and well-planned: the company's telephone number appears in the page title, so that customers interested in the products can call and speak to a representative. The site's content is also out-of-the-ordinary with a detailed printer's guide, a Social Conscience section (which contains links to local charities and Amnesty International chapters), and a Fun Zone that links to the Twinkie Project and to air guitar sites. Mirror's requisite shirt catalog is unusually well designed; visitors view only three or four images at a time, so loading is quick and painless.
✓**www**→http://www.digitalrag.com/index.html

Net Sweats & Tees A free T-shirt contest, a T-shirt of the month club, and an extensive collection of Net-themed clothing entice customers to this page. In case there's any doubt about the success of these tactics, the site also offers testament to its powers in the form of customer mail. Larry writes, "Best T-Shirt designs on the Internet Highway. Wearing one of these Ts will launch conversations," while Buffie sums it all up with "I love you guys…this page is so cool!!!"
✓**www**→http://www.icw.com/netsweat/netsweat.html

Ties

Artist's Collar Neckties Artist's Collar Neckties has created a series of tie collections based on the works of contemporary artists from Romero Britto to Matisse to Frank Lloyd Wright. The copy portrays the customer as an individualist intellectual who wants to stand out from the red power-tie crowd but isn't the hula-girl type either. Showcasing the ties with richly colored images, the catalog also offers an illustrated profile of each artist, which lends the collections an air of authenticity. Everything is available for online ordering, and a free gift comes with purchase.
✓**www**→http://www.necktie.com

The Shirt & Tie Musuem The selling point of this enormous, eclectic online catalog is exactly that: it is enormous and eclectic. Every possible genre has been covered, from sci-fi to animals to art, the ties range from tacky to almost-tasteful, whatever the customer's fetish—Buckwheat, the Shuttle Discovery, the Chicago White Sox, Van Gogh's *Starry Starry Night*, Bob Marley, Speed Racer—the Shirt & Tie Musuem lets him proclaim it to the world.
✓**www**→http://www.shirtandtie.com

Wild Ties This small netshop

doesn't have a huge catalog, but its underdog status results in a loose, humorous site that fits the product perfectly. Each novelty tie is showcased with an image and some extremely silly copy, from poetry— "Starry, starry night, Everything will be all right, Pretty sunflowers and you can't fail, When Vincent's tie comes in the mail"— to narratives—"Unbeknownst to Speed, Chim Chim has installed a top secret homing device...." The site promotes itself and its customers as laughing in the face of convention.

✓**www**→http://branch.com/wild ties/home.htm

Print catalogs

CatalogMart On its opening page CatalogMart boasts of 10,000 catalogs in over 800 topics—a claim impressive enough to attract even the most jaded direct mail shopper. Topics to choose from range from the very specialized (kaleidoscopes, aquatic therapy, afghans, personalized embroidery) to more general areas of interest (fishing equipment, apparel, home repair products, or art supplies).

✓**www**→http://catalog.savvy.com

CatalogSelect Part of Time Warner's massive Pathfinder site and one of the most recent entries into the online catalog clearinghouse business, the CatalogSelect site gives consumers the ability to put their names on the mailing lists for free catalogs in product categories that range from gourmet foods to movie memorabilia. At the checkout, consumers can also opt to receive special offers by email on categories they select.

✓**www**→http://www.Pathfinder .com/CatalogSelect

The Catalog Site Even if con-

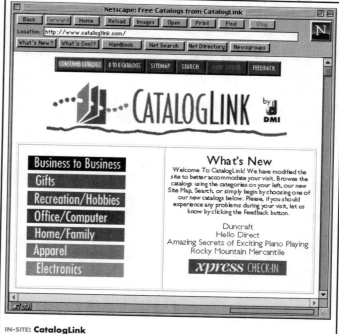

IN-SITE: **CatalogLink**
http://www.cataloglink.com

Shoppers are invited to CatalogLink to collect all the catalogs they can click on. CatalogLink's clients—the companies advertising their catalogs—feature short descriptions of their catalogs and CatalogLink then sets up a program to collect the names and addresses of consumers interested in the merchandise of their clients. The process is especially easy for consumers: just click the "send free catalogs" button under the catalog description.

sumers can't find exactly what they want on the Net (hard to believe), the Net can still lead them to it! This site represents thousands of catalogs in over 250 categories from accessories to yard products. It's a team effort here—the company provides a description, the Catalog provides contact information and an order form for each offline catalog, as well as links to the online versions, if available. The site also places great importance on customer feedback, with no less than five bulletin boards on subjects such as favorite catalogs and comments about the Catalog Site.

✓**www**→http://www.catalog

site.com

Mall of Catalogs The site has over 1,600 catalogs to choose from, some already with Web pages, and each with a concise review and an email button for ease of ordering. There is also a "green" button which customers can use to submit their name to a "never send me anything" list—in case anyone was worried about their name winding up on a list for Mexican forged iron fittings, pepper spray vendors, or collectible cars by mistake.

✓**www**→http://csn.net/market eers/mallofcatalogs

Florists

In the old days when people forgot Mother's Day or their Valentine, they could never be

sure that the florist miles away wasn't padding the bouquet with wilted carnations and baby's breath. No longer. Online florists like **Flower Power** provide pictures of all arrangements, and easy online ordering. Others like **1-800-Flowers**, **FTD Internet**, and **PC Flowers & Gifts**, have inaugurated gift reminder services that will notify subscribers via email, several days in advance of birthdays, anniversaries, holidays and other occasions. Convenience is an ever-more valuable commodity in today's world, and as a marketing strategy this one comes up smelling like a rose.

On the Net

1-800-FLOWERS 1-800-FLOW-ERS goes online with a stylized home page designed to look like the entrance to a nature park. Net-surfers can visit the Garden and find special offers, a list of retail stores, and a Floral Reference Center full of flower facts. Visitors can also head directly to the Store, questions of the Gift Concierge, or sign up for the Gift Reminder service (1-800-FLOWERS will email customers just before an important gift-giving date).
✓**www**→http://www.800flower-scom

FTD Internet The FTD man prevails in Cyberspace, offering dependable flower delivery and an Internet Reminder Service. Three days before the birthday, anniversary, or other special day that a customer needs to remember, FTD emails a reminder—just in time for the customer to order one of FTD's more than 80 arrangements on display at the Website.
✓**www**→http://www.ftd.com

The Flower Shop Floral arrangement graphics, a toll-free number, and links to other Web pages are all here, and are all common enough features for the Web-

sites of florists online. But this one certainly takes the bouquet for the best domain name!
✓**www**→http://www.theflower shop.com

Flower Power Sometimes companies affect a "cyberimage" to ingratiate themselves with the medium. Sometimes florists pretend that instead of being stem cutters they're really soldiers on a petal-laden rocket bound for Planet Earth. Roses? Meteors? What's the difference? Flower Power explores new galaxies of floral arrangements and accepts orders by email.
✓**www**→http://www.flowerpower .com

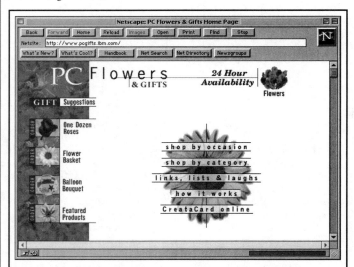

IN-SITE: **PC Flowers & Gifts**
http://www.pcgifts.ibm.com
PC Flowers & Gifts uses colorful graphics and a wide range of products—from Balloons to Flowers to Teddy Bears—in the hope that visitors will make this homepage their bookmark for gift shopping. Consumers can browse by category or occasion (get well, wedding, anniversary); each item gets an image and descriptive text, and flowers are delivered via Next-Day UPS. Special features such as create-a-card, and a reminder service add value to this attractive, service-oriented site.

Chapter 13

Politics
&
Charities

Government

Many government agencies have realized that the Net can provide both a means of

reaching out to its citizens and a method of saving tax dollars that would otherwise be spent on printed matter. As a result, government agencies have been actively establishing Websites. **The White House**, home of cyberpal Al Gore (who coined the term "Information Superhighway," offers plenty of important information and fun features like sounds from Socks the Cat. The **Internal Revenue Service** is using the Net to combat its negative image, with a tremendously user-friendly Website that offers a wealth of taxation information while promising painless taxpaying online. And selling America to itself is the business of **The National Park Service**. The Net has provided a boon to this American institution, enabling families in Georgia to preview the glories of the Rockies or even a National Monument closer to home through virtual brochures.

On the Net

DefenseLINK The Department of Defense (DOD) has several ready-made audiences (veterans, contractors, war buffs), and its

IN-SITE: IRS-The Digital Daily
http://www.irs.ustreas.gov/prod

In something of a marketing gaffe, the new and improved IRS home page (sponsored by Digital Planet) can only be accessed by a Java-enabled browser—perhaps not the best way to butter up a public that already associates the IRS with overwhelming frustration. But the site itself will woo them back. Features include Tax Stats, Tax Info For You, Tax Info For Business, Taxpayer Help, IRS Newsstand, Forms & Publications, and much more. There are even detailed instructions and links to all necessary software for online filing. Friendly copy make even the most daunting tax info seem manageable, and the fantastic campy graphics are worth the browser update.

crowded home page holds something for everyone. Style is key here; the DOD enables everyday citizens to play online General with its current hit BosniaLINK, which follows the campaign tank by tank. The site has also retained GulfLINK to attract those interested in reminiscing about past glories. Easy to use, contractors and taxpayers alike can use the site's search function to find out about upcoming rocket contracts and Star Wars research, which is thankfully not written in "Pentagonese."
✓**www**→http://www.dtic.dla.mil/defenselink

Federal Bureau of Investigation Thanks to *The X-Files* and Clarice Starling, the FBI is the most fascinating of all government entities. Adopting a serious tone on its Website, the FBI FAQ doesn't even address the question of whether there actually are X-Files. Instead the site emphasizes the FBI's crimebusting side, with information about ongoing investigations and the perennial favorite "Ten Most Wanted Fugitives Program." In a quiet, blue-suited, wing-tipped, manner the FBI combats its critics, and posts its positions on wiretapping, electronic surveillance, Ruby Ridge, and computer crime with little fanfare. Repeat visits are encouraged by the online Law Enforcement Bulletin and the ever-changing crime statistics.
✓**www**→http://www.fbi.gov/home page.htm

Fedworld Fedworld has a wealth of information from tax forms to the FDA's report on fat-free potato chips, and makes a solid attempt to resell the government back to its owners with a user-friendly site. Providing lots of guides, the site lists resources both by agency and

subject (Department of Agriculture and soybeans). There are also FTP and telnet options to ensure availability to the greatest number. Big government seems less like Big Brother and more like a cyberpal here.
✓**www**→http://www.fedworld.gov

National Park Service WWW Server This well-illustrated site is doing its best to remind visitors about their product—they're all over the country, they're beautiful, they're intriguing, and best of all, they're ours—hundreds of national parks, historic sites, monuments, and recreation areas. At this wonderful site, prospective travelers can make a virtual visit to areas as diverse as the green grasses of Gettysburg National Battlefield, the rugged peaks of Grand Teton National Park, the sands of Cape Hatteras National Seashore, and the silent ruins at Chaco Canyon. Each area is featured online with an illustrated brochure, complete with hours and contact numbers, and many have a great deal more —virtual tours, campsite reservations, maps, and historical essays. The friendly "Ask a Ranger" feature caps this effective sell of the All-American family vacation.
✓**www**→http://www.nps.gov

Securities and Exchange Commission The SEC is entrusted with one of our nation's most important commercial responsibilities—processing, and then publishing, companies' financial disclosure forms. The SEC Website reviews the legal reasons for this responsibility, as well as linking to a number of related sites where consumers can download everything from lists of major shareholders to details of initial public offerings.
✓**www**→http://www.sec.gov

Small Business Administration Brilliant blue, with red and white highlights, are the colors which open this agency's online sale of the American Dream. Descriptions of the SBA's programs are peppered with hypertext links to guides, business links, and local resources. Playing up its accessibility, the SBA offers a BBS, gopher and FTP options, and a good search function for gathering information on everything from pollution control to low interest loans.
✓**www**→http://www.sbaonline.sba.gov

Social Security Online The SSA tries to make itself as helpful, and indispensible as possible, providing lots of clearly written information in both English and Spanish, online forms, and even an online benefit computing program. Quick and easy email links make the system seem a little less distant, and a lot more manageable.
✓**www**→http://www.ssa.gov

The White House The elegant front page that greets visitors to the White House Website knows that its job is to make the nation's First Residence seem at once magisterial and approachable. The site does an excellent job, employing a cursive script and faux relief graphics to deliver information about President Clinton, Vice President Gore, and more. The big draw here is information, of course—visitors can link to online speech databases, photo archives, history lessons, and news—but the White House also targets America's littlest citizens, with a special children's area overseen by a cartoon Socks the Cat that teaches prospective voters to love and respect their nation.
✓**www**→http://www.whitehouse.gov

Politics

In the U. S. of A., the medium is the message, and if you want the biggest prize of all,

you really have to work for it. Everyone knows that Richard Nixon lost the 1960 TV debate to JFK because he was less effective at using the new medium, and anyone who doesn't cut it in Cyberspace is also going to be at a disadvantage. Thus parties and candidates flood the new medium with red, white, and blue images and cyber-speechbytes. At Republican front-runner **Bob Dole**'s site, excellent use is made of the Web's interactivity—custom email postcards and trivia quizzes attempt to ensure that potential voters stick around. At **Pat Buchanan's Internet Campaign Headquarters**, the sound of the columnist/candidate's down-home philosophizing is featured in a number of audio clips. And not the sort to let a little thing like the "Republican Revolution" dampen its spirits, the **Democratic Senatorial Campaign Committee Home Page** attempts to spur voter action with a color-coded, interactive map of House and Senate seats up for grabs in November and beyond. The polls are waiting.

IN-SITE: Democratic National Committee
http://www.democrats.org
The committee's site serves as an excellent spot for those looking for information about the Democratic Party, whether on the national, state, or county level. This is an easy-to-use site, with lots of emphasis on what is still positive in the days of the 104th Congress. The "What's Hot" section includes press releases and talking points from the DNC, presented with verve, to raise the ire of dyed-in-the-wool liberals. "Connecting with America" plays on the Party's old image as the people's advocate by offering audio clips from the President and the DNC's chairman.

On the Net
Candidates

Bob Dole for President
Whether or not he is America's choice for the highest office in the land, Dole is certainly America's choice for the most Hard-Bitten Washington Insider Whose Dedicated Staffers Know How to Make the Most of the Internet. The official Bob Dole home page is the best candidate Website online, hands down. Why? Because it has a lavish biography of ol' Bob. Because it lets you track the Dole campaign's progress with an inter-

active map of the United States. Because it includes a trivia quiz about the candidate. And because it's even beautiful, in a faux-Rockwellian way. A subtle suggestion is made by all this material—Bob knows how to reach out to the public and touch them.
✓**www**→http://www.dole96.com

Pat Buchanan's Internet Campaign Headquarters Fervid Buchananites treat the pugnacious candidate as the American messiah, and this official site doesn't divert from that view, presenting Pat's portrait at the center of a mosaic of eagles and flags. This is a huge resource that tracks Pat's appearances on television and radio, collects his journalism, lists contact numbers for local regiments of the Buchanan Brigade, and even furnishes dozens of sound clips of Pat sounding off on domestic policy. The wealth of Pat material has proved an effective sell—*Time* magazine declared this the "most information-packed" candidate site on the Web.
✓**www**→http://www.buchanan.org

Steve Forbes for President During his presidential run, Steve Forbes used his campaign site to distinguish himself from his celebrity father and from the other Republican challengers. His presentation relied largely on his claim to understand economic issues (noting that he has won the prestigious Crystal Owl award for financial reporting four times). The Steve Forbes site also included news articles, position papers, and a speech archive. The site contained no links to the online Flat Tax calculator, but in an effective bid for converts, Forbes provided the illusion of intimacy with an email link.
✓**www**→http://www.forbes96.com

Parties

Democratic Senatorial Campaign Committee Home Page As the 1996 elections approach, the few remaining Senate Democrats aren't taking defeat lying down. The overall strategy here is designed to encourage activism among the faithful. A color-coded map (open seats, Republican incumbents) is reminiscent of a battle plan and is complete with links leading to strategy and volunteer organizations. Each day there are new "talking points"—Republican pronouncements demanding contradiction. The Democrats also know the value of humor as a political tool to encourage positive feelings (there's a large cartoon collection), and the Committee updates its content frequently enough that return visits are a musts—witness the daily *Newtgram.*
✓**www**→http://www.dscc.org/d/dscc.html

GOP Main Street The GOP's Web presence is designed to evoke a quaint American small town. Travelers can stop by the newsstand for the latest from the Republican National Committee and the recent issue of *Rising Tide* magazine. In the comfy café Republicans can chat with others about welfare information or try to balance the budget. The Post Office offers quick email links to Congress and local GOPers. The School primes youngsters with Republican takes on defense, the economy, and Bill Clinton. Like good free traders everywhere, this Republican street also offers gifts—how about a Cross pen for signing welfare reform acts or a Swiss Army knife for whittling little elephants from soap?
✓**www**→http://www.rnc.org

Political ideologies

The Right Side of the Web The approach of this conservative site is to be as far right and as provocative as possible. Indeed, the Thought for the Day may criticize Republican Orrin Hatch, insinuating he's "in bed with Louis Freeh." The site lures visitors with an astonishing amount of information, links, and interactive features, including a conservative comic strip ("DeMOCKracy"), the Speaker's Corner, and Campaign '96 nostalgia like the unofficial Alan Keyes for President page. Other highlights at the Right Side include a Question of the Week, solicitations for ideas on casting Whitewater: the Mini-Series, and the Right Side Message Wall, which encourages conservative cyberpundits to scrawl their opinions for all to see.
✓**www**→http://www.clark.net/pub/jeffd/index.html

Town Hall Gathered here are the best and brightest of American conservatives—from Newt's own Progress and Freedom Foundation to Empower America. Town Hall plays up its stable of conservative columnists like Pete du Pont and the timeless William F. Buckley (whose ultraconservative magazine, the *National Review*, sponsors the site). But these savvy rightists also rely on the twin tenets of American culture to attact visitors—tax resentment and consumerism—offering a flat-tax calculator in the online boutique. Other links lead to sanctioned organizations and a search engine capable of finding any mention of "Hillary," "multiculturalism," and other dirty words within the pages of sixteen conservative entities.
✓**www**→http://www.townhall.com

Advocacy groups

When it comes to marketing, nonprofit organizations are more like politicians than

corporations. They have three things to "sell": the issues, community involvement, and themselves. Image and interaction are as important to nonprofits as they are to political campaigns, but these sites also provide what some politicians unfortunately shy away from—comprehensive information. Their sites argue their cases to gain new supporters and give the converted both a voice and faster, easier access to information and direct involvement. Perhaps most importantly, they attract those who truly want to help but who are intimidated by the time and effort involved. From the **Feminist Majority Foundation** to the **NRA**, these home pages act like community centers where the visitor can read a leaflet or research the issue in depth, sign a petition or dive into a heated debate, give a donation or sign up to be a volunteer, all without the pressuring of lobbyists.

On the Net

ACLU The American Civil Liberties Union doesn't exactly have customers to cater to or a product to promote, but the ACLU has created an informative online outpost that puts the customer service and public relations departments of most major businesses to shame. With a crisp and clean design, the ACLU foregrounds its political program—links to Congressional action, Supreme Court decisions, and a state-by-state rights review help civil libertarians cry freedom—but doesn't skimp on community orientation (features about online issues position the organization as an expert in the newborn field of cyberliber-

ties). In addition, there's plenty of interactivity; visitors can email a character named Sibyl Liberty to get answers to topics ranging from drug testing to the laws requiring parental notification of girls seeking abortions.
✓**www**→http://www.aclu.org

Amnesty International Online Renowned offline for its human rights letter-writing campaigns, Amnesty hasn't changed its tune in its move to the online world. Thanks to the speed of the Web and the convenience of

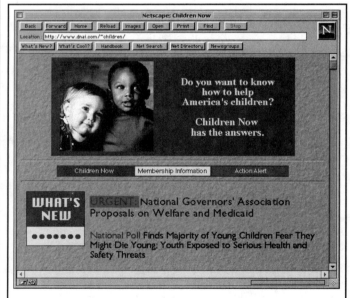

IN-SITE: **Children Now**
http://www.dnai.com/~children
With pictures of children of all races (but not all genders—only boys), this site uses primary colors and bold lettering to collect a wide variety of resources on children's issues, from education to health to family economic security. The Take Action section features interactive urgent actions, membership forms, a mailing list, a "Contract With America's Children" that can be signed online, and even special features (such as a national poll that finds that a majority of young children fear they might die young).

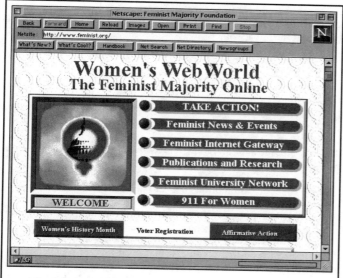

IN-SITE: **Feminist Majority Foundation**
http://www.feminist.org

Dedicated to bringing more women into the political arena, this organization has a clean, well-designed home page that emphasizes urgent-action alerts, news, and the group's 1996 Expo. The FMF lets visitors sign up for membership, explore the feminist career center, or sign up for the "We Card," a slick fundraising/membership drive offering new FMF members participation in a feminist buying club. And the site also works to reach out, especially through its 911 for Women section, which contains material on professional organizations, domestic violence hotlines, and sexual harassment hotlines.

email, Amnesty can now reach more supporters and get quicker responses than ever before. In addition to the Worldwide Appeals section, Amnesty includes a special section targeted at women's rights, reports on the status of human rights worldwide, links to other resources, and information on Amnesty's interactive CD-ROM.
✓**www**→*url* http://www.amnesty.org

The Carter Center Dedicated to "fighting disease, hunger, poverty, conflict, and oppression," the Carter Center has created a friendly, unassuming home page anchored by online excerpts from *Faces of Conflict*, a CD-ROM joint venture with CNN. The rest of the page offers press releases and articles, a multi-faceted organization profile, and a huge hypertext bio of former President and successful humanitarian Jimmy Carter.
✓**www**→http://www.emory.edu/CARTER_CENTER/homepage.htm

Easter Seals Though the URL is more suggestive of harp seals than the national disabilities-assistance organization, the Easter Seals Website leaves no question about its central concern, offering a variety of online brochures about programs and services, employment resources, and sponsors. In addition, the group positions itself as an authority on online disability resources, linking to Websites and newsgroups dealing with disability, disability employment, and dis-

ability law.
✓**www**→http://seals.com

GLAAD While this site gives excellent multimedia coverage of the GLAAD Media Awards, the majority of the site is devoted to a hypertext history of the organization, info on volunteerism and jobs, and announcements of regional events. Unfortunately, GLAAD has buried its motherlode—urgent-action alerts and hundreds of original articles on lesbian and gay politics and media representation.
✓**www**→http://www.glaad.org

National Coalition for the Homeless While there's a spare, almost skeletal look to the National Coalition for the Homeless Home Page (no irony intended, presumably), the organization's Website includes two excellent multimedia features that help communicate the terrors of homelessness. "One Family's Path to Homelessness" presents the actual plight of one clean-cut, white suburban family using scanned letters, email, images and more; it's updated daily to intensify the sense of urgency. The other feature, "Homeless Voices," collects images and sound clips of real homeless people, of all races, ages, educational and economic backgrounds.
✓**www**→http://nch.ari.net

National Right to Life Committee Overseen by a picture of a baby and the slogans of the pro-life movement ("Choose Life," "Partial Birth Abortion"), the National Right to Life Committee offers an audio greeting from director Dr. Wanda Franz, as well as information on the various arms of this anti-abortion effort. In addition, the site includes a few key interactive features, including an online form for subscribing to NRL News and a guestbook that surveys guests for name, address, age, and position on abortion.

✓**www**→http://www.nrlc.org/nrlc

NOW NOW's home page, which forgoes splash for simplicity, positions itself as an offline organization with a modest online component—most online features relate to real-world events such as marches, letter-writing campaigns, and volunteer drives. In addition, the site works to build a community (of both men and women) with its extensive list of state and local email addresses.

✓**www**→http://now.org/now/home .html

NRA The NRA uses its site to build a sense of community for supporters and sympathizers. Low on graphics and high on text—including hundreds of articles, legislative reports, federal delegation info, state firearms alerts, a firearm glossary, and a bibliography—the site also includes ads for NRA multimedia (a gun safety program for children with activity books and a video hosted by teen heart-throb and soap opera stalwart Jason Priestley), an NRA store, and a large library including some books on banned firearms.

✓**www**→http://www.nra.org

PETA The popular animal-rights organization diverges from its enormously effective offline strategies—celebrity endorsements and shock-tactic images of vivisection—with its Website, which is short on pictures of animals and fur-less celebs and long on news and analysis. The one exception to this toned-down strategy is the interactive tour of Animal Research Laboratories, which bludgeons visitors with images of dead animals and stomach-churning text ("At Wright State University in Dayton, Ohio, one dog was cut open

and autopsied while another live dog watched, waiting his turn on the bottom shelf of a stainless steel cabinet").

✓**www**→http://www.envirolink.org /arrs/peta

Positively HIV Strikingly designed in Pride Purple, this site is a support center for people living with HIV. With an optimistic URL, the site includes everything from nutritional charts to White House watchdogging, from a celebrity cookbook promotion to hundreds of archived articles and reports. As might be expected, the site is powered by its sense of community; the online Cyberquilt invites visitors to add electronic "patches" for friends and loved ones who are living with HIV or have died from AIDS.

✓**www**→http://www.hivnalive .org

Sierra Club For an environmental group that has been around since 1892, the Sierra Club puts on a persuasively modern face. This clean and unthreatening site not only focuses on the Club's illustrious history but also demonstrates its commitment to key issues such as pollution control, offshore drilling, grazing rights, and public land usage.

✓**www**→http://www.sierraclub .org

Zen Hospice Dedicated to supporting the terminally ill and disseminating Buddhist teachings on death and dying, this San Francisco hospice has a low-key Website that features a mission statement, schedules of events and volunteer training events, and even a Zen newsletter.

✓**www**→http://www.well.com/user /devaraja/index.html

IN-SITE: **Red Cross**
http://www.crossnet.org/
The Red Cross uses bold graphics—including its own red cross, which has a Q rating higher than even Bill Cosby's—to showcase its blood drives, disaster relief, and biomedicine. In addition to positioning itself as an international force (there's a link to BosniaNow), the organization emphasizes its local relevance with a Red Cross Chapter locator.

Going to Market: Not-For-Profits

Most of this book has concentrated on the ways in which businesses can profit from joining the online revolution, but the Web is also valuable for nonprofit organizations, which can use the Web to serve their various constituencies—at very low cost. Moreover, the benefits of using the Web are applicable to nonprofits of all types, from advocacy groups to health-oriented organizations.

Most not-for-profit groups need to educate the organization's members and the public about the activities of the organization; provide information about local activities where appropriate; deliver information to potential constituents in order to convince them that they should become involved with the organization and its efforts; answer questions from the general population; and communicate with professionals such as researchers, clinicians, and lawyers about specific progress or "technical developments." The Internet facilitates all of these activities at relatively low cost.

Probably, the best way to explain how the Web can be effectively used by nonprofits is to select one example and describe, in detail, what this organization is doing. The National Neurofibromatosis Foundation seeks to foster research and awareness about neurofibromatosis (NF), a genetic disease more common than multiple sclerosis (MS) or cystic fibrosis (CF). The NF Foundation was one of the first medical foundations to use the Web as an active part of its marketing efforts, and the NF site (**http://www.nf.org**) stands as one of the first examples of online medical not-for-profit marketing.

The NF Website serves a number of purposes, chief among them news delivery. The site allows the foundation to post any recent news on research or treatments related to the disorder; individuals with the disorder—or family members—can check out the site to follow progress in research and clinical efforts related to the disorder. A bulletin board can also carry common questions along with answers supplied by physicians and researchers.

The Website successfully anticipates the emotional needs of those diagnosed with the disease. The NF Foundation has digitized a substantial amount of information about the illness, but this site, and others like it, are perhaps most powerful for their potential as community-builders. An individual diagnosed with the illness, or just interested in it, can tap into the information provided on the NF Foundation's Website wherever they live. The NF Foundation is currently planning to offer Web-based bulletin boards to help forge a sense of community for afffected individuals and their families. This virtual community should work in harmony with the greater NF community.

Nonprofits can also use the Web to forge ties with related professional communities, publicly announce research grants, and build relationships with researchers. For example, the NF Foundation sponsors annual research grants to scientists, as well as holding conferences on specialized topics around the world. The Website publicizes both programs.

Finally, the Web can help not-for-profits with their business operations. Like any business, not-for-profits have existing and prospective "customers," and they rely on a continued influx of new "customers"—or financially supportive members, to stay afloat. By including a Web-based form on the site that new members can fill-in and send, foundations can add to their membership rolls. And with secure transaction capabilities, they can even collect membership fees and donations.

Appendices

Marketing resources

In preceding chapters, this book has demonstrated how best to take advantage of the

new marketing opportunities offered by the Internet, from setting up your Website to ensuring visibility within the Net community. The services that follow are representative of an ever-expanding list of marketing resources, from Net-specific services such as **InBusiness**'s cheerful, step-by-step beginners tutorial on Web marketing, to **The Web 100**, the online version of *Fortune*'s list, to a formidable list of job opportunities at sites like **Executive Search Professionals**, to marketing chat areas where, as at the **International Trade Forum**, you can find out what is the bestselling soft drink in Kuwait. The agora is there to be entered.

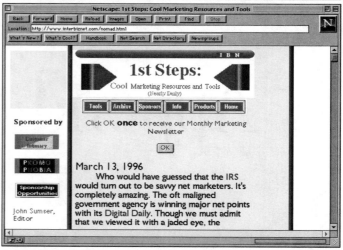

Screenshot from 1st Steps: Cool Marketing Resources on the Net

On the Net

Online marketing

1st Steps: Cool Marketing Resources on the Net This site design firm focuses its attention on the GenXer entrepreneurs flooding the Net ("cool" marketing resources?). This site is a good place to watch the new technology, through reviews of sites, browsers, and online tech tests. A new feature shows how Java will track site traffic minutely.
✓**www**→http://www.interbiznet
.com/nomad.html

ActivMEDIA Online Marketer Help Desk Although the main goal of this site is to sell ActivMedia's Net business reports, they do offer some useful tidbits as lures. A sample of the final product offers gems from surveys of money-making Web businesses, inside success stories, and hot Net news. A recent finding is the news that travel and tourism sites are outpacing computers and software in online revenue.
✓**www**→http://www.activmedia
.com

Biz Online Much of the effort here is directed at selling marketing products, but there is some free advice worth perusing here too. A quirky how-to piece focuses on marketing worm farms online. Another feature invites marketers to test their emotional intelli-

gence—essential for connecting with the customer. In attempting to attract people back to their site, the creators offer an email question and answer link through which they promise to flow waves of marketing wisdom.
✓**www**→http://ourworld.compu
serve.com/homepages/MCS
marketing

Blitz Marketing Resources What appears to be just a simple list of marketing-related links is really an eclectic selection of marketing know-how. Marketers can choose from book reviews of the hottest marketing titles, take a personality assessment test, or find out the broadcast profile of the major U.S. markets.
✓**www**→http://www.blitzmedia
.com/resources.html

InBusiness The basics of Net marketing from the ground up.

The authors are targetting beginners, but while you'll find an occasional "Wow! This is cool!", the resources here are anything but sophomoric. Learn what type of Website is right for your company and how to get started setting it up. Tune in to seminars like "Putting Newsgroups to Work for Your Business," and "What Makes Business Sites Great on the Net." Or head to the message boards to talk with other marketers about their plans and strategies (don't worry—the messages are organized by industry, so you'll be able to find your friends quickly).
✓**AMERICA ONLINE**→*keyword* inbusi ness

Internet Publishing Forum
Chip, who just started his own clerical services company last year, is interested in marketing his business online. He writes, "How do I get my home page on the search engines? Has anyone found any particular search engine to be particularly effective?" Gary responds, "I believe they will register your site for a fee, or you can just go to each of the sites individually and register yourself." As Chip discovered, the message board at this site is a great place to ask and get answers about online marketing. The library also offers many resources for Net marketers; articles like "Internet Marketing Tips," "Six Internet Marketing Disasters to Avoid," and "Online Market Research Book Review" help Net marketers get started and keep them well-informed once they've set up shop.
✓**COMPUSERVE**→*go* inetpublish→ Messages *and* Libraries→Internet Marketing

Media Central: Interactive
Monitor What's at the Interactive Monitor? Well, a little bit of everything. Top stories in interactive marketing. Reviews of Websites. A monthly list of Website dos and don'ts that, while relatively general, is indispensable for marketers arriving online ("Don't use multimedia applications in essential, information-intensive areas"). And don't forget to consult the Media Central Digest—an invaluable insider's report on "new and noteworthy" developments on the Web.
✓**www**→http://www.mediacentral .com/IMonitor

MouseTracks New South Network Services has created an admirable resource for marketers, which, despite its precious name, contains lots of serious information. MouseTracks teaches by example and theory, providing hypertext essays on Net demographics, innovations in online payment schemes, HTML instructions, links to online marketing journals, online marketing services, upcoming marketing conferences, and even numerous "syllabits" links to marketing research from universities worldwide. Added to this is a wry sense of humor and clear presentation, making MouseTracks one of the best overall marketing resources available.
✓**www**→http://nsns.com/Mouse Tracks

Online Marketing Advisor
John Child, Marketing Manager for the online division of a major newspaper in Utah, has created a well-rounded resource for online marketers. John's weekly articles include tips on target marketing, making money on the Net, and increasing interactivity on commercial Websites. Child also reviews two or three advertorial pages per week rating their overall effectiveness on a scale of one to three money bags. In addition, visitors find links to related marketing sites like Web Trak, Bur- maShave, and Trader's Connection.
✓**www**→http://intele.net/~johnc

SoftMail Direct Selling marketing services or running a class on direct marketing? You decide. SoftMail is a direct response agency for the software and new media industry. On its Website, the company maintains a database of information on past software mailing offers, writes weekly critiques of recent software mailings (see what SoftMail thought of GNN's or QuickBook's mailing), continually adds articles to its Direct Response Handbook ("Birth of the Direct Response Web Site," "How to Make the Most of a Mailing List," "The 20-Second Tour a Direct Mail Piece," etc.), and runs a mailing list for direct-marketing discussion. The company also advertises its services.
✓**www**→http://www.softmail.com

The online industry

Commerce on the World Wide Web Thank God for student projects. Several eager virtual entrepreneurs have put their class project online here. Nicely presented with eye-catching graphics, this page asks and answers heady questions such as "Is anyone making money?" and "What's in the way?" Each essay is packed with hypertext links to graphs, charts, and stats mapping the world of Net commerce.
✓**www**→http://www.deltanet.com /users/dplumley/eticket/index.html

The Information Economy A professor from Berkeley's School of Information Management has placed his entire course online. Here, eager Net business types will find lots of interesting links, in-depth research on Net commerce, and fun electronic developments.

An entire page focuses on the laws of electronic commerce, another of the newest technology in site traffic measurement. For the serious marketing analyst, there is no better source.

✓**WWW**→http://www.sims.berkeley.edu/resources/infoecon

News & publications

Adrap A weekly column with the scoop on the advertising industry written by Toronto marketer Peter Mosley.

✓**WWW**→http://www.magic.ca/magicmedia/adrap.html

Advertising Age What's at Advertising Age (AA) to entice a busy marketer to visit? Daily news briefs (for the online and offline marketing/advertising world), features on Web-marketing technology and innovations, profiles of America's 50 most important marketers, descriptions of the top 100 most-successful ad campaigns running, and more. On Prodigy, AA even offers a message board where readers can discuss marketing and advertising issues. Without a question, AA lives up to its subtitle "It's all about marketing."

✓**WWW**→http://www.adage.com
✓**PRODIGY**→*jump* ad age

Business Database Plus Access news articles on products, markets, and industries from over 750 business-related publications worldwide. This fee-based service archives newsbriefs for five years, and its archive is searchable by keyword. Strangely, the site does not list the names of the publications from which it draws its information.

✓**COMPUSERVE**→*go* busdb

Business Week Online Any marketer who doesn't read BWO will certainly feel left out in the

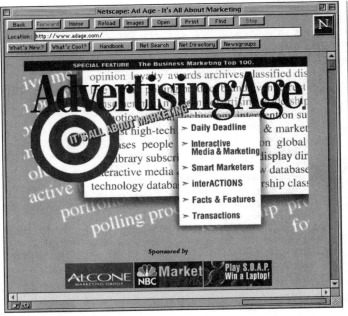

Screenshot from Advertising Age

cold. With in-depth company and industry news, topical feature articles (many of them with an online slant), and message boards geared specifically towards marketers, this site gives marketers a solid foundation.

✓**AMERICA ONLINE**→*keyword* bw

The Entrepreneur's Forum

Thinking about launching a mail-order program to market your product? Looking to put together a catalog for your growing business, but you just don't know where to get started? Wondering how to diversify the assets accumulated by your business? Then check in here where you can find articles that address these and other issues important to self-marketers, including marketing tips, industry trends, and marketing scams. All articles are excerpted from *Entrepreneur* magazine.

✓**COMPUSERVE**→*go* entmagazine→Libraries→Marketing

Fortune Looking for the scoop on potential employers? *Fortune* features articles on companies from Crisco to Microsoft. For a more extensive, if purely financial, collection of profiles, the Fortune 500—in its various forms—gives company profiles by revenues, profits, assets, stockholder equity, market value, total return to investors, and profits as a percent of revenues. Fortune 500 also links to Hoover's for more in-depth company information.

✓**WWW**→http://www.pathfinder.com/fortune/fortune.html

Guerrilla Marketing Online Although this site is primarily a plug for the Guerrilla Marketing Series of offline publications (visitors can read about the books and even order them online), the page also offers a weekly column for online marketers. Recent articles have included "Ten Reasons Why Internet Marketing Fails," "Four

Rules of Great Websites," and "Ten Guerrilla Selling Tips." In addition, the Website offers instructions on joining its mailing list and on signing up for contests.
✓**www**→http://www.gmarketing.com

Marketing Tools Both the online and offline marketer will find this mag a useful tool. With articles and regular columns on Net marketing technology, new marketing strategies, demographics, and other topics of concern to marketers, this magazine will soon become indispensable reading to visitors.
✓**www**→http://www.marketingtools.com/mt_current/default.htm

Marketing Week On-Line (UK) Global marketers shouldn't pass up the weekly news available from this British publication. Articles cover marketing industry events in the UK—everything from new management appointments at large corporations to announcements of new products and brands. Response forms at the end of every story encourage readers to voice their opinions about the issues. Subscription information for the newsstand version of MWOL is also available at the page.
✓**www**→http://www.marketing-week.co.uk/mw0001

Netrepreneur News This site monitors the mainstream media and trade magazines for news related to the Internet and commercial online services, which it then condenses into "succinct summaries to give online entrepreneurs and marketers quick access to the information that most concerns them." The tone of the articles is at times tongue-in-cheek, making NN both informative and entertaining.
✓**www**→http://www.conceptone

.com/netnews/netnews.htm

Newspage This site was obviously created by savvy marketers. If you want access to those tantalizing stories behind the hypertext headlines, registration is a prerequisite. Since there is no fee involved, advertising and marketing strategists have nothing to lose and much news to gain. The top stories on everything in the industry from campaigns to electronic media are updated daily.
✓**www**→http://www.newspage.com/NEWSPAGE/cgi-bin/walk.cgi/NEWSPAGE/info/d17/d6

Recruiting Magic A rather unattractive little purple gnome welcomes visitors to Microsoft's Internet Explorer's marketing newsletter. Each month new articles on how to create online business success appear here. Hypertext essays provide strategies for raising money without bank assistance and the marketer's mantra "power, purpose & success." After all, Bill Gates is the richest man in the galaxy so why not give his strategies a try?
✓**www**→http://home.earthlink.net/~fpearce

Web Digest for Marketers Nothing but reviews, more reviews, and even more reviews of company and promotional Websites. The reviews are brief and very focused, often touching on innovative uses of Net technology. The site is updated regularly, and faithful readers can subscribe to a service that automatically sends an email notice to them every time WDfM is updated. Bonus: Many marketing-related companies (including American Demographics/Marketing Tools and USA Data) offer special deals at this page.
✓**www**→http://wdfm2.com/wdfm/index.html

Web Marketing Today With tips on how to increase hits on your company's Website, articles on customizing your company's domain, and success stories by others who are marketing in Cyberspace, this bimonthly publication will keep you up on developments in Net marketing.
✓**www**→http://www.garlic.com/rfwilson/wmt

WebTrack Keep track of what's going on in Web advertising with the help of this page. Its extensive offerings include a collection of links to company home pages (organized neatly by industry and alphabetically), a database of company pages that provide advertising space at their sites, a searchable database of online and offline advertising/marketing personnel, subscription info for WebTrack's newsletter *InterAd Monthly*, and press releases about the site itself (WT recently published its findings from the first-ever Web advertising survey).
✓**www**→http://www.webtrack.com

Market research

American Business Info Yellow Pages Marketers interested in a good old-fashioned snail mail or telemarketing campaign will appreciate this database of names, addresses, telephone numbers, and even credit ratings for American businesses. Search the database by company name or industry and get those stamps and telephones ready.
✓**AMERICA ONLINE**→*keyword* abi

Biz*File A huge online Yellow Pages that lists more than ten million businesses in the U.S. and Canada. Search by company name, geographical location, telephone number, or type of business. There is a fee for this service.

Marketing Resources

✓**COMPUSERVE**→*go* bizfile

Company Research Know your key competitors inside and out with the help of this site, which provides company news, in-depth spotlight features on specific companies, and Company Profiles that list the intimate details of hundreds of companies (from basic company overviews to the names of their mailroom personnel). On the message boards, there is a section called Company Research ,which contains more company profiles, targeted stock reports, financial statements, earnings and estimates info, and more.
✓**AMERICA ONLINE**→*keyword* company research

Hoover's Business Profiles
Search the full text of Hoover's Handbook for detailed profiles of nearly 2,000 of the largest and fastest-growing public and private companies in the U.S. and the world. Profiles are exhaustive with info that includes assets, sales figures, number of employees, CEO and CFO salaries, and company products. In addition, the profiles feature long and gossipy descriptions of each company's history and culture. You can use the profiles to get the location of a company's office, its future goals and ongoing programs, and its recent stock prices, plus phone, address, and fax information. The exhaustive resources at Hoover's Business Profiles will help you get to know the market one company at a time. Note: To search the database on the Web, you have to subscribe at a cost of $9.95 per month.
✓**AMERICA ONLINE**→*keyword* hoover
✓**COMPUSERVE**→*go* hoover ✓**WWW**→ http://www.hoovers.com/profiles 3/profile_search.html

Hoover's Industry Profiles
Facts and figures on nearly 200

Screenshot from Guerrilla Marketing Online

U.S. industries ranging from construction to health care to transportation. The comprehensive list includes 30 service and 150 manufacturing industries. Filled with projections, trend analysis, and statistics from American companies (supplies, expenditures, employee numbers), the reports are long and detailed. If you want a quick but smart rundown of issues and challenges facing an industry for your market analysis, these reports spell those out well.
✓**AMERICA ONLINE**→*keyword* industry profiles

S&P Online For a fee this service distills the recent business histories of more than 5,000 companies to bring you essential information, including recent market activity, dividend info, product line summaries, and earning estimates.
✓**COMPUSERVE**→*go* s&p

The Web 100 America's top 100 companies (rated by revenue) are listed along with links to their

home pages.
✓**WWW**→http://fox.nstn.ca/~at _info/w100_table.html

General demographics

American Demographics
Browse the current issue of *American Demographics* magazine (currently articles on America's standard of living and the booming prison population are running); search an archive of previous issues by keyword (the archive holds articles from the past year); download a data table of "America's Hottest Markets"; or pick up details on how to subscribe to the offline version of this demographics magazine.
✓**WWW**→http://www.marketing tools.com

Business Demographics A wealth of facts and figures regarding specific markets and their employees.
✓**COMPUSERVE**→*go* busdem

FIND/SVP This fee-based service offers its catalog of demographic/industry reports online. Browse hundreds of reports on groups ranging from African-Americans to grandparents to the college market to the affluent. The service also collects information on hundreds of industries, including manufacturing, chemicals, and the Internet. Read descriptions of the reports and, if interested, purchase them online. Prices for these studies vary widely (anywhere from $10 to $2,000).
✓**www**→http://www.findsvp.com

Gallup Brief articles at the site present Gallup's statistical findings regarding topical national issues (presidential races, the Internet, etc.). Visitors can even participate in online Gallup polls at the page.
✓**www**→http://www.gallup.com

U.S. Census A treasure chest of facts and figures on who makes up the market today, how much money they earn, and who will lead the market tomorrow. Use the site's search engine to look for a particular topic by keyword, or browse any of the site sections, which include population and housing, economy, and geography, among others. In case you can't find the information you need, the "Ask the Experts" topic lets you pose specific demographic questions to Census personnel.
✓**www**→http://www.census.gov

Internet demographics

CommerceNet/Nielsen Surveys The television ratings giant, Nielsen, and an online site dedicated to promoting business on the Internet, CommerceNet, jointly conducted a survey of online users during the second half of 1995. The controversial results cover everything from the age and sex of users to their incomes and education levels. The survey is available in both HTML (open with your Web browser) and .PDF (you'll need to download it and use an Adobe Acrobat Reader) formats.
✓**www** ...→http://www.nielsenmedia.com/demo.htm ...→http://www.commerce.net/information/surveys

GVU's WWW User Survey Twice a year GVU holds a yardstick to the Web and measures it from all angles, and its findings are published at this page (along with the results of GVU's three previous surveys). Online marketers may be interested in the past year's trends; according to GVU, the Net's audience is getting older (the average age is now 32.7 years) and more feminine (women surfers are 30 percent of the total audience, up from 20 percent in the previous year). Visit the site for more info on who comprises the cybermarket.
✓**www**→http://www-survey.cc.gatech.edu/cgi-bin/Entry

The Hermes Project Consumer Survey of WWW Users Who's online? What types of products and services are they buying online? How comfortable are they paying for products? What are people willing to spend for Net access? This annual survey conducted by the University of Michigan Business School is easy to understand and available in both HTML and .PDF formats.
✓**www**→http://www-personal.umich.edu/~sgupta/hermes/survey4

Internet Domain Survey How many sites are running NCSA Web server software? What are the top 50 host names? Check for the annual results of a survey on Internet domains.
✓**www**→http://www.nw.com/zone/WWW/top.html

Screenshot from Hoover's Business Profile

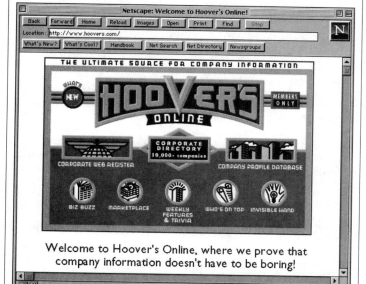

Marketing Resources

Internet Facts An excellent overview of the reports and articles published about Internet growth, demographics, and levels of business involvement. The site not only summarizes findings, it also links to them.
✓ **WWW**→http://www.echonyc.com /~parallax/interfacts.html

Market Research Center The Market Research Center's main interest is in selling its services, but this site is still peppered with interesting links, all collected here for ease of use. In addition to lists of online marketing services, publications, and "marketing secrets," there are links to numerous demographic surveys (including the famous U.S. sex practices report). There is also an attempt at creating a marketing community here through a marketing employment page.
✓ **WWW**→http://www.asiresearch .com

Marketing/Management Center The findings of hundreds of market research groups (Econ Base, PR Newswire, and Public Opinion Online are among them) are collected in this enormous archive of searchable info. For a fee you can access the full text of articles from major U.S. and international business, management, and technical literature, plus market and industry research reports, market studies, statistical reports, and U.S. and international company news releases.
✓ **COMPUSERVE**→*go* mktgrc

Measuring the Growth of the Web An article describing the growth of the Web from June 1993 to the present.
✓ **WWW**→http://www.netgen.com /info/growth.html

MIDS Internet Demographic

Survey Is the Internet all male? At what speeds are most organizations connecting to the Internet? What types of organizations are online? What percentage of Internet users are students? Check for the results of an annual survey conducted by Matrix Information & Directory Services.
✓ **WWW**→http://www1.mids.org /ids2/index.html

Open Market's Internet Index If you've seen the Harper's Index, Net-fanatic Win Treese's odd collections of facts and statistics about the Internet will seem familiar. To wit: "Number of daily newspapers in Iran with Websites: 2."
✓ **WWW**→http://www.openmarket .com/diversions/internet-index /index.html

The Tenagra Awards for Internet Marketing Excellence Each December a panel of Internet marketing experts choose between five and seven sites that have either achieved significant financial return or public relations success, or made significant contributions to the development of marketing on the Internet. Winners in 1995 included FedEx and Ragu. Consider it the Clios of the electronic medium.
✓ **WWW**→http://arganet.tenagra .com/awards.html

Vital Statistics *Ad Age* sums up the projected investment in each segment of the interactive industry, from 1994 to 1998.
✓ **WWW**→http://www.AdAge.com /bin/viewdataitem.cgi?stats&stats3 .html

Marketing chat

Biz-Marketing Consulting Advertising, public relations, product positioning, corporate identity, product strategy, and marketing

communications from the consultant's point of view.
✓ **EMAIL**→majordomo@world.std.com
✍ *Type in message body:* subscribe biz-marketing consulting

Forbes Forum "With all of the changes in technology, does good ol' marketing work in this new environment? What do you feel IS good ol' marketing?" asks Scott about making the transition to online marketing. There are plenty of folks at this message board to discuss this topic (and others) with Scott, and you too can visit this board to tackle the issues surrounding this new way of doing business.
✓ **COMPUSERVE**→*go* forbes→Messages→Marketing

Free-Market Just opened a travel agency and thinking about marketing your new business on the Net? You'd do well to subscribe to Free-Market, an unmoderated list dedicated to discussion of Internet marketing.
✓ **EMAIL**→listserv@ar.com ✍ *Type in message body:* subscribe free-market <your full name>

GINLIST Approximately 400 marketing professionals from over 25 countries meet at this online forum to discuss international marketing news and trends.
✓ **EMAIL**→*email* listserv@msu.edu ✍ *Type in message body:* subscribe GINLIST <your full name> *Archives:* ✓ **WWW**→http://ciber .bus.msu.edu/ginlist/archive .htm *Info:* ✓ **WWW**→http://ciber .bus.msu.edu/ginlist

IndustryWeek Forum Tips and hints from other marketers about general marketing issues and getting started marketing on the Net.
✓ **COMPUSERVE**→*go* iwfor→Libraries→ Sales & Marketing

International Trade Forum Mostly posts asking for market research help (e.g., "Does anyone know the top ten soft drink flavors in Egypt, Israel, and Kuwait?"), it's a great place to visit if you need informal assistance.
✓**COMPUSERVE**→*go* trade→Messages→Int. Marketing

Internet Marketing Discussion List "During my surfing I have noticed that large companies often don't connect to the customer in a personal way. When no names are given on a site, a Netsurfer cannot develop an emotional connection with a vendor. On Websites, the principle of personal contact is often missing. Many sites are as impersonal as a magazine ad. A particular message may work in magazines, but the Internet is a more intimate medium. People who surf the Net *want* an interactive relationship. It seems to me that this is best accomplished with an individual personality," writes Joan. Her comments are typical of the informed, professional conversation about Internet marketing that occur on this mailing list. Subcribe to this list and find yourself in good professional company.
✓**EMAIL**→*email* im-sub@i-m.com *Archives:* ✓**www**→http://www.i-m .com/#archives *Info:* ✓**www**→ http://www.i-m.com

List of Marketing Lists The mysteries of mailing lists with names like ADMODLMKT and KAWASAKI are solved here. (The first is devoted to the use of applied modeling issues in marketing; the second not to bikers, but to the theories of marketing guru Guy Kawasaki.) This list of lists provides subscription information and a brief description for dozens of marketing-related talk sessions.
✓**www**→http://www.bayne.com

/wolfBayne/htmarcom/mktglist.html
Market-L Marketers gather at this mailing list to discuss promotion and advertising, segmentation, surveys, service quality, positioning, exporting, market models, product design, and marketing information systems, among other topics.
✓**EMAIL**→listproc@mailer.fsu.edu ✍ *Type in message body:* subscribe market-l <your full name> *Archives:* ✓**www**→gopher://postoffice.cob .fsu.edu:4070/11/other/serials/ml *FAQ:*✓**www**→http:// nsns.com /MouseTracks/Market-L.FAQ.txt

misc.business.consulting Recently, Jim wrote, "Think about it. We are all marketers to some extent. When looking for a career/job, we market ourselves. You get a bad receptionist on the phone and an opinion is formed of that firm. To some extent, everyone in the organization is marketing that firm. From a line person on the floor, to the receptionist, to the CEO." Jim's post to the newsgroup is characteristic of the almost philosophical marketing discussions that occur here. But if you're more in the market for practical advice, there is also plenty of that available, especially for those seeking tips on how to market professional services (e.g., law firms).
✓**USENET**→misc.business.consulting

misc.consumers/misc.consumers.frugal-living (ng) Marketers get a look at the fruits of their labor at these newsgroups, where discussion of advertisements, new products, and consumer-related issues ("Is sending a gift certificate as a wedding gift rude?") are the topics of the day. The conversation here is primarily about discount stores (Wal Mart is a favorite), but junk mail and cold-call telemarketing are also discussed widely, most-

ly about how to "deal" with them.
✓**USENET** ...→misc.consumers ...→ misc.consumers.frugal-living

MktSeg Target marketers should take aim at this mailing list. According to its mission statement, the discussion group is devoted to target marketing to "ethnic segments, lifestyle and lifestage segments and interest group segments," and topics might include "advertising creative material, media issues, research, database marketing, direct marketing, promotions or education relating to all the above, and other segmentation information resources."
✓**EMAIL**→listserv@mail.telmar.com ✍ *Type in message body:* subscribe mktseg *FAQ:* ✓**www**→http://nsns .com/MouseTracks/tloml/mktseg.txt

Mousetracks List of Marketing Lists Like all sciences, marketing has fractured into numerous specialties, and there's a mailing list for every interest group imaginable. This list has links to home pages and subscription instructions for everything from product development to doctoral students to online auto sales.
✓**www**→http://nsns.com/Mouse Tracks/tloml.html

PR & MKG Forum The place for marketers to hang out online, you'll find every level of the business operating here. Vice presidents of marketing talk shop with one-horse, home-business owners; Web-savvy denizens give tips to Net beginners on building home pages for their businesses; marketing news and trends (especially high-profile advertising campaigns) are discussed; marketing jobs nationwide are sought and found. Although Net marketing is the primary topic here (how does one get started? which tactics are most successful? etc.), talk about marketing in the traditional media is also common.

✓ **COMPUSERVE**→*go* prsig→Messages *and* Libraries

Guides

20 Reasons to Put Your Business on the Net Just in case you needed another 20, this list provides them in easy-to-understand terms. Reason #6: To release time-sensitive material. Reason #8: To make pictures, sound, and film files available. Reason #9: To reach a desirable demographic market. Pretty simple stuff, but it drives the point home.

✓ **www**→http://www.net101.com /reasons.html

Blacklist of Internet Advertisers Many Websites offer advice on the correct way to advertise online. This site shows you the wrong way to go about the business, and it offers a glimpse into the ugly consequences of misusing the Net (especially Usenet) with inappropriate marketing schemes. One obnoxious advertiser angered a large number of Usenet users with a random SPAM; the newsgroups mounted a counterattack against his fax machine and home phone in retaliation.

✓ **www**→http://www.cco.caltech .edu/~cbrown/BL

Doing More Business on the Net Excerpts from Mary Cronin's bestselling book, *Doing More Business on the Internet*, which addresses everything from creating a Web page to developing an appropriate Internet plan for your business to the best business information resources and tools on the Net.

✓ **COMPUSERVE**→iwfor→Libraries→ *Search on file name:* CRONIN.TXT

Entrepreneur Weekly "Inter-

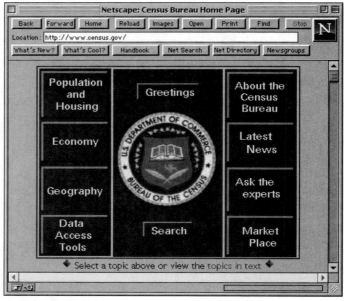

Screenshot from U.S. Census

preneur" Chris Donnell publishes new doses of his Net marketing wisdom every week. Visit the site to read Chris' viewpoint on such topics as "Ways to Market on the Internet Without Getting Flamed," "Guerrilla Marketing on the Net," and "Is Anybody Making Money on the Net?" (Chris swears the answer is "Yes!")

✓ **www**→http://www.eweekly.com

Internet Marketing Strategies and Implementation This extensive online marketing textbook hits all the high points of online and uses all the industry buzzwords—chapter titles include "Push/Pull Strategy," and "How to get people to come and have a look at your site." This hypertext primer provides an excellent beginners' guide with a clear discussion of the benefits and glitches of online selling from security to spamming. There's even a booklist for further edification. Best of all, these folks are selling anything but

free marketing insight.

✓ **www**→http://www.iib.qld.gov.au /publish/seminar/inetmrkt/index .htm

Setting Up Shop on the Internet It's a brave new world when someone can boast of industry longevity by proclaiming they've "been around since 1994." Evidently two years is enough to claim founding father status, backed up here by a hypertext essay with links to Internet statistics, surveys, and even a list of Internet marketing do's and don'ts. Perspective is the name of the game here, industry speculators would do well to check out the essays on the future (and past) of Net selling.

✓ **www**→http://www.netrex.com /business.html

Employment

Bloomberg Online Calling all marketers! Companies all over the world need your skills, and many

of them express that need at this page, often in great detail. Most entries include a brief description of the job (duties, location, and starting date) and telephone numbers or email addresses for those who wish to apply. Some listings even mention benefit and salary info. The list is updated daily, so come here for some fresh marketing material.
✓**www**→http://www.bloomberg .com

Business Job Listings If you're searching for a job in marketing, this page is definitely worth a visit. National and local companies (Walgreens, Philadelphia Insurance Company, and other businesses) looking for marketing personnel post detailed job descriptions and email addresses for those interested in further information or in submitting a resume. The site also offers a collection of links to other Web pages with marketing jobs listings.
✓**www**→http://www.cob.ohio -state.edu/dept/fin/jobs/jobslist .htm

Direct Marketing World Job Center Besides an extensive listing of direct-marketing jobs, the page also offers links to the home pages of other direct marketers and to related professional organizations. Don't leave the site without checking out the extensive online library, which features an impressive collection of material excerpted from topical direct-marketing publications.
✓**www**→http://www.dmworld.com

Executive Search Professionals This placement agency updates its list of marketing jobs nationwide every day. Positions typically include account executives, directors of marketing, and direct-marketing copywriters. To express

interest in any of the positions, applicants fill out and submit an on-line survey.
✓**www**→http://www.NakedPC .com/esn/contact.html

JOBS-SLS Entry-level marketers need not apply! This moderated list of employment opportunities for sales and marketing, advertising, customer service, market research, and public relations professionals caters to experienced workers in these fields.
✓**EMAIL**→obs-sls@execon.metro net.com ✍ *Type in message body:* subscribe <your full name>

Nationjob Marketing Page Hundreds of job listings for marketers all over the country. Click on any of the entries—marketing analyst for Hartford Insurance Company, marketing coordinator for New York City bank, marketing director for Omaha information service—and get job and company descriptions. Apply directly to the company for any job using the information provided at the site.
✓**www**→http://www.nationjob .com/marketing

Organizations

American Marketing Association A cornucopia of resources for marketers online, this page outlines membership rules for joining the AMA, lets members network with colleagues on its message board, provides an online library of articles from prominent marketing publications and journals (including the *Journal of Marketing*), lists a calendar of marketing-related conferences and seminars nationwide, offers support to college students studying marketing with a special collegiate section, and even hosts a search engine to guide visitors through its

larges.
✓**www**→http://www.ama.org

Events

Marketing Conventions and Conferences An online calendar of mostly offline meetings, seminars, classes, and camps for the marketing world.
✓**www**→http://www.yahoo.com /Business_and_Economy/Marketing /Conventions_and_Conferences

Indexes

The Internet Advertising Resource Guide A helpful collection of links to resources for advertisers and marketers, which includes links to primers on acceptable online marketing practices, advertising magazines online, the Blacklist of Internet Advertisers, professional advertising and marketing organizations, and even a small collection of links to sites on basic Website construction for marketers who want to create their own pages.
✓**www**→http://www.missouri.edu /internet-advertising-guide.html

Shelia's WWW Marketing Resource List California-based marketer Shelia has assembled an impressive collection of links to all types of marketing Websites, including discussion groups, commercial rate databases, ad agencies, and promotional companies.. From Shelia's page you can link to Advertising Age, GVU's WWW User Survey, the American Marketing Association, the Internet Marketing Discussion List, and even *HotWired* magazine. If you've just arrived online and you want to go to some of the best first stops for marketing, this index should be among them.
✓**www**→http://www.nsmi.com /links.html

@	Separates the **userid** and **domain name** of an Internet address. Pronounced "at."
anonymous FTP	Method of logging in to public file archives over the **Internet**. Enter "anonymous" when prompted for a **userid**. See **FTP**.
Archie	A program that lets you search **Internet FTP** archives worldwide by file name. One variant is called **Veronica**.
ASCII	A basic text format readable by most computers. The acronym stands for American Standard Code for Information Interchange.
bandwidth	The data transmission capacity of a network. Used colloquially to refer to the "size" of the Net; some information transmittals (e.g., multitudes of graphic files) are considered to be a "waste of bandwidth."
baud	The speed at which signals are sent by a **modem**, measured by the number of changes per second in the signals during transmission. A baud rate of 1,200, for example, would indicate 1,200 signal changes in one second. Baud rate is often confused with **bits per second (bps)**.
BBS	"Bulletin-board system." Once referred to stand-alone desktop computers with a single modem that answered the phone, but can now be as complicated and inter-connected as a commercial service.
binary transfer	A file transfer between two computers that preserves binary data—used for all non-text files.
bits per second (bps)	The data-transfer rate between two **modems**. The higher the bps, the higher the speed of the transfer.
bounced message	An **email** message "returned to sender," usually because of an address error.
bye	A log-off command, like "quit" and "exit."
carrier signal	The squeaking noise that modems use to maintain a connection. See also **handshake**.
cd	"Change directory." A command used, for example, at an **FTP** site to move from a directory to a subdirectory.
cdup	"Change directory up." Can be used at an **FTP** site to move from a subdirectory to its parent directory. Also **chdirup**.
chdirup	See **cdup**.
client	A computer that connects to a more powerful computer (see **server**) for complex tasks.
commercial service	General term for large online services (e.g., America Online, CompuServe, Prodigy, GEnie).
compression	Shrinkage of computer files to conserve storage space and reduce transfer times. Special utility programs, available for most platforms (including DOS, Mac, and

Amiga), perform the compression and decompression.

cracker	A person who maliciously breaks into a computer system in order to steal files or disrupt system activities.
dial-up access	Computer connection made over standard telephone lines.
dir	"Directory." A command used to display the contents of the current directory.
domain name	The worded address of an **IP number** on the **Internet**, in the form of domain subsets separated by periods. The full address of an **Internet** user is **userid@domain name**.
email	"Electronic mail."
emoticon	See **smiley**.
FAQ	"Frequently asked questions." A file of questions and answers compiled for **Usenet newsgroups**, **mailing lists**, and games to reduce repeated posts about commonplace subjects.
file transfer	Transfer of a file from one computer to another over a network.
finger	A program that provides information about a user who is logged into your local system or on a remote computer on the Internet. Generally invoked by typing "finger" and the person's **userid**.
flame	A violent and usually *ad hominem* attack against another person in a **newsgroup** or message area.
flame war	A back-and-forth series of **flames**.
Free-Net	A community-based network that provides free access to the **Internet**, usually to local residents, and often includes its own forums and news.
freeware	Free software. Not to be confused with **shareware**.
FTP	"File transfer protocol." The standard used to transfer files between computers.
get	An **FTP** command that transfers single files from the **FTP** site to your local directory. The command is followed by a file name; typing "get file.name" would transfer only that file. Also see **mget**.
GIF	Common file format for pictures first popularized by CompuServe, standing for "graphics interchange format." Pronounced with a hard *g*.
gopher	A menu-based guide to directories on the **Internet**, usually organized by subject.
GUI	"Graphical user interface" with windows and point-and-click capability, as opposed to a command-line interface with typed-out instructions.
hacker	A computer enthusiast who enjoys exploring computer systems and programs, sometimes to the point of obsession. Not to be confused with **cracker**.
handle	The name a user wishes to be known by; a user's handle may differ significantly from his or her real name or **userid**.
handshake	The squawking noise at the beginning of a computer connection when two modems settle on a protocol for exchanging information.
Home Page	The main **World Wide Web** site for a particular group or organization.
hqx	File suffix for a BinHex file, a common format for transmitting Macintosh binary files over the **Internet**.
hypertext	An easy method of retrieving information by choosing highlighted words in a text on the screen. The words link to documents with related subject matter.
IC	"In character." A game player who is IC is acting as his or her **character**'s persona.
Internet	The largest network of computer networks in the world, easily recognizable by the format of Internet **email** addresses: **userid**@host.

NetSpeak

Internet provider	Wholesale or retail reseller of access to the **Internet**. YPN is one example.
IP connection	Full-fledged link to the **Internet**. See **SLIP**, **PPP**, and **TCP/IP**.
IP number	The unique number that determines the ultimate **Internet** identity of an **IP connection**.
IRC	"**Internet** relay chat." A service that allows **real-time** conversations between multiple users on a variety of subject-oriented channels.
jpeg	Common compressed format for picture files. Pronounced "jay-peg."
ls	"List." A command that provides simplified directory information at **FTP** sites and other directories. It lists only file names for the directory, not file sizes or dates.
lurkers	Regular readers of messages online who never post.
lynx	A popular text-based **Web browser**.
mailing list	Group discussion distributed through **email**. Many mailing lists are administered through listserv.
mget	An **FTP** command that transfers multiple files from the **FTP** site to your local directory. The command is followed by a list of file names separated by spaces, sometimes in combination with an asterisk used as a wild card. Typing "mget b*" would transfer all files in the directory beginning with the letter *b*. Also see **get**.
Net, the	A colloquial term that is often used to refer to the entirety of Cyberspace: the **Internet**, the **commercial services**, **BBSs**, etc.
netiquette	The rules of Cyberspace civility. Usually applied to the **Internet**, where manners are enforced exclusively by fellow users.
newbie	A newcomer to the **Net**, to a game, or to a discussion. Also called **fluxer**.
newsgroups	The **Usenet** message areas, organized by subject.
newsreader	Software program for reading **Usenet newsgroups** on the **Internet**.
port number	A number that follows a **telnet** address. The number connects a user to a particular application on the telnet site. LambdaMOO, for example, is at port 8888 of lambda.parc.xerox.com (lambda.parc.xerox.com 8888).
posting	The sending of a message to a **newsgroup**, bulletin board, or other public message area. The message itself is called a **post**.
pwd	A command used at an **FTP** site to display the name of the current directory on your screen.
real-time	The **Net** term for "live," as in "live broadcast." Real-time connections include **IRC** and **MUDs**.
remote machine	Any computer on the **Internet** reached with a program such as **FTP** or **telnet**. The machine making the connection is called the home, or local, machine.
RL	"Real life."
server	A software program, or the computer running the program, that allows other computers, called **clients**, to share its resources.
shareware	Free software, distributed over the **Net** with a request from the programmer for voluntary payment.
sig	Short for **signature**.
signature	A file added to the end of **email** messages or **Usenet** posts that contains personal information—usually your name, email address, postal address, and telephone number. **Netiquette** dictates that signatures, or **sigs**, should be no longer than four or five lines.
SLIP and PPP	"Serial line **Internet** protocol" and "point-to-point protocol." Connecting by

	SLIP or PPP actually puts a computer on the Internet, which offers a number of advantages over regular **dial-up**. A SLIP or PPP connection can support a graphical **Web browser** (such as Mosaic), and allows for multiple connections at the same time. Requires special software and a SLIP or PPP service provider.
smiley	Text used to indicate emotion, humor, or irony in electronic messages—best understood if viewed sideways. Also called an **emoticon**. The most common smileys are :-) and :-(
snail mail	The paper mail the U.S. Postal Service delivers. The forerunner of **email**.
spam	The posting of the same article to multiple **newsgroups** (usually every possible one) regardless of the appropriateness of the topic (e.g., "Make Money Fast").
sysop	"System operator." The person who owns and/or manages a **BBS** or other **Net** site.
TCP/IP	The "transmission control protocol" and the "**Internet** protocol." The basis of a full-fledged Internet connection. See **IP Connection**, **PPP**, and **SLIP**. Pronounced "T-C-P-I-P."
telnet	An **Internet** program that allows you to log into other Internet-connected computers.
terminal emulator	A program or utility that allows a computer to communicate in a foreign or non-standard **terminal mode**.
terminal mode	The software standard a computer uses for text communication—for example, ANSI for PCs and **VT-100** for UNIX.
thread	Posted **newsgroup** message with a series of replies. Threaded **newsreaders** organize replies under the original subject.
timeout	The break in communication that occurs when two computers are talking and one takes so long to respond that the other gives up.
URL	"Uniform resource locator." The **World Wide Web** address of a resource on the **Internet**.
Usenet	A collection of networks and computer systems that exchange messages, organized by subject in **newsgroups**.
userid	The unique name (often eight characters or less) given to a user on a system for his or her account. The complete address, which can be used for **email** or **fingering**, is a userid followed by the @ sign and the **domain name** (e.g., Bill Clinton's address is president@whitehouse.gov).
Veronica	See **Archie**.
VT-100 emulation	Widely used terminal protocol for formatting full screens of text over computer connections.
WAIS	"Wide area information server." A system that searches through database indexes around the **Internet**, using keywords.
Web browser	A **client** program designed to interact with **World Wide Web servers** on the **Internet** for the purpose of viewing **Web pages**.
Web page	A **hypertext** document that is part of the **World Wide Web** and that can incorporate graphics, sounds, and links to other **Web pages**, **FTP** sites, **gophers**, and a variety of other **Internet** resources.
World Wide Web	A **hypertext**-based navigation system that lets you browse through a variety of linked **Net** resources, including **Usenet newsgroups** and **FTP**, **telnet**, and **gopher** sites, without typing commands. Also known as WWW and the Web.
zip	File-compression standard in the DOS and Windows worlds.

Index

Index

Index

Index

Iams, 179
IBM, 50, 215
IBM at Wimbledon, 207
IBM Global Network, 12
IBM Internet Connection, 214
IBM Telecommuncations and
     Media, 211, 119
ICS Webstats, 108
id Software, 76, 204
IDG Books, 199
Il Fornaio, 252
Imark, 238
In@veda, 156
In Your Face T-Shirts, 295
InBusiness, 310
incentives, 78-79
India Tourist Office, 248
industry hubsites, 112-115
   auctions, 290
   automobiles, 112, 113, 171
   real estate, 238
   restaurant, 253
   travel, 241
Industry.Net, 113, 222
IndustryWeek Forum, 316
Indy Racing League—Official
     Home Page, 205
Information Economy, The, 311
Infoseek, 110
Ingalls, Quinn & Johnson, 87
InnSite: The Internet Directory of
     Bed & Breakfasts, 251
Insignia Solutions, 100
Insomnia, 282
Inspiration, 76
Instant Travel, 241
insurance, 235-236
InsuranceNet, 115
Intel, 58
Intelligent Agents Make Shopping
     a Pleasure, 141
Intelligent Agents-A Technology
     and Business Application
     Approach, 140-141
Intelligent Agents/Information
     Agents, 141
Intelligent Software Agents Re-
     sources, 141
Inter@ctive Week, 6
Interactive Publishing Alert On-
     line Advertising Index, 99
Interactive Yellow Pages, 102
interactivity, 52-53

Internal Revenue Service, 32, 300
International Channel Network,
     60, 186
International Male, 294
International PGP Home Page,
     The, 126
International Trade Forum, 316
Internet, 4-20
   directories, 111
   demographics, 7-11, 315-315
   search engines, 110-111
   service providers, 212-214
   speed technology, 15-18
Internet access, 10-12
   cable, 17-18
   ISDN, 15-16
   service providers, 12, 212-214
Internet Advertising Resource
     Guide, The, 40, 319
Internet Audit Bureau, 108
Internet Domain Survey, 315
Internet Facts, 315
Internet Kitchen, The, 26
Internet Libri Bologna, 286
Internet Mall Listings, 84, 85
Internet Marketing Discussion
     List, The, 40, 317
Internet Marketing Mailing List
     Archive, 5
Internet Marketing Strategies and
     Implementation, 318
Internet MCIaccess, 214
Internet Plaza, 85
Internet Providers, 12
Internet Publishing Forum, 311
Internet Screenwriters Network,
     259
Internet Shopping Network, 127,
     130
Internet Shopping Plaza, 85
InterNet Travel Mall, 241
Internet Truckstop, 264
Internet Web Shopping, 85
InterNIC, 42
Interplay, 29, 29
Intuit—The Quicken Financial
     Network, 217
investigators, 258
investment services, 231-233
Iomega, 216
IRS-The Digital Daily, 300
ISDN lines, 15-16
Isuzu Motors, 170

ITT Hartford, 235

J

J.B. Hunt Transportation Services,
     263
J.C. Penny, 291
J. Dyer Animation, 295
Jack Daniel's, 52, 81, 165
Jackson Hewitt, 234
Jacqueline Gail Gorton—Ovum
     Donorship Services, 257
Jamaica, 248
Japan Travel Update, 248
Java, 48, 99
Jeep Unpaved, 168
Jekyll and Hyde Home Page, 193
jewelry, 177, 278
   direct selling, 293
Jiffylube, 173
JOBS-SLS, 319
Joe Boxer MegaCorp, 150
John Lennon Glasses, 179
John's Town & Country Office &
     Carpet Care Systems, 269
Jolt, 72, 162
Jorvik Viking Center, 195
Julia Haskett's BeautifulControl
     Brochure, 296
JWT (J. Walter Thompson), 47

K

K.V.S. International Homepage,
     270
KALL 910, 190
KBNP-AM 1410, 190
Kelloggs, 71, 75, 161
Kelly Services, 265
Ketchum Advertising, 87
KFC (Kentucky Fried Chicken),
     252
KIAK-FM, 190
Kilgannon Group, The, 87
KING FM 98.1, 190
Kinko's, 275
Kirk Originals, 179
Kirschenbaum Bond & Partners,
     87
Kitty Hawk Air Charter, 262
Klein Dytham Architects, 257

Index

Index

Index

X, Y, Z

Wolff New Media

Wolff New Media is one of the leading providers of information about the Net and the emerging Net culture. The company's NetBooks Series, presently at 13 titles—*NetGuide, NetGames, NetChat, NetMoney, NetTrek, NetSports, NetTech, NetMusic, Fodor's NetTravel, NetTaxes, NetJobs, NetVote,* and *NetMarketing*—will expand to more than 25 titles in 1996. This will include *NetDoctor, NetKids, NetOUT, NetSpy, NetSciFi, NetCollege,* and *NetHomework.* The entire NetBooks Series (to date) is now available on the companion Website YPN—Your Personal Net (http://www.ypn.com). And *Net Guide*—"the *TV Guide*™ to Cyberspace," according to *Wired* magazine editor Louis Rossetto—is now a monthly magazine published by CMP Publications.

The company was founded in 1988 by journalist Michael Wolff to bring together writers, editors, and graphic designers to create editorially and visually compelling information products in books, magazines, and new media. Among the company's other projects are *Where We Stand—Can America Make It in the Global Race for Wealth, Health, and Happiness?* (Bantam Books), one of the most graphically complex information books ever to be wholly created and produced by means of desktop-publishing technology, and *Made in America?*, a four-part PBS series on global competitiveness, hosted by Labor Secretary Robert B. Reich.

The company frequently acts as a consultant to other information companies, including WGBH, Boston's educational television station; CMP Publications; and Time Warner, which it has advised on the development of Time's online business and the launch of its Website, Pathfinder.

About the Author

One of the first marketers to recognize the power of the Internet in shaping the future of business, Bruce Judson is involved in virtually every aspect of the online world. As General Manager of Time Inc. New Media, Judson is one of the senior executives who founded—and continues to oversee—Time Warner's Pathfinder, one of the most popular and successful Web ventures in the world. Judson is also a member of the Board of Directors of Open Market, one of the leading publishers of software designed to enable easy commerce on the Internet; chairman of the Magazine Publishers Association Committee on New Media, where he has spearheaded the industry's effort to develop standards for online advertising; and Senior Vice-Chairman of the National Neurofibromatosis Foundation, where he was instrumental in investigating ways in which the Web could meet the marketing needs of nonprofit organizations.

In 1995, *Advertising Age* named Judson one of the nation's leading figures in cutting-edge marketing, calling him a "marketer's marketer." Judson, and his views about online marketing, appear in publications such as *The Wall Street Journal*, *The New York Times*, and *Advertising Age*. He lives in Manhattan with his wife and children.

Notes

NYNMA
NEW YORK
NEW MEDIA
ASSOCIATION

New York New Media Association

is a not-for-profit organization whose mission is to support the development of the new media industry in the New York area.

For membership information call 212.785.7898

http:// WWW.NYNMA.ORG

Packing for your first trip on the information superhighway?

Don't forget your roadmap.

Where to go. How to get there.

the net is your unique guide to cyberspace. We'll show you how to get involved in the Internet, how to get the most out of it and, with our web site at www.thenet-usa.com, we even give you a place to begin your travels.

Each issue of *the net* includes a CD-ROM disc, packed with great software to help you get the most out of your time online.

Subscribe today to receive 12 issues and 12 discs for only $39.95.

Call us at 800-706-9500. Outside the U.S. call 415-696-1661. E-mail your subscription to subscribe@thenet-usa.com. Or, mail your subscription to: *The Net*, P.O. Box 56141, Boulder, CO 80322-6141.

Canada: $53.95 (includes GST). Foreign: $US 63.95. Send foreign and Canada orders prepaid in US funds.   5TSCI

It's All Clear Now.

THE BEST WAY TO ATTRACT CUSTOMERS TO YOUR WEB SITE.

UUNET® Web hosting services give you fast, reliable site performance – at about a quarter of the cost of hosting your own. Our high-performance servers connect directly to UUNET's 45 Mbps backbone. So each visitor you attract has a top-quality experience.

    We provide 24-hour site monitoring and customer support. Complete traffic reports. Even content development if you need it. And, since your site is on our network, there's no security risk to your internal systems. Best of all, you retain control, choosing your own domain name and updating your site at any time. Sound attractive? Then call us at 1 800 465 6970.

THE INTERNET AT WORK™

http://www.uu.net   info@uu.net

3060 Williams Drive, Fairfax, VA 22031 +1 703 206 5600. Official Internet Access Provider to The Microsoft Network™